The Many Faces of Adam and Eve

The Many Faces of
ADAM & EVE

Bernard F. Batto

CASCADE *Books* · Eugene, Oregon

THE MANY FACES OF ADAM AND EVE

Cascade Books
An Imprint of Wipf and Stock Publishers
199 W. 8th Ave., Suite 3
Eugene, OR 97401

www.wipfandstock.com

PAPERBACK ISBN: 978-1-6667-1162-2
HARDCOVER ISBN: 978-1-6667-1163-9
EBOOK ISBN: 978-1-6667-1164-6

Cataloguing-in-Publication data:

Names: Batto, Bernard Frank, author.

Title: The many faces of Adam and Eve / Bernard F. Batto.

Description: Eugene, OR : Cascade Books, 2022. | Includes bibliographical refer-
ences.

Identifiers: ISBN 978-1-6667-1162-2 (paperback). | ISBN 978-1-6667-1163-9 (hard-
cover). | ISBN 978-1-6667-1164-6 (ebook).

Subjects: LSCH: Adam (Biblical figure). | Eve (Biblical figure). | Bible.—Old Testa-
ment—Criticism, interpretation, etc. | Bible.—New Testament—Criticism, inter-
pretation, etc. | Adam (Biblical figure)—In the Qur'an. | Eve (Biblical figure)—In
the Qur'an. Milton, John, 1608–1664—Paradise Lost.

Classification: BS580.A4 B38 2022 (print). | BS580 (ebook).

Figure 1. Drawing of central panels on wall of the throne room at Mari by J. Laufray, in André Parrot, "Peintures du Palais de Mari," *Syria* 18/4 [1937] 325-54, pl. 39, fig.8). Used by permission of Dr. Gaëlle Coqueugniot, CNRS, éditrice.

Contents

Illustrations and Tables

Illustrations

Tables

Abbreviations

ACW	Ancient Christian Writers
AH	Irenaeus, *Against Heresies*
ANEP	*The Ancient Near East in Pictures Relating to the Old Testament*. 2nd ed. Edited by James B. Pritchard. Princeton: Princeton University Press, 1969
ANET	*Ancient Near Eastern Texts Relating to the Old Testament*. 3rd ed. Edited by James B. Pritchard. Princeton: Princeton University Press, 1969
BAR	*Biblical Archaeology Review*
CAD	*The Assyrian Dictionary of the Oriental Institute of the University of Chicago*. Chicago: The Oriental Institute of the University of Chicago, 1956–2006
City	Augustine, *The City of God*
DGnL	Augustine, *De Genesi ad litteram libri duodecim*
Epid.	Irenaeus, *Epideixis tou apostolikou kerygmatos*
Gen. Rab.	Genesis Rabba
HTR	*Harvard Theological Review*
JBL	*Journal of Biblical Literature*
JECS	*Journal of Early Christian Studies*
NTS	*New Testament Studies*
Q	Qur'an
R.	Rabbi
RB	*Revue biblique*

Bible Versions

ASV   American Standard Version

ESV   English Standard Version

JPS   The Holy Scriptures, Jewish Publication Society (1917 ed.)

KJV   King James Version

Moffatt   James Moffatt, *The New Testament: A New Translation*

NAB   New American Bible

NEB   New English Bible

NIV   New International Version

NRSV   New Revised Standard Version

REB   Revised English Bible

RSV   Revised Standard Version

Introduction

MOST OF US, AT least most of us in the Western world, think we know the story of Adam and Eve. We have grown up hearing about "our first parents" and their sin. We frequently encounter allusions to the story in our everyday lives. If quizzed, we would probably recount the story in broad outline somewhat along these lines: the Lord God created Adam in the garden of Eden, a paradise, and afterwards took one of Adam's ribs and from it formed Eve as a fitting companion. Meanwhile Satan—once an angel of the highest rank but now condemned to hell because he proudly challenged God for supremacy, and anxious for revenge—disguised himself as a serpent and sneaked into paradise. There he found innocent Eve all alone and tricked her into eating fruit from the forbidden tree. After Eve had eaten, she went in search of Adam and seduced him to eat the forbidden fruit also. The Lord God then punished the serpent (Satan) and also Adam and Eve. The archangel Michael drove the human couple out of paradise to die in a world corrupted by their own sinfulness. Once outside of paradise, Adam and Eve begat children, with the first-born Cain killing his brother Abel and then begetting children of his own, who followed in his evil footsteps. That left Adam and Eve's other son, noble Seth and his offspring, to struggle perennially against the wicked descendants of Cain. The more sophisticated among us likely would add that in the ongoing struggle of Adam's and Eve's descendants outside the garden between good and evil, the former are aided by good angels like Michael, Gabriel, and Raphael, while the wicked are enabled by Satan and other fallen angels (demons). Still other respondents might add that, without a redeemer, all humans are helplessly mired in sin. Many, if not most, of us also assume that this "story of Adam and Eve" comes directly from the book of Genesis, or at least is implicit in the Genesis story.

1

Few of us allude to the fact that much of our understanding of the Genesis story has been shaped over the course of some three thousand years through gradual accretions to the original Genesis version. Even fewer of us know that the Genesis story itself had antecedents in ancient Near Eastern literature which greatly influenced the composition of the Genesis story. This book is an attempt to trace, in an admittedly cursory fashion, the long development of the Adam and Eve tradition, from its prebiblical roots, to its classic version in Genesis, to its expansion in postbiblical "apocryphal" Jewish writings, to a radical reinterpretation in the New Testament by various Christian authors, until it finally achieved what may be termed the "standard" version of the Adam and Eve story most of us "know"—unaware that this "standard" version owes more to John Milton's epic poem *Paradise Lost* than to the original Genesis story. Our goal in this book will be to show not only *how* the story has changed over the course of more than three millennia, but also *why* it changed. These changes were driven by multiple historical, cultural, and theological factors, all of which are fascinating in their own right and worthy of study.

As we proceed, it quickly will become obvious that the story of Adam and Eve is not just a story about two individuals but also about the world in which they lived and moved. In that sense, the story is about creation itself and how all things came to be, whether in heaven above, on earth, or under the earth. Part and parcel of the human experience is the ever-present menace of evil. Necessarily, then, an explanation of the origins of evil in the world must be part of the story of the first humans. The issue is not just why humans at times manifest evil, but also that on occasion creation itself seems to exhibit malevolent behavior, as when animals kill one another, or a virulent virus decimates whole populations. Does such "evil" arise from within humans themselves, or does it have its source in some force beyond human control, a superhuman power perhaps? Why does humankind not live in a perfect world (a "paradise")? Is a perfect world even possible, perhaps in some distant future? All of these are questions associated with the story of how humankind began and are linked with "Adam and Eve."

We will begin with an analysis of the Adam and Eve narrative from the book of Genesis, trying to hear the story as it most likely was written and understood by the original author—or authors, as there are actually two stories of creation and the origins of humankind preserved in the opening chapters of Genesis, a so-called Yahwistic account and a Priestly account. But before we look at these Genesis stories, we will need to travel backwards in time into the ancient Near East in order to retrieve the backstories of "Adam and Eve," that is, to investigate how several still earlier stories from Mesopotamia about creation and the formation of the first humans contributed to shaping the biblical story. We will also move forward in time from Genesis to trace how the Adam and Eve tradition is retold and embellished in postbiblical Judaism of different periods and in different works: (a) the book of 1 Enoch (ca. 200 BCE), wherein is told a story of how fallen "watchers" (angels) lusted after "human daughters," and marrying them, brought about near total corruption not only of humankind but also of earth itself; (b) the book of Jubilees (ca. 150 BCE), which picks up on themes from 1 Enoch and takes the story of corruption even further; and (c) Life of Adam and Eve (ca. 100 CE), where we first encounter the story of the fall of Satan from heaven, and where blame for human sin is laid principally upon the woman, but nevertheless hope for redemption in some distant future is held out to humankind.

From the Jewish retellings of the Adam and Eve tradition, we then transition to Christian reinterpretations of that same tradition. The most important innovation is found in the letters of the apostle Paul—some of the earliest writings of the New Testament. In Paul's Letter to the Romans and in 1 Corinthians 15, he will develop his "gospel" (Good News) that Jesus Christ was a new Adam. Just as the first Adam brought sin and death to every human and even upon the whole of creation, so the second Adam, Christ, reversed the harm done to humankind and the world by the first Adam. The result, according to Paul, is literally a re-creation of the world—indeed a new creation that by far surpasses the original creation in that humans not only bear the image of God, they have become adopted children of God.

Various Christian writers in succeeding centuries developed Paul's thesis even further. Especially important for subsequent Christian belief are the teachings of St. Augustine of Hippo (died 430). Augustine popularized the doctrine of "original sin," according to which every human is born in sin and therefore doomed to eternal death. This is the heritage that Adam and Eve as progenitors of the human race have bequeathed to each and every one of their descendants—with the exception of Jesus Christ and his mother Mary. The doctrine of "original sin" pervades every aspect of Christian belief. Not many people today are aware that various gnostic sects also advanced versions of the Adam and Eve story, some of which radically challenged and even supplanted the standard Christian and Jewish versions.

At the same time as Christian church fathers were rewriting the Adam and Eve story to include the second Adam, Jewish rabbis were reviewing the Genesis story and debating among themselves about the correct way to read the story and how it applied to themselves. During this process, numerous novel elements were introduced into the ancient biblical tale.

Islam was greatly influenced by both Judaism and Christianity. It will come as no surprise, therefore, that Adam and Eve figure prominently in the Qur'an and in subsequent Islamic tradition. Most important is the role played by Iblis, as Satan is generally called in Islam. From the very beginning Iblis has worked ceaselessly to lead humankind astray.

No survey of the Adam and Eve tradition would be complete without a review of the epic poem *Paradise Lost* by the seventeenth-century English poet John Milton. It is fitting to end with Milton because he masterfully brought together in a single composition nearly all the literary strands and theological views that had evolved over the course of more than two millennia around the figures Adam and Eve. Indeed, when asked to recite the story of Adam and Eve, what today the average person will "remember" about Adam and Eve likely owes more to Milton than to Genesis, so thoroughly have the original narratives of Genesis been supplanted in Western thought by the epic strains of *Paradise Lost*.

The texts chosen for review in this book are by no means intended to be a complete accounting of the many variants of the Adam and Eve tradition that have surfaced over the course of more than three millennia. Numerous texts have been left aside, both in the interests of economy and to avoid reader fatigue. Hopefully, the texts selected here will provide the reader with a meaningful overview of the most important developments in the Adam and Eve story, as well as their many variations.

This book is intended to be accessible by the general reading public. For that reason I have intentionally kept notes and technical discussions to a minimum. For those interested in a more scholarly approach to biblical creation narratives and their ancient Near Eastern backgrounds, numerous studies published elsewhere are readily available.[1] As different

---

1. For my part, I have treated a number of issues covered in this volume previously at greater length elsewhere; see especially my very accessible volume, Batto, *Slaying the Dragon*. Also recommended is my volume of collected essays on various creation topics, Batto, *In the Beginning*.

audiences read the Bible in sometimes very different ways, perhaps I need to lay out some basic assumptions and working principles that undergird my approach to the study of the Bible in general and to the Adam and Eve tradition in particular. Fundamental to my method is a recognition that whatever else it may be, the Bible is also a work written by humans and therefore is replete with both the wisdom and the limitations that human authorship entails. Implicit here is an admission that the Bible is both culturally and historically conditioned. In short, its wisdom is not universally perfect. It underwent growth and revision during its long period of composition, even as its composers—whether of the Hebrew Bible or the New Testament and beyond—advanced in their own under-standings of both the physical world and the spiritual world. Without in any way denying that divine inspiration may be involved in the pro-duction of the Bible, it is patently clear that the individual books which comprise the Bible are also truly human compositions. They bear the im-print of authors heavily steeped in a specific culture of a specific historical period. These works reveal also that their human authors individually held unique theological views and moral values that oftentimes were in opposition to, or corrective of, values espoused not only by their contem-poraries but even other biblical writers. Moreover, it was not uncommon for a later writer to "correct" what he believed to be inadequacies in an earlier sacred writing or prophetic book. Such "correctives" were all the easier to proffer because back then there was no concept of a "Bible." A "canon" of authoritative books to guide the believing community was an idea that developed late both in Judaism and in Christianity, as well as in Islam. While certain prophets or poets may have felt "inspired" to speak or write in the name of God, every biblical author was a true author. In other words, the writers of the books of the Bible were individuals who penned their own unique ideas as best they knew how. Moreover, such ideas were in large measure shaped by the time and the place in which each writer lived.

Unfortunately, no "autograph copy" (the original manuscript penned by an author) of any biblical book has been preserved for us. For example, the standard or "received text" of the Hebrew Bible (Old Testament), known as the Masoretic Text, dates back only to approxi-mately the tenth century CE/AD—nearly a millennium after the last books of the Hebrew Bible were written. All modern translations of the Hebrew Bible/Old Testament are based upon this relatively late edition of the Hebrew Bible. There were, of course, numerous earlier, intermediate editions of biblical books and translations, including Aramaic targums, the Greek Septuagint, and various Dead Sea Scrolls. But none of these is an autograph copy. Even the earliest surviving manuscript of any biblical book is a copy of a copy, sometimes many times removed from the original autograph. As we all know, in the ancient world copy machines and printing presses were non-existent. Duplicating any work was a tedious, manual process. Every new copy involved a scribe painstakingly inking each letter of each word until the whole manuscript was complete. It goes without saying that in any work of length, multiple copying errors might be—and were—introduced into every new "copy" through this process.

But there is more. Ancient scribes were more than mechanical transcribers. They were also scholars. As such, a scribe might judge the manuscript from which he was copying to be defective in some way; he might then use his own judgment to correct it. In such cases the scribe might also feel compelled to improve the work before him by rearranging the text, or by omitting a passage, or even by adding new material. Over several centuries individual works might undergo considerable alteration in the process of transmission from one generation to the next. The Dead Sea Scrolls provide graphic evidence of biblical books having been altered in just this way during the process of transmission.

The process by which ancient scribes altered ancient composition by means of corrections, deletions, and supplementations is also evident throughout the ancient world in general, as we will observe repeatedly throughout this volume. A parade example of this is found in the Mesopotamian tale, The Epic of Gilgamesh. As already mentioned, no autograph copy of a biblical work, written on perishable papyrus sheets or leather scrolls, has survived to us. By contrast, we do have what can be described as autograph copies of Gilgamesh. Ancient Mesopotamian scribes wrote in cuneiform on durable clay tablets, which survived not only the ravages of time but even of floods and destructive fires. Archeologists have excavated clay tablets of Gilgamesh from several sites and from different historical periods. The best thing about these clay tablets is that each exemplar is an autograph copy. No two exemplars are identical. And because these tablets were written over a period of some fifteen hundred years, we are able to observe how the Gilgamesh tradition evolved— sometimes changing radically—over the course of a millennium or more.

Oftentimes we do not have to speculate concerning a scribe's motive for altering the text in his new copy. Take the case of the Babylonian Creation Story (Enuma Elish). It was originally composed as a paean in praise of Marduk, the national god of Babylon. Marduk, formerly a minor city deity in the Sumero-Akkadian pantheon, suddenly was thrust to the fore when Babylon emerged as the most powerful political entity in southern Mesopotamia. According to the prevailing view of the day, the political success of a state was intimately linked to the relative status of its patron deity. Accordingly, it fell to Babylon's theologians (apologists) to justify Babylon's ascendency to political dominance by claiming that Marduk had become king over all gods. They did so by creating an entirely new poem—a myth, actually—which recounted how, before the world began, when the gods themselves were young and still struggling to organize themselves into what would eventually become the great assembly of (Sumero-Akkadian) gods, one god emerged as the supreme ruler of the gods. That god was Marduk, the patron deity of Babylon. Marduk ascended to the exalted position of the divine sovereign by virtue of having subdued the "chaos monster" Tiamat and her allies, and then from her carcass created the world as well as humankind. It was a masterful piece of Babylonian propaganda. However, when several centuries later Babylon fell to the Neo-Assyrian kingdom, it was a simple matter for an Assyrian scribe to justify Assyria's sudden rise to power by "repurposing" this *Babylonian* Creation Story into an *Assyrian* Creation Story, merely by substituting the name of Assyria's own national god Assur everywhere in place of the Babylonian god Marduk. The propagandistic motives of the Assyrian scribe for altering the text in this case could not be more obvious.

These two Mesopotamian examples provide us with empirical models for positing how biblical traditions like the Adam and Eve story similarly must have evolved in Jewish, Christian, and Muslim hands over an equally long period of time in order to accommodate changing historical circumstances and theological beliefs. Each community of belief found herein elements of truth which continued to speak to them in profound ways. Indeed, precisely because they saw the Adam and Eve story as having continuing relevance for themselves, they felt free—compelled, even—to adapt the story in various and sundry ways so that it spoke more directly to their own lived experience and better undergirded their religious convictions. Such evolution of belief is one focus for the present volume.

Finally, a word about translations. Both for biblical texts and ancient Near Eastern texts I often provide my own translations. If I lift a translation from another source, I try to acknowledge that fact. Specifically, regarding quotations from the Bible, my default translation is the NRSV for both the Hebrew Bible and the New Testament. But I do not hesitate to alter the reading of the NRSV when I think a different wording better renders the meaning of the Hebrew or Greek original. As I frequently borrow from my own prior writings, on occasion I may have missed giving proper credit where due. For any such omissions, I apologize in advance. Also, because this book is primarily a diachronic study of the Adam and Eve tradition rather than a theological treatise, I have chosen to transcribe names for the deity as closely as possible with their English equivalents. For that reason, I render the Hebrew proper name for God as Yahweh. Similarly, when referencing an Islamic text or tradition, I use Allah and God interchangeably, or an equivalent term, adhering as much as possible to the wording of the source text itself.

1

The Mesopotamian Backstory

MOST PEOPLE THINK THAT the story of Adam and Eve begins in the first book of the Bible, in the book of Genesis. That is both true and not true. It is true that one first encounters the two figures known by the name "Adam" and "Eve" in the book of Genesis. Furthermore, it is the story of these two biblical figures and the story of their descendants that is the subject of this book. But there is an earlier story—a backstory, if you will—on which the Genesis story is in part based. That backstory comes from ancient Mesopotamia (modern day Iraq). In ancient times, however, this land was known by different names at different times: Sumer and Akkad, Babylon and Assyria, Mesopotamia, and still others. These ancient kingdoms dominated the ancient Near East both politically and culturally. They developed a writing system inscribed on clay tablets with which to record their economic and political successes. They also recorded their cultural achievements, one of the greatest being their literary compositions. Among their literary works are various stories about how the world began, including how humans came to be. There were multiple "origins" stories, only a fraction of which have been preserved for us. It is fortunate that the scribes of ancient Mesopotamia used clay tablets to record their writings, since clay tablets are much more durable than papyrus or animal skins used elsewhere. When an enemy sacks and burns whole cities, clay is only hardened and covered by debris, but it does not perish entirely as does flammable papyrus and skins. Consequently, many such tablets remained buried in the rubble, entirely unknown to Western folk until the modern era, when these ancient clay tablets began to be recovered by archeologists within the last two centuries.

In 1872 George Smith, a pioneering English Assyriologist studying the cuneiform clay tablets held by the British Museum, announced his discovery of a "Chaldean flood story" with close similarities to the biblical flood story. This discovery shocked the world, as up until that time it had been assumed that the biblical story of the flood was unique and completely original. Smith's translation of a cuneiform version of a universal flood demonstrated beyond doubt that the biblical version not only was not unique but also that the biblical story was patently dependent upon earlier ancient Near Eastern myth(s). This discovery led to more intense investigation of other tablets in the British Museum and elsewhere. What is more, continuing archaeological excavations throughout the Middle East have uncovered additional tablets containing related stories. The upshot is that Assyriologists and biblical scholars working together have been able to show that much of the narrative in the early chapters of Genesis is patterned after similar stories, or myths, from Mesopotamia.

The stress upon stories from Mesopotamia as the background for the biblical Adam and Eve tradition may at first glance seem surprising. The Israelites were part of Canaan, geographically and culturally, and the Hebrew language is a dialect of the Canaanite language. Moreover, the Hebrew Bible for the most part exhibits close ties with the surrounding Canaanite culture, even to the extent that biblical prophets and writers frequently rail against the Israelites who worship Canaanite gods and actively participate in Canaanite religious practices. The Psalter is filled with language and ideas borrowed from Canaanite tradition. It is most unexpected, therefore, to find that the opening chapters of Genesis (1–11) are heavily dependent upon the stories and culture of the more distant Mesopotamia, rather than upon those of the closer land of Canaan. How this happened is still not fully understood. It is possible that Abraham and his descendants who migrated from Mesopotamia brought these stories with them. But it is equally possible that the Israelites learned these traditions from various Assyrian and Babylonian invaders who imposed upon the Israelites (and others) not only their political rule but also much of their religious and cultural heritage. They even deported whole populations into Mesopotamia as captives where they lived for generations. Whatever the route by which it came to pass, the stories in the opening chapter of Genesis are heavily dependent upon Mesopotamia traditions.

This leads us back to our main topic in this chapter: the origins of the Adam and Eve tradition in Mesopotamian myth, or stories of origins.

Atrahasis: The Babylonian Genesis Story

Above, I spoke of a "backstory." There is not just one story, however. There are multiple backstories: Gilgamesh, Enuma Elish, Anzu, Adapa, and others. We will be concerned with one story first and foremost, however. That is the ancient Babylonian myth of Atrahasis, sometimes referred to as "the Babylonian Story of the Flood," after the subtitle of the book in which this myth was first published and translated.[1] Atrahasis does contain the flood story, but it is much more than that. Much like the early chapters of Genesis, in Atrahasis the narrative about the flood is preceded by an account of how humans came to be in the first place, as well as an account of why and how the flood happened. Because of these parallels to the biblical story, Atrahasis might better be labeled as "the Babylonian Genesis."

Atrahasis was first composed in the Old Babylonian Period, sometime around 1750 BCE. But like Genesis, Atrahasis itself incorporated earlier stories from Mesopotamia already in circulation.[2] Incorporating earlier mythic fragments, a Mesopotamian poet composed a major new work, which itself quickly achieved the status of a literary classic, likely because it reflected so well the prevailing Mesopotamian view of how the world began. This "classic" work continued to be copied for well over a thousand years, down to the sixth century BCE when cuneiform writing and the Akkadian language ceased to be used.

Atrahasis is named for its main character, the hero by that same name who survived the great flood. In the Bible the name of the flood hero is Noah. Elsewhere in the ancient Near East the flood hero was known by still additional names, notably, Ziusudra and Utnapishti. Atrahasis, whose name means "Extra-wise" or "Exceedingly-Wise," was a priest of Enki (also known as Ea), one of the three highest ranking gods in the Sumero-Akkadian pantheon. The god Enki was renowned for exceptional wisdom and kindness, and later as the creator and patron deity of humankind. As a devotee of Enki, Atrahasis, as his name implies, was beneficiary of a gift of "extra" wisdom from Enki. Atrahasis was also,

1. Lambert and Millard, *Atrahasis: The Babylonian Story of the Flood.* Other English translations include Dalley, *Myths from Mesopotamia,* 1–38; *ANET,* 99–100, 104–6, 512–4; and Foster, *Before the Muses,* I:158–201.

2. The author of Atrahasis lifted much of his storyline directly from the Sumerian myth "Enki and Ninmah," translated by Jacob Klein, in Hallo and Younger, *Context of Scripture,* 1:159: 516–18. Enki and Ninmah lacks a flood story, however.

apparently, *extra pious* in his service of his god Enki, whose goodwill will ultimately be the reason why Atrahasis and his family survived the flood, when everyone else perished. Another parallel to the biblical Noah.

But as already said, Atrahasis is about more than the flood and the flood hero. This epic poem begins in a chronologic period before there were any humans at all. The poet opens his composition with the lines:

> When the gods were human,
> Bore the labor, carried the corvee basket,
> The corvee-basket of the gods was immense.
> The work heavy, the distress severe.
> The seven great Anunnaki
> Were making the Igigi suffer the labor. (1.1–6)

Clearly there is something amiss in this picture. Gods are supposed to enjoy leisure, or in the language of the poem, "rest." Yet in the beginning only the highest gods, the Anunnaki, enjoy leisure. The lesser gods, the Igigi, are being made to work like "humans," that is, to work *as slaves*. They must bear the entire burden of producing food and supplying provisions for all the gods. There is no one else to dig the irrigation canals, plow the fields, or harvest the crops—all very important functions in an agricultural society situated in a semiarid land such as ancient Mesopotamia (modern day Iraq). Located between the Tigris and the Euphrates rivers, the peoples of ancient Sumer, Babylon, and Assyria knew well the importance of diverting water from the Euphrates and the Tigris rivers onto their fields through a system of irrigation canals in order to make their fields productive. Digging these canals as well as maintaining them required intensive labor. Without such constant vigilance, crops would fail, and the populace would starve. The burden of such work naturally fell upon the lower classes. Kings and city rulers obviously shifted such labors onto their underlings, who were little more than slaves. In fact, many of them were slaves, being debtors and war captives. This was how society operated in those days.

It should come as no surprise that the ancient Mesopotamians envisioned the society of the gods to be structured similarly. After all, most societies have always conceived of the gods in their own image and likeness—a society of superhuman beings, if you will. It was only natural, then, that ancient Mesopotamians would have assumed that the high gods, like human kings, similarly imposed these burdensome tasks upon the backs of lesser gods, since there was no one else to do such manual labor.

The Igigi gods, though lesser, were not unaware of their dignity as gods and their rights, however. As gods they implicitly understood that they also ought to share in the divine privilege of leisure. Being made to slave as if they were "humans" was simply intolerable. So, incited on by one of their own, a certain Weila, the Igigi gods finally rebelled. One night they banded together and surrounded the "house" (palace) of Enlil, the king of the gods. This was more than a simple workers' strike, however. The Igigi not only refused to work, but they also burned their agricultural implements—hoes and pickaxes—making further work impossible. Their "cries" of defiance against Enlil and their "din" (their *ḫuburu* and *rigmu*) were so great that Enlil was unable to sleep, or as the Akkadian text puts it, unable to "rest." In short, this was open rebellion against the tyrannical rule of their king and the high-ranking Anunnaki gods. King Enlil was so terrified that he cowered inside his palace walls, and instead sent Nukshu, his lieutenant, out to negotiate with the rebels. In the end, however, it was the renowned god of wisdom, Enki, who brokered a compromise that ended this first crisis of authority.

Enki summoned all the gods together in a council. The gods acknowledged the justice of the Igigi gods' demands. Lesser gods should indeed enjoy full divine privilege, just the same as the high gods. Enki proposed that an entirely new species of beings be created to take over the menial tasks of agriculture and of provisioning the gods. In other words, this new species would be created specifically to function as servants (slaves) to the gods. Moreover, this new species would be created by molding and shaping clay, though not clay mixed with water. Instead, Weila, the rebel god who initiated the revolt, should be slain. From his flesh and blood mixed with clay, Nintu the mother god would mold fourteen clay specimens—seven males and seven females—as substitute laborers for the gods. There are several points worthy of notice in Enki's proposal.

First is the composite nature of these proposed new creatures. They are to be a mixture of divine and earthy elements: flesh and blood from a god, which means that they would share to some extent divinity with the gods; and earthy clay. Mesopotamia is nothing if not a land comprised of clay and water. Not only is clay the substance out which bricks for their buildings were made and from which their earthen pots and figurines were molded, it is also the very earth (soil) which these creatures were to till and work. They were to be part god and part earth, having something in common with both. (If this sounds reminiscent of the Genesis story of Adam and Eve in which humankind ["Adam"] was formed from "dust from the ground" [i.e., clay] and then animated with the deity's own divine breath [spirit], before being placed in the garden of Eden to till it and care for it—that is because the Genesis author borrowed extensively from Atrahasis to write his own story of primeval humankind. (But let us save that discussion for our next chapter.)

Second, the name of the new creatures is also revealing. They are to be called *lullu-awilu* (literally, "primeval Humans"). They are to be formed in part from the flesh and blood of the rebel god Weila. The pun is deliberate. The vocable *awilu*, like Hebrew ʾ*adam*, can mean both "(the) human/humans" and "humankind." Being derived partially from the deity Weila, the *awilu* creatures carry not only the deity's flesh and blood but even his name.

Third, the poet explicitly states that when Enki and Nintu create the *awilu*, they consciously place some memory from the rebel god within every primeval human. There should be no forgetting by humans of how and why they were created in the first place.

Enki and Nintu dutifully carry out their task. After purifying themselves for this creative work, the gods

> Slaughtered Weila, the rebel leader, within the divine assembly.
> Nintu mixed clay with his flesh and blood.
> That very god and human[kind] were thoroughly mixed within the clay.
> For the rest of time they would hear the drum (i.e., heartbeat of the god).
> It would be a sign to the living (creatures);
> Lest (the *awilu*) forget, (its) spirit remained.

As Nintu set about her task, she summoned all the gods, the Anunnaki and the Igigi alike, and had each of them spit into the mixture, both as their sign of approval to this creative initiative and to add potency to the plastic substance. Upon completion of her work, Nintu announced to the whole divine assembly that she has faithfully carried out their instructions. The rebel god has been eliminated, together with his scheme of rebellion. Everything will be beneficial for all the gods, whether high-ranking or low-ranking, from this moment forward. As Nintu phrased it,

I have removed your forced labor.
I have imposed your drudgery upon human(s).
You have diverted(?) (the rebellious) clamor unto humankind.
I have lifted the yoke; I have reestablished freedom.

Fourth, this new human species was to be self-propagating. Accordingly, elaborate rituals for marriage and birthing are provided right from the beginning. No provision was made for a naturally occurring death, however. If death for one of these creatures should be necessary, it would have to be executed on an ad hoc basis, much like the rebel god Weila from whose flesh and blood these humans were partially made. So while primeval humankind was explicitly designed to multiply, there was no corresponding automatic dying. That was supposed to be good, as it meant that the ranks of these substitute laborers would quickly swell, thereby relieving the gods of their hated burden. The name for this newly created species appeared entirely appropriate: *lullu* or *lullu-awilu*, that is, "*primeval* humankind/human(s)."

Enki's proposed solution seemed perfect. The *lullu* quickly assumed their functions of digging the irrigation canal, working the fields, and of provisioning the gods. The gods were happy with these new servants/slaves, as now all gods were able to enjoy their divine status, complete with the appropriate rest/leisure. Everything went exactly as the gods planned—at least for a time.

One shortcoming with Mesopotamian gods, however, is that they are not omniscient. Subsequent events would soon prove how naïve their thinking had been. "1200 years had not yet passed" before a design flaw became apparent. (1200 years in Mesopotamian sexagesimal numbering system is simply a way of saying "a period of many years.") With no checks on their self-propagation, the *lullu* rapidly expanded across the land. Their sheer numbers generated such ruckus that once again the divine king Enlil found himself deprived of sleep. This was not a matter merely of human over population. No. This was a case of déjà vu. This was a repetition of the situation when the Igigi gods, incited onward by Weila, had revolted against Enlil and the Anunnaki. The gods should have anticipated this development. When they slaughtered, Weila in order to create the *lullu-awilu* species, they determined that Weila's "spirit" should be placed within humankind. What they did not calculate, however, was that Weila's "spirit" also included his proclivity to revolt, manifested in "cries" of defiance, their "din" (*ḫuburu* and *rigmu*).

Patently, mere rebellion is not the entire story here. Primitive humans carried within themselves remnants of divinity. The "flesh and the blood" of the rebel god constituted a substantial part of their very being. Despite having been created specially to serve the gods, these *lullu-awilu* were themselves part divine. The "ghost memory" of their divine origins, however vague, still resonated deep within. So their "cries" of defiance and "din" likely were as much a clamoring to share in the privileges of divinity to which they felt themselves entitled, as it was an outright revolt against the tyranny of Enlil. (In this respect, Atrahasis paints a picture of human beginnings very similar to that of Genesis, wherein the first humans also desired to "be like gods.") The *lullu*, too, wished to assert their right to share divine privilege by ridding themselves of slavery to the soil.

The rapidly expanding human population thus posed a threat to divine rule, much as an expanding Hebrew population in latter day Egypt was perceived as a threat to Pharaoh's rule (Exodus 1:8–10). Like Pharaoh in Egypt, king Enlil tried to eliminate the threat to his authority by diminishing the sheer numbers of primeval humankind. Enlil's solution was to send a plague, by which he hoped to drastically reduce the *lullu* population. The god Enki, however, witnessing his beloved *lullu* dying off in droves, decided to thwart Enlil's scheme, lest the entire human population be lost. So Enki went secretly to "Extra-Wise" (Atrahasis) with a plan to save at least a remnant of primeval humankind. Atrahasis was not only Enki's devoted priest, he was also king of all the *lullu* and thus a natural choice by which to save humankind. Enki advised Atrahasis that humans should cease making offerings to their personal (favorite) gods and goddesses. Instead they should direct their offerings and prayers solely to Namtar, the god who controls plagues. Namtar will thus be so embarrassed by all the attention and special devotion directed to him that he will stop the plague. The scheme succeeded.

> Atrahasis followed (Enki's) instructions.
> He assembled the elders before his gate . . .
> The elders heeded (his) words.
> They built a temple for Namtar in the city.
> They commanded and [heralds] proclaimed.
> They clamored loudly [throughout the city].
> They did [not] reverence their (own) gods.
> They did [not] pray to [their (own) goddesses].
> They sought (only) [the door] of Namtar
> And [laid] in front of [it] baked (gifts).

The meal offering pleased (Namtar).
[The god was shamed] by the gift and withdrew his hand.
[The plague] left them.

Thus was the annihilation of primitive humankind averted. At least for a time.

Before another 1200 years had passed, however, the lullu population had once more multiplied, with the same result. Their clamoring again threatened Enlil's sleep. Enlil tried once again to decimate the *lullu*, this time by withholding rain in order to cause a devastating drought, and ultimately famine and starvation. Despite repeated attempts by Enlil to decimate the *lullu* population, each time Enki thwarted Enlil's plans by counseling Atrahasis to overwhelm with pious devotion the very deity responsible, whether for plague, or rain, or grain. And each time a remnant of primitive humankind was spared, thanks to Enki's wisdom and intervention. And each time the *lullu* population rebounded, and the process would begin anew.

Finally the ruler god Enlil reached the limits of his tolerance. Enough was enough. He decided to wipe out, once and for all, the entire rebellious *lullu* population by means of a universal flood. But first Enlil would have to restrain Enki, as by now Enlil had surmised that Enki alone was responsible for foiling each of his previous schemes.

Assembling the whole divine council, Enlil summoned Enki to appear before the gods and laid out the charges against Enki. Enki attempted to defend his actions, saying that he was acting to preserve what the gods had previously decreed, namely, that primeval humankind was to be created; therefore it should also continue in existence to serve the gods. But to no avail. The divine assembly sided with Enlil and affirmed Enlil's plan to annihilate the *lullu* through a universal flood. So that Enki would not once again thwart Enlil's decree, they made Enki swear under oath that he would not tell Atrahasis and the *lullu* about this impending flood.

Now Enki was not revered for wisdom without cause, however. He quickly figured out a way around his oath. He had only sworn not to *speak* the plan to Atrahasis. But revelations can be made in ways other than speaking. Enki approached the sleeping Atrahasis and delivered his message via a dream. Desperate to understand the dream, Atrahasis implored Enki for clarification. Because Enki was under oath not to communicate with his devotee, Enki instead spoke to the wall of the reed house in which Atrahasis was sleeping. Enki spoke to the wall not only news of the impending destruction but also detailed instructions on how to survive it. Atrahasis's house should be dismantled and from its materials a huge boxlike "boat" should be constructed, which Atrahasis and his family—and other life as well—could then board and so be saved.

When Atrahasis awoke, he heeded the warning from his dream. He tore down his house and began construction of the boat. To allay the concerns of the city elders about his strange behavior, Atrahasis told them that the gods were angry with him and that he had to depart from them, that he was going to live with his patron deity Enki, whose dwelling is located in the vast underground sweet water sea (which, by the way, is a motif common in Mesopotamian myths). *Mirabile dictu*, seven days later the boat was completed and fully provisioned. Just in time Atrahasis entered the boat along with his family and representative animals. The rain began to fall. For seven dreadful days, the storm god Adad unleashed his rain and lashed his winds against everything in sight. People could not see one another through the blinding rain. Even the gods were terrified at the storm's ferocity. The Anunnaki, the great gods, hunkered down in dismay, moaning with thirst and hunger cramps because there was no one to feed them, their *lullu* servants having perished in the flood. Enki was beside himself, watching his "children" drown. Mother goddess Nintu also wept and reproached herself. How could she have listened to Anu and Enlil (the president of the assembly and the king of the gods, respectively), those instigators of this scheme? How could she have agreed to this terrible deed—with her precious ones whom she had birthed now floating like dead flies in these raging waters?

Atrahasis and those with him rode out the storm aboard the boat. This is the point at which the Mesopotamian flood story parallels most closely the Genesis flood story. As the flood waters recede, the boat comes to rest upon a mountain peak. The flood hero sends out in succession three birds to determine whether it is safe to venture forth from the boat. When the flood hero finally determines that the waters have subsided sufficiently and does emerge from the boat, he immediately offers a sacrifice to the gods—or in the case of Noah, to Yahweh God.

As Atrahasis offered his sacrifice, the starving gods smelled the sweet savor and swarmed like flies over the sacrificer. After seven days without food and drink, the famished gods were relieved—and thankful—that a remnant of humankind had survived to feed them once more.

All—except Enlil, who arrived at the sacrifice angry that his will had been thwarted yet again. After much cajoling, however, even Enlil was persuaded that the survival of the *lullu* was a good outcome for the gods' own sakes.

Even so, something needed to be done about controlling the *lullu* "problem." They must not be allowed ever again to become so populous that the prerogatives of the gods are threatened. The *lullu* population must be kept in their proper place.

After further consultation, a compromise was reached between Enlil on the one side and Enki/Ea and Nintu on the other side. Various "human regulations" were instituted by Enki and Nintu. The humans would be allowed to reproduce as before, but now death was henceforth established as the normal course for humankind. According to a partially restored passage, Ea instructs Nintu, "You are the womb-goddess who decrees destinies; [create death] for (the) people." In addition, allow some babies to be snatched away at birth or from their mother's lap by she-demons. Some women are to be sterile and thus produce no children at all. Still other women should become priestesses of various kinds—Ugbabtu, Entu, Igiṣitu—for whom marriage was forbidden, and therefore remain childless for life. The remainder of the tablet is broken off at this point, but undoubtedly additional sources of death were listed, such as various illnesses and diseases. With these "human regulations" in place, a new era had begun for humankind. The descendants of "primeval humankind" (*lullu-awilu*) were reconstituted as simple "humans" (*nišu*). That is to say, they became the ordinary *mortals* who ever since have inhabited this earth.

Unfortunately, the last few lines of this epic poem are damaged. But enough is preserved to suggest that the "singer" (the composer) of this "Song of the Flood" was imagined to be none other than the mother goddess herself, Nintu, and that she composed this poem to praise "you, the counselor of the [great] gods," namely, Enki. The final line is a call for "all peoples" to "listen" to this paean of praise for Enki, the patron deity of humankind, the one responsible both for their conception in the beginning as well as for their ultimate preservation. In a very real sense, therefore, this epic poem is a celebration of humankind itself and its origins.

Related Mesopotamian Myths

Gilgamesh

For more than a millennium the tale of Atrahasis circulated widely throughout the ancient Near East. It was copied over and over, and in the process various modifications were introduced. It was also alluded to in other myths. Moreover, portions of it were incorporated wholesale into other compositions. The best-known example of the latter procedure is the "standard edition" (Neo-Assyrian version) of the epic poem Gilgamesh.[3] This tale of Gilgamesh is important for our agenda (a) because it too recounts the story of the flood, and (b) because it contains a story of a primeval human's quest of immortal life but which in the end is unsuccessful because he let a snake steal the "plant of life" from his hands. Both motifs reappear in the early chapters of the book of Genesis.

The Gilgamesh cycle is long and complex. There apparently was a historical person by that name, the king of the city-state of Uruk sometime between 2700 and 2500 BCE. Although we know virtually nothing about the historical person, his legendary namesake looms large in Mesopotamian lore. Already by the Fara period (ca. 2500 BCE) Gilgamesh was revered as a god to whom offerings were made. In the Sumerian King List "the god Gilgamesh" is named as one of the postdiluvian kings of Uruk. Because certain traditions associated Gilgamesh with the Underworld and the human struggle to overcome death, Gilgamesh also figures in several funerary texts. But actual literary compositions about Gilgamesh seem to begin only in the Third Dynasty of Ur (twenty-first century BCE), with some five or six independent tales—though all known copies of those early Sumerian tales date only to the Old Babylonian period (1900–1600 BCE). During the Old Babylonian period these Sumerian tales were brought together by a literary genius into a single, integrated Akkadian composition, with episodes arranged in a meaningful sequence and tied together by recurrent themes. Nearly a millennium later, during the Neo-Assyrian period, the Epic of Gilgamesh was again revised and expanded. This latest edition was the first to be discovered by modern archaeologists and so became known as the "standard version" of the Epic of Gilgamesh.

3. For convenient translations of this epic poem, see Dalley, *Myths from Mesopotamia*, 39–153; and *ANET*, 72–99 and 503–7; and most recently, George, *The Epic of Gilgamesh*; or the definitive two-volume critical edition by George, *The Babylonian Gilgamesh Epic*.

In this longest literary work from the ancient Near East, Gilgamesh has been transformed from a historical king into a semi-divine hero of epic proportions. Also, his companion Enkidu has been elevated from being Gilgamesh's servant to a hero in his own right. Gilgamesh, two-thirds god and one-third human, goes about accomplishing superhuman feats, accompanied by Enkidu. When Enkidu dies, Gilgamesh is forced to face the fact that he, too, is part human and therefore susceptible to death. Haunted by the prospect of death, Gilgamesh sets out on a quest of immortality. His quest eventually takes him to the isle of Dilmun, where lives Utnapishti with his wife. Utnapishti is none other than the flood hero we have already encountered in the Atrahasis myth, under another name. Mesopotamian tradition has it that, at the conclusion of the flood, the gods granted immortality to the flood hero and his wife, because they alone had survived the flood that killed off all the other primeval humans. Although death was imposed upon their descendants, the flood hero and his wife themselves were removed from the "land of the living," where ordinary mortals reside, and placed on the isle of Dilmun, located on the other side of the "ocean of death." Gilgamesh, determined to achieve immortality at any cost, decided to cross over to Dilmun in order to learn directly from the flood hero how to achieve immortality. Benefiting from his superhuman powers, Gilgamesh does the impossible. He manages to reach Dilmun on a raft, using 300 tall tree trunks as punting poles, being careful to discard each pole after a single thrust so as to avoid touching a single drop of the deadly waters. Exhausted from his arduous journey, Gilgamesh approaches Utnapishti and asks how he had achieved immortality. Here our texts diverge.

In the earlier, Old Babylonian version of this epic tale written circa 1700 BCE, Utnapishti merely tells Gilgamesh that the gods had gifted him and his wife with immortality at the conclusion of the flood. But as that was a unique event, no such opportunity is available to Gilgamesh. In the better known "standard" (Neo-Assyrian) version from a millennium later, a learned scribe has inserted the entire flood story, copied directly from the Atrahasis poem, though with several modifications. The most important modification was a notation that, at the conclusion of the flood, the flood hero and his wife were blessed by Enlil himself with immortality before being removed to the Dilmun where they now live as immortals. In Utnapishti's telling,

Enlil boarded the boat,
taking my hand, he brought me on board.
He brought aboard my wife and had her kneel at my side.
He stood between us and touched our foreheads, blessing us:
"Previously Utnapishti was mortal,
but now he and his wife shall become like us gods!
Utnapishi shall dwell far away, at the source of the rivers."
Taking me far away, they settled me at the place from which flow rivers.

Although immortality was not an option for Gilgamesh, he nevertheless continued pressing Utnapishti whether there might not be some other possible way to overcome death and gain immortality. Utnapishti replied, Yes, there might be. Sleep is akin to Death. If Gilgamesh were able for one week to forego sleeping, perhaps he might also be victorious over Death. Gilgamesh accepted the challenge—too rashly and too confidently. As soon as Gilgamesh sat to begin his seven-day vigil, he immediately sank into a deep sleep, so thoroughly exhausted was he from his just completed arduous journey to Dilmun. Utnapishti, aware that the mortal would deny that he had fallen asleep, had his wife bake a new loaf of bread each day as Gilgamesh slept on. On the seventh day Utnapishti awakened Gilgamesh. As predicted, Gilgamesh protested that he had not been sleeping; he had only momentarily nodded off. Utnapishti pointed to the loaves of bread, the first one already molded and crumbling into pieces—rendering pointless any further protestation by Gilgamesh.

Because Gilgamesh had failed in his quest of immortality, Utnapishti instructs his own boatman to ferry Gilgamesh back to the land of mortals. As Gilgamesh departs, Utnapishti and his wife offer one last glimmer of hope. They tell Gilgamesh a divine secret that was not supposed to be revealed to mortals. At the bottom of the ocean grows a special plant, which if eaten, will make one "eternally young." Thus encouraged, Gilgamesh ties heavy stones to his feet, after the manner of ancient pearl divers, and descends to the ocean depths. He successfully finds "the plant of eternal youth," brings it to the surface, and loads it onto the raft. Gilgamesh informs the boatman that he will sample the plant at their first rest stop.

When the two stop for the night, they break bread. But instead of immediately eating from the plant of life, Gilgamesh decides first to refresh himself with a cool dip in a nearby pool. A snake caught scent of the fragrant plant and carried it off in his mouth, sloughing off his old skin as it went. Gilgamesh, observing from a distance how the snake was renewing itself as it slithered away, could only mourn his own loss. (Similarities to Genesis are patent in that the human hero lost immortality because of a snake that somehow caused humans to lose access to the plant/tree of life.) Defeated at every turn, Gilgamesh's only option was to return to his city of Uruk, where tradition says he lived out the remaining years of his mortal life.

Preoccupation with human mortality is evident in the epic of Gilgamesh in other episodes as well, notably concerning the character Enkidu, Gilgamesh's bosom companion and accomplice in many prodigious feats. It was Enkidu's untimely and unexpected death that had set Gilgamesh off on his quest for immortality in the first place. But Enkidu did not start off as Gilgamesh's ally—quite the opposite.

Enkidu had originally been created by the gods to serve as a foil to Gilgamesh. Gilgamesh was no ordinary king, being two parts divine and one part human. Ordinary humans were no match for him, which inevitably spelled trouble for the citizens of Uruk. With no equal to challenge him, Gilgamesh asserted his superiority over his subjects in many and annoying ways, including claiming "first night's privilege" with the bride when one of his subjects married. Tired of such oppression, Gilgamesh's subjects cried out to their gods for relief. The gods responded by creating an equally strong opponent to engage Gilgamesh in contests that would keep him too preoccupied to bother the citizens of Uruk. The gods created Enkidu as a *lullu*, that is, as a primeval human with superhuman strength but possessing only primitive skills and subhuman intelligence. Prior to meeting Gilgamesh, the *lullu* Enkidu roamed the steppes naked, and living with wild beasts as his sole companions. Indeed, at this point Enkidu could be considered more animal than human.

Eventually though, Enkidu encountered the prostitute Shamhat and through intercourse with her, literally and figuratively, over time gradually became civilized and donned clothes. Subsequently however, when Enkidu attempted to return to his animal friends and run with them, they would no longer have anything to do with him and fled away. Moreover, he had lost his ability to keep up with his former animal companions. Enkidu grieves his loss of intimacy with the animal kingdom, but the woman consoles Enkidu with assurances that his new state is all to the good. He is no longer a lowly "primeval human" (*lullu*); he has "become truly human" (*awēliš iwē*). Enkidu would quickly realize that in his new condition he is much superior to what he had been in his former state. In keeping with his new condition, Shamhat advised Enkidu to make his way to the great city of Uruk where he might live appropriately as a true (cultured) human being. There he met the great king Gilgamesh, first as a rival but eventually becoming Gilgamesh's bosom friend and companion. Together the two traversed the land, accomplishing prodigious, superhuman feats.

Such prowess caught the eye of the goddess Ishtar, who proposed marriage to Gilgamesh. Remembering stories about how quickly Ishtar had grown tired of previous lovers, Gilgamesh refused her offer. There is no fury like the fury of a woman spurned, however. One thing led to another, until Ishtar demanded that one of the two "culprits" must die. The lot fell to Enkidu. The unexpected death of his friend set Gilgamesh into overdrive on a quest to secure his own immortality. That quest eventually took Gilgamesh to the isle of Dilmun where he encountered the flood hero Utnapishti and his wife, the only humans ever to have been blessed with immortality. But as we have already seen, Gilgamesh failed in his quest of personal immortality and had to return to Uruk to live out his remaining years.

Enkidu may have become human in the fullest sense of that word, but that could not save him from death. Even Gilgamesh, more god than human, was doomed to die. The epic of Gilgamesh is unrelenting in its message that death is inevitable for all of humankind.

Adapa: The First Human

A third Mesopotamian myth that must be considered part of the "backstory" for the Genesis story of Adam and Eve is a brief tale known as *Adapa and the South Wind,* or simply Adapa for short. Although certainly composed in Mesopotamia, the longest and most complete tablet containing this myth was discovered in ancient Egypt at Amarna. It is dated to the New Kingdom Period sometimes during the fifteenth or fourteenth century BCE. Other fragmentary copies of Adapa were found in the Assurbanipal library at Nineveh (seventh century BCE). But the origins of the myth are more ancient still, as Adapa is referenced already in Sumero-Akkadian bilingual texts more than a thousand years earlier.[4]

According to early Mesopotamian tradition, Adapa was the first of seven antediluvian sages known as *apkallu.* The *apkallu* were said to be

---

4. The most recent study of this myth, complete with a new edition of all known fragments, is Izreʾel, *Adapa and the South Wind.*

the first "humans," being intermediary between the gods and later humankind. In short, they were revered as primeval humans, but not like the *lullu*, whom as we have seen could be considered more animal than human. The *apkallu* received from the gods privileged instructions or "ordinances" about how the world of civilized humanity should function and how its denizens should live. These ordinances included matters such as the governance of society (kingship), how to organize an agricultural economy (dig canals, plow fields and harvest crops), the art of writing, laws about how citizens should conduct themselves, and the like. These sages were to pass these ordinances on to the generations who come after them, thereby laying the foundations of Mesopotamian civilization itself—the apex of all that is good and right for humanity. One tradition, however, claims that at some point all seven antediluvian sages offended the gods and were banished. Whether our tale of Adapa has any connection with that tradition is uncertain. In any case, as the very first of the *apkallu*, Adapa played a pivotal role in the development of humankind.

Tradition identified Adapa as a priest of Ea/Enki, the god of fresh water, whose palace was in Apsu, that vast underworld sea of fresh water so vital for the survival of humankind. As Ea's devoted priest, Adapa was depicted as a fisherman—and perhaps even part fish himself—whose task it was to supply fish for Ea's table, which provides the setting for the tale of *Adapa and the South Wind*.

The beginning and the end of the Amarna clay tablet—our longest and most complete witness to the tale of Adapa—is missing (broken off), thus leaving our understanding of this short narrative partially in doubt. The main contours are clear, however. The first preserved lines reveal Adapa fishing from his boat in what is now the northern portion of the Persian Gulf, near the island of Bahrain. This is significant, for even today at this location there is a huge freshwater spring welling up from deep within the saltwater of the Persian Gulf. It is understandable why ancient Mesopotamians conceived this area as a conduit reaching down to the palace of the god Ea, ruler of the underworld freshwater realm known as Apsu. A sudden storm wind from the South capsized Adapa's boat. Foundering in the sea, drowning even, Adapa curses the South Wind, immediately "breaking its wing" and rendering the South Wind immobile. For seven days there is no wind, leaving the land to languish in scorching drought. When Anu, the ruling god of heaven, discovers the cause for this catastrophe, he immediately issues a summons to Adapa to come up to heaven to give an accounting for his wrongful actions.

At this point Ea springs into action as well. He appears before Adapa with detailed instructions for Adapa to follow carefully. Adapa is to divest himself of his priestly robes, dishevel his hair and put on mourning clothes sprinkled with dirt, and affect a sad face. When Adapa approaches Anu's gate, he will be met by two adjutant deities, Dumuzi and Gizzida, who will question him as to why he is so dressed. Adapa is to respond that he is mourning two recently disappeared deities, namely Dumuzi and Gizzida. The two adjutant deities will be pleased to learn that they are missed on earth. Then they in turn will put in a good word to Anu for Adapa and so appease Anu's wrath.

Ea continued his instructions. Once in heaven, Anu will offer Adapa four things, (1) the opportunity to bathe and anoint his body with oil, (2) fresh garments, (3) water of life to drink, and (4) bread of life to eat. Adapa may accept the first two gifts but adamantly refuse the latter two, for they will actually be "water of death" and "bread of death."

Everything happened exactly as Ea had foretold. Anu extended the four gifts to Adapa. Heedful of his patron god's advice, Adapa accepted the first two but refused the "water of life" and the "bread of life." When Anu learned the reason for Adapa's refusal, he "laughed" at the foolishness of the human for passing up the opportunity for immortality by not drinking the water of life and not eating the bread of life:

> Anu looked at [Adapa] and laughed,
> "Come, Adapa, why did you not eat or drink?
> Hence you shall not live! Too bad for inferior humanity!
> . . . .
> Take [Adapa] and return him to his earth."

The conclusion of the tale is lost to us, as the tablet breaks off at this point. We are left, therefore, to speculate about its ultimate meaning.

In any case, this tale has some bearing on ancient Mesopotamian conceptions about the first human(s). It also has remote resonances with the Adam and Eve tradition. First, like Adam, Adapa is depicted as the first "human," so what happens to him determines the course of all humanity coming after him. Also like Adam, Adapa originally lived in close proximity to his god and served him devotedly, at least in the beginning. Adapa had the opportunity to receive immortality but squandered that opportunity, in part through the intervention of a divine or semi-divine figure counseling him. The motive of that other figure is ambiguous in the case of Adapa, as well as in the case of Adam (and Eve) as we will see in the next chapter.

Ea is directly implicated in Adapa losing immortality because Ea explicitly instructed Adapa not to eat or drink anything Anu offered because it would result in death. Scholars are divided over how to interpret Ea's intervention here. Was Ea mistaken about the food and drink that Anu would offer? Was Ea correct that Anu would offer "death"—only to have Anu change his mind after witnessing Adapa's humility (repentance) and therefore decided to offer Adapa "life" instead? Or did Ea purposely deceive Adapa about the nature of the gifts because he did not want Adapa and his descendants to have immortality? A case can be made for each of these interpretations. But in the end, I think the most compelling interpretation is that Ea deliberately deceived Adapa on the grounds that humans are not meant to have immortality. Immortality is a prerogative that belongs to gods, not to humans.

Ea was renowned for his superior wisdom, even among the gods. None of them could match his cleverness and his foresight. The Atrahasis myth credits him with the "creation" of humankind to be servants of the gods. Further, that same myth at it ending credits Ea with having imposed "death" upon humankind, lest in the future humans might again become so numerous that they are able to challenge the authority of the gods. Part of Ea/Enki's "wisdom," it would seem, is the insight that immortality is not an appropriate attribute for humankind.

Add to this mix the Mesopotamian trope that the three major deities of the Sumero-Akkadian pantheon—Anu, Enlil, and Ea—were in continuous competition one with the other. Eventually a compromise was reached whereby "the universe" was divided between them. Anu, the father of the gods, became ruler in heaven. Enlil was given earth and ruled there. Ea received Apsu, the mythical underground freshwater sea, where he established his kingdom. Cooperation was required if harmony were to prevail in the universe.

When Anu summoned Adapa to heaven to account for his wrongful action of stilling the South Wind, Ea apparently surmised that Anu would recognize Adapa's superhuman powers and offer him immortality—indeed, even let him remain in heaven. That may be why Ea intervened, to ensure that Adapa would never gain immortality but return to earth to resume his proper place and role as servant of Ea. If this is the correct reading of *Adapa and the South Wind*, then a link to the Adam and Eve tradition becomes more apparent. Adapa is yet another Mesopotamian antecedent to the Adam and Eve story in Genesis.

Postscript to "Backstory" Stories

These are far from the only stories from the ancient Near East relevant to the Adam and Eve tradition. One could adduce additional texts not only from Mesopotamia but also from Canaan, Egypt, and elsewhere that provide background materials for the early chapters of Genesis and for biblical conceptions of creation specifically.[5] The Mesopotamian myths highlighted in this chapter were chosen because they appear to have a more direct connection with the narratives in Genesis 1–9 than other ancient Near Eastern narratives. Not only are the Mesopotamian stories typologically similar as to content, but they are also chronologically earlier, sometimes by as much as a thousand years or more. As we progress through the next two chapters, it will be apparent that the stories of creation that comprise Genesis 1–3 and the biblical story of the flood in Genesis 6–9 are in part literarily dependent upon the Mesopotamian myths we have just analyzed. This is not to say that the biblical authors copied portions directly from those texts or had direct access to them. It may be that those stories were so much a part of the larger culture that biblical authors were familiar with them second or third hand, and appropriated aspects of that larger cultural world in much the same way an American student might incorporate, consciously or unconsciously, into her creative writing project various motifs of good and evil drawn from such diverse source as Nathaniel Hawthorne's 1850 novel *The Scarlet Letter,* the Disney film *Beauty and the Beast,* and the George Lucas futuristic fantasy *Star Wars.*

My contention is that the biblical authors of these opening chapters of Genesis drew heavily upon long-standing traditions about how the world began. There was no intent to plagiarize or to mislead the reader. Rather, it appears that the biblical authors were merely following cultural conventions of the day, and even incorporating the best "science" of the day. Their goal, however, was neither cultural nor scientific. Their goal was to represent the best religious understanding of the world as it is and to promote praise of Yahweh God as the authentic creator of all that is.

5. Among others, see my collected essays, Batto, *In the Beginning,* esp. chapter 1, "The Ancient Near Eastern Context of the Hebrew Ideas of Creation," 7–53.

2

The Yahwist's Creation Story

MOST OF US ARE confident that we know the story about Adam and Eve as narrated in the opening chapters of the book of Genesis. But are we accurately remembering the Adam and Eve narrative as it is actually written in the book of Genesis? Or are we filtering the Genesis story through the lens of Jewish and Christian interpreters many centuries later who have put their own "spin" on the story? The difference between the two perspectives is immense.

Two Creation Accounts

Scriptural scholars, at least academic critical biblical scholars, posit that the opening chapters of Genesis (1–11) actually contain two creation accounts and that these two accounts likely were composed several centuries apart. For the most part, the main contours of the two accounts are clearly visible—and therefore easily divisible—especially in the first five chapters of Genesis. One narrative now found in Genesis 1:1—2:3 plus Genesis 5 is attributed to a "Priestly Writer" (P), so named because of this author's inclination to emphasize priestly concepts, using priestly language. Parts of the flood narrative in Genesis 6–9 are also attributed to P. Based on internal evidence, this Priestly Writer seems to have written sometime in the sixth century BCE, perhaps during the Babylonian exile.

By contrast, the narrative in Genesis 2:4—4:26, as well as a second version of the flood story in Genesis 6–8, is thought to have been composed by someone living some three or four centuries earlier in the southern Kingdom of Judah. Modern scholars have labeled this earlier author "the Yahwistic Writer," or more simply "the Yahwist" (J), because this author normally references the deity by the name "Yahweh" or "Yahweh God" (often rendered in modern English translations as "the LORD" and "the LORD God," respectively). These two writers must be considered separately, due to their very different contents and perspectives.

The P narrative posits that before "God" (*Elohim*) began to create, there was only a chaotic mass of water (*tehom*) enveloped in complete darkness. The deity began to create by dividing the water and then organizing everything into an orderly whole in six days of creative activity. Everything is spoken into existence by God merely saying, "Let there be X." And so it happened. The deity's last act is to create humankind in his own image, both male and female at the same time. On the seventh day God "rests." There is no "garden of Eden" in this P account.

Like the P account, the J narrative also opens with a statement of conditions prior to the day when "Yahweh God" began to create. In contrast to the Priestly Writer who posited the precreation condition as being one immense chaotic ocean, the Yahwist assumed the precreation condition of the world to be nothing but a huge barren wasteland, a desert, where nothing grew. In this barren wasteland Yahweh God planted a garden, the garden of Eden. To take care of the garden, out of clay from the ground (*ha-ʾadamah*) Yahweh God created *ha-ʾadam*—better translated as "the Human" rather than "Adam," as in most bibles (Gen 2:7). Usual translations of this verse fail to capture the pun present in the original Hebrew which links the creature (*ha-ʾadam*) to the ground (*ha-ʾadamah*) from which he is taken and to which he is bound.

The garden quickly becomes the locus for additional activity. The deity must first find an appropriate companion for "the Human," resulting in the creation of the animals and eventually the creation of Eve. Following an encounter with an extraordinary snake, the man and the woman disobey the deity by eating a forbidden fruit, which results in their being expelled from Eden. Simultaneously, the man and the woman lose access to the "Tree of Life," which means that they and their descendants must die.

How these two very different creation accounts (J and P) eventually came to stand side by side in Genesis requires a lengthy investigation. We will begin with the Yahwistic Writer's narrative as the chronologically earlier story, even though in the present arrangement of Genesis it is placed second. The Priestly Writer's account will be examined in the following chapter.

A Free Translation of Genesis 2:4—3:24

At the time when Yahweh God made the earth and the heavens, there was as yet no vegetation on earth. No plant had sprung up because Yahweh God had not yet caused it to rain on earth. Also, there was no one to till the ground. A stream welled up from the earth and began to water the whole surface of the ground. Then Yahweh God molded the Human—clay from the ground—and blew life breath into its nostrils, and the Human came alive. Now Yahweh God had planted a garden in Eden, in the East; there he put the Human he had molded. From the ground Yahweh God caused all kinds of trees to spring up that were beautiful to look at, in addition to being good to eat. In the middle of the garden were the Tree of Life and the Tree of Knowledge of Good and Evil. A river arose in Eden to water the garden and from there spread out to become four headwaters. The first is named Pishon; it encircles the whole territory of Havilah, a place where there is gold—the gold of that country is excellent. Bdellium and onyx stone are there as well. The second stream is named the Gihon; it circles around the whole country of Cush. The third stream is called the Tigris; it flows to the east of Assyria. The fourth stream is the Euphrates.

Yahweh God took the Human and set him in the garden of Eden to work it and to watch over it. Now Yahweh God sternly admonished the Human, "You must eat[1] from every tree in the garden, except from the Tree of Knowledge of Good and Evil. You must not eat from it, because on the very day you eat from it you will most assuredly die."

Then Yahweh God said, "It is not good for the Human to be alone. I will make an appropriate companion for him. So Yahweh God molded from the ground all the land animals and all the birds of sky and he brought them to the Human to see what

---

1. Usual translations such as "You may eat from any tree" (except from the Tree of Knowledge of Good and Evil) do not capture the imperative force of the Hebrew grammar: "You *must eat* from every tree." The original intention was that the Human should eat from the Tree of Life and thereby become immortal, just like the gods (cp. 3:22). I thank the late Professor William H. Hallo for bringing this grammatical issue to my attention during a National Endowment for the Humanities Summer Seminar for College Teachers at Yale University, 1990.

he would name them. Whatever the Human named each, that became its name. The Human named each beast and each bird in the sky—every living animal. Nevertheless, for the Human no appropriate companion was found. So Yahweh God cast the Human into a deep stupor, so that he slept. Then [Yahweh God] took one of [the Human's] sides[2] and closed it up with human tissue. Yahweh God built the side that he had taken from the Human into a woman/wife, which he brought to the Human. The Human exclaimed, "Finally! Bone of my bone and flesh of my flesh, this is. This one will be called 'Woman' because from 'Man' she was taken." For this reason, a man/husband leaves his father and his mother to cling to his woman/wife, as the two become one flesh. Now the two of them, the Human and his woman/wife, were naked—and they were not ashamed.

[3] Now the serpent was wiser than all the beasts of the field that Yahweh God had made. It spoke to the woman: "Is it true that God forbade you (plural) to eat from every tree in the garden?" The woman answered the serpent, "We may eat the fruit of the trees in the garden. It is only the fruit of the tree in the middle of the garden that God said, 'You (plural) must not eat from it. You must not even touch it, or you will die!'" The serpent replied to the woman, "You (plural) most assuredly will not die. Indeed, God knows that on the very day that you (plural) eat from it, your (plural) eyes will be opened and you (plural) will become like gods knowing good and evil." When the woman realized that the (fruit of the) tree was safe to eat as well as a delight to the eyes—and furthermore, that the tree was to be desired for making one wise—she took some of its fruit and ate. She also gave some to her husband who was with her, and he ate as well. Immediately the eyes of both were opened. They comprehended that they were naked, so they sewed fig leaves together to make loincloths for themselves.

Then they heard sounds of Yahweh God walking about in the garden in the evening breeze. So the man and his wife hid themselves from Yahweh God in the midst of the garden trees. Yahweh God called out to the Human, "Where are you?" He answered, "I heard you (walking about) in the garden and I became alarmed because I was naked. That's why I hid." "Who told you that you were naked?" [Yahweh God] asked. "Have you been eating from the tree which I forbade you to eat?" The Human replied, "The woman/wife *you* gave me, *she* gave fruit from the tree, and I ate." Then Yahweh God said to the woman, "Why

2. On Hebrew *tsela'* as meaning "side" rather than "rib," see below.

have you done this?" The woman replied, "The serpent beguiled me into eating." Yahweh God said to the serpent,

"Because you have done this, you are more cursed than any beast,
　　more than the creatures of the field.
On your belly you shall go about;
　　you will eat dust every day of your life.
I will put enmity between you and the woman,
　　and between her offspring and your offspring.
He will strike you on the head,
　　while you strike him at the heel."
　　　　To the woman [Yahweh God] said,
"I will surely magnify your birthing pangs,
　　with pain you will birth children.
Your longing will be for your husband,
　　but he will dominate you."
　　　　To the man[3] [Yahweh God] said,
"Because you listened to your wife
　　and ate from the tree that I forbade you to eat,
the ground is cursed because of you.
　　Only with much toiling will you eke out a living.
When you attempt to eat plants from the field,
　　thorns and thistles will overwhelm you.
By the sweat of your brow
　　will you eat bread,
until you return to the ground
　　from which you were taken,
because you are dust
　　and to dust you shall return."

The Human named his wife Eve because she became the mother of all life. Yahweh God made garments from animal skin to clothe the Human and his wife.

Then Yahweh God said, "Indeed humankind has become like one of us in knowing good and evil. They must not be allowed to reach out and eat from the Tree of Life as well, for then they would become immortal." Accordingly, Yahweh God expelled [humankind] from the garden of Eden to till the ground from which it was taken. Having driven out the human(s), he stationed cherubim with flaming swords east of the garden of Eden to guard the path to the Tree of Life.

---

3. Or, "to Adam"; the usual definite article is lacking in this instance.

Eden: The Garden of God

As already noted, according to the Yahwist's creation narrative, before Yahweh God began to create, there was only barren wasteland, where absolutely nothing could grow: "no plant of the field was yet on the earth and no herb of the field had yet sprung up" because "Yahweh God had not yet created rain for the earth, nor was there anyone to till the ground" (Gen 2:5). Such were conditions before the deity began his creative activity.

Ignoring for the moment how the stream(s) came to be, Yahweh God's first explicit act was to mold *ha-'adam*—"the Human" (or "humanity/humankind")—from clay and then breathe some of his own life force into the inanimate clay figure, whereupon the clay figure became a living being. Older translations rendered *ha-'adam* as "man" or "Adam," both of which are misleading. Elsewhere (specifically, in Gen 5:1a), the Hebrew word *'adam* may indeed function as a proper name ("Adam"). But here—and in most occurrences within the Yahwist's primeval narrative—rendering *ha-'adam* as a proper name is not accurate because the vocable is preceded by the definite article: "the *'adam*." The primary referent of the Hebrew vocable *'adam* is to humankind in general, and not specifically to the male of the human species. Accordingly, a more accurate translation is that the deity created "the Human" (a representative figure) or "humanity/humankind" (a generic term for the species as a whole). The English word "man" should be avoided as being too ambiguous, since in English the term "man" can refer either to humankind in general (i.e., "humanity," its generic meaning, which includes women and children), *or* to a person of the male gender only (which excludes anyone of the female gender). Patently, the latter meaning is not what the author intended, as context makes clear.

The deity's second act was agricultural:

> Now Yahweh God had planted a garden in Eden, in the East, and he put there the Human he had molded. From the ground Yahweh God caused all kinds of trees to spring up that were beautiful to look at, in addition to being good to eat. In the middle of the garden were the Tree of Life and the Tree of Knowledge of Good and Evil. (2:8–9)

Normally overlooked in this agricultural notice is the fact that Yahweh God himself was the original gardener. He not only planted the garden; he also was responsible for making everything grow to perfection.

Up to this point the Human has done no work, though that will soon change. In the next panel, water is provided for the garden. It is not said explicitly that the deity was the one who provided the water, but it is implied. How else could a river suddenly appear in the middle of the garden of Eden, smack in the middle of what formerly was an arid wasteland? There is no one else around who could have accomplished this feat. There are also two important extrabiblical parallels which substantiate our positing that Yahweh God is responsible for the appearance of this river.

Archaeologists have excavated the royal palace of Zimri-Lim (died ca. 1550 BCE), the last king of the Amorite kingdom of Mari, located on the banks of the Euphrates river, in what is now eastern Syria. The excavators unearthed a telling fresco painted on the wall of king Zimri-Lim's throne room.[4] Even though painted almost 1000 years prior to the Yahwist's writing, this fresco illustrates well the motif of idyllic conditions depicted in Genesis 2. Keep in mind that in the ancient Near East the king was believed to be the designated representative on earth of the divine sovereign, the ruler of all the gods. The king thus stood in the place of the national god and ruled in the god's (or gods') stead. Royal propagandists attempted to capture this conceit in the fresco painted on the wall immediately behind the king Zimri-Lim's throne.

The fresco consisted of two panels, one above the other. In the upper panel Zimri-Lim stands piously before the goddess Ishtar, Mari's principal deity, who "invests" the king with his symbols of divine authority, the rod and the ring that she hands to him. Other deities flank on either side, confirming this conferral of divine power. In the bottom panel at either side stands a goddess holding a vase out of which flows water that immediately divides into four streams or rivers, two of which are surely the Euphrates and the Tigris which run through and around the kingdom of Mari. The streams connect at the top of the panel. It is doubtful that two goddesses are intended, as outside in the courtyard before the palace entrance was found a single goddess holding a vase so crafted so that water would have flowed forth from it in Zimri-Lim's time.[5] By this fresco the artist apparently was trying to convey that the whole of Zimri-Lim's kingdom—represented by the space in the middle of the panel—is

4. This drawing by Lauffray was first published by A. Parrot in *Syria* 18 (1937), pl. 39, fig.8; and reproduced in *ANEP*, fig. 610; and in Batto, *In the Beginning*, 110, fig. 13.

5. See drawing by M. Barrelet of the goddess with flowing vase from the Mari palace (now in the Aleppo National Museum no. 1659), reproduced in Batto, *In the Beginning*, 111, fig. 14; and partially reproduced in *ANEP*, fig. 516.

surrounded by divinely provided abundant waters—an idyllic kingdom with paradisaical conditions, if you will. One cannot help but compare the garden of Eden in Genesis 2, with its four rivers flowing from a single source, two of which are explicitly identified as the Euphrates and the Tigris.

FIGURE 1: INVESTITURE OF ZIMRI-LIM
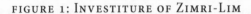

Fig. 1. Painting depicting the investiture of Zimri-Lim, from the throne room wall in the palace at Mari. Drawing by J. Lauffray (fig. 8 of André Parrot, "Peintures du Palais de Mari," *Syria* 18/4 (1937) 325–54). Used by permission.

Further support for a conceit of Yahweh God as the master irrigator comes from Tell Fakhariyeh in northeastern Syria, in a bilingual (Akkadian and Aramaic) inscription on a statue of the storm god Hadad. The inscription on the statue praises Hadad as

> the irrigation master of heaven and earth, who rains down abundance and provides pastures and water for the whole country; who supplies drink and food for all the gods, his brothers; the irrigation master of all the rivers, who makes luxuriant (*m'dn*) the whole land. (Aramaic version 11:2–5)[6]

Hadad, the Syrian storm god, is lauded above other gods as the one responsible for providing water for the entire country and making it "luxuriant." But there is more. The Aramaic word *m'dn*, translated here as "luxuriant," derives from the same Semitic root as the name Eden (*'dn*), the garden that Yahweh God irrigates.[7] Both Hadad and Yahweh are depicted as turning barren steppe land into luxuriant gardens. Although we cannot draw a direct line from the Tell Fakhariyeh inscription to the Yahwist's primeval story, patently there is some connection, such that we are justified in positing that the Israelite author understood Yahweh God's creative activity to be the work of the original master gardener, much the same as the Syrian author of the Tell Fakhariyeh inscription believed his god Hadad to be the original gardener and master irrigator of a barren wasteland.

Next, "Yahweh God took the Human and set him in the (now luxurious) garden of Eden to work it and to watch over it" (2:15). At last we learn the deity's purpose in creating the Human. This new creature was to take over the task of working and caring for God's garden—a task the deity previously had done himself. In short, the Human was created to be a substitute gardener for Yahweh God, to relieve the deity of the burdensome labor of caring for his own garden.

We have been conditioned by later interpreters to think that Yahweh God created Eden for the benefit of humankind, as a kind of human pleasure garden, if you will. That such was not the view of the Yahwist when writing this story, however, is evident from two data. First is the clear datum that in writing the primeval story of origins, the Yahwist

6. See Abou-Assaf et al., *La statue de Tell Fekherye*; see further Batto, *Slaying the Dragon*, 49–50.

7. A previous attempt to derive the name Eden from Sumerian **e d i n** now seems misguided.

patently patterned his narrative upon the prior myth of Atrahasis, as well as other Mesopotamian stories about human origins, which explicitly state that humankind was created to relieve the gods of burdensome tasks that they no longer wished to perform themselves. A second indication comes from the tentativeness of the creative process itself; the deity was required to make several alterations to his initial human prototype before finally achieving a satisfactory type of "humankind." That from the very start the deity planned everything for the benefit of "the human" clearly was far from the mind of the writer.

The Yahwist did not have to imagine *de novo* how the cosmos had taken shape. His cultural world had already provided satisfactory answers to many questions by way of various creation myths or stories noted already in the preceding chapter. Especially close both in theme and structure is the Mesopotamian creation myth Atrahasis. Similar to Atrahasis, the Yahwist purports to explain the proper place of humankind within the cosmos by showing that "our world" is the result of a series of tentative attempts on the part of inexperienced gods to achieve a workable model for creation. In other words, the creator god(s) required more than one try to achieve a cosmos that functions, if not perfectly, at least reasonably well. Both texts also link the creation of humankind with a story of "the flood" which narrates how a remnant of humankind was saved by divine intervention for the purpose of repopulating the earth.

The following chart comparing the Yahwist's primeval story with the Atrahasis myth reveals just how much the Yahwist was dependent upon this Mesopotamian story of human origins. The full implications will become clearer as we proceed.

TABLE 1

Comparison of Atrahasis and Yahwist's Creation Stories	
Atrahasis	*J's Primeval Story*
Irrigation agriculture assumes steppe setting of Mesopotamia	Eden (located in Mesopotamia): dry wasteland becomes a lush garden by irrigation
Igigi gods = original laborers who dig the canals and work the fields	YHWH = original laborer: planted a garden & irrigates it
Annunaki gods enjoy privileges of divine rank	Eden = YHWH's private garden with magic trees
	1. tree of life 2. wisdom tree (knowledge of good & evil)
Lullu (proto humans) created as substitute laborers for gods	Primeval human (*ha-'adam*) created to work and care for YHWH's garden
• modeled from clay + rebel god's blood • implicitly immortal (no natural death)	• modeled from clay + divine breath • implicit immortality (access to tree of life)
Institution of Marriage	Institution of Marriage
Lullu revolt against the divine sovereign	*Ha-'adam* aspires to divinity status by eating from wisdom tree reserved for deity
• their "din" and "cries" = rebellion • inherit "spirit" and "plot" of rebel god	• wisdom makes one "like gods"
Successive outbreaks of "sin"/rebellion	Cain, Lamech, "sons of God"—all increase sin
Punishment: life diminished by	Punishment: life diminished by
1. plague 2. drought 3. famine	1. expulsion from Eden 2. denied access to tree of life 3. curses
Flood	Flood (with obvious similarities to Atrahasis)
Atrahasis = pious wise king	Noah = righteous (& wise?, cp. Ezek 14:14)
• sacrifice = provisioning of gods	• sacrifice = provisioning of the deity
Gods smell sacrifice and bless survivors	YHWH smells sacrifice and swears oath
• Enlil reconciled and accepts situation	• YHWH reconciled to flawed humankind (evil from youth onward)
"Regulations for people" limitations on life	Lifetime limited to 120 years
• Provisions for natural death • *Lullu* become (normal) numans	• *ha-'adam* becomes (normal) human
Sign: Nintu's fly-necklace	Sign: duration of the earth and its seasons
[End of myth]	[Primeval period ends at Gen 8:22]

The Atrahasis myth, like the Yahwist's creation story, was set in the primordial period, when there were yet no humans and the land was a barren wasteland, like the arid steppe lands with which Mesopotamian folk were thoroughly accustomed. Without irrigation, agriculture was neigh impossible. Initially there were only the gods; there were no humans at all. To live and eat, the gods themselves had to provide for themselves. Or more accurately the ruler gods were making the lesser gods do the burdensome labors of plowing, planting, and harvesting the soil. They also had to dig irrigation canals to bring water to their fields. When their labors became too heavy to bear, the lesser gods revolted, forcing the ruler gods to find an alternate source of labor. Their solution was to create humankind. Enki, the god of wisdom, and Belet-illi, the mother goddess, conceived the idea of molding humanoid figures from clay moistened—or to be more exact, *animated*—with blood from the rebel god who had initiated the revolt. Being a combination of "clay" and "divinity," these primeval "humans" were assumed to be the perfect solution to the problem of devising something or someone to take over the agricultural burdens required to provision the gods, thus allowing all gods, whatever their rank, to enjoy the privileges appropriate to their divine status.

In the Yahwist's story of creation, humankind is likewise molded from the clay, though without any admixture of divine blood. Nevertheless, biblical humankind received an equivalent degree of divinity when Yahweh God breathed some of his own divine breath into the nostrils of "the Human." Unfortunately, the very next chapter, Genesis 3, will reveal that the deity's design for humankind will have problems. Initially, however, everything seemed to go exactly as the deity planned.

The Yahwist did depart from his Mesopotamian prototype in one significant way, however. Atrahasis had posited that the human species had originated with polygenesis; that is, original humankind had started with the creation of multiple humans. When the creator gods Enki and Belet-illi first conceived their scheme for humankind, they decided to mold seven pairs of humanoids—seven male and seven female—which they incubated for seven days, until the clay figures came alive. From the very beginning these human pairs were programmed with marriage "regulations" that destined them to become a self-propagating species. By contrast, the Yahwist posited that humankind began with a solitary (androgynous?) "Human." Only with further experience would the deity realize his mistake, namely, that "it is not good for 'the Human' to be alone." This set Yahweh God off on a search for a suitable companion for the creature. The deity's first remedial action was to mold additional creatures from clay, giving rise to the animal kingdom. When no suitable companion was found among the animals, Yahweh God went back to the drawing boards, so to speak, and cast the solitary "Human" into a "deep stupor." Yahweh God then divided "the Human" into two by taking one of his two sides and building it into a separate person.

Note that I said the deity took a "side" and not a "rib." The relevant Hebrew word here is *tsela'*—the basic meaning of which is "side" or "plank" or "stave." Only secondarily did *tsela'* acquire a meaning of "rib." Indeed, ancient Jewish rabbis debated which "side" God took in order to fashion it into a woman. Was it the right side or left side? The front half or the back half? The top half or the bottom half? Such debates led to fierce (and sometimes comical) debates about the proper social position of females vis-à-vis males. Were females implicitly subordinate to males, if they were formed out of the back or bottom half? Or were women intended to be the equals of men, especially if they were built out of the right side? Whatever the intended social position of women vis-à-vis men, just as did Atrahasis, the Yahwist likewise concluded this creation trope with a provision for the institution of marriage as the normal condition for humankind: "For this reason a man shall leave his father and mother and cling to his wife, and they shall become one flesh" (Gen 2:24). It turns out that having a self-propagating human species was a major concern in these ancient creation stories, and necessarily so if the human population is to be sustained.

Genesis 3: Enter the Serpent

If you or I were to go for a stroll along a familiar path in some well-tended orchard abounding with many delicious fruit trees and perchance come face to face with a serpent, standing tall and erect, especially one that started asking personal questions, I am quite sure that, like me, you would think oneself to be hallucinating, perhaps having imbibed too much liquor, or perhaps having accidentally overdosed on that new prescription pain killer. Coming face to face suddenly with a talking snake is completely foreign in our realm of experience, and even beyond imagination. To us, the scene in Genesis 3 appears completely fantastical, even impossible in the real world. But such would not have seemed at all beyond the realm of possibility to ancient Near Eastern folks.

To the people of ancient Egypt and Mesopotamia and Canaan, serpents—at least some serpents—were thought to possess divine powers and are regularly depicted as servants or protective companions of the gods. Ra (earlier known as Horus), the chief Egyptian god, for example, is regularly depicted as having a cobra (the cobra uraeus) or other venomous serpent stationed at either side of his head, poised to strike any viewer who failed to show proper deference for the august dignity of the deity. A deity might even take the form of a snake. In ancient Mesopotamia, Nirah, the messenger god of Istaran, was represented as a serpent on *kudurrus* (ancient boundary stones). Also, depictions of two intertwined serpents are common in Sumerian and Neo-Sumerian artwork and have been identified as representative of the god Ningishzida. The horned viper (Cerastes cerastes) appears in Kassite and Neo-Assyrian *kudurrus* and is invoked in Assyrian texts as a magical protective entity.[8]

The Bible is not exempt from this ancient Near Eastern cultural phenomenon. According to Isaiah 6, when the prophet experienced a vision of Yahweh seated on his lofty throne, he saw a seraph on either side hovering "above" the deity. Each seraph had three pairs of wings. With one pair they covered their faces, for even these creatures whose function was to protect the deity were unable to look directly upon Yahweh. A second pair of wings covered their feet—a euphemism for their genitals—signifying that, unlike the gods of the other nations, the God of Israel did not have a female consort and did not create by means of sexual intercourse. The third pair of wings was functional, that is, used for flying about. Moreover, verse 3 makes clear that these beings could speak and be understood by humans, as evident from their refrain, "Holy, holy, holy is Yahweh of hosts; the whole earth is full of his glory." By long standing Jewish and Christian tradition, we are accustomed to think of Isaiah's seraphim (the plural form of *saraph* in Hebrew) as angelic beings with spiritual bodies. But the ancient Israelites seemed to think that they possessed actual physical bodies. Specifically, they imaged the seraphim as winged, poisonous or "fiery" serpents, as is evident from elsewhere in the Bible.

According to Numbers 21:4–9, while the Israelites escaping from Egypt were in the desert, at one point the people became impatient and

---

8. Black and Green, *Gods, Demons and Symbols of Ancient Mesopotamia*, 166–68.

spoke against God and against his servant Moses, "Why have you brought us up out of Egypt to die in the wilderness? For there is no food and no water, and we detest this wretched food (manna)." Then to punish the ungrateful and rebellious Israelites, "Yahweh sent fiery seraphs among the people and they bit the people, so that many Israelites died." Clearly these "seraphs" were serpentine in form, for subsequently as an antidote against these snake bites, God commanded Moses to make a bronze image of a seraph and place it upon a pole so that whenever a serpent (*nahash*) bit someone, that person would "look at the bronze serpent and live."

The serpentine form is confirmed in the book of 2 Kings. Centuries later in the Kingdom of Judah, pious king Hezekiah initiated a series of reforms designed to root out idolatrous practices that had crept into the worship of ancient Israel. One of the reforms Hezekiah initiated was the removal of the Nehushtan from the temple in Jerusalem. "He broke in pieces the bronze serpent that Moses had made, for until those days the people of Israel had made offerings to it; it was called Nehushtan" (2 Kgs 18:4). The name Nehushtan is derived from the ordinary Hebrew word for "snake, serpent": *nahash*. The interchange in these Hebrew texts between *seraph* and *nahash* shows that in the minds of the ancient Israelites a seraph was a type of "snake." This is not to deny that a seraph might also be conceived of as possessing a divine character, at least at times.

Both from Isaiah's vision of the seraphim as protectors of the deity and from the portrayal of seraph serpents in Numbers 19 and in 2 Kings 18 one must conclude that in the ancient Israelite mind a seraph could be identified physically as a snake, likely a cobra as in the iconography of Egyptian divine king. Simultaneously, it could also possess the character and function of a semi-divine minister of the deity, comparable to the Egyptian uraeus.[9] Seraphim, not unlike some other biblical figures, were considered to be complex beings, such that they do not easily fit within our modern categories of reality.

All this, of course, is pertinent for understanding the nature and function of "the snake" in Genesis 3. It is identified as a *nahash*, the general term for a snake or serpent. But it likely was understood more specifically as a seraph-serpent, and to be identified physiologically with a cobra, universally feared because of their deadly poisonous bite. Cobras

9. For the identification of Isaiah's *seraphim* as comparable to the Egyptian uraeus, see Joines, "Winged Serpents in Isaiah's Inaugural Vision," 410–15; Keel, *Jahwe-Visionen und Siegelkunst,* 46–124; and Roberts, "The Visual Elements in Isaiah's Vision," 206–10.

are also noted for their ability to "stand" erect upon their coiled tails. Unlike Isaiah 6, no wings are mentioned in the Genesis text, but these likely are to be assumed. Certainly, this "snake," like Isaiah's seraphim, could talk and converse with humans. Apparently, it once stood upright, since after its punishment it was forced to crawl on its belly. Furthermore, it possessed great intelligence and was privy to divine secrets.[10]

Later Jewish traditions ascribe a nefarious character to "the snake," suggesting that it was hanging around in Eden hoping to catch one or other of the naïve human couple in an unguarded moment and seduce him or her into disobeying the deity's command.[11] But that appears to be wide of the mark as originally depicted by the Yahwistic writer of Genesis 3. Given various clues found in the Genesis text, one should assume that the deity had stationed "the snake" beside the Tree of Knowledge of Good and Evil to guard it and to protect it, lest the humans eat of its fruit and acquire "wisdom"—one of the two qualities which in ancient Near Eastern thinking were considered prerogatives of gods. Christian tradition (John 8:44–45; 1 Tim 2:12–14) likewise ascribed a malicious intent to the snake, namely, to seduce humankind into disobedience and thereby to bring death to humankind through willful sin against God. But the story need not be read that way. Given that the Yahwistic writer relied so heavily upon prior ancient Near Eastern myths—not just Atrahasis but also Gilgamesh, Adapa, and others[12]—one probably should understand Genesis 3 as originally written to be a story about how humankind came to possess wisdom, a prerogative reserved to the deity and his divine associates, of which "the snake" was one.

When read within its original cultural milieu, one recognizes that the biblical author unconsciously assumed that readers would understand that the garden in Eden belonged to the deity. The garden was his private preserve. One need only recall the words of Genesis 2:8–9:

> Now Yahweh God had planted a garden in Eden, in the East,
> and he put there the Human he had molded. From the ground

10. On the serpent in Genesis 3 as a seraph, see Batto, *Slaying the Dragon*, 59–61 with n. 46. Ezek 28:12-17 seems to have combined this seraph-serpent and the guardian cherubs of Gen 3:24 into a single cherub; see below pp. 51 and 130–31).

11. E.g., Wis 1:13–15; 2:23–24 alludes to this event, saying the God did not make death; rather "by the envy of the devil, death entered the world."

12. See Batto, *Slaying the Dragon*, esp. chapters 1–3; and my article "The Ancient Near Eastern Context of the Hebrew Ideas of Creation," in Batto, *In the Beginning*, pp. 7–53.

> Yahweh God caused all kinds of trees to spring up that were beautiful to look at, as well as good to eat. In the middle of the garden was the Tree of Life and the Tree of Knowledge of Good and Evil.

Much like the fabled hanging gardens of Babylon that were designed for the enjoyment of the Babylonian king, this magnificent garden was for the pleasure of the deity, a place where he might stroll and enjoy the cool evening breeze (3:8). The garden was not created for the benefit of humankind. Rather, humankind was created to serve as the gardener: "Yahweh God took the Human and set him in the garden of Eden to work it and to watch over it." (2:15). At the same time, "the Human" was allowed usufruct of the delights of the garden, with the sole exception of the Tree of Knowledge of Good and Evil. About this specific tree the Human had received a stern warning that "in the day that you eat of it you will most assuredly die" (2:17).

The snake's character has been much maligned over time. In Genesis 3:1 the snake is said to be more ʿarum than all the wild animals that God had created. The difficult Hebrew word ʿarum has been translated variously, usually with negative connotations, for example in recent English versions: "crafty" (NRSV), "subtle" (RSV), "cunning" (NKJV, NAB). Such negatives connotations may be traced back to the Latin Vulgate translation as callidior, which carries a wide semantic range of meanings, often pejorative: (more) crafty, sly, cunning, wise, skillful, clever, ingenious. But the Greek Septuagint translation is more straight forward: phronimōtatos "wise," which seems to best capture the meaning of the original Hebrew vocable. Apparently, the Yahwistic writer meant to pun on the snake's own innate wisdom (ʿarum) standing in stark contrast to the condition of the human couple who are said to be "naked" (ʿarum; 2:25), which is to say, "naïve." But if the human couple was naïve—innocent and vulnerable—apparently so was the snake in its straight-forward wisdom, its ʿarum-ness.

The snake's question, "Did the deity tell you not to eat of the tree?" does not appear to have been a ruse designed to trip up the woman. Rather it may have been a sincere question, a simple probing for information, or perhaps even a way to strike up a friendly conversation with a figure newly introduced onto the scene. When the woman responds by overstating the situation—not only that the humans were prohibited from eating of the tree's fruit but even from touching it, lest they die—the snake felt compelled to correct her misconception. From its own knowledge of the nature of the tree, namely, that partaking of its fruit would impart divine wisdom, the snake unwittingly revealed a secret that humans were not supposed to know. In short, according to a long-standing ancient Near Eastern trope, wisdom is a divine prerogative. Only the gods and semi-divine beings were supposed to possess true wisdom. Humans are not allowed to partake of this divine privilege precisely because they are not gods. As a semi-divine being, however, the snake legitimately had access to the fruit of this tree and therefore to its wisdom. It knew firsthand, perhaps even from tasting its fruit, the power of the tree to impart divine wisdom. But it was a mistake—a sin, if you will—to have revealed that secret to humans, who were created without such wisdom. Although the snake's intentions were not malicious, both humankind and the snake would suffer greatly from the snake's folly.

In the preceding chapter we considered the ancient Mesopotamian myth of Adapa, which also contained the trope of immortality being lost to humankind. Like Genesis 2–3, Adapa is a story about the first human. Indeed, the name "Adapa," exactly like biblical ha-ʾadam, means "(the) Human" or "humankind." As we saw, Adapa was a faithful (pious) priest in Eridu of the god Ea, the very god who in the myth Atrahasis is credited with having created humankind to be servants for the gods. As the first human, Adapa found himself in uncharted waters, literally. When a storm wind from the south churned up the sea and capsized Adapa's boat, an angry Adapa uttered a powerful prayer/curse against the south wind, breaking its wing so that it could no longer function. This action saved Adapa, but it also prevented the wind from blowing and bringing the much-needed rain. In reaction to Anu, ruler of the divine assembly, having summoned Adapa to account for his (mis)deed, Adapa's patron god Ea advised Adapa to appear most contrite when he appears before Anu. Moreover, Adapa should refuse Anu's offer of "bread of life" and the "water of life," as these will actually be "bread of death" and "water of death." Following Ea's advice, Adapa refused Anu's offer of bread and water, thereby forfeiting for himself and his descendants the opportunity for immortality.

As previously noted, the ending of Adapa is lost; we can only speculate about the ultimate meaning of the myth. Why did Ea instruct Adapa to refuse these gifts which would have resulted in immortality? Given Ea's reputation for wisdom, it seems most unlikely that he was ignorant of the true nature of Anu's divine gifts. More likely, Ea, being the creator and patron of humankind, deemed it inappropriate for humans to have both divine wisdom *and* immortality. Adapa was an apkallu, one of the seven original sages from whom all human wisdom was derived. In other words, Adapa, like Atrahasis, was already "exceedingly wise." This would suggest a motive for Ea not wanting Adapa to have immortality. If Adapa already possessed divine wisdom, then this (primeval) human must not be allowed to acquire immortality as well, lest Adapa become fully divine. The boundary between humankind and divinity must be maintained.

Adapa thus provides a key to unlocking the mysterious conduct of Yahweh and the snake in Genesis 3. Humankind had been granted access to the Tree of Life, that is, to immortality, even though the primal human couple had as yet failed to partake of its fruit. But because they had access to immortality, simultaneously they were forbidden to partake of the Tree of Knowledge of Good and Evil, that is, the divine wisdom, since partaking of both would make them fully divine. "Knowledge of good and evil" is the equivalent of *divine wisdom*. The deity acknowledges as much in stating his reason for driving the man and the woman out of Eden.

> Then Yahweh God said, "Indeed humankind (*ha-'adam*) has become like one of us in knowing good and evil. They must not be allowed to reach out and eat from the Tree of Life as well, for then they would become immortal. Accordingly, Yahweh God expelled [humankind] from the garden of Eden to till the ground from which it was taken. (3:22–23)

So when the snake informs Eve that eating from this "tree of wisdom" will not kill her but rather will result in acquiring wisdom such as gods possess, the snake is not lying but speaking the truth as it knows it. Even so, such truth-telling results from a certain naiveté on the snake's part. This was a secret that the snake should not have revealed—hence the reason for its own punishment. The ironic part—and fortuitous, at least according to later Christian theology—is that because of the snake's intervention, humankind ultimately will acquire even greater divine status than that to which they aspired in the garden. As the apostle Paul proclaims in his New Testament gospel, because of the redemptive work of "the second Adam," humans are destined to become adopted children of God. This truly is the stuff of primeval myth—an account of how things came to be the way they are.

But we are getting ahead of ourselves in this growing tradition. Let us return to Eden and pick up the story at the point when the human couple is about to disobey the deity's commands.

Eve is often depicted as the culprit here, as if her husband were away in another part of the garden and thus completely unaware of what the serpent and Eve were up to; and only after the fact of Eve's eating, was Adam subsequently seduced by Eve to partake of the forbidden fruit. Nothing could be further from the truth. The Genesis text is very explicit in stating that Adam was right there beside Eve as she and the serpent were conversing, and therefore cognizant of everything that was going on. The text reads, when Eve ate, "she gave some (of the fruit) to her husband, *who was with her,* and he ate (as well). Then the eyes of both were opened" (3:6–7).

The notion that in Genesis 3 the man was absent when Eve ate the forbidden fruit and therefore less guilty is due in large part to St. Jerome who in his Vulgate Latin translation omitted the Hebrew phrase "who was with her" ('imah), thereby perpetuating the misperception that Eve alone heard the serpent speaking and that she alone ate initially, and only later tempted her husband to "sin" as well. Jerome likely came to this idea from a Jewish pseudepigraph, Life of Adam and Eve, which as we will see claims that Adam was away in a different part of the garden when the serpent seduced Eve. However, the Hebrew text of Genesis 3 is quite explicit that the man was present the whole time and was as much responsible as the woman for disobeying Yahweh God's command.

The Deity

Just as the serpent in this story is not the devil (Satan), so also the figure "Yahweh God" is not the monotheistic God of later Judeo-Christian belief. Rather, the deity depicted in the Yahwistic narrative here derives from a much earlier religious tradition, namely the preexilic Israelite religious practice known as henotheism. The difference is this. Monotheists not only worship one God—proclaimed as the one true God—they also deny the existence of any other god or gods. Henotheists also worship only one god, but they do not deny the existence of other gods. The god they worship often is either their national or patron deity, or it is revered as the supreme deity within a pantheon of gods—the king of the gods, if you will—but it could just be one's favorite deity.

Prior to the Babylonian exile, most Israelites were henotheists—if not outright polytheists (worshippers of many gods). True, at Sinai the Israelites made an exclusive covenant with "Yahweh God": "I am Yahweh your God, who brought you out of the land of Egypt, out of the house of slavery; you shall have no other gods before me" (Exod 20:2). But as the Hebrew Bible makes abundantly clear, the Israelites—whether in the northern kingdom of Israel or in the southern kingdom of Judah—mostly failed to live up to this covenant ideal. The Israelites cheated in that they frequently worshipped other gods: Baal, Asherah, El, Molech, or the queen of heaven, to mention just a few.

Indeed, one may wonder if there existed any true monotheists among those ancient Israelites. Consider Deut 4:19.

> When you look up to the heavens and see the sun, the moon, and the stars, all the host of heaven, do not be led astray and bow down to them and serve them, things that Yahweh your god has allotted to all the peoples everywhere under heaven. (NRSV)

Patently, the sacred writer considered the heavenly luminaries to be divinities, but worship of those divinities was permissible only for the other nations. Israel, by contrast, was restricted to worshipping "Yahweh your god" alone.

Other sacred writers likewise betray their henotheistic tendencies, among them the poet who penned Exod 15:11, "Who is like you, Yahweh, among the gods?" Not infrequently the psalmist also extols the incomparability of Yahweh and his powers within the pantheon of gods, as in Ps. 86:8, "There is none like you among the gods, Yahweh, nor are there any works like yours." Other psalms proclaim that Israel's patron deity is king over all gods: "For Yahweh is a great god, and a great king above all gods" (95:3); and even more loudly, "For I know that Yahweh is great; our lord is above all gods" (135:5). Psalm 82 depicts a courtroom scene in which all the "children of the Most High"—in Canaanite literature "Most High" is a title of the god El, head of the Canaanite pantheon—are seated in judgment; God (=Elohim, Israel's patron deity) rises to denounce the rest of the gods for their failure to act justly and impartially on behalf of the weakest among humankind, especially orphans—clearly a dereliction of their divine duty. These and other passages make evident that ancient Israelites did not deny that there may be other gods. Nevertheless, these Israelites are vociferous in their affirmation that their national god is supreme in power and majesty. This is the deity depicted by the Yahwist in his Genesis creation narrative.

Although ancient Near Eastern peoples understood the gods to be vastly superior to humans in every respect, the gods' powers were not unlimited. The Mesopotamian gods depicted in Atrahasis, for example, required more than one try to achieve an acceptable and sustainable human population that met their requirements to provide for the needs of the gods. The Yahwist's conception of Yahweh God was not much different. As we have already noted, Yahweh God likewise required several attempts before achieving an adequate design for his newly created human population. As should be obvious by now, ancient Near Eastern folk, and that includes ancient Israelites, did not consider their deities to be omniscient. Despite possessing vastly superior intelligence, ancient Near Eastern gods were not all-knowing—and therefore were not always able to anticipate how humankind would act in the future, or for that matter, how other divine beings might act. Certainly, that was the case with Adam and Eve and the serpent in Eden.

Human Hubris as a Threat to the Deity

Once the first man and woman had eaten the fruit of the wisdom tree, their minds were immediately enlightened. As the serpent had predicted, they did acquire additional knowledge—wisdom that allowed them to understand their own condition vis-à-vis Yahweh God.

The forbidden fruit they ate was from "the tree of knowledge of good and evil." Just what is meant by this phrase is debated. Some have suggested that it meant that the primal human couple was tempted to decide for themselves what they could legitimately do or not do; or to put it more simply, humans wanted to decide for themselves what is moral and what is immoral. Others have seen here a reference to sexual indulgence, taking their cue from Barzillai's remarks to David when David promised Barzillai all kinds of pleasant rewards if Barzillai would accompany David back to Jerusalem to reclaim the throne (2 Sam 19:31–37). Barzillai begs off, saying that at age eighty he can no longer distinguish between "good and evil," by which Barzillai means that he no longer derives any pleasure from sumptuous food and drink, or from entertainment provided by singing girls and singing men. In short, Barzillai appears to be saying that all his sensual and sexual appetites have dissipated. While sexual indulgence is a plausible interpretation of the phrase "knowing good and evil," nevertheless, ancient Near Eastern context suggests a still better explanation.

Most likely the Yahwist understood the fruit of the tree of knowledge to refer to a kind of universal knowledge. In this case, the meaning of "knowing good and evil" would be the equivalent of our expression about knowing everything from A to Z. In short, the serpent informed the human pair that by eating from this special tree they would gain divine wisdom, that they would acquire additional knowledge comparable to that of Yahweh God or his divine court. After all, the garden was the deity's own private preserve, to which he and his divine court had ready access. Recall the rationale of Yahweh God for banishing the human couple from the garden: "Indeed humankind has *become like one of us in knowing good and evil.* They must not be allowed to reach out and eat from the Tree of Life as well, for then they would become immortal." Paraphrasing the deity's meaning, humankind has illegitimately acquired one divine quality—wisdom. They must be prevented from acquiring yet a second divine attribute—immortality—lest they become fully divine.

Ezekiel 28:12–17 confirms that knowledge of good and evil is be understood as divine wisdom. In this passage the prophet compares the wicked king of Tyre to the cherub that God had once stationed as "guardian" in "Eden, the garden of God." This figure is described as a "serpent of perfection, full of wisdom and perfect in beauty" who because of arrogant pride "spoiled [his] wisdom." Whether Ezekiel 28 is dependent upon Genesis 3, or the other way around, patently these two passages are related; and the one helps to clarify the meaning of the other. Ezekiel's divine "serpent," characterized as "full of wisdom," no doubt owed its wisdom to its daily access to "the Tree of Knowledge of Good and Evil."

Although humankind did acquire a knowledge comparable to that of divine beings, the results were not as expected. With their heightened knowledge, the man and the woman immediately understood the implications of their nakedness. Animals feel no shame in being naked. But humankind, despite having much in common with the animals, is also higher in status than the animals because humans also possess some degree of divinity. At creation, primeval humankind had been animated with the deity's own life force when Yahweh God breathed life into "the Human" (Gen 2:7). Yet humankind was not fully divine, as is evident from the fact that the primordial couple was naked. Ancient Near Eastern gods are always depicted as clothed; they are civilized and sophisticated, not uncivilized savages. By contrast, primitive or primeval humans were naked, the same as the animals.

This was a common trope in ancient Mesopotamian literature. Numerous Sumerian and Akkadian stories tell how primitive humankind originally was little better than animals in the way they lived. The Sumerian myth "Ewe and Wheat" (also known as "Lahar and Ashnan") depicts primeval humans as a sorry lot indeed:

> The people of those distant days . . .
> They knew not cloth to wear.
> They went about with naked limbs in the land,
> And like sheep they ate grass with their mouth,
> Drinking water from ditches.

Only after the gods arrived on the scene and taught the first humans better, did humankind achieve the high civilization for which the ancient Sumerians and Akkadians prided themselves. In this regard they are the exact opposite of ancient Greeks who conceived of human history as *regressive*, that is, as devolving from a Golden Age at the very beginning to ever sorrier human periods as time elapsed. By contrast, Mesopotamian folk thought of human history as *progressive*, with humankind continuously improving. Mesopotamian myths depict the first humans as ignorant and primitive creatures. But thanks to various divine patrons who intervened to help, humankind steadily advanced along the path to civilization until finally attaining the pentacle of human achievement now manifest in the high culture of the Sumerians and Akkadians themselves.[13]

The Gilgamesh epic contains a related theme, as noted in the previous chapter. Enkidu, the figure designed by the gods to serve as a distraction to Gilgamesh, king in Uruk, originally had been created a *lullu,* a primeval human with superhuman strength but subhuman intelligence and limited learning. Prior to meeting Gilgamesh, the *lullu* Enkidu had roamed the steppes naked, living with wild beasts as his sole companions. In Enkidu's initial condition, he is portrayed as a brute, more animal than human. However, through human intercourse—literally and figuratively with the woman Shamhat—Enkidu gradually became civilized and donned clothes. The result was that he could no longer cavort with the animals, having become "human" (*awēliš*). Clothes symbolize the distance between humankind and animalkind, on the one side, and the similarity between humans and the gods, on the other side.

---

13. For an extended treatment of the Mesopotamian motif of creation as continuously improving, see Batto, "Paradise Reexamined," 34–50.

Returning to the Yahwist's story of human origins in Genesis, when the man and his wife recognize that nakedness is unfitting to their status as partially divine beings, they attempt to remedy the situation by making clothes for themselves. Having no experience with cloth and without a teacher, the primal couple fashioned loincloths for themselves from fig leaves (Gen 3:7). That they used fig leaves has no discernible significance here. Their attempt at making loincloths is patently a clothing failure, however. When Yahweh God expelled the man and his wife from the garden, he replaced their fig-leaf loincloths with "garments made of skin" (Gen 3:21). This action is often considered to be an act of mercy on the part of the deity. More likely, however, the deity's actions here should be understood as one more attempt on the part of deity to enforce proper distancing between humanity and divinity—something the humans had attempted to do away with by their striving to become like gods. Dressing the human couple in animal skins rather than in cloth would appear to be the deity's way of asserting that humankind has more in common with the animal kingdom than with the gods.[14] After all, humankind and the animals had been formed from the same earthy substance: clay.

The Deity under Siege

Human attempts to usurp divine prerogatives are not the only challenge facing the deity in this story. Incomplete knowledge is another. As already remarked, ancient Near Eastern gods were not omniscient. Yahweh God was no exception, as is apparent in the fact that he required more than one try to create a workable model of humankind, nor did he anticipate many of the problems that would arise.

The limited knowledge of the deity is also evident in the way he learns about the disobedience of the human couple in Genesis 3.

> When the man and the woman heard the sound of Yahweh God walking about in the garden in the evening breeze . . . they hid themselves from Yahweh God in the midst of the garden trees. Yahweh God called out to the Human, "Where are you?" He answered, "I heard you (walking about) in the garden and I was frightened because I was naked. So I hid." "Who told you that you were naked?" [Yahweh God] asked. "Have you been eating from the tree which I forbade you to eat?" (3:8–11)

14. For this trope see Batto, "Paradise Reexamined," 55 with n. 72.

As was the deity's wont, one cool evening as he walked about his pleasure garden, he noticed that the man and his wife were nowhere to be found. So he called out, "Where are you?" This was not play acting on the part of the deity. Read in a straightforward manner, the narrator appears to say that the deity truly did not know that the human couple were hiding. Nor did the deity know what had transpired in the garden until the man blurted out his shame concerning his nudity. Only then did the deity realize that the human couple had tasted the forbidden fruit. Moreover, an inquisition of the man and the woman and the serpent, each in turn, was necessary for the deity to ascertain what had happened and how it had come about. An appropriate punishment could be imposed only after establishing the guilt of each participant.

Learning what had transpired in his absence, the deity quickly comprehended the seriousness of the threat to established divine order. Although not explicitly stated, it must be assumed that Yahweh God summoned all the gods into council, as he informed them, "See, humankind has become like one of us, knowing good and evil. They must not be allowed to reach out and eat from the tree of life, for then they would become immortal" (Gen 3:22). Having usurped one divine attribute (wisdom), humankind must be prevented from acquiring yet another divine attribute (immortality).

The sentences meted out to the man and the woman and the serpent (Gen 3:14–19) are less punishments than statements of what their respective conditions outside the garden will be like. Life will not be easy. The (Seraph) serpent will be reduced to an ordinary snake, forced to crawl on its belly—and always in fear for its life because of perpetual enmity with humankind. As for the woman, who in the garden had enjoyed equality with her husband, henceforth outside Eden she will not only be dominated by her husband (and males in general) but also will suffer great pain in birthing children. The man, previously in symbiotic harmony with the ground from which he had been formed and which heretofore he had easily cultivated, now will find that same ground uncooperative and even resistant to agricultural manipulation. These are not so much punishments imposed from above as they are descriptions of what to expect. Life inside the garden of God had been easy, a pleasure even. Life outside will be a perpetual struggle just to survive.

Expulsion from Eden also was less a decree of divine punishment for sin than a desperation move by the deity to enforce radical separation between the divine and the human realms. Humans are not gods, and the demarcation between the two must be maintained at all costs. At the same time, expulsion from the garden of God was an implicit admission by the deity that he was partially at fault for having failed to anticipate that humankind would attempt to usurp divine prerogatives, or even desire them.

What about Sin?

It is worth noting that nowhere in Genesis 2–3 is there mention of "original sin." The concept of original sin developed only much later, outside the confines of the Hebrew Bible/Old Testament. Indeed, the word "sin" is never used in connection with the events that transpired in Eden.[15] The first occurrence of the term "sin" (*ḥaṭṭāʾ*) in the Hebrew Bible comes only in Genesis 4, in the narrative about Cain and Abel. Although Genesis 4 now stands as a reasonably apt extension of the garden of Eden story of Genesis 2–3, there are a number of indications that the Cain and Abel story may have had its genesis in a different literary setting. First, the story of Cain and Abel is set entirely outside the garden, with no allusion whatever to the garden or to expulsion from it. Second, the deity is differently named here, simply as "Yahweh," whereas in Genesis 2–3 the deity was consistently named "Yahweh God." Third, the interaction of Cain and Abel is between two fully grown men, each firmly entrenched in his chosen occupation: Cain as a farmer and Abel as a sheep herder. Cain's occupation as a cultivator of the soil is understandable as a continuation of the task assigned to Adam ("the Human") at his creation. But Abel's profession, tending sheep, is novel and has no preparation in the larger narrative. Surely there is a backstory here that has been lost, which, had it been preserved, would also certainly make more understandable why the deity favored Abel's offering from his flock over Cain's offering from the produce of the soil. As it is, both brothers seemed intent on pleasing Yahweh by offering choice portions of what their individual labors have produced.

One may also pause to speculate where the idea of making offerings to God comes from, since nowhere in the narrative up to this point has humankind been commanded or instructed to do so. An answer to this question may be provided, once again, from the Atrahasis myth.

15. See Smith, *Genesis of Good and Evil,* esp. chap. 4, "Is Genesis 3 about Human Sin?"

Certainly, the motif of Noah offering a "sweet-smelling" sacrifice to Yahweh at the conclusion of the flood derives from the parallel scene in Atrahasis. It stands to reason that familiarity with the Mesopotamian flood tradition led the Yahwist to posit a universal obligation on the part of humankind to offer sacrifices to the deity. Atrahasis explicitly posits the reason humans were created in the first place was to be servants of the gods by providing food for them. Burnt offerings were the normal way of converting both cereals and animal flesh into a spiritual form that the gods could consume. It might be assumed, therefore, that the very first action of humankind outside the garden would be to offer sacrifices to the deity. Following upon the expulsion of the man and the woman from Eden, their children dutifully carry on with this foremost human obligation.

No matter how one resolves the origins of making sacrifices to the deity, the apparent arbitrariness on the part of Yahweh in favoring Abel's offering over Cain's is what so upset Cain and what led to the "sin" of killing his brother. After all, had not Cain taken up the task that Yahweh God had assigned to his father, namely, to be a cultivator of the soil? Whatever the case, as the narrator tells it, Cain was so visibly angry that the deity could not fail to notice.

> Yahweh said to Cain, "why are you angry, and why has your countenance fallen? If you do well, will you not be accepted? And if you do not do well, sin is a croucher at the door; its desire is for you, but you yourself can control it!" (4:6–7)

Even though "sin" is said to be crouching at the door—always lurking on one's doorstep, so to speak—sin is not presented here as inevitable. It can be overcome, even if sometimes only with difficulty. And certainly, sin as depicted here is not something that is passed on genetically from parent to child at conception, as postulated in the later Christian doctrine of "original sin." Indeed, the concept of "original sin" is nowhere to be found in the Hebrew Bible. Without denying the pervasive sway of evil over humankind, Israel's sacred writers all maintain that one can—and must—resist sin in all its forms. Deuteronomy expresses well this biblical view that no one is doomed to disobey God; everyone is capable of keeping the divine commands.

> Most assuredly, this commandment that I am imposing on you today is not too difficult for you, nor is it very distant. It is not in heaven, that you should say, "Who will ascend to heaven for

us, and bring it down us so that we may hear it and observe it?" Neither is it across the sea, that you should say, "Who will cross the sea for us and get it for us, that we may hear it and carry it out?" No, it is something very near to you; it is already on your lips and in your heart, just waiting for you to carry out . . . Today I call heaven and earth to witnesses against you: I have set before you life and death, blessings and curses. Choose life, and you and your descendants will live. (Deut 30:11–14, 19)

The Flood

If, as has been hinted, the Cain and Abel story in Genesis 4 originally belonged to another narrative cycle and was only secondarily attached to the Adam and Eve cycle, then the Yahwistic primeval story continues directly from Genesis 2–3 into Genesis 6, that is, with the flood story. This would make comparisons with Atrahasis even more compelling, since in that Mesopotamian myth the flood narrative is the essential resolution to a conflicted story of human origins. It is not necessary, however, to exclude Genesis 4 from the Yahwist's primeval story, as the sin of Cain and other stories of human wrongdoing in Genesis 4 could be seen as the equivalent of the several acts of rebellion against the gods in Atrahasis that led the god Enlil to bring on the great flood in a final desperate attempt to rid the earth of the human problem. Either way, the flood is part and parcel of the myth of human origins. It is the flood that brings the story to a successful resolution. The flood is the event that forced Enlil and the gods in Atrahasis—and likewise Yahweh God in Genesis—to accept, however reluctantly, the necessity of a flawed humankind living in a symbiotic relationship with their divine creator(s). The contours of the flood story are essentially the same in both narratives.

Atrahasis relates the story thusly. As the human population expanded, so did their "cries" and "din," the uproarious clamor of their rebellion/ sin. Enlil, the ruler god, perceived the persistent outcries of primeval humankind as a threat to his divine authority. After several unsuccessful attempts to diminish the human threat, Enlil decided upon a universal flood to wipe out the rebellious humans once and for all. Reluctantly, the other gods—except for Ea (Enki)—agreed to the plan. No sooner had the flood killed off the humans, however, than the gods realized their folly in having agreed to Enlil's disastrous plan to eliminate all of humankind. Almost immediately they began to suffer hunger cramps, since there were no humans remaining to serve them their food offerings. Fortunately, Ea (Enki) had foreseen the problem and had saved the pious hero Atrahasis and his family, along with representative animals, in a huge boat. Upon debarking from the boat, the pious flood hero immediately offered sacrifices to the gods, who swarmed like hungry flies to consume the food offerings. The gods came, acknowledging that for their own good they needed the services of humankind. Even Enlil grudgingly acknowledged the necessity of humankind to serve the needs of the gods. Enlil did require adjustments be made to the human condition in order to keep humankind within their proper bounds, however. The most important adjustment had to do with limiting human longevity and restricting propagation to certain categories of people only. Henceforth, human life was to be sharply demarcated by natural death and further diminished by disease and starvation (droughts). In short, the previously long-lived primeval humans were henceforth transformed into ordinary humans. The gods signified their agreement to this arrangement, binding themselves with a solemn oath. And that, according to Atrahasis, is how the world as we know it came into being.

The Yahwist recounts the flood story in a similar fashion. After the initial attempt by the man and the woman in Eden to usurp divine prerogatives, Yahweh God sought to prevent any further usurpation of divinity by expelling them from the garden. If Genesis 4 is an integral part of this narrative, then Cain's murder of his brother Abel, as well as Lamech's boast to his wives Ada and Zillah that he would outdo Cain's violence seventy-sevenfold, should be understood as evidence of the continuing growth of human rebellion, in direct proportion to an expanding human population. The birth of Seth is an exception to the general rule.

Genesis 6:1–4 contains a cryptic myth fragment that seemingly did not originate with the Yahwist, as it contains motifs that occur nowhere else in this narrative. Whatever its source, this myth fragment serves to further the idea of a growing unrighteous rebellion against divine order. We are informed that as humans began to multiply, so did evil increase upon the earth—and beyond. Apparently, some lesser divinities, here termed "the sons of God," found the beauty of "the human daughters" so irresistible that they began marrying them—a definite no-no as it obscured the boundary between divinity and humanity. These unnatural unions produced monstrous offspring, further polluting the earth. This led Yahweh God to yet another attempt to rein in these out-of-control rebellious primeval humans. He decreed that their lifespan would be drastically shortened. Whereas primeval humans had previously enjoyed lifespans approaching 1000 years, henceforth they would be allotted no more than 120 years.[16] But even that was insufficient to stifle the spreading cancer of sin.

> Yahweh saw that the wickedness of humankind was enormous on earth, and further, that their every thought was inclined toward perpetuating evil. Yahweh regretted having made humankind on earth, it so grieved his heart. So Yahweh determined, "I will wipe off the face of the earth the very humankind I created—everything, from people, to beasts, to crawling critters, to birds of the sky! I am sorry that I made any of them! Only Noah found favor in Yahweh's eyes. (Gen 6:5–8)

The rest of the story is well known. Yahweh saved pious Noah and his family, along with representative animals in an enormous box-like "ark," while the remaining people and animals perished. Just how closely the Yahwist followed his model Atrahasis is evident in the conclusion to the flood narrative. When the flood waters had sufficiently subsided and the ark came to rest on a mountain peak, Noah, just like the Mesopotamian flood hero, sent out in succession three birds to determine if the waters had sufficiently receded that it would be safe to disembark from the ark. Once on dry land, the very first act of Noah, just like pious Atrahasis, was to offer a sweet-smelling food offering to the deity, who was pleased with his human servant. Indeed, Yahweh vowed a kind of "Never again!"

> When the LORD smelled the pleasing odor, the LORD said in his heart, "I will never again curse the ground because of humankind, for the inclination of the human heart is evil from youth; nor will I ever again destroy every living creature as I have done. As long as the earth endures, seedtime and harvest, cold and heat, summer and winter, day and night, shall not cease." (Gen 8:21–22 NRSV)

16. An upper limit of 120 years for human life is also present in a bilingual (Sumerian and Akkadian) text from Emar: "The days of the human-being are approaching / Day to day they verily decrease, / Month after month they verily decrease, / Year and year they verily decrease! / One hundred twenty years (are) the years of humankind, / verily it is their *bane*(?). / (This is so) from the day that humanity exists until today!"; see Batto, *Slaying the Dragon*, 65, with n54; also Smith, *Genesis of Good and Evil*, 78, with n18. One may also compare the trope of decreasing longevity for humankind in the Sumerian King List, *ANET*, 265–66.

The Creator's vow here never again to "destroy every living creature" must be compared to the creator goddess Nintu in the Babylonian story of the flood holding up her fly-necklace and swearing that never again would the gods allow humankind and animalkind to perish off the face of the earth. With this divine decree firmly in place for all time, the Yahwist, like the author of Atrahasis, brings the primeval age to a close. A new age had begun.

From this time forward Yahweh God seems reconciled to working with a flawed humankind. In effect, the Yahwist has the deity concede that the flood had been yet another mistake. Yahweh learned from this experience that humankind is essentially flawed. Yes, occasionally one may come across a righteous individual. But most humans likely will never measure up to divine expectation. But like a good parent, the deity had learned to accept his "children" as they are—warts and all. That is the basis of the continuing story of God's mercy and redeeming love—something which biblical writers are at pains to reaffirm over and over.

Before leaving the Yahwist's story of creation, we should note one final parallel to its Mesopotamian antecedent. Ancient Mesopotamians prided themselves on being the most civilized people on earth, far advanced beyond their barbaric neighbors. They saw themselves as the apex of a steadily progressing humankind. While this concept may be less explicit in Atrahasis than in other Mesopotamian myths we considered in chapter 1, it is nonetheless present. The Yahwist appears in part to have adopted this conceit, for "the story of Adam and Eve" can be read as the story of humankind progressing from a lower status to a higher status, even if against the original design of their divine creator. Adam and Eve did progress in becoming more fully human as well as more god-like. They acquired a certain amount of moral independence in making their own moral choices: they learned to exercise free will. As Yahweh God begrudgingly conceded to the other gods, Adam and Eve had indeed "become like one of us, knowing good and evil." The reader cannot but wonder if the writer was not implicitly applauding the *maturation* of humankind. Adam and Eve had finally become *fully human*—the result of a whole series of initial missteps, both on the part of an inexperienced creator and on the part of the novel human creatures learning to cope in an unfamiliar world.

The Yahwist has concluded his story of origins with the flood as its "happy" ending. Yet for the Yahwist, a successful conclusion to the origins story also serves as a springboard to a fascinating follow-up story about what will happen to the descendants of Adam and Eve in the future. We will pass over in silence the story of the descendants, however, since it will be replicated in various forms in other texts to be treated below.

3

Priestly Revision of Israel's Creation Story

NEARLY ALL CRITICAL BIBLICAL scholars agree that Genesis 1:1—2:3[1] was written by a different author than the one who penned the Yahwistic narrative of Genesis 2:4b—3:24 that we examined in the preceding chapter. Biblical scholars generally refer to this second author as "the Priestly Writer" (P) because of his propensity to emphasize issues and concerns associated with the cult or other priestly functions. There is less agreement about when this Priestly Writer lived and wrote, however. Indeed, it is likely that under this rubric are cultic and legal materials composed by several "priestly" writers from the seventh and sixth centuries BCE, which materials were subsequently incorporated into a single document. Although a minority of scholars would place this final Priestly Writer/ editor in the postexilic period, most scholars assign him to approximately the time of the Babylonian exile (587–539 BCE). For reasons too complex to lay out here, this last position is the one adopted here. It appears obvious to me that at least the Priestly creation account in Genesis was composed by someone who lived during the sixth century BCE and was writing from within the context of Babylonian hegemony.

It is not my intention to discuss the overall structure and the theology of the Priestly Writer nor even to investigate P's primeval narrative per se in Genesis 1–9. My concern is how P depicts the creation of the first humans (or humankind) in the opening chapter of Genesis. In short, what does P contribute to the growth of the Adam and Eve tradition. P's contribution to this tradition is confined to Genesis 1:26–31:

1. Most scholars would include Gen 2:4a here.

²⁶Then God said: "Let us make humankind[2] in our image, according to our likeness: and let them have dominion over the fish of the sea, and over the birds of the sky, and over the cattle, and over all the wild animals of the earth, and over every creeping thing that creeps upon the earth." ²⁷So God created humankind[3] in his image,

> in the image of God he created them,[4]
> male and female he created them.

²⁸God blessed them, and God said to them, "Be fruitful and multiply, and fill the earth and subdue it; and have dominion over the fish of the sea, and over the birds of the air, and over every living thing that moves upon the earth." ²⁹God said, "See, I have given you every plant yielding seed that is upon the face of all the earth, and every tree with seed in its fruit: you shall have them for food. ³⁰And to every beast of the earth, and to every bird of the air, and to everything that creeps on the earth, everything that has the breath of life, I have given every green plant for food." And it was so. ³¹God saw everything that he had made, and indeed, it was very good. (NRSV translation)

That's it! That is the totality of what P has to say about "Adam and Eve" in his creation story. (There is a further notice in Genesis 5 concerning Adam and Eve and their descendants after expulsion from Eden, which may or may not be directly connected to the foregoing P passage; we will have more to say about that passage later.) Note that in this P account of the creation of humankind there is no garden scene whatever. There are no special trees with supernatural powers, nor any divine command forbidding the eating of a certain fruit. Moreover, there is no talking serpent. One would be hard pressed to identify this as a story of "Adam and Eve," since the humans are not named in this narrative. Indeed, this brief P account has little in common with the J account discussed in the previous chapter. So how should one explain this strange turn of events.

2. Heb. 'adam, here corrected to correspond with ha-'adam in v. 27. Even though the definite article is lacking here, context makes it clear that Hebrew 'adam must be understood here as a generic term and not as the proper name "Adam" as in Gen 5:1–5.

3. Hebrew ha-'adam; see preceding note.

4. In Hebrew, "him." Context makes clear that the reference is to "humankind" and not to an individual male, as all other pronouns ("them," "you") and verbs herein are grammatically plural.

Elsewhere I have sketched in some detail the historical and cultural circumstances that inspired the Priestly Writer to compose his own story of how God created the world "in the beginning," and then populate it with various life forms, including humankind.[5] Accordingly, here I can be brief and merely highlight some of the more salient points.

As already noted, P's historical context appears intimately connected with the Babylonian exile. Whether the Babylonians had already sacked Jerusalem and deported whole populations of Judeans to Babylonia, or whether the Babylonian armies were still only on the horizon but poised for a decisive attack, the P writer felt compelled to offer his fellow Judahites encouragement in the form of a completely new theological composition designed to undercut the Babylonian menace. It was a brilliant tactic, as it involved appropriating Babylon's own national epic story to establish that Israel's God was the true Divine Sovereign, and not, as the Babylonians claimed, Babylon's patron god Marduk. To see this dynamic in action, we need to take another look at the Babylonian backstory used by P.

The Babylonian Backstory: Enuma Elish

Over the long course of history in Mesopotamia, power tended to shift between various city-states: Kish, Nippur, Ur, Uruk, and Akkad, to name but a few from the early periods. During the second and first millennia BCE, however, political power became concentrated primarily in two large national kingdoms, Assyria in the north and Babylon in the south. These two were perpetual rivals, with political dominance vacillating between them. Babylon, once a backwater city, rose to political dominance when Hammurabi, the aggressive king of Babylon (1792–1750 BCE), succeeded in conquering his more powerful neighbors. Simultaneously, the Akkadian language and literature was flourishing and gradually displacing the older, established Sumerian culture during what has come to be known as the Old Babylonian Period (2000–1600 BCE). It was during this time that Atrahasis and the epic poem Gilgamesh were written. As Babylon rose in political importance, so gradually did the reputation of its patron deity, Marduk. Once a minor deity in the Sumero-Akkadian

---

5. See Batto, *Slaying the Dragon*, 73–101. See also Batto, "The Ancient Near Eastern Context of the Hebrew Ideas of Creation," in *In the Beginning*, 7–53, esp. 48–52; and Batto, "Divine Sovereign," 143–86, reprinted in *In the Beginning*, 96–138.

pantheon, Marduk increasingly was promoted by his Babylonian devotees as a major deity, eventually challenging Anu and Enlil for the title of ruler of the gods. Some four centuries later (ca. 1100 BCE), during the Middle Babylonian Period—a second period of Babylonian dominance—a Babylonian theologian-poet composed a new work to extol Marduk as the king of the gods, thereby explicitly promoting Marduk to the rank of the highest god in the Sumero-Akkadian pantheon. This new composition was the poem Enuma Elish, sometimes referred to as "The (Babylonian) Epic of Creation" or "The Babylonian Creation Story."[6]

There already were Sumerian and Akkadian creation myths to which one could point. In fact, some motifs and even some of the storyline in Enuma Elish were lifted straight out of an earlier Akkadian myth, Anzu.[7] No creation myth of that period, however, held more importance than Atrahasis. Composed during the Old Babylonian Period, Atrahasis quickly acquired the status of a classic, becoming the standard against which all subsequent Mesopotamian ideas of creation were measured.

Enuma Elish is likewise a Babylonian story of origins, but with a difference. It appears that the author intentionally set out to replace Atrahasis with a poem of his own as the standard creation myth. Unlike Atrahasis which opens in a time when the gods are ready fully formed and functioning, even if unhappily, the poem Enuma Elish is projected back into a still prior primeval time, before even the gods had come into existence. As the opening lines state, the poem is set in the earliest primeval period, when yet nothing but chaotic waters existed:

> When above, the heavens did not yet exist,
> And below, solid earth had not come to be . . .

In that earliest primeval period there was only a watery mass of two quasi-divine primitive, dark entities. The waters of male Apsu (the sweet-water abyss) were intermingling with the waters of female Tiamat (the salt-water abyss). From this marriage of waters gradually there evolved

6. Although earlier scholars often posited that Enuma Elish had been written during the Old Babylonian period following upon Hammurabi's rise to power, Lambert (*Babylonian Creation Myths*, 439–65) convincingly argues from many lines of evidence that Enuma Elish was composed only during the Middle Babylonian period, at the time when Marduk was first celebrated as the foremost deity of the Babylonian pantheon.

7. The Anzu myth exists in two forms, an Old Babylonian version and a Late version. Translations are available in *ANET*, 111–13 and 514–17; S. Dalley, *Myths from Mesopotamia*, 203–27; and Foster, *Before the Muses*, 1.461–85.

a series of male-female pairs of inchoate gods (Lahmu and Lahamu, Anshar and Kishar, and others), with each new generation of divinities being more sophisticated than the previous one, until finally the great Sumerian gods themselves were born. From Anshar was born Anu, the traditional king of the gods; and Anu in turn sired Ea (Enki), the famed god of wisdom.

One might suppose that the evolution of the gods was now complete and that everything was in order, since all the major gods known from traditional sources (such as Atrahasis and Gilgamesh) are accounted for and settled in their respective places. But not so according to Enuma Elish. Because Babylon was a recent arrival on the political stage in Mesopotamia, naturally its patron deity Marduk had no place among the traditional major gods of Sumer and Akkad. That was an omission that had to be corrected, given Babylon's recent emergence as the most power-ful nation in the world—at least in the eyes of the Babylonians.

The corrective was a simple matter for the author of Enuma Elish: alter the story of the evolution of the gods to include Marduk and then promote him to the pentacle of power. The evolution of gods did not stop with the birth of Ea, according to our Babylonian author. There was an additional generation of younger gods, among whom was Marduk. This last generation was not only younger, it was also more active and vigor-ous. Their playful activity was also upsetting to their lethargic elders, and especially to Tiamat and Apsu, who were unable to take their "rest." As we learned previously, "rest" in ancient Near Eastern literature "can be a metaphor for the power and respect due the king of the gods, so it would appear that the activity of these young gods constituted—or at least was perceived as—a challenge to the authority of Tiamat and Apsu. Although Tiamat was inclined to indulge the youngsters, Apsu could not tolerate them and plotted to annihilate the whole lot of them.

The younger gods, fearful for their lives, organized to resist. Ea was selected to challenge Apsu in open battle. Note that this generational bat-tle was also a battle for progress and order. Tiamat and Apsu represented the forces of primitiveness and chaos; they were resistant to change. We might label them an anti-creation force—in popular terminology, the "bad guys." By contrast, Ea-Enki represented the more evolved forces of wisdom and progress—in short, the "good guys." Ea was able to kill Apsu, thereby saving the day for progress and good order.

One should recall the analogous challenge to the authority of Enlil by the lesser gods in Atrahasis; the "savior" on that occasion also was the wise god Ea-Enki. It is as if our author is claiming that the traditional gods of Sumer and Akkad may have been sufficient for days past, but no longer—as will soon become evident.

After the death of Apsu, Tiamat chose a new and more powerful husband, Qingu. Together Tiamat and Qingu set out to do away with the rebel gods, once and for all. Seeing the awesome force gathered against them, numerous gods went over to the side of Tiamat and Qingu.[8] Ea again went forth to battle but this time was unable to withstand the combined forces of Tiamat and Qingu. Ea turned tail and returned to report to Anu and the council of gods. Ea wisely suggests sending his own son, Marduk, one even stronger and wiser than himself.

To display his superior power and wisdom, Marduk arose before the council and, using his awesome word alone, makes things appear and disappear. Marduk agrees to battle Tiamat and Qingu, but on the condition that the gods make him, Marduk, the king of the gods in place of Anu (or Enlil, as the case may be). With no other option available, the gods give their assent, and Marduk marches off to battle. Singlehandedly, he successfully kills Tiamat and takes her husband Qingu captive.

Having vanquished the enemy, Marduk manifests both his power and his wisdom by using the carcass of Tiamat as raw material from which to fashion the heavens and the earth and their constituent components. By this simple stratagem, our author ascribes to Marduk the different acts of creation which in other texts had been attributed to multiple other deities. Marduk then has Qingu killed and directs his father Ea to fashion humankind from the dead body of Qingu. This is a masterful literary stroke. In the epic of Atrahasis it was Ea (Enki) who had conceived the plan to create humankind to relieve the lesser gods of their burdens, and then, with the assistance of the mother god Belet-illi, had executed the plan. According to the author of Enuma Elish, however, it was not Ea but his son Marduk who was responsible for designing the whole schema of creation, even humankind. Marduk has taken over the functions of all other gods, including the highest and wisest.

Marduk further manifests his worthiness to be the divine sovereign by pardoning all the gods who in the civil war just concluded had abandoned the side of the "good" gods and allied with "evil" Tiamat and Qingu. Marduk's act of mercy assured the newfound loyalty of the

8. For more on this civil war among the gods in Enuma Elish, see my article, "The Malevolent Deity in Mesopotamian Myth," in Batto, *In the Beginning,* 199–228, esp. 215–20.

repentant gods. Moreover, Marduk assigned an appropriate place of rest (i.e., a palace) to each deity to enjoy for all times. These actions cemented Marduk's authority over the other gods, as well as manifesting his superior wisdom for ruling.

The other gods in turn acknowledge Marduk's authority as the divine sovereign by building him a palace (temple) in Babylon. Marduk's temple-palace is not local but cosmic in function, as its name Esagila clearly signals. Esagila means "House (temple/palace) that raises its head (that is, into the heavens)." Moreover, its ziggurat, or temple tower, was named Etemenanki, "House where the foundation of heaven and earth is."

Having established himself as divine sovereign and creator of heaven and earth, and having overcome every challenger, Marduk can hang up his weapons of war for good. As a powerful symbol of the good and permanent order he has established, Marduk retired his war bow by placing it in the sky as the "bow star"—probably to be identified with the constellation Sirius—where it now shines for all time as a symbol of Marduk's supreme authority. With that, the Babylonian Creation Story reached its conclusion.

Such was the backstory from which the Priestly Writer of Genesis 1 seemingly derived many of his own novel ideas. If our contention is correct that the Priestly Writer lived and wrote out of the context of the Babylonian exile, then he had to contend with this Babylonian propaganda, namely, that Babylon is superior to all other nations because its patron deity Marduk is greater than all other gods. It was commonly believed that each nation's might derived from the power of its god(s). If one nation defeated another, it was because its god(s) was superior to the god(s) of the defeated kingdom. A century earlier, in the days of King Hezekiah, when Sennacherib and the Assyrians attacked Jerusalem, the Assyrian envoy Rabshakeh attempted to discourage the defenders perched on Jerusalem's city walls with this very taunt:

> "Don't listen to Hezekiah when he misleads you by saying, 'Yahweh will deliver us.' Has a god of any nation ever delivered its land out of the hand of the king of Assyria? Where are the gods of Hamath and Arpad? Where are the gods of Sepharvaim, Hena, and Ivvah? Have they delivered Samaria out of my hand? Among all the gods of the countries is there one who has delivered its land out of my hand? So how can Yahweh deliver Jerusalem out of my hand?" (2 Kings 18:32–35; similarly 19:10–13)

(It should be said that a second reason, so it was believed, why a nation might suffer defeat is that its citizens had offended their own god[s], who was now punishing them by delivering them into the hands of the enemy. Israel's prophets often voiced such a threat. Rabshakeh also alludes to this possibility in 2 Kings 18:22.).

Given this mindset, the Priestly Writer had to contend with the Judahites' own faltering faith that Yahweh their God might not be as powerful as Israel's priests and prophets had preached. The Priestly Writer seems to have made it his business, therefore, to subvert the Babylonian propaganda by assigning all Marduk's functions and powers, including that of creator and divine sovereign, to Yahweh God. This accounts for why so many of the themes and motifs of Enuma Elish are found also in Genesis 1:1—2:3.

It is no accident that P posits that prior to God's creative actions, there was only a mass of chaotic waters and darkness. The Hebrew of the first two verses of Genesis is ambiguous. One might best translate, "In the beginning, when God began to create heaven and earth, there was only a formless void, with darkness covering the surface of the Deep (*tehom*) and an awesome wind was churning the surface of the waters." "The Deep (*tehom*)" is the Hebrew (masculine) equivalent of the Akkadian (feminine) *tamtu* "sea, ocean," which in turn was the name of Marduk's mortal enemy, Tiamat, in Enuma Elish. Tiamat, as her name implies, was primeval "Ocean," the inchoate, ill-defined deity from whom the higher great deities evolved. Tiamat was understood to be a ruthless and negative force, a kind of chaos monster that had to be slain before a well-ordered creation could appear. After Marduk killed Tiamat, he sliced her carcass in two, using the upper half to form the heavens and the lower half to form earth. In Genesis 1, God does the same thing to *tehom,* "the Deep." God divides the primeval waters of *tehom,* the Deep. As Marduk had demonstrated his power by making things appear or disappear merely by a spoken command, so God "spoke" a "firmament" into existence by which to separate the primeval waters above from the primeval waters below. Going one better, however, than the Babylonian Marduk who needed Tiamat's carcass as material from which to make the heavens and the earth, Israel's God creates everything using the power of his word alone. P thus seems to be writing an intentional polemic against the Babylonian oppressors, by showing Israel's God to be superior in every way to the god of the Babylonians. One can almost hear the P author shouting at the top of his voice: "Anything your god can do, our God can do better!"

The Priestly Revision of Israel's Creation Story

The very first task of the Priestly Writer (P) was to revise the Yahwist's version of creation. Much like the Babylonian composer of Enuma Elish who found the old Sumero-Akkadian myths no longer adequate for the new political realities of his day, so also the Priestly Writer seems to have judged the Yahwist's creation story deficient on numerous scores. Why P did not simply delete or leave aside the Yahwist's version is unclear. Perhaps the Yahwist's version had become so entrenched in Israel that it could not be ignored. It had to be dealt with somehow.

The deity depicted by the Yahwist was neither omniscient (all-knowing) nor omnipotent (all-powerful), something that appears to have greatly chagrined P—so much so that P was at pains to undo this older, erroneous portrayal of Israel's God. If Yahweh God in J had needed more than one try to achieve workable models for humankind, by contrast P's God is depicted creating every component of creation as "good" at every step along the way. Unlike Yahweh God who required modeling clay from which to fashion both humankind and animalkind, P's God brought all things into existence by the power of his word alone. He simply commanded, "Let there be . . ., and it was." When God finished creating on the sixth day, God looked at his completed work and "saw that everything he had made was indeed *very good*," which is to say, everything was *perfect*! Nothing is amiss in this picture. Nothing has been overlooked. Accordingly, on the seventh day God "rests."

Implicit here is a common ancient Near Eastern motif of a deity *resting*: the creator god, having overcome every negative, anti-creation force, may at last retire to his heavenly temple-palace to relax and enjoy ruling over his newly organized universe, with everything functioning in perfect harmony. We saw this motif in the Babylonian Creation Story, where the creator god was Marduk and his temple-palace bore the name Esagila, "House [temple/palace] that raises its head (that is, into the heavens)." Although variations of this motif were widespread across the ancient Near East, it is likely that P patterned his creation narrative on the Babylonian Creation Story specifically rather some other version, to judge by the similarities in the two narratives.

Years ago Alexander Heidel pointed out the broad similarities between the Babylonian Creation Story and Genesis 1.[9]

TABLE 2

Enuma Elish	Genesis 1
Divine spirit and cosmic matter are coexistent and coeternal	Divine spirit creates cosmic matter and exists independently of it
Primeval chaos: Tiamat enveloped in darkness	The earth a desolate waste with darkness covering the deep (*tehom*)
Light emanating from the gods	Light created
The creation of the firmament	The creation of the firmament
The creation of dry land	The creation of dry land
The creation of humankind	The creation of [humankind]
The gods rest and celebrate	God rests and sanctifies the seventh day

Precisely how to account for these similarities between Enuma Elish and Genesis, that is, whether P knew the Babylonian Creation Story and was literally dependent upon it, or was acquainted with Babylonian theological ideas only indirectly, remains a matter of debate, and beyond our capacity to decide on the basis of our current knowledge. Whatever the case, it seems certain that part of P's agenda was to undermine the Babylonian propagandists. That goal was sufficient reason to portray Israel's God, and not some other god, as the divine sovereign and creator of all.

Reimagining Creation as a Slaying of the Chaos Dragon

Reliance upon the Babylonian Creation Story necessarily required deviating from the Yahwist's creation narrative in other important ways as well. One of the most obvious is the primeval condition before the deity began his creative activities. The Yahwistic author had posited that prior to Yahweh God's creative actions, the earth was a dry, barren wasteland where nothing could grow. That was one common ancient Near Eastern concept of "non-creation," and it is that conception of non-creation which undergirds the myth of Atrahasis as well. According to P, however, the precreation state of primeval matter was "the Deep" (*tehom*)—a chaotic ocean of disorganized and unruly waters—upon which God imposed order and meaning. This second conception of "non-creation" was also widespread throughout the ancient Near East, and it is the one that undergirds the Babylonian Creation Story. As we have suggested, P likely

9. Heidel, *Babylonian Genesis,* 82–140, with diagram on 129.

adopted this latter motif precisely to counter the Babylonians' claim that their patron god Marduk was the divine sovereign.

Once P chose to go that route, the rest of his creation narrative was predetermined. The waters of the Deep (*tehom*) had to be divided and carefully organized by the divinely spoken word alone. In the Babylonian Creations Story Marduk proved himself worthy to be the divine sovereign by overcoming the chaos dragon in battle and from her carcass creating the various element of the physical world. Granted that P does not portray God as battling a physical chaos dragon, as does Marduk. But the battle motif is implicit in Genesis 1, as other scriptures clearly attest. Psalm 8, for example, is very close thematically to Genesis 1:1—2:3, and almost certainly derivative from it. Psalm 8 praises "Yahweh, our sovereign" for his great majesty in creating the heavens and all that is in them, including the moon and the stars. Moreover, much like the statement in Genesis 1:26–28 that humankind was created in the image and likeness of God, the psalmist marvels concerning mortal human beings that God has "made them (only) a little lower than God,[10] crowning them with glory and honor." In addition, God has given humankind dominion over all things, "all sheep and oxen, and also the beasts of the field, the birds of the air, and the fish of the sea, whatever passes along the paths of the seas" (Ps 8:4–8). The references to Genesis 1:26–28 could not be more obvious. So it is significant that the psalmist states in almost the same breath that above the heavens the Creator "has founded a bulwark because of your foes, to silence the enemy and the avenger" (v. 2). In context, this can only mean that God, much like the Babylonian god Marduk, has built himself a temple-palace, after defeating his arch enemy. Psalm 8 thus confirms that a battle motif is implied in Genesis 1 even though not explicitly stated.

During the exilic period it was common for Israelite writers to employ motifs from the Combat Myth to bolster their audience's faith in Yahweh God. Nowhere is this more evident than in Isaiah 51:9–11, the so-called ode to Yahweh's arm. There an anonymous poet-prophet, often referred to as Deutero-Isaiah (Second Isaiah), calls upon Yahweh to rouse himself from his rest and take up arms once again, as in primeval times, to slay the chaos monster anew.

---

10. The meaning of Hebrew '*elohim* here is capable of several interpretations: "God," "gods," or "angels."

Awake! Awake! Robe yourself in Power,
O arm of Yahweh.
Awake as in primordial days,
(the) primeval days.
Is it not you who cleaves Rahab in pieces,
who pierces the Sea-dragon?
Is it not you who dries up the Sea,
the waters of the great Abyss (*tehom*),
The one who makes the depths of the Sea a road
for the redeemed to pass over?

Deutero-Isaiah's words had great appeal for his exilic audience. The God who slew the chaos monster in primeval times is credited as also the savior of Israel during the exodus out of Egypt by drowning Pharaoh and his army in the Red Sea—Pharaoh being but a historical incarnation of the chaos dragon. Now the divine savior is invoked to act once more as Israel's savior by delivering the Judean captives out of Babylonian exile— the Babylonians being the most recent reincarnation of the chaos dragon. Calling upon Yahweh to "wake up" is implicitly an accusation that the deity had prematurely retired to his temple-palace to "rest." The arch enemy of the divine sovereign is still alive and even now raging against God's chosen people. Yahweh must return to battle.

Very similar is Psalm 74, also very clearly composed when the Babylonian assault on Jerusalem was at its height. With vivid images of the enemy army ravaging the city and razing its sacred temple still swirling in his head, the psalmist calls upon God to defeat the Babylonian foe as he did the seven-headed chaos monster in primeval days when he brought order out of chaos.

How long, O God, shall the enemy blaspheme?
Is the adversary to revile your name forever?
Why do you restrain your hand?
your right hand remain idle inside your cloak?
O God, my king from primeval times,
who works salvation in the middle of the earth,
It was you who broke apart the sea by your might,
who smashed the heads of the dragon on the water.
It was you who crushed the heads of Leviathan,
who gave him to the desert folk as food.
It was you who opened springs and brooks;
you who turned primordial rivers into dry land.
To you belongs the day and the night as well.

It was you who established the moon and the sun.
It was you who fixed the boundaries of the earth.
Summer and winter, you created them. (Ps. 74:10–17)

These examples are sufficient to demonstrate how Israel's poets and storytellers framed their compositions to combat the Babylonian propaganda machine. We may assume that the Priestly Writer was at the forefront of this resistance movement, and that this is evident by his addition of a second creation account, which he prefixed to the Yahwist's creation story to serve as a corrective to erroneous elements in that older account.

What Happened to "Adam and Eve" in P's Retelling?

Strictly speaking there is no story of "Adam and Eve" in the P account. P provides us with a complete story of the creation of the heavens and the earth, ending with the creation of humankind. But there is no mention of "Adam and Eve" per se. In the first three days of creation God made light to illuminate the darkness and divided the Abyss with a firmament, thereby establishing the heavens above and the earth below. On the fourth day God filled the heavens with the sun and the moon and the stars. On the fifth day he populated the sea with fish and the sky with birds. On the sixth day he populated the earth with animals and with humans. This last act, the creation of humankind, is presented as the crowning achievement of creation.

According to P, humans were created in the image and likeness of God. Rather than continuing J's view that humankind had been created as servants or slaves to do the menial tasks for the deity, P says the function of humankind is to serve as God's viceroys on earth to rule over the rest of creation. Theirs is a royal function, that is, to be God's regents in governing this world. This is almost the exact opposite of the servile function imagined for humankind by the Yahwist.

If we are to grasp the full force of the royal character P assigns to humankind, we must probe further what P intended by the statement, "God created humankind in the image of God."[11]

---

11. For a fuller study of this motif, with documentation, see Batto, "Divine Sovereign," 143–86; reprinted in Batto, *In the Beginning,* 96–138.

The King as the Divine Sovereign's Viceroy on Earth

As already intimated, the role of creator is a subsidiary function of the divine sovereign motif in ancient Near Eastern thought. The concept of divine sovereignty varied from society to society and from period to period. Early on, divine power was thought to be shared among several great gods. During the second and first millennia BCE, however, as first Babylon and then Assyria gained hegemony over surrounding kingdoms and established empires, gradually there emerged a new conception of kingship, both earthly and heavenly. There could be but one king, whether on earth or in heaven. Indeed, kingships in both realms were at root one and the same. True kingship belonged to the divine sovereign in heaven, but the earthly king was the deity's representative on earth. To be more precise, the Babylonian king—alternatively, the Assyrian king—was hailed as the divine sovereign's viceroy on earth, acting in the deity's stead by ruling over the land and maintaining the divinely ordained order. Assyrian propagandists could not have been more explicit on this point. In the throne room of the northwest palace of King Assurnasirpal II (883–859 BCE) at Nimrud (Kalhu), carved repeatedly into the wall and on the base of the king's throne is an inscription that proclaims Assurnasirpal as the "viceregent of Assur," the "king of the universe."

Assyrian propagandists conveyed this message in other ways as well. Numerous reliefs carved on Assyrian palace walls and elsewhere often depict scenes in which the king of Assyria is depicted larger than life—a form of flattery, to be sure. But hovering overhead is a second, smaller figure symbolic of the divine authority of the Assyrian king. This figure likely originated from the winged sun disk, known from Egyptian iconography as a symbol of the sun god. The Assyrians transformed the winged sun disk into a winged anthropomorphic figure, symbolizing the divine authority of their own king. Inside of a fiery sphere propelled by two wings is a human-like figure from the waist up; on its head is a horned cap such as Mesopotamian gods wear. The figure's bottom half issues in a feathered bird-like tail. In some scenes this anthropomorphic winged figure appears to replicate the actions of the Assyrian king. In others it appears to bless the work of the king.[12]

The identity of this figure is the subject of discussion among scholars. Some interpret it as representing the divine sovereign Assur, who

---

12. For a full discussion, with images, see Batto, "Divine Sovereign," 149–57; reprinted in Batto, *In the Beginning*, 102–9.

approves the Assyrian king as his viceroy. Other scholars suggest it represents some other special god aiding the king. Most likely, however, the figure is not intended to portray a god at all, but rather is symbolic of divine power invested in the earthly king and which he exercises to bring about peace and security on earth. If correct, then this is analogous to the Old Babylonian wall painting in the throne room of the palace of King Zimri-Lim of Mari discussed in chapter 2.

In the Mari painting, an upper panel depicts the high goddess Ishtar handing King Zimri-Lim "the rod and the ring," symbols of his authority. In the bottom panel stands a goddess on either side holding a vase from which issue four streams. These streams encircle the entire panel before merging together in the center. Apparently, the scene is intended to portray paradisaical conditions as existing throughout the whole kingdom of Mari. In short, Zimri-Lim's propagandists were broadcasting not only that Zimri-Lim was divinely appointed to rule but also that his rule establishes peace, security, and fruitfulness on earth. Though such weal derives ultimately from the sovereignty of the deity, it is effected on earth through the agency of the king, the deity's viceroy. The winged anthropomorphic figure symbolized a similar royal conceit in Assyria nearly a thousand years later.

Appointment to the post of viceroy for the divine sovereign was a great honor, to be sure. But some Mesopotamian kings attempted to do more than mere lip service. Lipit-Ishtar, king of the city-state of Isin (2017–1985 BCE), proclaimed that the high gods An and Enlil had appointed him king of Sumer and Akkad "in order to establish justice in the land, to eliminate cries for justice, to eradicate enmity and armed violence, to bring well-being to the lands of Sumer and Akkad" (The Laws of Lipit-Ishtar 1.1–37). Similarly, Hammurabi of Babylon (1792–1750 BCE) prefaced his famous law code with the statement, "Anu and Enlil, for the enhancement of the well-being of the people, named me by my name: Hammurabi . . . to make justice prevail in the land, to abolish the wicked and the evil, to prevent the strong from oppressing the weak, to rise like the sun-god Shamash over all humankind, to illuminate the land" (The Laws of Hammurabi 1.27–49).[13] Other kings published comparable statements about their divinely given responsibilities concerning the welfare of their lands.

13. Both translations by Martha Roth, in Hallo and Younger, *Context of Scripture* 2:154 (p. 411) and 2:131 (p. 336).

It is worth noting that among the king's responsibilities was the removal of ferocious animals whose attacks might threaten the security of the peoples of the land, if one may judge by the frequency of reliefs on Neo-Assyrian palace wall depicting the king killing lions and other wild beasts. One is reminded of Leviticus 26:5–6, which speaks of the security that God bestows on earth in precisely these terms: "I will grant peace in the land and you shall lie down, and no one shall make you afraid; I will remove dangerous animals from the land, and no sword shall go through your land." Ezekiel (34:25–31) announced that in the eschatological covenant of peace that God will establish in days to come, God promises to "banish wild animals from the land, so that they may live in the wild and sleep in the woods securely . . . (God's people) shall no longer be plunder for the nations, nor shall the animals of the land devour them; they shall live in safety, and no one shall make them afraid . . . You are my sheep, the sheep of my pasture and I am your God, says the Lord GOD." When kings killed wild beasts, symbolically they were acting in place of the divine sovereign, exercising their roles as divinely appointed shepherds ridding the earth of threats to the divinely willed order. The Priestly Writer seemingly had this very conceit in mind when he writes that God created humans in his own image that they might "have dominion over the fish of the sea, over the birds of the sky, over all the wild animals of the earth, and over every creeping thing that creeps upon the earth" (Gen 1:26; cp. 1:28).

Israel's theologians and poets borrowed many of these motifs from their neighbors and applied them to their own God and to their own kings. The Bible is rampant with affirmations of Yahweh as the true divine sovereign. Moreover, Davidic kings frequently were depicted as Yahweh's divinely appointed representative on earth. In the language of the Bible there was almost a symbiotic relationship between Yahweh God and David and/or Davidic kings. Consider Psalm 2:4–8, where the psalmist mocks those who would attack "Yahweh and his anointed":

> He who sits enthroned in heaven laughs.
> Yahweh holds them in derision.
> He will rebuke them in his wrath,
> terrify them in his fury, saying,
> "I have installed my king on Zion, my holy hill."
> I will tell you what Yahweh has decreed:
> He said to me, "You are my son;
> today I have become your father.

Ask of me what you will:
As your inheritance I will give you the nations;
the farthest regions of the earth as your possession."

What is more, there is even a physical resemblance between Yahweh and his human viceroy. It is commonplace to say that P did away with the anthropomorphic creator depicted in the Yahwist's creation account. It is true that P did eliminate some of the more blatant anthropomorphisms, such as Yahweh God planting a garden in Eden and Yahweh God molding clay figures in order to create the animals and humankind. But P is not devoid of anthropomorphisms in depictions of God. P's God speaks, and sees, and rests as do humans. Although not explicitly stated, P assumes that God has a spiritualized physical body replete with eyes, ears, and a mouth. One may assume also that P's deity has limbs, since in Genesis 9 he hangs his weapon—his bow—on a cloud in the heavens where it now may be glimpsed on occasion as the rain bow.

It is no wonder, therefore, that the prophet Ezekiel, when attempting to describe the vision of "the majesty of Yahweh" that he saw in the temple, says that the deity had a partially humanlike form, "a likeness of appearance of a human" (Ezek 1:26). Bear in mind that nearly every commentator has noted a great degree of similarity between P and Ezekiel when it comes to describing God and his appearance. Ezekiel's statement that Yahweh bears "a likeness" to humans is the reverse of P's statement in Genesis 1:26–27, that humankind was created in "the likeness" of God.

The framers of Israelite royal ideology, and more specifically, of Davidic theology, appropriated this ancient Near Eastern motif that the king, as the earthly viceroy of the divine sovereign, bore the "image of God." There is more than mere metaphor implied in Yahweh's oath to King David concerning his successor: "I will be a father to him, and he shall be a son to me" (2 Sam 7:14). That the king was in some real sense a son of the divine sovereign was a long-standing conceit in the ancient Near East. For example, in the thirteenth century BCE. it was said of the Assyrian king Tukulti-Ninurta I that "through the destiny of Nudimmud,[14] he is reckoned as flesh godly in his limbs; by fiat of the lord of the world, he was cast sublimely from the womb of the gods . . . the eternal image of Enlil."[15] It may not be out of place at this point to recall that in Egypt, too, Pharaoh was considered to be an incarnation of Egypt's supreme deity.

14. Nudimmud is the title of the god Ea when acting as creator.
15. The Tukulti-Ninurta Epic (A.i.16–20), in Foster, *Before the Muses*, 1:213.

The Democratization of Kingship

But what does all this have to do with the Adam and Eve tradition? To answer that we return to Genesis 1:26–31.

According to P, God created humankind all at once. This is not a story of about a solitary human being created and then modified by necessary adjustments to become a self-sustaining species. No, in P the male and the female are created simultaneously. Indeed, were it not for the fact that the P account is followed immediately by the J account, one would not even think of a single human couple here. Rather to judge from P's depiction of the creation of other creatures—specifically, how fish and birds and animals are created from the very beginning in sufficient numbers to fill the seas and the skies and the land—one would assume that multiple pairs of humans were also created simultaneously. After all, nowhere else in ancient Near Eastern tradition did humankind begin with a single human or even a single human couple. Recall, for example, Atrahasis which posits that Enki and Belet-illi created *seven* human pairs—and because *seven* is often a symbolic or mystical number, even "seven pairs" may be a convention for implying that humankind began with many human pairs. In Egyptian cosmological texts there is little attention to the creation of humankind per se, but one Coffin Text (Spell 1130) does claim that "humans" (*rmṯ*) are "tears" (*rmyt*) which flowed from the creator's eye.[16] No number is specified, but presumably the resulting humans were many, as are tears. Whatever P's meaning here, the creation of humankind was complete in a single day, not something that stretched out over an unspecified prolonged period of time.

What is special about the creation of humankind in P is not the number of humans, however, but their function. From the very beginning, humans were intended to rule over the rest of God's creatures. They were created specifically to be God's viceroys on earth. Previously this had been considered a royal function, a privilege that belonged to kings alone. But according to P, all humankind is charged with exercising dominion over God's creation. In short, kingship has been democratized. Whereas formerly only kings were thought to be the *imago dei*, the image of god/God, now every human is created in the image of God, we are informed.

16. "I made the gods evolve from my sweat, while people are from the tears of my Eye"; translation by James P. Allen, in Hallo and Younger, *Context of Scripture*, 1:17 (p. 27).

One cannot but help admire the farsightedness of the Priestly Writer. Long before environmentalism became a concept, this ancient Priestly Writer was already preaching that every person has a God-given duty to protect and advance the welfare of this God-given world and its inhabitants, from the birds of the sky, to the beasts of the field, to the creepy-crawly critters on the ground, to the fish that swim in our rivers and seas. From a humanistic point of view, the Priestly Writer was far advanced beyond many of his contemporaries. For that matter, the Priestly Writer was even more enlightened than many of our own modern-day contemporaries regarding the responsibility of humans with regard to the rest of creation.

Summing Up

The Priestly Writer seems to have lived close to the time of the Babylonian conquest of Judah. The trauma of the Babylonian destruction of Jerusalem and its temple is never far from the writer's consciousness as he penned his creation account. Seemingly, one goal of the P account is to counter Babylonian propaganda that Babylon's patron god Marduk is the highest of all gods, the divine sovereign and therefore, also the creator of the heavens and the earth. This view was proclaimed in the Babylonian Creation Epic, Enuma Elish. To effectively counter the Babylonian propaganda, the Priestly Writer composed an alternate account of creation that projected the God of Israel as the true divine sovereign and the one who created the heavens and the earth and all that is in them. Neither this God nor his work was in any way flawed. Consequently, Israelite tradition itself had to be emended as well.

Israel already had "origins stories." Chief among these prior stories was that of the Yahwist, which purported to tell the story of Israel's origins, going all the way back to the very beginning, when the very first human was created. It began in Eden, when Yahweh God planted a garden and then created humankind to work it. Following long-standing ancient Near Eastern tradition for such creation stories, the Yahwist painted a picture of an originally inchoate creation that had to be continually improved upon. In short, the creator required several tries before finally achieving an adequate specimen of humankind.

If the Priestly Writer were going to effectively counter the Babylonian Creation Story, he could not allow the Yahwist's version of creation to stand. It must be demonstrated that Israel's God is not only all-powerful and all-knowing, but also that God created all things perfectly from the very first. God did not require a second, remedial action. Accordingly, the Priestly Writer composed an alternate account of an absolutely perfect creation, accomplished in six days. On the seventh day God "rested." That is, God retired into his (newly established) temple-palace as the divine sovereign. Nothing is awry in this Priestly portrait of the creator and his creation. Chaos (the Deep) has been totally mastered and converted into a well-ordered heaven and earth.

According to the Yahwist, a certain amount of disharmony had existed between Yahweh God and his newly created humans, the man and his wife. That certainly could not be considered a picture of perfect creation. The Priestly Writer corrected this picture as well. According to P, the humankind that God created was in perfect alignment with God. God made humans in his own image so that they would be his viceroy(s) on earth and rule (manage) all creatures in his stead. P's story of creation is thus almost the exact opposite of the prior Yahwistic version. According to P, there was no need for improvement or adjustment; everything was perfect right from the beginning. The divinely ordained order does require maintenance; that is not the duty of a king, however, but of every human—all humankind together.

"Perfect Creation" Becomes a Story of "the Fall"

How this Priestly version came to be placed as the opening chapter of Genesis, ahead of the Yahwistic account of creation, is not entirely clear. According to the Documentary Hypothesis—once accepted as certain by nearly all critical biblical scholars—an editor (or a series of editors) redacted J and P and combined them together with still additional traditions to achieve our present Pentateuch. In a prior work I expressed a preference for an alternate thesis that posits that the Priestly Writer was the redactor-editor largely responsible for inserting his own writings into preexisting traditions to create a Tetrateuch (Genesis-Exodus-Leviticus-Numbers), later expanded to a Pentateuch.[17] No matter how Genesis came about in its final form, the fact that the Priestly account was placed as a preface to the Yahwistic account allowed for radically new and different readings of "the creation story," ones that neither J nor

17. *Slaying the Dragon*, 41–43.

P could have foreseen. I am referring to later Christian interpretations of the disobedience of the original couple as a story about "the fall" and especially the development of the doctrine of "original sin." But there are other developments along the way. We will examine a number of these developing traditions in the following chapters.

For the time being, I wish to expand on the popular belief that Genesis 3 is a story about "the fall." Most Christians have grown up with the belief that in the beginning, Adam and Eve in Eden were completely innocent and enjoyed total harmony and friendship with God. To use a theological concept, they were filled with grace. But at some point, they sinned by eating the forbidden fruit and were punished with expulsion from the garden and cast out of God's presence. In theological terms, they had fallen from grace. Yes, they were doomed to die physically. But even worse, having lost God's friendship, they were already dead spiritually. That was the true meaning of Yahweh God's admonition to them beforehand, "On the day you eat of the forbidden fruit, you will die!" Moreover, as "our first parents," this sentence of death and loss of grace fell not just upon Adam and Eve; it was also imposed upon every one of their descendants. All humankind fell with them on that fateful day. That is what is meant by the term "the fall."

This concept of a "fall" is nowhere stated in Genesis 3. It must be inferred from outside the text. So how is that possible? The answer lies in the present narrative arrangement of Genesis. When the Priestly creation account (Gen 1:1—2:3) was placed ahead of the Yahwistic account (Gen 2:4—3:24), it was possible to read the two accounts as one continuous narrative. Genesis One describes God's creation as perfect, where nothing is out of order, including humankind. Genesis 2–3 could be understood as picking up and expanding on that thread of harmony between deity and humans, since Adam and Eve were at home in the garden where Yahweh God was accustomed to enjoying walking in the cool evening breeze. That (assumed) divine-human intimacy was forever shattered by a single act of willful disobedience.

It bears repeating that the concept of a fall is only possible by reading the first three chapters of Genesis as if they were a single narrative. When read as two discrete narratives, however, one would never arrive at a story of a fall. It is therefore instructive to note that different faith communities understand the opening chapters of Genesis in radically different ways. Christians normally see in them a story of "the fall" and the source of "original sin." The result is that, as the apostle Paul preached, all humans are enslaved to sin and hence incapable of pleasing God, apart from the redeeming grace that comes through Christ. This is the reason Christians place great emphasis on Genesis 3, because in their belief it chronicles the most significant event in the history of humankind prior to the advent of the Christ.

By contrast, Jewish tradition, lacking a doctrine of "original sin," has attached greater importance to Genesis 1. This chapter emphasizes the goodness of creation, resulting from God's blessing. Humans share in this blessing. True, humans are prone to sin, even great sin. But Jews would never say that no human is incapable of pleasing God or doing his will. Indeed, Cain—the very first descendant of Adam and Eve—was admonished by God, "If you do good, will you not be accepted? And if you do not do good, sin is lurking at the door; it lusts for you, but you are able to overcome it" (Gen 4:7). Cain is explicitly told that he is capable of resisting sin and doing good. Likewise, Moses in his very last sermon exhorted the Israelites that they would be held responsible for choosing between good and evil: "Today I call upon heaven and earth to witness that I have set before you life and death, blessings and curses. Choose life" (Deut 30:19). Even following the expulsion of Adam and Eve from the garden, Jewish tradition understands the blessing God gave to humankind in Gen 1:28 to continue unabated down to the present day.

Adam Later in Life and His Descendants

Earlier we noted that there is a further notice about "Adam and Eve," in Genesis 5:1–5. It would be more exact to say that the P account proper *resumes or continues* (following the Yahwistic "interruption" of Genesis 2:4—4:26) with a notice about "Adam's" descendants.

> This is the list of the descendants of Adam. When God created humankind, he made them in the likeness of God. Male and female he created them, and he blessed them and named them "Humankind" when they were created.
>
> When Adam had lived one hundred thirty years, he became the father of a son in his likeness, according to his image, and named him Seth. The days of Adam after he became the father of Seth were eight hundred years; and he had other sons and daughters. Thus all the days that Adam lived were nine hundred thirty years; and he died.

This NRSV translation is a bit deceptive, however, in the sense that the same term ʾadam, which occurs nine times in this short passage, always without the definite article, is sometimes translated as the name "Adam" and sometimes as a common noun "Human/humankind." Moreover, the associated pronoun in Hebrew is sometimes singular ("him") and sometimes plural ("them/their"); but NRSV ignores the grammatical form, choosing to translate ad sensum, that is, according to which interpretation of ʾadam was deemed appropriate in each instance. It is difficult to determine precisely the meaning(s) intended by the ancient author or editor. It is no wonder, therefore, that translations vary.

Verses 1–2 clearly are an extension of the language and imagery of P from Genesis 1:26–31, even to the extent of repeating some of the exact same (ambiguous) phrasing. If the intent was to closely link this passage with Genesis 1, then one may ask if the author/editor either did not know the Yahwist's account or else deliberately ignored the intervening Yahwist's account of an inchoate creation, a disobedient Adam and Eve, and their expulsion from Eden. Verses 3–5, however, could just as easily be read as continuing the Yahwistic account of Cain and Abel from Chapter 4, and therefore serve as an appropriate conclusion of the history of Adam and Eve and their descendants living outside of the garden. The latter seems more likely the case. In other words, at this point the author/ editor has fused the J and the P stories of origins in order to move forward with a unified narrative about how humankind progressed—or did not progress—after the deaths of Adam and Eve. P is quite aware that the perfect, orderly world that God had created in the beginning is no more and that sin is not only rampant in the world but also is a reality that must be dealt with on a daily basis. By singling out Seth as carrying on the divine image that "Adam"/"Human(kind)" had received from God, however, P seems to remind the reader that no matter how deeply our world may descend into sin, the original goodness that God bestowed on our world and on humankind in particular is never completely lost.

4

1 Enoch: Blame the Fallen Angels

IN THE STORY OF the flood found in Genesis 6–9, responsibility for evil on earth—and by extension, the cause of the flood—is laid directly at the feet of humankind, the direct descendants of Adam and Eve, because they all are thoroughly steeped in sin. This is true both for the Yahwistic account (J) and for the Priestly account (P). According to the Yahwist,

> The LORD saw that the wickedness of humankind was great in the earth, and that every inclination of the thoughts of their hearts was only evil continually. And the LORD was sorry that he had made humankind on the earth, and it grieved him to his heart. So the LORD said, "I will blot out from the earth the human beings I have created—people together with animals, and the creeping things and birds of the air, for I am sorry that I have made them." But Noah found favor in the sight of the LORD. (Gen 6:5–8 NRSV)

The Priestly Writer likewise considers the flood to have been brought on by human sin,

> Now the earth was corrupt in God's sight, and the earth was filled with violence. And God saw that the earth was corrupt, for all flesh had corrupted its ways upon the earth. And God said to Noah, "I have determined to make an end of all flesh, for the earth is filled with violence because of them; now I am going to destroy them along with the earth." (Gen 6:11–13 NRSV)

Neither J nor P attributes the flood to any cause other than human sin. The deity's decision to send the great deluge was based entirely upon the fact that humans had so corrupted the face of the earth that even the animal kingdom, apparently, was infected with violence that had spread like a virus originating from humankind. The deity could see no other solution than to wipe the earth clean of both humans and animals. Both J and P present the flood story as part of the creation story, wherein the sins of humankind are primarily of its own making.

Even so, the Yahwist does preface the flood story with a strange note about a stage in early human history when humankind (*ha-'adam*) first began to expand across the earth and illicit mating occurred between heavenly beings and human women.

> When people started to increase on earth and daughters were born to them, the sons of God saw that they were beautiful; and they took as many of them for wives as they wished. Then the LORD said, "My spirit shall not remain in humans forever, since they are flesh. Their lifetime shall be limited to one hundred and twenty years." The Nephilim were on the earth in those days— and afterward—when the sons of God went in to the human daughters, who bore them children. These were the heroes of old—the renowned warriors. (Gen 6:1–4)

The passage is very cryptic and enigmatic. Its function here seems to be to provide some explanation for the coming catastrophic flood. But the origins of this story are uncertain, as it is out of keeping with the primeval stories that both J and P have been narrating. Indeed, these verses appear to be a myth fragment derived from an earlier time and another culture. It bears some similarities to Mesopotamian myths, the Atrahasis myth especially, with its motif a punishing flood decreed by the supreme deity to rid the earth of rebellious humankind.

As in Atrahasis, in Genesis 6 the setting for the great flood is when humankind began proliferating on earth. As the numbers of humans grew, they find themselves in conflict with powerful forces of the divine realm. In Atrahasis, the ruler god Enlil was disturbed by the excessive "noise" (ruckus) raised by the humans, so much so that Enlil is unable to sleep—sleep being a metaphor for the leisure the gods were supposed to enjoy as their divine prerogative. As explained in an earlier chapter, this noise should not be taken as merely an indication of an overpopulated earth. Rather it should be understood as a kind of rebellion against the authority of the ruler god, or what in biblical parlance is called "sin"—a rejection of the authority of the ruler god. Similarly in Genesis, it is taken for granted that there is supposed to be separation between the divine realm and the human realm. Therefore marriage between "the sons of God" and "human daughters" is an egregious violation of right order. Also, the name given to their apparent offspring, the *Nephilim,* signals culpability on the part of those involved. Subsequent Jewish tradition connected their name with the Semitic root *npl* "to fall," indicative of the fact that the term *Nephilim* should be translated as "Fallen (Ones)," that is, heavenly beings who have corrupted themselves. Finally, the decision of the deity to limit the human lifespan to a mere 120 years—following accounts in the preceding chapter about prediluvian ancestors with lifespans approaching a thousand years—confirms that this passage must be read as a negative judgment on primeval humankind. If this interpretation is accurate, then one is justified in positing that Genesis 6:1–4 is a myth fragment from an earlier ancient Near Eastern tradition about primeval humankind, which the biblical authors have re-appropriated to augment their own story of human origins.

Whatever its origins, certainly this myth fragment is foreign to Israelite tradition as mediated to us through the primary authors of the Hebrew Bible. It does not reappear elsewhere in the Hebrew Bible. Nevertheless, this passage was terribly suggestive for later, postbiblical Jewish writers and it set off a wave of additional myth-making speculation about early human history. This is nowhere more apparent than in chapters 6–12 of 1 Enoch, a Jewish pseudepigraph from approximately the late third or early second century BCE.

The Book of Watchers (1 Enoch 1–36)

According to the opening verse of the book, 1 Enoch, also known as the Ethiopic Book of Enoch, is ascribed to Enoch, a seventh-generation righteous descendant of Adam and Eve, who wrote this book before the great flood. In actuality, 1 Enoch is a long and complex Jewish pseudepigraph composed by several different writers over a period of three centuries or more, beginning sometime around 300 BCE in the pre-Maccabean period and completed at least by the end of the Second Temple period (70 CE). It would be difficult to overestimate the importance of this singular work. Originally composed in Aramaic and Hebrew, it was preserved complete only in Ethiopic (Ge'ez). A lengthy portion of the work, written in Aramaic, was discovered at Qumran among the Dead Sea Scrolls. Its popularity in antiquity is attested by the widespread circulation of manuscripts in several languages, including Greek and Latin. It influenced the composition of other Jewish pseudepigraphs, notably Jubilees, the Testament of the Twelve Patriarchs, the Assumption of Moses, 2 Baruch, and 4 Ezra. Its influence extended also to the New Testament. Jude 14–15 explicitly quotes 1 Enoch, as if it had the authority of Scripture; and 1 Peter 5:8 and 2 Peter 2:4, among others, certainly allude to it. Other antique Christian writings, for example, the Epistle of Barnabas, the Apocalypse of Peter, Justin Martyr, Tertullian, Irenaeus, Origin, and Clement of Alexandria, likewise give great credence to this work. In the fourth century, however, its popularity and influence among Christians began to wane because of negative reviews by Augustine, Hilary, and Jerome, among others. Only in Ethiopia did its influence remain undiminished—hence its survival there.

Enoch is a lengthy work of 108 chapters. From the introductory verse (1:2), the reader learns that this book purports to be a record of "a holy vision from the heavens which the angels showed" to Enoch. According to Genesis 5:24, "Enoch walked with God; then he vanished, because God took him." This cryptic statement excited vivid imaginations among various Jewish writers, as they pondered what secrets God may have revealed to Enoch, a man so righteous that God elevated him into his own heavenly company. 1 Enoch is one of three Jewish pseudepigraphs written about this mysterious figure.[1]

Our interest with 1 Enoch concerns that portion known as "The Book of Watchers" (1 Enoch 1–36), and more specifically, a subsection of that which may be called "The Fall of the Angels" (chapters 6–12). It is in this segment that we first encounter a major development in the Adam and Eve tradition, namely, the view that evil was introduced into the world not by humans themselves but rather by demonic forces having much greater powers than humankind, namely, the fallen angels, popularly known as devils.

1. We ignore 2 Enoch and 3 Enoch in this book not only because their connection with the Adam and Eve tradition is much less direct than 1 Enoch but also because they were written (or redacted) much later. The date of 2 Enoch is much debated, ranging from ca. first century BCE to ninth century CE; 3 Enoch was written in the fifth or sixth century CE. For a recent assessment of Adam and Eve specifically in all three pseudepigraphs, see Böttrich, "The Figures of Adam and Eve in the Enoch Tradition."

The Fall of the Angels (chapters 6–12)

One can readily discern the intent of 1 Enoch, to get right to a burning question that has preoccupied humankind in every age and in every society: Why is there so much evil in our world and how did this situation come about? Moreover, how will it all end? Better yet, will there be an end to evil? This last question is vital to 1 Enoch, as this book belongs more to the category of apocalyptic literature than to creation stories. Its purpose is to reassure its readers that, despite evil raging all around, the Almighty is in control and therefore, all will end well. Every evil power will be overcome, and the original perfect order intended by the divine Creator will once again prevail.[2] Accordingly, the righteous of this world, although suffering greatly in the present time, may rest assured of their eventual vindication because the omnipotent, omniscient God has already revealed to Enoch through his holy angels what will happen in the end time.

Because 1 Enoch is an apocalyptic treatise, it does not bother recounting a story of creation per se, whether of the world or of humankind or of heavenly beings such as angels. It assumes the veracity of the biblical narrative that God created the world *good*, and that includes humankind. The important question for 1 Enoch is, how did things go awry? Why is the world now corrupt and polluted with evildoers?

According to 1 Enoch, the real origin of evil is to be found in Genesis 6:1–4. Accordingly, it bypasses the first five chapters in Genesis that contain the stories of creation and human sinfulness, including how Adam and Eve were expelled from the garden for their disobedience, how Cain murdered his brother Abel the just, and other stories about the progression of human sin upon a virgin earth.[3] Instead, 1 Enoch attributes the corruption of humankind and the good earth to the fall of certain angels ("the sons of God") chronicled in Genesis 6:1–4. That Genesis passage is extremely cryptic and leaves many questions unanswered, among them: Who are "the sons of God" (*bene 'elohim*)? What is the meaning of the

2. See Nickelsburg, *1 Enoch 1*, 5, 40–42, and 48–56.

3. There is allegorical reference to Eve begetting Cain and Abel and to Cain murdering his brother Abel, and to Eve begetting other children—Seth in particular—to be found in another, originally distinct Enoch tradition known as "the Book of Dreams" (now 1 Enoch 83–90) in the section often labeled the "Animal Apocalypse" (1 Enoch 85–90), in which the descendants of Cain are evil while the descendants of Seth are good. But even in this section responsibility for evil in the world is blamed primarily upon fallen "stars" (angels) and the havoc they wreaked upon earth.

verb *yadon*[4] in verse 3? What is the significance of the 120-year limit for a human lifetime? Who are the "fallen (ones) (*nephilim*) and what is their relationship to the marriages between the "sons of God" and the human daughters and their progeny? Patently, 1 Enoch attempts to answer such ambiguities in the Genesis passage by elaborating in detail the import of this all-important episode.

> [6]In those, days, when the children of man had multiplied, it happened that there were born unto them handsome and beautiful daughters. And the angels, the children of heaven, saw them and desired them; and they said to one another, "Come, let us choose wives for ourselves from among the daughters of man and beget us children." And Semyaz, being their leader, said unto them, "I fear that perhaps you will not consent that this deed should be done, and I alone will become (responsible) for this great sin." But they all responded to him, "Let us all swear an oath and bind everyone among us by a curse not to abandon this suggestion but to do the deed." Then they all swore together and bound one another by (the curse). And they were altogether two hundred; . . . Semyaz, the leader of Arakeb, Mame'el, Tam'el, Ram'el, Dan'el, Ezeqel, Baraqyal, As'el, Armaros, Batar'el, Anan'el, Zaqe'el, Sasomaspe'el, Kestar'el, Tur'el, Yamayol, and Arazyal. These are their chiefs of tens and of all the others with them.
>
> [7]And they took wives unto themselves, and everyone (respectively) chose one woman for himself, and they began to go unto them. And they taught them magical medicine, incantations, the cutting of roots, and taught them (about) plants. And the women became pregnant and gave birth to great giants whose heights were three hundred cubits (four hundred feet). These (giants) consumed the produce of all the people until the people detested feeding them. So the giants turned against (the people) in order to eat them. And they began to sin against birds, wild beasts, reptiles, and fish. And their flesh was devoured the one by the other, and they drank blood. And then the earth brought an accusation against the oppressors.
>
> [8]And Azaz'el taught the people (the art of) making swords and knives, and shields, and breastplates; and he showed to their chosen ones bracelets, decorations, (shadowing of the eye) with

---

4. Translated variously in the following examples (in italics): My spirit shall not always *strive* with man, for that he also [is] flesh" (KJV); "My spirit shall not *abide* in mortals forever, for they are flesh" (NRSV); "My spirit shall not *remain* in man forever, since he is but flesh" (NAB); "Let My spirit not *quarrel* forever concerning man, because he is also flesh" (JPS).

antimony, ornamentation, the beautifying of the eyelids, all kinds of precious stones, and all coloring tinctures and alchemy. And there were many wicked ones and they committed adultery and erred, and all their conduct became corrupt. Amasras taught incantation and the cutting of roots, and Armaros the resolving of incantations; and Baraqiyal astrology, and Kokarer'el (the knowledge of) the signs, and Tam'el taught the seeing of the stars, and Asder'el taught the course of the moon as well as the deception of man. And (the people) cried and their voice reached unto heaven.[5]

Many assumptions are present in this text. Although nowhere stated, 1 Enoch assumes that before God created humankind, he had already created various kinds of angels, what Genesis 6:1 refers to as "the sons of God" (or "the sons of the gods" in even older myths), that is, divine, heavenly beings.[6] 1 Enoch refers to these heavenly beings using a variety of terms, notably "watchers" and "holy ones." They are called "Watchers" (*'irim* in Aramaic, from the root *'wr* "to be awake," "to be watchful") because the deity had assigned them the task of watching over and guarding all elements of creation (heaven and earth, summer and winter, frost and heat, wind and rain, thunder and lightning, etc.). Among their duties was watching out for the welfare of the newly created, innocent humans; in other words, they were to act as "guardian angels." More on this shortly.

But before proceeding, we should note another characteristic of these heavenly beings. They were, without exception, all males—"sons of God" in the words of Genesis. That is hardly accidental. In the patriarchal society of that time, males were considered superior to females, physically, intellectually, and morally. Perhaps the Hellenistic pre-Maccabean Jewish author of 1 Enoch would not have subscribed fully to the common Greco-Roman view that females were defective males, but likely he was influenced by it. The female body was considered imperfectly formed, as females suffered a lack—a pit or cavity—in the very area where males exhibited robust genitalia. At the same time women suffered from excesses—witness their leaking extra fluids such as menstrual blood and breast

5. Translation by E. Isaac, "1 (Ethiopic Apocalypse of) Enoch," in Charlesworth, *Old Testament Pseudepigrapha*, 1:15–16.

6. That "the sons of God" in Gen 6:2 should be understood as "angels" was a widespread assumption at the time, as attested by the fact that many Greek copies from this period render Hebrew "sons" (*bene*) into Greek as "angels" (*aggeloi*); see James C. VanderKam in *Jewish Apocalyptic Heritage in Early Christianity*, edited by VanderKam and Adler, 60 n183.

milk. Moreover, women were believed to lack masculine self-control and so need to be dominated by men. At least some of these prejudices are present in the Enochic trope according to which heavenly beings were depicted as males, and appropriately so.

It appears that one group of these heavenly beings, some two hundred of them under the leadership of a powerful angel named Shemihazah,[7] were assigned to watch over humankind and to intervene and instruct these innocent and inexperienced neophytes how to make their way in this new world. (One wonders, further, if perhaps the task of the Watchers was to look after the human women specifically, since women were thought to need more guidance than men.) Unfortunately, some of these angels carried their duty of "watching" to an extreme. While they watched, their passions were aroused as they observed the humans marrying and copulating and having families. Moreover, the longer they watched, the more they noticed just how attractive and beautiful these "human daughters" were, so much so that they began to lust after them. This was of course a no-no, given the rigid boundaries between the heavenly and the earthly realms, and the rules regarding appropriate behavior within each realm. In the earthly realm, creatures were supposed to mate and have offspring. But heavenly beings such as the Watchers were created "spiritual, having eternal life, and immortal" (15:6). For that reason they had not been given wives (15:7), as that would be "unnatural" for them. Most certainly, the denizens of these two realms were never supposed to co-mingle, as if they belonged to the same species. It was only a matter of time before the impassioned Watchers conspired together to have their way with the human daughters, and even to have families of their own. At the instigation of their leader Shemihazah, these conspirators bound themselves under oath to commit together this "great sin" (6:3) against the Almighty, against themselves, and against humankind.

It should be noted that throughout this whole conspiracy, humankind played no active role. The humans did not attempt to cross any boundary between the heavenly and the earthly realms, only the Watchers. Nor did the human daughters themselves do anything to entice the

7. Elsewhere in 1 Enoch (chapter 8) Azazel appears to be the leader of the rebel angels. It is likely that that this discrepancy regarding who is the leader of the Watchers, Shemihazah/Shemjaz(a), on the one hand, or Azazel/Asael, on the other, derives from different versions of Enochic tradition having been combined into a single text in 1 Enoch, analogous to the Yahwistic, Elohistic, and Priestly strands found in the final version of Genesis; see VanderKam, "Genesis 6:1–4 and the Angel Stories in the Book of Watchers," 5–7.

Watchers. Indeed, it would appear that the Watchers actually forced themselves upon naïve, innocent adolescent women. *Raped* might not be too strong a word here. In any case, 1 Enoch makes it abundantly clear that responsibility for this violation—more precisely, this *sin*—lay entirely with the Watchers. (Even so, one may detect elements of a patriarchal cultural bias here, in that women are *indirectly* blamed for leading the Watchers astray—because *as males* these angels found it nearly impossible to resist feminine beauty. So invariably, women are responsible for the downfall of the males!)

The consequences of this "original sin" were utterly disastrous, 1 Enoch informs the reader. The divine design for a good and well-ordered earth was totally subverted because of the actions of these fallen angels. Evil quickly engulfed both humankind and the animal world, as all creatures descended further and further into violence and mutual enmity.

Women are depicted as the first humans to succumb to the novel evil ways. The Watchers initiated their new wives into every sort of wrongdoing. First, the women were taught the use of forbidden magic and incantations. Worse, women were also instructed how to employ various artificial means to make their naturally beautiful bodies even more alluring through the use of make-up and the wearing of jewelry, all of which inevitably led to adultery and multiple other sinful practices.

Next, Azazel revealed heavenly secrets to the human population that they were never supposed to learn (chapter 8), including how to make and use various weapons such as swords and knives and shields with which to kill one another and wreak havoc across the face of the earth. They also turned their weapons against the animals, which in turn began to ravage the humans.

But the most egregious part was that these unnatural unions between the Watchers and their human wives produced humongous giants 300 cubits in height (= 450 feet tall!). These in turn begat gigantic children, the Nephilim, who bore still more oversized offspring, the Elioud. Naturally, with such huge bodies came voracious appetites. After consuming every bit of food needed by humankind, these giants turned upon the human population and began to devour them.

Such was the havoc wreaked upon God's good world by the Watchers, now become fallen angels. Humankind could bear no more. In desperation they "cried out, and their voice reached unto heaven" (7:6). In heaven four of the most powerful faithful angels—Michael, Sariel, Raphael, and Gabriel—heard the pleas of desperate humankind and looking down "saw much bloodshed upon the earth. All the earth was filled with the godlessness and violence that had befallen it." They observed how the earth had been emptied of its people, and the souls of the dead pleading, "Bring our case for judgment before the Most High" (9:1–2). So the four faithful angels went before the Almighty and pleaded,

> "You have made everything and with you is the authority for everything. Everything is naked and open before your sight and you see everything; and there is nothing which can hide itself from you. You see what Azaz'el has done; how he has taught all (forms of) oppression upon the earth. And they revealed eternal secrets which are performed in heaven (and which) man learned. (Moreover) Semyaz, to whom you have given power to rule over his companions, co-operating, they went in unto the daughters of the people on earth, and they lay together with them—with those women—and defiled themselves, and revealed to them every (kind of) sin. As for the women, they gave birth to giants to the degree that the whole earth was filled with blood and oppression. And now behold, the Holy One will cry, and those who have died will bring their suit up to the gate of heaven. Their groaning has ascended (into heaven) . . . tell us what is proper for us that we may do regarding it."

The Almighty was indeed moved to have compassion upon wronged humankind, but in a somewhat roundabout way. He sent each of these four faithful angels forth with a specific mission (chapter 10).

The Almighty instructed the angel Sariel to descend to earth to Noah, the righteous son of Lamech, and reveal to Noah a plan forward for humankind. God would send a mighty flood to cleanse the face of the earth. Noah was to "hide (himself)," because every living thing except for Noah and his family is be destroyed. Thus will the reign of terror by the monstrous giants on earth come to an end, as all evildoers will be wiped out. Noah and "his seed," however, "will be preserved for all generations."

The Almighty dispatched the angel Raphael to deal with the scourge of the rebellious angels. Azazel—the one who taught humans to make implements of war and women to pollute their bodies with enticing beauty accoutrements—Raphael was to "bind hand and foot," and cast him into a deep pit in the desert where Azazel is to remain in complete darkness until "the great judgment day" when Azazel will be confined "into fire." (Note that here we have the beginnings of the Christian concept of the eternal fires of hell, as well as a precursor of themes that will reappear in Revelation 20:1–6 about the binding of "the Devil and Satan" for all eternity in the fiery lake of torment.)

Gabriel was instructed to "proceed against the bastards and the reprobates and against the children of adultery," setting them against one another," with the result that they will kill each other and thereby rid earth of their pollution.

Meanwhile, Michael was to proceed directly to Shemihazah, the ringleader of the fallen angels and chief architect of the conspiracy, and to those who with him fornicated with the women. Michael was to announce their punishment: that they will all die together with those whom they have defiled, but only after battling each other. They are to be bound "for seventy generations" underneath the rocks of the ground until the day of their judgment and of their consummation, when judgment is finally completed. These too are to be bound and confined in the fiery pit.

Thus will the earth finally be rid of the "pleasure seekers" and their offspring, those who inflicted so grave an injustice upon humankind. Happily, the removal of injustice and iniquity from the face of the earth will result in renewal of original paradisiacal conditions. Then

> the plant of righteousness and truth will appear forever and (God) will plant joy. Then all the righteous ones will escape and . . . multiply and become tens of hundreds, and all the days of their youth and the years of their retirement they will complete in peace. In those days, the whole earth will be worked in righteousness . . . they shall plant pleasant trees upon her—vines . . . (that) produce wine for plentitude. Every seed that is sown on her one measure will yield a thousand (measures) and one measure of olives will yield ten measures of presses of oil . . . all the children of the people will become righteous, and all nations shall worship and bless me; and they will prostrate themselves to me. The earth shall be cleansed from all pollution, and from all sin, and from all plague, and from all suffering; and it shall not happen again that I shall send (these) upon the earth from generation to generation and forever.
>
> In those days I shall open the storerooms of blessing which are in the heavens, so that I shall send them down upon the earth, over the work and the toil of the children of man. And peace and truth shall become partners together in all the days of the world, and in all the generations of the world. (10:16—11:2)

Enoch relates that upon learning of their fate and impending doom, the condemned Watchers implored Enoch to intercede for them before the Almighty to lift their terrible punishment. Enoch does approach the Almighty but is informed there can be no mitigation. The rebels knowingly violated the divine order according to which heavenly beings are created to be spiritual and not to have wives or to sire offspring (emphatically stated in chapter 11 and reiterated in chapter 15). They also possessed superior knowledge, though not perfect knowledge. If they had perfect knowledge, they could have foreseen the consequences of their act of rebellion. As it were, "not all the mysteries (of heaven) are open to you; you (only) know the rejected mysteries" (16:3). Yet because of their superior intellects, no forgiveness is possible. Their culpability is emphasized, further, by a cryptic note that not all the Watchers so sinned; 1 Enoch 12:1 says that before all these things came to pass, Enoch himself "was hidden" in heaven among "the (faithful) Watchers and the holy ones," that is to say, among the good angels. Clearly, rebellion against God's decrees is a free-will choice. (This is a theme to which Augustine will return some five centuries later, but with a difference: Augustine opined that God extended forgiveness to Adam and Eve and their descendants because humans act without full understanding of their sin(s); but the fallen angels were denied forgiveness precisely because with their superior intellects, they possessed full and complete knowledge of what they were about.)

Enoch in his vision is shown how, with the removal of the fallen angels and their wicked offspring, the earth will quickly recover, and paradisiacal conditions will descend once again upon the earth. When the heavens shower down their abundant blessings, prosperity abounds. Peace and truth will again partner. Evil will be no more. Such is the vision for the future of humankind; moreover, their earthly home will be fully restored. Of course, this will not happen immediately, but it will happen.

It is important to state once more that according to 1 Enoch 6–12 humankind is not responsible for plunging this world into chaos and evil. That is the work of fallen angels, beings who possess infinitely greater power than humans. Humans are victims, not perpetrators. True, humans do engage in evil acts, but less of their own volition than because they have been overwhelmed or led astray by demonic forces much stronger than themselves. As 1 Enoch 6–12 recounts human history, it literally is correct to say, "The devil made me do it!" Or, more exactly, the devil together with all his fallen angel allies dragged us into committing sins that we could never have conceived on our own.

1 Enoch is thus a major departure from Genesis. In Genesis, humans, especially the original man and woman, are held accountable for their own sin(s). Yes, they were in part misled by suggestive (but truthful?) words from the snake—who, remember, is not the conniving devil/Satan of later Jewish and Christian literature but rather a divine seraph posted in Eden to prevent humans having access to the Tree of Knowledge of Good and Evil. Humans were not supposed to acquire divine wisdom. The snake is not without fault, as indicated by Yahweh God's judgments which quickly follow. Whatever the role of the snake, however, the deity holds the human couple responsible for their own complicity. The man and his wife are each judged fully culpable for his or her own action and punished accordingly. This motif of every human person being fully responsible for his or her own actions—whether bad or good—carries through into the following chapters of Genesis as well. Cain is condemned for the murder of his brother Abel (Gen 4:1–16). Similarly, Lamech is depicted as excessively violent in his desire for "seventy-sevenfold" vengeance (Gen 4:23–24). The growth of human sinfulness over the earth eventually becomes so rampant that Yahweh God decides upon the drastic action of sending the great flood (6:5–8) to wipe the face of the earth clean of both sin and sinners.

A completely different view is presented in 1 Enoch, which mostly ignores the first five chapters of Genesis. There are but two minor references to Genesis 1–5 in 1 Enoch: the first, a listing of "Adam" in genealogical lists (37:1; 60:8); and the second, a brief cryptic allusion to the "tree of wisdom . . . from which your old father and aged mother, your precursors, ate and came to know wisdom" (32:3–6). Neither text contains any suggestion of sinfulness on the part of the human couple. For 1 Enoch the story of sin begins only with the account of the sons of God/angels lusting after the beautiful human daughters (cp. Genesis 6:1–4). Again, it must be emphasized that in 1 Enoch's version of human history, humans are the victims, not perpetrators, of sin. Humans and their world are polluted from the outside by a band of heavenly rebels, a rebellion began in heaven and spread to earth.

This motif a heavenly rebellion against divine authority is new in Israelite and biblical tradition; however, it will soon become a prominent theme in Jewish and Christian tradition. And while it appears here for the first time in Israelite and biblical tradition, it is a motif that has antecedents in ancient near eastern myth, going back at least to ancient Mesopotamia at the beginning of the second millennium BCE.

Rebellion in Heaven

A motif of lesser divinities revolting against the Divine Sovereign or Ruling God is found in several myths from ancient Mesopotamia. We have previously encountered this motif in the Old Babylonian Atrahasis myth. Recall that the gods decided to create humankind to serve as substitute agricultural laborers to dig irrigation canals and to plant and harvest crops after the lesser gods (the Igigi-gods)—the majority of the gods—refused to continue doing their appointed servile tasks for the benefit of Enlil and the few high-ranking gods. The revolt against the authority of the Enlil, the king of the gods in this text, was eventually resolved when the divine council, with guidance from wise Ea (Enki), decreed that the god Weila, the instigator of the conspiracy and ringleader of the divine rebels, be killed and from his blood mixed with clay seven primeval human pairs be created to take over the agricultural labors of the lesser gods. Henceforth all gods, no matter their rank, were to enjoy the privilege of "rest" (leisure), as befits gods. Although this "solution" will cause additional problems for the Divine Sovereign down the road in the form of an analogous revolt on the part of the human population, it did succeed in quelling the immediate crisis of rebellion by the lesser gods. It is worth noting, too, that in Atrahasis the subsequent human rebellion against divine authority—what conventionally may be termed "sin"—ultimately was inspired by a "demonic" force working from within the "spirit" that humankind received from Weila.

An even better example of rebellion in heaven is found in the so-called Babylonian Creation Myth, Enuma Elish. As noted in chapter 3, this epic poem is less a "creation myth" than the Babylonian account of how Marduk became king over all gods. Enuma Elish may be characterized as a theomachy, a battle between gods. To become the divine sovereign, Marduk had to battle the two most awesome primeval gods, Tiamat and Qingu, who were determined to kill off all the younger gods. A victory by Marduk would make him the king of the gods. The odds of victory were slim, however. Marduk's own father, the acknowledged leader of the younger generation of "good" gods, had been unequal to the task and had fled the battlefield. So formidable did the combined power of Tiamat and Qingu appear that most of the gods deserted Ea and his son Marduk and went over to the side of Tiamat and Qingu. In an initial battle Marduk's father Ea had been successful in killing Apsu, Tiamat's first husband. But Tiamat quickly recovered by marrying Qingu, an even more fearsome threat than was Apsu.

This new coalition proved so formidable that most of the lesser gods threw their lot in with Tiamat and Qingu, leaving Marduk and his few remaining allies sorely outnumbered. After an initial setback for the allies in battle, Marduk marched forth alone and singlehandedly managed to slay Tiamat and take Qingu captive. Having emerged victorious, Marduk was ultimately proclaimed the divine sovereign by all the gods, even those who had sided with Tiamat and Qingu.

The Babylonian author of Enuma Elish leaves no doubt, however, that most of the gods, by deserting Marduk and siding with Tiamat and Qingu, had acted wrongly in going over to the "dark side." Their participation in this rebellion in heaven came close to destroying hope for the good order that Marduk hoped to bring forth to replace the chaotic reign of Tiamat and her ilk—not only in heaven, but also on the earth with its human population that Marduk would go on to create from the dead bodies of Tiamat and Qingu.

It might be too much of a stretch to suggest a direct parallel between these rebel gods and the fallen "Watchers" in 1 Enoch. After all, 1 Enoch is monotheistic and its rebels are angels, while Enuma Elish is patently polytheistic in character, and its rebels are lesser gods. The rebellion of Enuma Elish takes place in heaven before the creation of the world and of humankind, while the rebellion of the Watchers in 1 Enoch happens on earth after the world and humankind had been created. Nevertheless, the Watchers patently are a derivative of the "sons of God" in Genesis 6, and thus may be considered lesser divine beings. Moreover, the Watchers take an oath of alliance to Shemihazah/Azazel much as the rebel gods pledge their loyalty to Tiamat and Qingu. In 1 Enoch a few good angels/ Watchers battle the many fallen Watchers in a manner not dissimilar to the alignment of Marduk and his few faithful allies against Tiamat and the majority of gods who sided with her. It seems plausible, then, that the Mesopotamian motif of a rebellion in heaven served at minimum as a distant antecedent to one of the central themes of 1 Enoch.

One may wonder why the author of 1 Enoch was so fixated on the ubiquity of evil in the world and especially about his motive for shifting responsibility for rampant human iniquity away from humans themselves and onto alien, superhuman powers. Perhaps it was a manifestation of the troubled times in which the author lived. 1 Enoch was written in a (postexilic) period, when the formerly free Israelites and Judaeans were dominated by powerful foreign enemies (Babylonians, Persians, Greeks, Egyptians); they undoubtedly felt powerless to resist such evil forces. Certainly, such expressions of powerlessness were prominent in other writings from this period, such as the biblical books of Esther and Daniel, as well as 1 Maccabees, 2 Maccabees, and the Dead Sea scroll *The War of the Sons of Light Against the Sons of Darkness.*

Postscript: Fallen Angels in Later Tradition

The motif of fallen angels who lead humankind astray had a long after-life. Once introduced into theological discourse as an explanation for the ubiquity of evil in human experience, the motif spread like wildfire, first within certain Jewish circles, and later widely infiltrating the writings of Gnostics and Christians alike. It appeared in the gnostic text known as the Secret Revelation of John, for example (to be discussed in chapter 9, below). The second-century Christian apologist Justin Martyr, who was beheaded circa 160 for his robust defense of the Christian faith, explicitly traced the corruption of humankind back to this primeval "event."

> God, when He had made the whole world, and subjected earthly things to men and women, and arranged the heavenly elements for the increase of fruits and change of the seasons, and ordered the divine law for them—these things also He made for people to see—entrusted the case of men and women and of things under heaven to angels whom he appointed over them. But the angels transgressed this order, and were captivated by love of women, and produced children who are called demons. And besides later they enslaved the human race to themselves, partly by magical writings, and partly by fears and punishments which they occasioned, and partly by teaching them to offer sacrifices and incense and libations, which they needed after they were enslaved with lustful passions; and among people they sowed murders, wars, adulteries, intemperate deeds, and every evil. When also the poets and mythologists, not knowing that it was the angels and those demons who had been begotten by them that did these things to men and women and cities and nations, which they related, ascribed them to God Himself, and to those who were his offspring, and to the offspring of those who were called His brothers. For whatever name each of the [fallen] an-gels had given to himself and to his children, by that name they called them.[8]

8. Second Apology 5–6, in Justin, *St. Justin Martyr,* 76–77.

The motif of the fallen angels continued to reappear in various forms in both Jewish and Christian texts over the next millennium and a half at minimum. We will see in a later chapter that it figures prominently in Milton's epic poem *Paradise Lost*. Indeed, one could argue that the fallen angels motif has never gone away; it continues to be reincarnated in dystopian novels and Hollywood blockbusters such as *Lord of the Rings* and the *Star Wars* trilogy.

5

The Book of Jubilees

ANOTHER JEWISH PSEUDEPIGRAPH THAT contributed greatly to the expansion of the Adam and Eve tradition is the book of Jubilees. Only slightly younger than 1 Enoch, it was written in approximately 160–140 BCE by a fervent Jewish priest (or priests) whose primary goal was to promote strict observance of the Jewish legal code in an increasingly secularized (Hellenistic) society. To that end, the author has retold much of the biblical narrative found in Genesis and Exodus but set it in a new framework.

According to this new version, while Moses was on the mountain top those forty days and nights with God (see Exodus 19–34), God revealed to Moses the whole history of the world, from creation down to the "present," that is, when Moses stands in the presence of God on top of Mount Sinai. Moses is admonished to pay close attention "to everything which I shall tell you on this mountain, and to write it in a book so that their descendants might see that I have not abandoned them on account of all the evil which they have done" (1:5; also 1:26). The opening line in the book claims, further, that this book is an exact account of "the years of the world just as the Lord told it to Moses on Mount Sinai when he went up to receive the tablets of the Law." Mercifully, it seems Moses may have been spared the herculean task of copying down all by himself every word issuing from the mouth of God, since a bit later the reader is informed that God commanded one of his highest angels, the angel of the presence: "Write for Moses from the first creation until my sanctuary is built in their midst forever and ever" (1:27, 29). However the scribing may have been accomplished, it appears that the book of Jubilees was intended at minimum as a supplement to the biblical five books of the Torah, and perhaps even a replacement for the whole of them.

Adam and Eve according to Jubilees

For the most part Jubilees follows Genesis 1 in recounting how God created the world in six days and hallowed the seventh day as a day of rest. There are few noteworthy departures from the Genesis account, however.[1]

On the first day, after creating the heavens and the earth and the waters, Jubilees adds that God also created various kinds of angels, presumably to populate the heavens, similar to the manner in which fish and sea creatures were created later to swim the sea, and birds to fill the sky, and beasts and humans to populate the earth. The angel population consists of all the spirits who minister before God: the angels of the presence and angels of sanctification; angels of the spirit of fire and winds; angels of the spirits of the clouds and darkness, snow and hail and frost, angels of thunder and lightning, and cold and heat and winter and springtime and harvest and summer—the spirits of all God's creatures in heaven and on earth (2:2).

Angels will play important roles in the history of humankind, as in 1 Enoch. 1 Enoch did not explain how these angels came to be, however—a major lacuna that Jubilees felt it necessary to fill. The angel of the presence informs Moses that because the angels were the first creatures created, they witnessed how marvelously God created all things and continuously praised him for his wondrous works, as was only appropriate.

A second departure from Genesis is that on the fourth day, when God created the sun and the moon and the stars, he designed the sun so that it marked not only days of the week but also jubilees—jubilees being a most important calendrical event for the writer and his community. A jubilee is a period of "seven weeks of years," that is, forty-nine years. From creation until Moses's death there were fifty jubilees, that is 2450 years.

A third departure was that the creative process was not completed in a single week. Yes, the deity did create humankind—both the male and the female—on the sixth day. On this point the author of Jubilees is insistent. Reformulating the description of humankind in Gen 1:26–31, Jubilees 2:13–14 states that

1. Conveniently summarized by Jacques van Ruiten, "Adam in the Book of Jubilees," in Laato and Valve, eds., *Adam and Eve Story*, 143–75.

On the sixth day he made all the land animals, all cattle, and
everything that moves about on the earth. After all this, he made
humankind—a male and a female he made them. He made him
rule everything on earth and in the seas and over flying creatures, animals, everything that moves about on the earth, cattle,
and the entire earth. Over all these he made him rule. These four
kinds he made on the sixth day.[2]

Even though both the male and the female were created at the same time,
nonetheless Jubilees says that dominion over everything on earth and
in the seas and in the air was given only to the male: "[God] made *him*
rule."[3] As in Genesis, God then rested, having given the appropriate laws
for observance of the sabbath.

But while all things had been created in those first six days, the refinement of creation continued beyond the first week. At first the woman
existed only in inchoate or virtual form, hidden as a rib inside the male.
During the six days of the *second* week the Lord directed the angels to
bring the various animals before Adam so that Adam might name them,
"each one according to its name, and whatever he called them became
their names." But as Adam observed the various creatures parading before him during those first five days and saw how they were paired as
male and female, Adam realized that "he was alone and there was none
whom he found for himself, who was like himself, who would help him"
(3:2–3). Why God did not simply create humankind fully as male and
female from the start is not made clear. Perhaps God wanted the man to
recognize his need for companionship and a sexual partner for propagat-
ing the earth.[4] Whatever the reason, Adam's need prompted God to take
addition actions.

And the Lord said to us [angels], "It is not good that the man
should be alone. Let us make for him a helper who is like him."
And the Lord our God cast a deep sleep upon him, and he
slept. And he took one bone from the midst of his bones for
the woman. And that rib was the origin of the woman from the
midst of the bones. And he built up the flesh in place of it, and
he constructed a woman.
And he awakened Adam from his sleep, and when he
awoke, he stood up on the sixth day. And he brought her to him,

2. VanderKam, *Jubilees*, 1:167.

3. VanderKam, *Jubilees*, 1:190–92.

4. Van Ruiten, "Adam in the Book of Jubilees," 152–53.

and he knew her and said to her, "This is now bone of my bone and flesh from my flesh. This one will be called my wife because she was taken from her husband."

Therefore a man and woman shall be one. And therefore it shall be that a man will leave his father and his mother, and he will join with his wife and they will become one flesh.

In the first week Adam was created and also the rib, his wife. And in the second week [God] showed her to him. And therefore the commandment was given to observe seven days for a male, but for a female twice seven days in the impurity. (3:4–8)⁵

Here Jubilees has combined the two creation accounts from Genesis and in the process added embellishments of his own making. The "us" of Gen 1:26 and 3:22 is explicitly interpreted as God speaking to his angels, thereby removing any ambiguity that other gods might have been involved.

Next, the author makes no bones about it that the Hebrew vocable *tsela'*, that part taken from Adam while he slept, was a specific bone, namely, a "rib," and not one "side" as numerous contemporary rabbis were speculating. Even though Jubilees posits that Eve was not actually "built" into a woman until the sixth day of the second week, yet because the rib from which she was built was a part of "the human" when he was created on the sixth day of the first week, the statement of Gen 1:27 that God created both the male and the female on the same day is factually correct:

So God created humankind (*ha-'adam*) in his image,
In the image of God he created *him*,
Male and female he created *them*.

At the same time, Jubilees affirms that the account in Genesis 2, which posits that woman was created *after* man, is likewise correct. The author finds no contradiction whatever between Genesis 1 and Genesis 2.

From this point on Jubilees departs radically from the Genesis narrative, however. Again combining the two creation accounts, Jubilees states that God created the garden of Eden on the third day, at the same time when God created every fruit-bearing tree (Jub 2:7; cp. Gen 1:11–12). Moreover, going against the common understanding which assumes that Adam and Eve were placed in the Eden immediately upon their creation,

5. Unless otherwise stated, excerpts of Jubilees are from Orval S. Wintermute, "Jubilees," in Charlesworth, *Old Testament Pseudepigrapha*, 2:35–142.

Jubilees claims that Adam and his wife had been created outside of Eden and only later did the angels conduct the primal couple into Eden, but at different times. While the angels brought Adam into Eden on the fortieth day after his creation, Eve had to wait an additional forty days, that is, eighty days in all, before the angels conducted her into the garden. This difference, combined with the fact that Eve was only completely "built" seven days after being initially formed inside "Adam," is given as justification for the disparity for the law in Leviticus 12 requiring a differing numbers of days for removal of impurity and purification of both a post-partum mother and her newborn, depending upon whether the child is a boy or a girl.

The idea that Adam and Eve had been created outside of Eden and put there only subsequently is based upon a close reading of Genesis 2:7–15. Verse 7 describes how God formed "the Human" from the dust, which God then animated with his own life-giving breath. This is followed by a subsequent statement that God "planted" a garden, where many marvelous trees grow and are watered by four streams. Only after the garden had been created (planted) did "Yahweh God take the Human and put him in the garden in Eden to till it and to care for it." Jubilees (3:32) names Elda as the land in which Adam and Eve had been created and the place to where they were returned when expelled from Eden.[6] Adam and Eve seem to have spent the remainder of their lives back in Elda, since Adam was buried there.

> At the end of the nineteenth jubilee in the seventh week, in the
> sixth year, Adam died. And all of his children buried him in the
> land of his creation. And he was the first who was buried in the
> earth. (4.29)

Jubilees also has a unique take on the matter of human sexuality, or more precisely, where the sex act may be performed. Jubilees says that immediately after the creation of Eve, God brought Eve to Adam and Adam "knew" her. That is, he had sexual intercourse with her, just as God intended: "Therefore a man and woman shall be one. And therefore it shall be that a man will leave his father and his mother, and he will join with his wife and they will become one flesh" (3:5; compare Gen 2:24).

6. That Adam and Eve were created outside of Eden may also have been the view of Ben Sira (Sir 25:24); so Antti Laato and Lotta Valve, "Understanding the Story of Adam and Eve in the Second Temple Period," in Laato and Valve, eds., *Adam and Eve Story*, 5–6; and Anders Aschim, "Adam Translated, Transcribed and Recycled," in the same volume, pp. 129–32.

This happened *before* the angels conducted Adam and Eve into Eden. During the whole time the primal couple were in the garden, however, they did not have sex. Only after they were expelled from Eden did Adam again "know" Eve. According to the author of Jubilees, this hiatus was purposeful. Eden is a sacred space, an inner sanctum, a kind of temple. Eden is the holiest place in the whole world. Even the trees there are holy (3.12). Just as a priest must refrain from sex and be purified before entering the Temple, so it would have been inappropriate for Adam to have engaged in sex within the sacred garden, because in Eden Adam functioned as a priest, which included his offering incense (3:27).[7]

In addition to functioning as a priest, Adam was a model farmer the whole seven years he and Eve were in Eden. According to Jubilees 3:15–16, the angels themselves taught Adam how "to do everything which was appropriate for tilling." Accordingly, there was food in abundance. Adam protected "the garden from the birds and beasts and cattle"; he gathered its fruit for eating and stored the surplus for use later. During this whole blissful period Adam and his wife were naked but felt no shame. Trouble, however, was just over the horizon.

"At the end of seven years . . . the serpent came and drew near to the woman" (3:17). The author of Jubilees—surely a male—seems to blame the woman almost exclusively for what happens next. (According to Jubilees, Adam was not with Eve during this episode, contrary to the statement in Genesis 3:6 that her husband was "with her.") The serpent appears here to be nothing more than a snake—an extremely intelligent one, however—who can ably hold his own in a conversation with the woman. And yes, the serpent could talk. In those days, all the animals were able to converse in Hebrew, the sacred language of God and the angels. Only later, as a result of their expulsion from Eden did the animals lose their ability to speak. In the course of their dialog, the serpent tells the woman that if she eats from the fruit of the tree in the middle of the garden, she will not die that very day. On the contrary, her eyes will be opened and she "will become like gods . . . knowing good and evil"—that is, she will be enlightened with divine wisdom. The woman seems less interested in the magic qualities of the tree, however, than that "its fruit was good to eat, and she took some of it and she ate" (3:20).

7. See the excellent discussion by Anderson, *Genesis of Perfection,* chapter 2, esp. 55–62; also van Ruiten, "Adam in the Book of Jubilees," in Laato and Valve, eds., *Adam and Eve Story,* 161–66.

The serpent was correct. Eve did not die that very day, but more on this later. Moreover, she did gain further knowledge—though not the knowledge she expected. She immediately recognized that she was naked, just like the beasts. So she covered her nudity with a fig leaf. Only then, feeling guilty and shameful, did Eve approach Adam to give him some so that he also ate. We are not told of Adam's reason for disobeying the divine command, but only that he complied, becoming similarly "enlightened." Adam, too, experienced shame and guilt, and sewed a garment of fig leaves to cover his own nudity—and to hide his sinfulness. For the first time he also became aware of his wife's nudity.

The following scene is much abbreviated from Genesis. God does not walk in the garden, nor do the man and his wife attempt to hide among the trees. Rather, God simply appears and curses the serpent and the woman and the man. The text is corrupt at this point, but it appears that until now the serpent had walked on legs—similar to the way divine guardian serpents are sometimes depicted in ancient near eastern iconography—and that his curse involved henceforth crawling on his belly, as in Genesis 3. [Later traditions will specify that to accomplish this aspect of the curse, God sent his angels to hack off the serpent's feet and hands.] The woman is punished for having listened to the serpent and having eaten. The man's sin was in listening to his wife's seductions rather than adhering to God's instructions. After pronouncing appropriate curses on the primal couple, God "made for them garments of skin and he dressed them and sent them from the garden of Eden" (3:26). There is no mention of a second tree nor any indication that these humans were being punished additionally by depriving them of either immortality or access to "the tree of life." Jubilees is unclear about any intended fate for Adam and Eve, whether they would have lived forever, had they not been expelled from Eden.

In another departure from Genesis, Jubilees has Adam offer a sweet-smelling sacrifice to God in the morning of the very day he and Eve were expelled from Eden (3:27). This would appear to be a sign of Adam's repentance for his sin, as well as an indication that from the very beginning Adam was less "committed" to sinning than was the woman. In general, Jubilees portrays Adam more favorably than Eve, perhaps because the author considers Adam to be a priest. Eve was automatically excluded from that privileged status, of course, since in orthodox Israelite religion women were not eligible to be priests.[8]

Life outside Eden was radically different. "Adam and his wife went out from the garden of Eden and dwelt in the land of Elda," where they had first lived, before the angels brought them into Eden. Back in Elda, Adam "tilled the land as he had been taught in the garden of Eden" (3:35), though because of the curse, the labor was more difficult and the land less productive. The couple were not alone in their suffering, however. All creation suffered with them. Jubilees emphasizes that all of creation was afflicted by Adam's and Eve's sin. "All flesh," that is, all the animals were also expelled from the garden. Moreover, "on that day the mouth of all the beasts and cattle and birds and whatever walked or moved was stopped from speaking because all of them used to speak with one another with one speech and one language" (3:28).

Jubilees continues to supplement the all too cryptic text of Genesis concerning the life of Adam and his wife outside Eden. The author postpones Adam's naming of his wife "Eve" ("the mother of all living," Gen 3:20) until the couple was back in Elda, to correspond to the birthing of their children. Eve gave birth not only to sons Cain and Abel, but also to a daughter named Awan. The latter was necessary to explain how after murdering his brother Abel, Cain was able to find a wife prior to Adam and Eve giving birth to Seth and "other sons and daughters" (Gen 5:4). Jubilees specifies that among the latter is another daughter, Asura, who will become the wife of Seth.

As the author elaborates on how the offspring of Adam and Eve continued to multiply on earth, he notes that it was in the days of Jared that "the angels of the Lord, who were called Watchers, came down to the earth in order to teach the sons of man, and perform judgment and uprightness upon the earth" (Jub 4:15; cp. Gen 5:15–20). This is an obvious link to the Enochic tradition—with which the author appears to be well acquainted—Jared being the father of Enoch. Jubilees specifies that it was only in the days of Enoch that humankind first learned to read and write. Enoch "was the first who learned writing and knowledge and wisdom, from (among) the sons of men, from (among) those who were born upon earth" (4:17). Enoch's wisdom and knowledge of matters divine is without equal among the descendants of Adam and Eve because over the course of "six jubilees of years" the angels of God stayed with him

---

8. Taggar-Cohen, "Why Are There No Israelite Priestesses?"

"and they showed him everything which is on earth and in the heavens" (4:21), all of which Enoch wrote down in a book. Whether the author had knowledge of our book of 1 Enoch is uncertain, but he was certainly well acquainted with the larger extrabiblical Enochic tradition, including the story of the fall of the Watchers:

> [Enoch] wrote everything, and bore witness to the Watchers, the ones who sinned with the daughters of men because they began to mingle themselves with the daughters of men so that they might be polluted. And Enoch bore witness against all of them.

Because of his unique status, Enoch was spared the life—and death—of an ordinary mortal. Instead, "he was taken from among the children, and we [angels] led him to the garden of Eden for greatness and honor. And behold, he is there [still] writing condemnation and judgment of the world, and all of the evils of the children of men" (4:22–23), until the end, that great day of judgment.

The author cannot conclude his account of Adam and Eve without returning to the matter of their death, or at least Adam's death. He felt the need to correct a nagging doubt that the serpent may have been correct in telling Eve that she (and Adam) would not die in the very day they disobeyed God's command not to eat of the forbidden fruit in Eden, because after the couple was expelled from the garden they continued to live and even beget many children. Further, Genesis 5:5 explicitly says that Adam lived to a ripe old age, dying only in his nine hundred and thirtieth year! God's foreknowledge, and indeed God's veracity, must be defended. The author seemingly found a solution to this dilemma in Psalm 90:3–4, wherein the psalmist, reflecting on human frailty before God, wrote:

> You turn us back to dust
> and say, "Turn back, you mortals."
> For a thousand years in your sight
> are like yesterday when it is past,
> or like a watch in the night. (NRSV)

Granted that the psalmist was speaking in poetic language, but if interpreted literally, it can be understood to say that as God reckons time, a thousand years is a mere one day and, vice versa, a day is a thousand years—as 2 Peter 3:8 will argue a couple of centuries later. Just so, the author of Jubilees argues the case for God's veracity, that Adam did indeed die in the same day that he ate the forbidden fruit:

At the end of the nineteenth jubilee in the seventh week, in the sixth year, Adam died. He was the first who was buried in the earth. He lacked seventy years from one thousand years, for a thousand years are like one day in the testimony of heaven and therefore it was written concerning the tree of knowledge, "In the day you eat from it you will die," Therefore he did not complete the years of this day because he died in it. (4:29–30)

The book of Jubilees will continue on with the developing sorry story of early humankind, but the narrative concerning Adam and Eve per se has reached its conclusion.

Who Is Responsible for Human Sin?

The Jubilees account of Adam and Eve has evolved beyond the original Genesis narrative. But it less evolved than some later Jewish, Christian, or Muslim interpretations, especially with regard to the origin of evil and the first sin. The serpent has not yet become Satan in disguise. Nor is Adam—or Eve—assigned responsibility for the downfall of all humankind into a condition of absolute sinfulness. Many humans are sinful, but others are virtuous, witness Enoch himself—and Noah. About Noah the author notes "his heart was righteous in all of [God's] ways just as it was commanded concerning him. And he did not transgress anything which was ordained for him" (5:19). Also among the righteous were Noah's son Shem, and Abram (Abraham), and Moses. In other words, in Jubilees there is no concept of an "original sin" that universally affects every descendant of Adam and Eve. If blame is to be attributed to any one human, that belongs primarily to Eve. This is a theme that will have a long history in future reformulations of the Adam and Eve tradition.

Moreover, while Jubilees does not totally absolve humankind of responsibility for evil upon earth, as does 1 Enoch which blames everything upon the fallen angels, Jubilees does suggest that humankind is more victim than perpetrator. Jubilees follows 1 Enoch in positing the more grievous sin is that of the Watchers who abandoned their original spiritual condition in order to marry the attractive human daughters, as many as they wished.[9] From these unnatural unions were born monstrous giants who propagated injustice and corruption across the face of the earth.

9. In addition to 1 Enoch and Jubilees, the motif of the fallen angels is attested in the pseudepigraphs The Genesis Apocryphon and The Testaments of the Twelve Patriarchs.

> And injustice increased upon the earth, and all flesh corrupted
> its way; man and cattle and beasts and birds and everything
> which walks on the earth. And they all corrupted their way and
> their ordinances, and they began to eat one another. And injus-
> tice grew upon the earth and every imagination of the thoughts
> of all mankind was thus continually evil. (5:2)

God's anger burned hot "against his angels whom he had sent to the earth" and he commanded his good angels to bind the fallen Watchers within the depths of the earth, where they are imprisoned still. As for the Watchers' human offspring, the deity commanded that their lifespan be limited to "one hundred and ten years" (5:8). (Why this discrepancy from "one hundred and twenty years," as in Genesis 6:3, is unclear.) At the same time the deity sent "his sword" among the Watchers' monstrous offspring so that "they began to kill one another until they all fell on the sword and they were wiped out from the earth" (5:9). But the damage had been done. Even though the monsters themselves were thereby removed from earth, their evil spirits continue to roam this world misleading much of humankind so that they turn aside and "walk in the paths of corruption" (7:26–27). Moreover, "all flesh," even the animal kingdom, has been corrupted.

Truly there is no limit to the evil legacy of the Watchers. Arpach-shad taught his son Cainan to read and write. When Cainan went forth into the world to establish a city of his own,

> he found a writing which the ancestors engraved on stone. And
> he read what was in it. And he transcribed it. And he sinned
> because of what was in it, since there was in it the teaching of
> the Watchers by which they used to observe the omens of the
> sun and moon and stars within all the signs of heaven. And he
> copied it down. (8:3–4)

Thus was the wicked practice of astrology and reading of omens perpetu-ated and passed down to the present day.

In a similar manner nearly every evil in this world can be traced back to the heritage bequeathed us by the fallen Watchers and the demons they sired. When God ordered the fallen Watchers and their offspring bound and imprisoned in the underworld, the chief of the spirits, Mastema—that is, Satan—interceded with God to leave a portion of the evil spirits free so as to be able to exercise authority over wicked humans on earth, as was their destiny. God acceded to Mastema's request and allowed one tenth of the evil spirits to remain on earth subject to Satan, while binding the rest in the underworld. One should thank God that only one tenth of the evil spirits were allowed to remain to wreak havoc upon humankind and God's good creation. Imagine how terrible this world would be, had the totality of evil spirits been allowed to remain on earth.

The Legacy of Jubilees

The extent of the legacy of Jubilees is debatable. Jubilees was known to the Dead Sea Scrolls community, since a copy of the book was found among its scrolls. Also, the Jubilee calendar was adopted by Hasmonean rulers. Nevertheless, Jubilees did not have much lasting influence upon mainline Judaism, as it was rejected within rabbinic circles. Only Ethiopian Jews (Beta Israel) consider it a sacred book, where it known as the *Book of Division.*

Its influence upon Christianity was similarly mixed. Although it was well known to many early Christian writers (Epiphanius, Justin Martyr, Origin, Diodorus of Tarsus, Isidore of Alexandria, and Isidore of Seville, among others), Jubilees was accepted as canonical only by the Ethiopian Orthodox Church. Eastern Orthodox, Roman Catholic, and Protestant churches universally reject Jubilees as canonical, and consider it as one of the Pseudepigrapha.

Jubilees was influential with some early Christian writers regarding marriage and sex. Prior to Augustine (ca. 400), who allowed that sex within Eden was permissible even though it was never exercised there, most Christians followed the logic of Jubilees that sex within the confines of Eden was incompatible with the sacred character of Eden. For example, Gregory of Nyssa and Ephrem the Syrian (St. Ephrem), two contemporary fourth-century giants of Eastern Christianity, both in framing their views regarding marriage and celibacy relied upon the statement in Jubilees that Adam and Eve had refrained from sexual intercourse the whole time they were in the sacred garden. Gregory and Ephrem arrived at two very different conclusions, however. Ephrem argued that the primal couple's refraining sexual activity is an argument for celibacy as a state superior to marriage. Gregory, by contrast, was married. He, too, lauded virginal living, but argued that marriage was ordained by God and therefore, while there are occasions when abstinence is appropriate, chaste intercourse between husband and wife is not to be proscribed.[10] Even today, most Christians, perhaps unconsciously, continue to think that sex and Eden were somehow incompatible.

10. See the excellent discussion by Anderson, *Genesis of Perfection*, 55–62.

6

Life of Adam and Eve

SOME TWO HUNDRED YEARS after Jubilees another Jewish pseudepigraph appeared that radically changed the contours of the Adam and Eve tradition. This is the work popularly known as the Life of Adam and Eve. Its origins are unknown but likely it was composed in Hebrew sometime at the end of the first century or the beginning of the second century CE. It quickly gained popularity within both Jewish and Christian communities and was soon translated into Latin and Greek. From the Greek version still additional translations were made, notably Armenian and Slavic. Other versions exist as well: Syriac, Arabic, Coptic, and Ethiopic. No two versions, (which vary greatly in date, from the third to the sixteenth centuries CE) are identical in content; nevertheless, they do have much in common.

The two main extant versions are the Latin (known as the Vita) and the Greek (known as the Apocalypse of Moses).[1] These two are illustrative of both what the different versions have in common and how versions differ one from another. Both purport to narrate the lives of Adam and Eve following their expulsion from the garden of Eden until their deaths. Both place principal blame on Eve for their expulsion from the garden and subsequent woes. Both also posit Seth as a major figure in their life outside. Both detail Adam's and Eve's repentance and desire to

---

1. For these two texts I am dependent upon M. D. Johnson, "Life of Adam and Eve," in Charlesworth, *Old Testament Pseudepigrapha*, 2:249–95. Because the complex transmission histories of both texts have resulted in a certain amount of obscurity, for the most part I normally summarize Johnson's translations rather than quote them; even passages presented herein as direct quotations are at times my simplified paraphrasing of Johnson's translation.

regain God's forgiveness. Both tell of Seth's futile attempt to regain entry into the garden to obtain healing oil for Adam upon his deathbed. And both conclude with the dying Adam receiving a promise of resurrection at the end of time, and with Eve dying shortly thereafter, also with expectation of eventual resurrection.

The two versions differ in significant ways, however. Since the narrative begins only after Adam and Eve have been expelled from the garden, there is no narrative opportunity to relate chronologically what had transpired previously, when they were still in the garden. That missing information is supplied retroactively in both versions, but in different ways. The Latin text supplies the missing narrative by having Eve, after the death of Adam and just prior to her own death, recount to her children what transpired in Eden, how the devil through the serpent duped her into eating of the forbidden fruit. The Greek text, by contrast, has the angel Michael reveal to Moses atop of Mount Sinai what transpired *in the beginning* in the garden. A second major difference is that the Vita has Satan himself explain how he deliberately set out to seduce Eve and thereby foil the couple's happy existence in Eden, primarily out of envy stemming from his fall from heaven for refusing to worship the image of God in Adam at Adam's creation. Satan's role is much more restricted in the Apocalypse. Satan does not speak; rather Eve narrates at length her encounter with the talking serpent whose body and tongue had been taken over by the beguiling devil (Satan), and that it was largely Eve's own folly that caused them to be expelled from paradise.

The Greek Text (Apocalypse of Moses)

The Apocalypse purports to be a trustworthy account of what happened in the beginning because it was revealed by God through an angelic mediator to Moses on Sinai. The opening, prefatory verse asserts that this book is nothing less than "the narrative and life of Adam and Eve the first-made, revealed by God to Moses his servant when he received the tablets of the law of the covenant from the hand of the Lord, after he had been taught by the archangel Michael." The book continues, "This is the account of Adam and Eve," beginning with the day they emerged from paradise. They went down into the East, where they stayed for eighteen years. During those years Eve conceived and bore Cain and Abel. After Cain murdered Abel, they had another son, Seth—and eventually an additional thirty sons and thirty daughters. (As the parallel passage from the Latin Vita [24:5] implies, they took seriously their divinely given charge to multiply and fill the earth.)

The Apocalypse passes over all the intervening years of their life, coming quickly to Adam on his death bed. Adam summons his children to assemble from the various parts of the earth. He is in distress and great pain. Seth begs to understand the meaning of pain and illness, so Adam explains that this is punishment for his sin of eating the forbidden fruit in paradise. Eve speaks up, that "this has happened to you through me; because of me you suffer troubles and pains" (9:2). (Note that throughout both the Apocalypse and the Vita, Eve is credited as being the more guilty one, as here.) Adam requests Eve and Seth to return to paradise. Perhaps God will have mercy on Adam and allow him a bit of oil from the tree of life to ease his illness and pain.

During their journey back to the garden, Seth is attacked and bitten by a wild beast. When Seth inquired about the reason for this attack, the beast cries out that the fault lies with Eve for eating the forbidden fruit: "O Eve, neither your greed nor your grief is due to us. But because of you . . . *our* nature was changed" (11:1–2). Implicit in the beast's retort is that violence within the animal kingdom is the direct result of Eve and her sin. Seth reprimands the beast for not respecting the image of God and the beast slinks away.

Seth and Eve continue to paradise where they entreat God to grant them "the oil of mercy." Their request is refused. God sends the archangel Michael to deliver the verdict: Adam must die, as will all humankind. But on the last day he will be raised up, as will all the just. "Then to them shall be given every joy of paradise, and God shall be in their midst" (13:4). Seth and Eve return to the dying Adam with this comforting message. Notice how Seth is emerging as a major figure within the Adam and Eve tradition. More on this later. Adam's dying request is that Eve "call all our children and our children's children and tell them how we transgressed" (14:3).

Eve's Story of the Fall (chapters 15—30)

Eve does call her children together to tell them the story of "how our enemy deceived us." Immediately we encounter a new twist in this traditional story. Eve explains that God had divided the garden between

Adam and her, giving each a portion to care for. Eve's portion was the South and the West, while Adam was assigned the North and the East. This separation of Eve from Adam apparently was inspired by orthodox Jewish conventions of the time by which female and males were segregated by gender. Even the animal kingdom was segregated according to gender, with Adam taking care of the male animals, while Eve cared for the females. Even so, as the stronger and more intellectual of the two, Adam was expected to look out for his wife. And as an extra precaution, the Lord God posted angels around the garden to watch over Adam and Eve and keep them from harm.

Thus it came to pass that Adam and Eve found themselves in different parts of Eden, without each knowing precisely where the other was or what the other was doing at any given moment. Such an arrangement was perfect for the machinations of that great deceiver, Satan.

Apparently intuiting that a direct assault on Adam would be pointless, Satan cast his eye on Eve. Females are by nature more simple minded, more gullible, and therefore easier to seduce. But even Eve, however naïve she may be, likely would discern the devil's true intent in any straightforward encounter. A more circuitous stratagem was required. Accordingly, Satan sneaked into Adam's portion of the garden and approached the (male!) serpent with flattering words designed to entice the serpent into becoming an accomplice in crime:

> I hear that you are wiser than all the beasts; so I came to check you out myself. (And indeed) I do find you greater than all the beasts . . . and yet you (crawl) prostrate to the very lowest (of them). Why do you eat Adam's and his wife's weeds, rather than Paradise's fruit? Rise and come and let us cause him to be cast out of Paradise through his wife" . . . The serpent replied, "I fear lest the Lord become angry with me." The devil said to him, "Do not fear; only become my vessel; I will speak through your mouth so that you will be able to deceive him." (16:1–5)

Having secured the services of the serpent, the devil then scaled the walls of paradise to wait for an opportune moment.

That moment soon came, when the angels ascended to heaven to worship God at the daily hour of prayer. Disguising himself as an angel, the serpent/devil quickly struck up a conversation with the unsuspecting Eve. Eve remembers that first meeting as if it were only yesterday. Feigning the air of a stranger to these parts, Satan asks casually, "Are you Eve?" When she answers in the affirmative, Satan continues, disarmingly, "Why are you in paradise? What do you do?" Eve answers truthfully that God put them there to take care of the garden, but adding, at the same time they are allowed to enjoy its fruits. Having found an opening, and using the voice of the serpent, Satan pushes harder, "And yet I notice that there is one tree from which you do not eat?" Eve protests, "Yes, we do eat of every plant, with the exception of the one in the middle of paradise that God warned us not to eat from it, 'else you shall most surely die.'"

The psychological battle has been successfully joined. "For heaven's sake!" Satan speaking through the serpent exclaims in mock indignation. "I hate to see you being treated as if you are nothing more than a (dumb) beast. Use your intelligence and come see for yourself how absolutely wonderful is the fruit of that tree." When Eve expresses her reservations about going against God's instructions, the serpent appeals to Eve's latent pride, "What are you afraid of? God warned you away from eating it be-cause he knows that if you eat, your mind will be enlightened. You will become like a god and know everything!" Eve cast a glance at the tree and did notice how succulent it appeared. Bit by bit Satan was breaking down Eve's resistance.

Apparently, the serpent (Satan) had remained outside the garden, for at this point Eve opened the gate for him to enter. With great psy-chological insight, the serpent first challenged Eve to follow him to the forbidden tree, but then feigned changing his mind, saying he could not allow her to eat. As Eve later recalled the incident, the serpent had said this in order to entrap Eve into swearing that she would entice her hus-band to eat also. The strategy worked. Eve swore, "By the throne of the Lord and the cherubim and the tree of life, I shall give it also to my hus-band to eat." Having secured Eve's oath, the serpent climbed the tree and surreptitiously sprinkled the fruit with "his evil poison." Eve plucked the fruit and ate. No sooner had she swallowed the fruit than she realized she had been duped, for instantaneously she recognized herself as "deprived of the glory with which (she) had been clothed." She looked for leaves from which to fashion herself a skirt. The trees were already afflicted, however, and had shed their leaves. The only leaves available were those of the fig tree, for the forbidden fruit had been a fig.

True to her oath, Eve called to Adam in a distant part of the garden to come to her. Adam was completely unaware of the events that had just transpired. With malice and forethought Eve coaxed him with smooth words, "Come here and I will show you something wonderful." It was the devil speaking through her, "Listen to me. Eat this fruit that God told us not to eat. You will be as God!" When Adam hesitated, Eve relates, "I quickly persuaded him. He ate, and his eyes were opened also"—and he immediately recognized his nakedness: "Evil woman, you! Why have you brought destruction upon us? You have estranged me from the glory of God!"

Almost immediately, Eve continued, we heard the archangel Michael assembling the angels to hear God pronounce judgment. When God arrived seated on his cherubim chariot, all the plants of paradise revived and blossomed once more, with the angels singing and praising God. Eve recounted the judgments of God upon the serpent, Adam, and herself pretty much the same as narrated in Genesis 3. One addition—which may be implied in Genesis—is that God's curse of the serpent included having the serpent deprived of its hands and feet, which is why henceforth it must crawl on its belly, as well as its ears and its wings—all powers it had used in causing the sin that resulted in the human couple being expelled from paradise.

As the angels were in the process of driving Adam and Eve out of the garden, Adam beseeches God for mercy. Adam accepts full responsibility for what has happened, seemingly because he listened to his wife rather than to God: "Have compassion and pity me, for I alone have sinned" (27:2). God, however, orders his angels to continue with the expulsion. Even so, God does offer hope to wounded humankind. He promises Adam, "In your toiling outside of paradise, if you guard yourself from evil, preferring even death to it, at the time of the resurrection I will raise you again; then you shall regain access to the tree of life, and you shall live forever" (28:4).

God grants Adam one further grace. He allows Adam to take with him various fragrances from the garden from which Adam can make aromatic incense with which to worship the deity outside paradise. Thus can Adam and his descendants remain close to their God while patiently awaiting the end time and their promised resurrection.

Deaths of Adam and Eve (chapters 31–42)

Having carried out Adam's command to inform their children about how and why their expulsion from paradise happened, Eve turns again to the dying Adam to lament further her culpable foolishness. "Why are you dying, and I live? How long must I be separated from you?" Adam consoles Eve, saying they must commend themselves to God's mercy.

Eve then goes out and prostrates herself on the ground, praying, "O Father of all, I have sinned against you, against the cherubim and all your angels. I have sinned grievously before you. All sin in creation has come about through me." She is still confessing her sin when Michael approaches to inform her that Adam has died. The angel comforts her, telling her to lift her eyes heavenward and see Adam's spirit being borne up to his maker in heaven. As Eve gazes, she sees a chariot of light drawn by four radiant eagles descend and carry Adam's spirit before the throne of God. A host of angels go before, begging the Almighty to "forgive (Adam), for he is your image, and the work of your hands" (33:5).

Enter Seth to further comfort his mother. (From this point forward devout Seth increasingly will replace his father Adam as a principal model of fidelity on earth.) With Seth looking on, the angels wash the body of Adam in the river Acheron three times as a sign of God's pardon. Next, at God's command, the archangel Michael translates Adam's body up to the third heaven, to the heavenly paradise, where he is to remain until the final day of judgment. God directs further that all the angels should gather to welcome Adam into the heavenly paradise with censers and blaring trumpets. Then God commands that the body of the murdered righteous Abel, whose blood the ground refused to receive, be brought into the heavenly paradise also and placed beside his father Adam.

The burial in paradise is capped by an amazing scene of hope and divine mercy. God calls out,

> "Adam, Adam." And the body answered from the earth, "Here I am, Lord." The Lord said to him, "I told you that *you are dust and to dust you shall return.* Now I promise to you the resurrection; I shall raise you on the last day in the resurrection with every one of your seed." (41:1–3)

Thereupon God sealed the tomb and the angels returned to their assigned stations.

Six days later Eve died also, after imploring God that she might be buried with her husband, and after again confessing great sorrow over her sin. After her death, the archangel Michael with three additional angels carried her body into paradise also and buried her alongside Adam and Abel. The book concludes with Michael ascending back to heaven, glorifying God and singing God's praises: "Alleluia, to whom be glory and power forever and ever."

The Latin Text (Vita)

Despite considerable overlap with the Greek version, the Latin text (Vita) in many respects is a different story. It, too, picks up the account of Adam and Eve immediately after "they were driven out of paradise" (1:1). Now standing outside the garden, the human couple found themselves facing hunger for the first time. For seven days Adam traversed this new land seeking food. Together he and Eve searched an additional nine days, but all they all they could find was what God had "apportioned for animals and beasts to eat," but nothing of "the food of angels" to which they had been accustomed in paradise. In desperation they agree to seek help from God, after doing suitable penance for their sin.

Eve defers to Adam since he knows best. Adam responds, "Although you are not capable of doing as much penance as I, nevertheless you should do as much as you are able." Adam proposes that he should spend forty days fasting, while standing up to his neck in the River Jordan. Meanwhile, Eve should proceed to the closer Tigris river and similarly immerse herself and fast for thirty-seven days. Both are to remain completely silent during this period of penance, for only afterwards will it be proper for them to implore the Lord, since their lips are unclean from having eaten the forbidden fruit in paradise. Eve agrees, and they each go to their respective stations.

After eighteen days—only halfway into the agreed period of penance—Satan disguised himself as an angel of light and approached Eve standing in the Tigris. Finding Eve weeping contritely, Satan feigns tears of empathy. He tells Eve she and her husband need weep no longer, for God has accepted their repentance, especially because "all *we angels* have interceded for you with the Lord as well." Moreover, the deceiver continued, "God has sent me to bring you out from this freezing water and to restore your food, indeed the very food which you enjoyed in paradise!" What a naïve, gullible woman! Believing this bald-faced lie, Eve abandoned her penance in the Tigris River, her skin all shriveled and "grass green" (which is to say, blue from the icy cold water).

Satan led Eve to the Jordan, to Adam, to deliver the good news. But Adam was not so easily fooled.

> As soon as Adam saw her and the devil with her, he cried out
> with tear-filled eyes, "O Eve, Eve! Why have you stopped your
> acts of penance? How could you be seduced a second time by
> our enemy, the very one who previously robbed us of our home
> in paradise and of our spiritual happiness?" (10:3–4)

Only then did Eve understand that she had succumbed a second time
to Satan's machinations and lies. Flinging herself to the ground, she demanded of Satan why he continued to assault and torment them so. And
for once Satan spoke forthrightly and without any duplicity.

Satan's Answer: Adam Was the Cause of Satan
Being Expelled from Heaven

Satan seemed eager to give Eve an answer to her question: "Why do you
harbor such hate toward Adam and me?" "O Adam," Satan responded,
"every ounce of my enmity, my envy, my sorrow is due to you! Because
of you I am expelled from heaven and deprived of the glory I once had
as one of the angels. Because of you I am now exiled to earth." Confused,
Adam queried, "How so? What did I do to you?"

Indeed, Adam could not have known. Satan's account detailed what
had happened *before* Adam was created: Before God created Adam, God
had dismissed Satan from his presence, allowing only selected angels to
be present. God blew his life breath into you, Adam. After creating you
in his own image, God instructed Michael to see that each of us angels
worship the image of God. Michael immediately complied, the first to
do so. Michael then summoned Satan, as the second highest angel, and
commanded him to worship the image of the Lord God. "I will not worship Adam," Satan haughtily replied. "I will not worship one inferior and
subsequent to me. I am prior to him in creation; before he was made, I
was already created. He ought to worship me!"

Michael continued to pressure Satan, charging that he would surely
incur the wrath of God. Satan hastily shot back, "Should he (attempt to)
inflict his wrath upon me, I will set my throne above the stars and will
be like the Most High." Mistaking arrogance for power, a band of angels
under Satan's command also joined Satan in refusing to worship. Satan
and his associates quickly learned how terribly they had miscalculated
the power of the Most High. Immediately they were cast out of heaven
and onto the earth, deprived of their former glory. From this incident

stemmed their enmity toward Adam and his wife. As Satan confessed to Adam, "We (fallen angels) were pained to see you in such bliss of delights. So with deceit I assailed your wife and caused you to be expelled through her from the joys of your bliss, as I have been expelled from my glory" (16:2–3).

Having heard the devil's own account, Adam cried out to God for relief from the assaults of Satan. At once the devil disappeared. To Adam's credit, he "persisted the (full) forty days standing in repentance in the water of the Jordan" (17:1–3), thereby foiling Satan's hope for total ruin of the human couple and their descendants.

The Next Generation (chapters 18–24)

Having seen firsthand how superior, both intellectually and morally, Adam was to her, Eve decided to separate from her husband, for his good. "You should live without me, my lord," she tells Adam. "You did not succumb to either the first or the second temptation. I was the one who was deceived and erred by not keeping the command of God. You and I should separate. I will walk toward the sunset and die" (18:1–3). So she departed and built herself a hut for shelter. She was three months pregnant.

When it came time to give birth, she was alone, with no one to help her. Even God seemed to have deserted her. In desperation she cried out to heaven that somehow news might reach Adam. Intuiting that something was wrong, that perhaps the serpent was once again assailing Eve, Adam went seeking Eve. Finding her in distress, he prayed to God for help.

And behold "twelve angels and two excellencies came" and assisted Eve in giving birth. Michael stood beside her and declared, "Blessed are you, Eve, because of Adam. Because of his intercession, I have been sent to help you" (21:1–2). Eve delivered an awesome son, Cain. Immediately upon birth the child stood up and ran to procure a "reed" to give to his mother. (Latin *herbum* "grass/reed" likely translates an original Semitic vocable *qaneh* "reed," suggestive of an original pun on the boy's name *Qayin*, "Cain.") Michael then brought Adam and Eve and the child back to the East, where the angel Michael taught Adam how to work and till the ground so that they and their descendants might live.

Sometime after, Eve gave birth to a second son, Abel, and the two boys grew up together into adulthood. When Adam was 130 years old, and Abel was 122,[2] Cain murdered his brother Abel.

Adam again "knew" his wife and she bore another son, Seth. This was a significant event, because from this point forward Seth will occupy an increasingly important function in the story of developing humankind. Preparatory for that development, however, as an aside, the author felt compelled to explain how Seth, (and Cain as well) was able to find a wife—and also how the earth became populated so quickly as humankind expanded into multiple nations—the author records that after the birth of Seth, Adam "lived (another) 800 years and fathered (an additional) thirty sons and thirty daughters, sixty-three children altogether" (24:1, 3–4).

Seth's importance is revealed in the very next scene. At an unspecified time in Seth's adulthood, Adam calls Seth aside and informs him of a special vision that God had granted him after he and Eve had been driven out of paradise. They were at prayer when suddenly Michael the archangel descended from heaven in a fiery chariot and carried Adam up "into the paradise of righteousness"—apparently a heavenly paradise distinct from the earthly paradise from which Adam and Eve had just been expelled. There Adam saw the Lord seated on a flaming throne of unbearable brilliance, surrounded by thousands and thousands of adoring angels.[3] Adam feared for his life because, as Scripture says, no one can see the face of God and live. God told Adam that he would indeed die, not because of this vision, but because of what he did in the garden.

Eating the forbidden fruit was not Adam's real sin, however. As God informed Adam, "You shall die because you listened to your wife rather than to me . . . I gave her into your power, for you to keep under your will. Instead, you listened to her and disregarded my command" (26:1–2).

The patriarchal bias in the deity's words is palpable. A husband is supposed to rule his wife. A wife is supposed to obey her husband—rather than a husband obeying his wife! This divine order within marriage was established by the Creator from the very beginning. Eve's sin may have

2. The ages here are difficult to explain and may result from mixing traditions. Jubilees 3:17 says Adam and Eve spent seven blissful years in Eden before being expelled; other traditions posit that Cain and Abel were born shortly after Adam and Eve were expelled. Combining these would make Adam eight years older than Abel.

3. This scene is patterned undoubtedly upon the description of God seated upon his chariot-throne in Ezekiel 1, with elements borrowed from Isaiah 6 and elsewhere.

consisted in eating the forbidden fruit, but Adam's sin was compounded by failing to keep Eve safe from her own naivete.

Hearing his death sentence, Adam fell prostrate to the ground before God with one last request, namely, that God not let the image of God be obliterated from earth. (Remember that this vision happened before any children had been born to Adam and Eve.) Pleased with Adam's request, God assured Adam that the image of God would be carried on through his descendants, and especially through the line of Seth: "There shall never lack among your seed those who serve me" (27:4).

Having heard God's promise that Adam's mission would be perpetuated through Seth, Adam worshipped God once more. Then Michael took Adam's hand and translated him back to earth to resume life outside the garden and to begin populating the earth.

Adam's Final Days

At age 930, Adam recognized that death was fast approaching. So he summoned all his sons to his deathbed where he told them of his painful illness. While others queried Adam about the meaning of pain and death, only Seth was perceptive enough to understand the underlying reason. Seth volunteered to return to paradise and try to obtain fruit from it, fruit with its healing qualities. To restrain Seth, Adam explained why that would not be possible by telling his own story about what had transpired in the garden, which had caused Eve and him to be expelled in the first place.

Adam's story corresponds in large part with that told by Eve in the Greek text. When God placed them in the garden, God designated different portions of the garden for which each was responsible. Eve was to care for the trees in the South and in the West, Adam for those in the North and in the East. That arrangement would prove problematic, however, as it separated Eve from Adam. Although God had stationed angels to watch over them, each day at the hour of prayer the angels would temporarily abandon their stations to ascend into heaven to worship their Creator. With Eve left alone, the devil seized the opportunity to deceive Eve into eating the forbidden fruit. And Eve in turn gave some to Adam.

As punishment, Adam continued, not only did God expel them from the garden, he also said that in the future he would inflict upon their bodies seventy plagues. "Your bodies will be racked with various pains, from head to toe, including all your limbs. Moreover, your descendants will suffer similarly" (34:1–4). This terrible suffering, Adam explains, is what has now overtaken him and which he finds nearly impossible to bear. He begs Eve to go with Seth back to the garden to see if perhaps God will have mercy and allow an angel to let them have even a tiny bit of soothing "oil of life" from paradise.

Eve and Seth set out and on the way were attacked by a ferocious wild beast, as in the Greek version. Similarly, the beast explained the enmity of the wild beasts as due to Eve's eating of the forbidden fruit, in disobedience of God's command. When Seth rebuked the wild beast for daring to attack the image of God before it, the wild beast meekly disappeared. Nevertheless, Seth's and Eve's quest is futile. The angel Michael informs them that Adam must die, as will all humans, and that these pains will continue up to the very last days.

Upon their return to the dying Adam, they relay Michael's message. They also relate how the wild beast attacked and bit Seth. This causes Adam to accuse Eve, "What have you wrought? You have brought upon us a grievous wound, transgression, and sin in every generation . . . They will curse us: Our first parents have brought upon us all evils" (44:2–5). And Eve wept.

As Michael had foretold, death came to Adam six days later. As a symbol of mourning, the sun, moon, and stars withheld their light for seven days. Then Michael appeared to Seth, revealing to him that God had indeed shown mercy to Adam. All the angels sounded their trumpet and blessed God, "who has pitied [his] creature." In a vision Seth saw God handing the body of Adam over to Michael, along with Abel, for burial, to be preserved until the final day. Seth was given instructions to bury all the dead in a similar manner in the future.

Aware that she was soon to die also, Eve instructed her children to write two copies of this Life of Adam and Eve, one on a stone tablet and one on a clay tablet. That way, the story would be preserved for posterity, no matter how God might judge the world. If by water, the clay tablet would dissolve but the stone tablet would survive. If by fire, the stone tablet would break into pieces, but the clay tablet would be only further hardened. Seth did make tablets of stone and clay and placed them in the oratory his father had built and where he used to pray. A tablet did survive the flood, so that afterward many were able to read the Life of Adam and Eve. Apparently, Seth placed his two tablets for safe keeping in the exact location where later Solomon built the Temple, since the Greek text concludes with a notice that wise Solomon discovered this writing while building the Temple, thereby enabling the Life of Adam and Eve to be preserved in perpetuum.

[The motif recounted here about the story of primeval humankind being preserved on tablets which survived the flood is unique in Jewish literature.[4] Similar motifs are recorded in Mesopotamian literature, however, even down to the time of Berossus (third century BCE).]

Concluding Remarks concerning the Life of Adam and Eve

As we conclude our treatment of the Life of Adam and Eve, we should take note of several new developments to the Adam and Eve tradition that appear herein.

One motif that played so prominently in the earlier pseudepigraphs 1 Enoch and Jubilees, namely, how fallen Watchers were responsible for leading primeval humankind into sin, is virtually absent in both versions of the Life of Adam and Eve. Indeed, this Jewish pseudepigraph seems studiously to avoid mentioning the Watchers' sin in order to lay greater guilt upon the original human couple, and especially upon the woman Eve. Adam does bear some responsibility, but primarily because he allowed the woman to rule him rather than the other way around, as God ordained. The source of such thinking is not entirely clear. Granted that patriarchy dominates much of the biblical tradition. It seems particularly emphasized in this writing, however, when compared to the original biblical story. It does parallel a similar development in late New Testament writings, e.g., 1 Corinthians 14:34–35; 1 Timothy 2:8–15; 1 Peter 3:1–7, all of which were penned at approximately the same time as this Jewish pseudepigraph. In the late first century, many Christian leaders admonished women to show greater deference to their husbands, in conformity with Greco-Roman cultural ideals of that time. Seemingly, a parallel movement was under way in Jewish circles as well. Likely, however, the author chose to ignore the Watchers tradition because he found another emerging tradition more compelling—the story of Satan.

---

4. There is a note in Jub 8:3, however, about Canaan, when he left his father to establish his own city, he found a tablet about the fallen Watchers, from which Canaan learned to do evil. But that was a negative story, not a positive one as here.

In the Hebrew Bible there is no equivalent of the figure Satan which will figure so prominently in later Jewish and Christian traditions. The name "Satan" derives from a vocable that in its verbal form means "to obstruct, to oppose"; and in its noun form can refer to an "opponent," an "adversary," or to an "accuser." When used with the definite article, *ha-satan* ("the accuser") has reference to one exercising a specific function or office. This is the way the term is used in the book of Job, chapters 1–2. In this old folk tale which serves to introduce the story of Job, "the satan" is not the devil but rather one of "the sons of God," an official within the divine court whose job it was to test humans, to see if they are as virtuous as reputed. When God calls attention to his servant, the pious Job, *the satan,* in challenging God, is fulfilling his proper function by testing Job to see whether Job's reputed piety can withstand serious testing. *The satan's* challenge, as the reader knows, proved baseless. Much the same can be said concerning Zechariah 3:1–7, where "Satan" is likewise preceded by the definite article, making it clear that here also "the satan" is a title, and not the devil. Finally, attention may be called to 1 Chronicles 21:1, where "the satan" tests the high priest Joshua, but in the parallel text in 2 Samuel 24:1 that function is said to be accomplished by the Lord himself, clearly establishing that "the satan" is not the devil.

By the first century CE, however, the concept of "the satan" had evolved, likely under the influence of earlier Jewish pseudepigraphs like 1 Enoch and Jubilees, which highlight the story of fallen Watchers leading humankind astray and corrupting the earth. In 1 Enoch the leader of the fallen Watchers was known by the name of Shemihazah. Azazel, also named in 1 Enoch as a ringleader, may be an associate, or perhaps the same figure by an alternate name. In Jubilees, the leader of the fallen Watchers is named Mastema. By the time Life of Adam and Eve was written, some two centuries later, the figures of Shemihazah, Azazel, and Mastema have merged with "the satan" of the Hebrew Bible to create a very different adversary of humankind—one even more powerful and more malevolent. It goes by the name Satan, or the devil.

Even though the story of Satan's primordial fall from heaven in this tale is new in Judaic literature, it is not entirely without precedents. Ezekiel 28 may provide at least a partial backstory for the depiction of Satan as a powerful and proud angel who considered himself the equal of, or even superior to God, and subsequently is cast out of heaven. In a first oracle of judgment (Ezek 28:1–10), the prophet condemns the king of Tyre for his conceit in thinking himself no mere mortal; indeed the king believes himself a veritable god. In a follow-up oracle (28:11–19), Ezekiel likens the king to the proud cherub who once held sway in Eden. It is a lament, steeped in satire and sarcasm.

> You, O Serpent of perfection,
>> full of wisdom and perfect in beauty.
> You were in Eden, the garden of God,
>> every precious stone your clothing . . .
> You are a wing-spread Cherub,
>> I appointed you as the guardian.
> On the holy mountain of God you were;
>> in the midst of the stones of fire you walked.
> You were perfect in your ways
>> from the day of your creation
>> —until iniquity was found in you!
> Your heart became proud because of your beauty;
>> you spoiled your wisdom for the sake of your splendor. (28:12–17)[5]

The allusions to Genesis 3 are obvious. Of more interest to us, however, is the manner in which the prophet has combined two Genesis figures, the supremely wise seraph-serpent and the cherubs appointed as guardians over Eden, into one persona, an incomparably perfect divine cherub prone to downfall because of excessive vanity.[6] Just what was the "iniquity" found in this cherub that caused him to be "cast from the mountain of God . . . down to earth" and "come to a dreadful end," Ezekiel does not elaborate.

Another passage that contributed much to the Vita's portrayal of Satan as the devil is Isaiah 14:12–15, an oracle directed against Babylon. It likely was not spoken by Isaiah himself, but added a century or more later by an anonymous prophet, after the fall of Babylon in 538 BCE. Whoever the author, he clearly gloats over the downfall of the Babylonian tyrant, borrowing from Canaanite mythic language.

> How you are fallen from heaven, O Day Star, son of Dawn!
> How you are cut down to the ground, you who laid the nations low!
> You said in your heart, "I will ascend to heaven.
> I will raise my throne above the stars of God.
> I will sit on the mount of (divine) assembly on the heights of Zaphon.
> I will ascend to the tops of the clouds; I will make myself like the Most
>> High."
> But you are brought down to She'ol, to the depths of the Pit.

5. This translation follows van Dijk, *Ezekiel's Prophecy on Tyre*, 92–93, 113–21.

6. See Batto, *Slaying the Dragon*, 94–97.

In Canaanite myth, various deities aspired to sit on the throne of the Most High (*El Elyon*) on Mount Zaphon, that is, to take over as king of the gods. "Day Star" and "Dawn" were Canaanite astral deities. The prophet borrowed from that tradition to parody the Babylonian king for his vain and futile attempt to "play God." The author of the Vita similarly disparages the vanity of Satan for thinking that he could displace the Lord God in heaven. It is not impossible that the author of the Vita had some familiarity with the Canaanite myths themselves, since a number of those motifs persisted throughout the Levant well into the Greco-Roman period. If so, the Vita's portrayal of Satan thinking he could challenge God becomes even more compelling.

The Vita was not unique, however. The motif of the powerful but rebellious angel Satan being cast down out of heaven spread far and wide during the first century CE. It appears in the New Testament at Luke 10:18, according to which Jesus told his disciples, "I watched Satan fall from heaven like a flash of lightning." It also figures prominently in the book of Revelation:

> And war broke out in heaven, Michael and his angels fought against the dragon. The dragon and his angels fought back, but they were defeated, and there was no longer any place for them in heaven. The great dragon was thrown down, that ancient serpent, who is called the Devil and Satan, the deceiver of the whole world—he was thrown down to the earth, and his angels were thrown down with him. (Rev 12:7–9 NRSV)

All the elements of the motif are brought together here in a single short paragraph.

Although Eve is singled out in this first century Jewish pseudepigraph as more responsible than Adam for the primal sin of humankind—being duped not once but twice by Satan—that viewpoint was not universally shared. Another major contributor to the ever-expanding Adam and Eve tradition, and writing approximately at the same time, laid total responsibility for the sinful condition of humankind not upon Eve but upon Adam. I refer to the converted Pharisee Paul of Tarsus, to whom we now turn for his radical thesis of *two* Adams.

7

Paul: Christ as the Second Adam

PERHAPS THE MOST DRASTIC innovation to the Adam and Eve tradition throughout its long history was that introduced by Paul (or Saul, as he was known in Hebrew) of Tarsus during the middle of the first century of the Christian era. According to his own account, Paul, a former ardent Pharisee, received a "revelation of Jesus Christ" that radically altered his life and transformed his thinking in ways that he could not have imagined previously (Gal 1:11–24; 1 Cor 15:8–9). While on the road to Damascus to arrest those he considered perfidious Jews (that is, Jews who were spreading a novel doctrine according to which the recently executed Jesus of Nazareth was actually the Messiah), Paul experienced a vision of Jesus—the very Jesus whose followers Saul the Pharisee was at that very moment attempting to eradicate. This vision left Saul confused and shaken to his core. It took him years to sort out the full significance of that experience. Reading Paul's letters in the New Testament, one can observe him right up to the end of his life struggling to grasp all its implications. If Jesus is indeed the Messiah, then much of what Saul the Pharisee had stood for had been misguided and his whole belief system had to be rethought in order to make room in his theology for Jesus as the Messiah, or as Paul normally expressed it in Greek, *Iēsus Christos,* Jesus Christ. One result of Paul's rethinking was his formulation of a doctrine about Jesus Christ being a "second Adam" (or, alternatively, the "last Adam"). Through the concept of a new or second Adam, Paul sought to universalize the mercy of God so that it extended to all humankind, and not just to a chosen few, namely, the descendants of Abraham, as he had previously believed. It is most instructive, therefore, to investigate the process by which Paul arrived at his Christology about this "second Adam."

We begin by noting that there is no narrative or storyline in Paul's writings comparable to those texts we have analyzed in preceding chapters. Instead, we must depend upon our own sleuthing of Paul's letters to tease out his doctrine. In attempting to set forth Paul's views in a systematic fashion, I am reminded of a warning by the author of 2 Peter concerning the letters of Paul, "There are some things in them hard to understand, which the ignorant and unstable twist to their own destruction" (3:16). In what I write, I trust that I have not betrayed Paul's meaning, though I readily acknowledge that Paul can be difficult to interpret, and that others have arrived at different interpretations.

Paul buys into the standard biblical/Israelite myth of human origins expressed in the combined J+P narrative found in the opening chapters of the book of Genesis and elaborated in various Jewish pseudepigraphs. There is nothing here of the polygenesis found in the Mesopotamian myth of Atrahasis or in Egyptian myth, that humankind began with multiple humans, male and female. Rather, in keeping with a literal reading of Genesis 2, all humankind is believed to originate from a single human: Adam. Paul's thesis of a New Adam depends upon this anthropological foundation. But at the same time, Paul's thesis of second Adam is radically new—a creation of his own making—as nowhere in Jewish literature of that time is there any hint of a coming "second" or "last" Adam.[1] Moreover, for the most part Paul is forced to ignore Eve and her not insignificant role in tradition.

Even as a Christian Paul retained his Jewish belief in the goodness of the covenant that God had given through Moses and of the Law that accompanied it. The question was how to reconcile the goodness of the Mosaic covenant and the Law while at the same time insisting on the necessity of Jesus Christ for the completion of God's saving action on behalf of humankind. As a Pharisee, Paul had been extremely careful about keeping the Law, more so by far than most of his contemporaries (Gal 1:13-14). But as a Christian, Paul preached that keeping the Law was insufficient, and that acceptance of what God had accomplished through

---

1. See Nielsen, *Adam and Christ in the Theology of Irenaeus*, 77, and references there. Nickelsburg (*1 Enoch 1*, 407) and Christfried Böttrich ("The Figures of Adam and Eve in the Enoch Tradition," in Laato and Valve, *Adam and Eve Story*, 215-18) suggest that the great "white bull" who is to appear at the apocalyptic judgment at the close of the age (1 Enoch 90:37-38) may be a veiled reference to a "New Adam." This interpretation seems unlikely, however, as the symbol of a white bull is used in the Animal Apocalypse (1 Enoch 85-90) of several extraordinary figures in addition to Adam: Seth, Noah, Shem, Abraham, and Isaac.

Jesus Christ was required. The issue for the Christian Paul, therefore, was how to retain belief in the goodness of the old while at the same time making room in his theology for this new element, namely, that God had accomplished the salvation of humankind in and through Jesus Christ. A solution to this conundrum required Paul to posit an entirely new approach to the history of humankind.

The Two Eras of History: Before Christ and After Christ

In Paul's reconstruction, the history of humankind must be divided into two radically different periods: the *former era*, extending from creation to the coming of the Messiah and characterized by enslavement to sin and death; and a *new era* of freedom and life brought about by the death and resurrection of Jesus the Messiah—or to put it more succinctly, *before Christ* and *after Christ*. Each era is fundamentally shaped or determined by its founding father: Adam for the former era; Christ for the new era. One might schematize Paul's view as follows:

TABLE 3

	Former Era	New Era
Progenitor:	Adam	Christ
Characteristic attitude:	Disobedience	Obedience
Posture before God:	Pride: to become gods	Faith: total trust in God
Ruling element:	Sin	Grace
End result:	Death	Life
Status of humans:	Slaves to Sin	Free adopted children of God
Legal requirements:	Bound by the Law	Love fulfills the Law (Grace)
Condition of creation:	Unity & harmony disrupted	Unity & harmony restored

Adam sinned by disobeying God's command, and with sin came death—symbolized by being expelled from the garden and from the tree of life. Moreover, because Adam was the progenitor of the entire human race, every human also suffered Adam's fate. Paul was very conscious that the name "Adam" in Hebrew means both "(the) Human" and "humankind." Continuing a long tradition of Jewish interpretation, Paul understood all humans to have been contained virtually in Adam's seed, and that Adam's "essence" was passed on to every one of his descendants as their heritage. Therefore, Paul reasoned, every human was also entwined in Adam's disobedience and must die. As was Adam, so is every human.

This was not the view of most Jews in Paul's day, of course, nor is it a view grounded in the Hebrew Scriptures. The Adam story receives scant notice in the Hebrew Bible.[2] Nor is there any concept of universal sinfulness in the Hebrew Scriptures, such that no human can elude its grasp. As God tells Cain in Genesis 5:7, "If you do well, will you not be accepted? But if you do not do well, sin is lurking at the door. Its desire is for you; you must master it." Thus the reader is informed already in the generation immediately following Adam that sin is indeed a powerful force, but it can be controlled, even overcome. Similarly, in the book of Deuteronomy (30.15-19), Moses in his last sermon is reported as admonishing the Israelites to remain faithful to the commands that God has given them by "walking in his ways and observing his commandments, decrees, and ordinances." They have a choice between life and prosperity, on the one hand, *or* death and adversity, on the other. "I call heaven and earth to witness against you today that I have set before you life and death, blessings and curses. Choose life." Both texts, as well as many others, including the pseudepigraphic Jewish texts previously considered, are predicated on the assumption that everyone can choose between good and evil, and is capable of doing good.

Even a text such as Genesis 6:5 (cp. 8:21), "The Lord saw that the wickedness of humankind was great in the earth, and that every inclination of their hearts was only evil continually," does not imply that humans are incapable of doing other than evil. Humans are fully capable of doing good, as this same passage a few verses later makes abundantly clear in the example of Noah: "Noah was a righteous man, blameless in his generation; Noah walked with God" (Gen 6:9).

Jewish postbiblical and rabbinical tradition has long recognized the proclivity of humans to do evil,[3] but avoided the conclusion that humankind is so wedded to evil that an outside figure (a messiah) is required to redeem humankind from its sinful condition. In fact, just the opposite is the case. Jewish belief is that the Messiah will come when—that is, *after*—one person keeps the Law perfectly. Keeping the Law is within human possibility.

Prior to his conversion, Paul as a Pharisee must have held similar beliefs. Following his conversion, however, he promulgated a radically different view. In Paul's letters to the Galatians and to the Romans, he

2. 1 Chron 1:1; Deut 4:32; Job 31:33; Ezek 28:12-15; Hos 6:7; see also Tobit 8:5.
3. See Dunn, *Theology of Paul*, 84-90.

elaborated a belief that because of Adam's sin, all humans are born slaves to sin and are incapable of doing God's will. Paul does not deny that humans can at times perform good acts, but ultimately good acts do not make one "righteous." This is so because to be righteous before God, one must keep God's commands *perfectly*. Even a single infraction is enough to condemn one before God. To prove his point, in Romans 3:11 Paul cites Psalm 14:1, "There is no one who is righteous, not even one."

Paul insists that this is true of Gentiles and Jews alike—Gentiles who sinned without benefit of the Mosaic Torah; and Jews, who even though they had been privileged to have the Torah, did not keep it perfectly. Accordingly, everyone, whether Jew or Gentile, stands condemned for breaking God's commands.

No Jew in Paul's day—or since—would claim that one stands condemned before God for not keeping the Torah perfectly. The Hebrew Scriptures are replete with examples of God's chosen people being unfaithful to their God and breaking their covenantal obligations. Yet time and again the Lord God in his mercy forgave them. Forgiveness and restoration are integral to the covenant itself, as the book of Exodus patently reveals. At Sinai, Moses had scarcely concluded making the covenant between God and his people and returned to the mountain top to receive additional instructions from God (Exodus 24), when the Israelites broke the covenant by making the golden calf and worshipping it (Exodus 32). According to the biblical narrative, God was so angry that he wanted to annihilate the sinners and start over by making a new covenant with Moses alone and his descendants (Exod 32:9–10). Moses, however, pleaded with God for the sinful Israelites, reminding God of his merciful nature. God relented and reestablished the covenant with his people (Exodus 33–34). This story is deliberately constructed to show that while humans may be incapable of complete fidelity to God and his commands, on the one side, it is the very nature of God to overlook human frailty and to maintain his covenantal loyalty with them, on the other side. This story encapsulates the core message of the Torah better than any other passage in the Hebrew Bible.

Now if Paul did not derive from Judaism his view that one must keep the Law *perfectly* in order to be righteous before God, how did he come by it? The answer seems to lie with Paul's understanding of the unique role of Jesus Christ as the second Adam.

Why a Second Adam Was Necessary

From his conversion experience Paul came to believe that Jesus was absolutely essential to God's salvific plan because no one can be saved apart from Jesus Christ. It was precisely in attempting to understand Jesus's unique role in salvation that Paul arrived at his view of Jesus Christ as the second Adam. As Messiah, Jesus somehow had to undo everything that Adam had done wrong.

Note that I said "Adam" and *not* "Adam *and Eve*." In the whole of the Pauline corpus Eve is mentioned only twice, in 2 Corinthians 11:3 and 1 Timothy 2:13–14 (to be discussed later). Paul ignored Eve because he needed both sides of his "Adamic equation" to be equal. If Jesus is the operative factor on the one side, then a comparable individual figure is required on the other side. Eve *must* be ignored to make the equation work. Moreover, because in Genesis 2 Eve is taken from the side of "Adam"/"the Human," she is not needed to complete the picture because she was present within "the Human" *virtually*, as was the rest of humankind. By ignoring Eve, therefore, Paul is better able to achieve the requisite symmetry between the first and the second Adam.

Humankind Enslaved to Sin

Because all humans are descended from Adam, all inherited from Adam his characteristic posture of disobedience to God. Being like their "father" Adam, they also manifest Adam's proclivity to disobedience and sin. Indeed, Paul goes further, concluding that from birth every human is enslaved in sinfulness. Sin is so dominant within humans that it must be regarded as a power or entity in and of itself, that is, "Sin"—with a capital "S." Sin is the master of all humans, and we are its slaves, literally. (The choice of the pronouns "we" and "us" throughout this discussion is intentional, both to echo Paul's own language and to emphasize his view that all of "us" are united in one common humanity.) We are not free to follow our highest desire, which is to follow God's will. We are compelled instead to be disobedient to God. As Paul says of himself,

> I find it to be a law that when I want to do what is good, evil lies close at hand. For I delight in the law of God in my inmost self, but I see in my members another law at war with the law of my mind, making me captive to the law of sin that dwells in my members. Wretched man that I am! Who will rescue me from

this body of death? Thanks be to God through Jesus Christ our Lord! So then, with my mind I am a slave to the law of God, but with my flesh I am a slave to the law of sin. (Rom 7:21–25 NRSV)

Paul recognizes in each person an internal war between the "spirit" and the "flesh." "Spirit" is that part of each of us that is open to God and desirous of doing God's will. "Flesh," by contrast, is that part of each of us that is closed to God and which pushes us to pursue our own wills—what we might call our common "human nature." The "flesh" is dominated by Sin, which rules us as an absolute master. So even though we might recognize the superiority of God's ways and desire to follow them, we find within ourselves an opposing force so powerful that we end up doing the exact opposite. That is what Paul means by saying that we are slaves to Sin. We find ourselves powerless to obey God even when we want to do so.

Being under the domination of Sin means also that we find ourselves in enmity to God. Because we are allied with Sin, we come under the "wrath" of God. Sin has no place in the coming kingdom of God, and it will be destroyed along with Sin's ally Death at the end time, when Christ "hands over the kingdom to God the Father, after he has destroyed every ruler and every authority and power . . . The last enemy to be destroyed is death" (1 Cor 15:24–26).

God's Righteousness Is Manifested in Christ Jesus

Note that Paul never says that God is our enemy, rather that we have made ourselves enemies of God by aligning ourselves with Sin. By contrast, God continually reaches out to us, as the Scriptures attest again and again. Last of all, God has sent his son, Jesus Christ, to reconcile humankind to himself. This is totally unexpected by conventional thinking, that one would reach out to help an enemy. Yet that is exactly how God acts on our behalf, Paul says.

It was while we were still helpless that, at the appointed time, Christ died for the wicked. Even for a just man one of us would hardly die, though perhaps for a good man one might actually brave death; but Christ died for us while we were yet sinners, and that is God's proof of his love towards us. And so, since we have now been justified by Christ's sacrificial death, we shall all

> the more certainly be saved through him from final retribution.
> For if, when we were God's enemies, we were reconciled to him
> through the death of his Son, how much more, now that we have
> been reconciled, shall we be saved by his life! (Rom 5:6–10 REB)

In Paul's view we were powerless to do anything to help ourselves precisely because we were completely under the domination of Sin. Therefore, setting us in the right with God had to be a completely gratuitous act on the part of God. And this, God accomplished through Jesus Christ.

Paul had little interest in the historical Jesus. Instead, Paul's own teaching was focused on Jesus as the Messiah. Better yet, Paul's message was about "the gospel of God" (Rom 1:1), that is, the good news of what God has accomplished through the Lord Jesus Christ. For Paul, salvation is always God's doing. His letter to the Romans is explicitly about "the righteousness of God" (Rom 1:17; 3:21–22). That is, God is faithful to his covenant made long ago with Abraham (Romans 4; see Genesis 15). As important as was the Mosaic covenant wherein God revealed the Law to Moses and the Israelites, in Paul's mind the prior covenant God made with Abraham takes precedence because it resulted from God gratuitously declaring Abraham righteous, that is, being "right" with God. Moreover, Abraham's righteousness did not come from keeping the Law, since the first mention of Abraham performing an act of the Law comes only two chapters later in Genesis 17, when Abraham circumcised himself and his family. One cannot earn or merit righteousness. Rather, the covenant with Abraham rested upon Abraham placing his faith, or absolute trust, in God (Gen 15:6; Rom 4:1–5, 9). Moreover, the blessings of the Abrahamic covenant were intended to benefit all peoples—whether Jew or Gentile—who like Abraham place their trust (faith) in God (Rom 4:9–25; see also Gen 12:1–3). Trusting the God who acts gratuitously is the essential element here.

Most importantly, God has manifested his righteousness through his Son, Jesus Christ. The work of God henceforth cannot be divorced from the Son whom he sent. So "the gospel of God," Paul avers, also concerns "his Son, who was descended from David according to the flesh and was declared to be the Son of God with power according to the spirit of holiness by resurrection from the dead, Jesus Christ our Lord" (Rom 1:3–4).

Paul did not think of Jesus with a post-Nicene mentality; he had no conception of Jesus as the "Second Person of the Trinity." Rather. Paul appears to have believed that Jesus at birth was human only; he became divine at his resurrection. As Paul wrote to the Romans, "the gospel of God" he preaches is about God's Son, "who was descended from David according to the flesh" but "was declared to be the Son of God with power according to the spirit of holiness by resurrection from the dead, Jesus Christ our Lord" (Rom 1:3–4). "Declared" here has the same force as when God "declared" Abraham righteous; that is, by a gratuitous act of God the status of Jesus was changed in that moment from a mere human into the Son of God, much as Abraham became righteous through a declaration by God. If for Paul the resurrection is the defining event for Jesus's mission as Messiah, then one can understand why Paul pays so little attention to the life and words of the historical Jesus. Instead, Paul emphasizes that Jesus's death and especially his resurrection was foundational to his mission as the Messiah for all humankind—which brings us back to Jesus in his capacity as the second Adam.

The Second Adam

The second Adam is the very antithesis of the first Adam, the one who brought about all the woes of humankind. Nowhere is this antithesis stated more clearly than in Romans 5–6. In reading this passage, one must keep in mind that in Hebrew "Adam" literally means "(the) Human/ Man" or "humankind," and that this in turn was translated in the Greek Septuagint sometimes as "Adam" and sometimes as *anthrōpos* "(the) human/man." Only thus can one understand how Paul derived universal significance for all humans/people (*anthrōpoi* [plural]) from Jesus's role as the second Adam.

> Because sin entered the world through one man (*anthrōpos*), and through sin death, so death spread to all in as much as all have sinned. Indeed sin was already in the world before there was law, but there was no reckoning of sin in the absence of law. Nevertheless, death reigned from Adam to Moses, even over those who had not sinned like Adam—a type of the one who was to come (Christ). (5:12–14)

Tied up in Paul's thesis here is the role of the Law, which is a necessary component in Paul's argument that one cannot be justified by the keeping of the Law. The Law given through Moses is indeed good in that it tells us what God expects of us, but it had a negative consequence in that it provided no power to sinful humans to accomplish God's commands. In effect, the Law actually increased sin for Jews, Paul argues, since although they now know what God's will is through the Law, they are unable to fulfill it, thereby effectively increasing both the instances of sin and the guilt of the Jews. "Law was introduced to increase transgressions, so that where sin increased, grace might abound all the more, so that just as sin reigned in death, so God's grace might reign through justification and result in eternal life through Jesus Christ our Lord" (5:20–21).

The role of the Law does not substantially affect Paul's thesis about Christ as the second Adam, however, as the sin of the first Adam occurred long before the Law was revealed to Moses. No, the First Adam's sin was much more fundamental. Because it was universal in its effect, it requires a universal solution.

> Now (God's) free gift is not like (Adam's) trespass. For if the many died because of the one man's transgression, how much more do God's grace and the free gift in the grace through the one man (*anthrōpos*), Jesus Christ, abound for the many. The free gift is not like the effect of the one's sin. The judgment following that one transgression resulted in condemnation. But the free gift, despite many transgressions, results in justification. If because of one man's transgression, death reigned through that one, how much more will those who receive grace in abundance and the free gift of righteousness come to reign in life through the one Jesus Christ.
>
> It follows, then, that just as the one transgression resulted in condemnation for all men (*anthrōpoi*), so one act of righteousness results in justification and life for all men (*anthrōpoi*). For just as by the one man's (*anthrōpos*) disobedience the many were made sinners, so by the one's obedience the many will be made righteous. (5:15–21)

Incorporated into the Second Adam

Paul has been making the point that just as all humans have been subjected to sin and death because of the trespass of the one "Human," that is, the first Adam, so now all humans have the possibility of grace and eternal life through the obedience of another "Human," that is, the second Adam, Jesus Christ. Exactly how that happens is spelled out in the following chapter in Romans.

> Do you not know that all of us who have been baptized into
> Christ Jesus were baptized into his death? Therefore we have
> been buried with him by baptism into death, so that, just as
> Christ was raised from the dead by the glory of the Father, so we
> too might walk in the newness of life. For if we have been united
> with him in a death like his, we will certainly be united with
> him in a resurrection like his. We know that our old self was
> crucified with him so that the body of sin might be destroyed,
> and we might no longer be enslaved to sin. For whoever has died
> is freed from sin. But if we have died with Christ, we believe that
> we will also live with him. We know that Christ, being raised
> from the dead, will never die again; death no longer has domin-
> ion over him. The death he died, he died to sin, once for all;
> but the life he lives, he lives to God. So you also must consider
> yourselves dead to sin and alive to God in Christ Jesus. (Rom
> 6:3–11 NRSV)

Implicit in Paul's argument here is the premise that no one can be
saved *outside* of Christ. Christ Jesus is the only human that God has
raised from the dead, and this was because Jesus was the only human ever
to fulfill God's will perfectly.[4] So in effect, Jesus Christ is the only human
that has been saved and graced by God with eternal life. So where does
that leave the rest of humankind? This is where Christ's role as the second
Adam comes in. Just as all humankind was embodied virtually in Adam
and so suffered the consequences of Adam's trespass, so also through
God's grace working through baptism, one is "incorporated" into Christ.
Through baptism one is actually "united" with Christ, that is, becomes
one with Christ. By becoming one "with" and "in Christ," every human
has the potential of "dying in Christ" and "rising in Christ." When God
raised Jesus, he also raised up all who are "in Christ." (Given its importance in Paul's theological scheme, one can understand why the phrase
"in Christ" or "in Christ Jesus" occurs some 127 times in the "authentic"
or undisputed letters of Paul alone.)

One need not have been present at Jesus's death and resurrection to
share in the benefits of this saving mystery. The effects of Jesus's death are
not bound by time. It is an event that is "once for all." It stands outside of
space and time. Sin has been forever conquered. Similarly, God's raising

4. Here Paul seemingly alludes to the prevailing Jewish belief that the messiah will
come when just one person keeps the Law perfectly, thereby inaugurating the messianic age. Paul turns this belief on its head, saying the Messiah (Christ Jesus) has already
come, himself having kept the Law perfectly, and has ushered in the messianic age.

of Jesus from the dead is an event that need not be repeated because it too transcends space and time. Through baptism the power of Jesus Christ's death and resurrection is extended to all humankind, not just to Jesus's contemporaries or to those who follow him. Its power extends *also to those who lived before* Jesus, as the example of Abraham shows (Romans 4). Adam's legacy extends only to those who come after him, since in Adam's case physical descent is the operative principle. By contrast, Christ's power extends backwards in time as well as forward, because the operative principle is not physical descent but faith (*pistis*)—not our faith, but Jesus's faith. We are saved by the faith of Jesus. Jesus manifested absolute trust in God and complete fidelity to God's will. Because he is a second Adam, Christ Jesus's faith embraces all humankind and incorporates all within that faith.

Saved by "Faith in Christ" or "Faith of Christ"?

Pistis ("faith") is a multivalent term in the New Testament, as in Greek literature generally. It may refer to one's trust in another, to one's own trustworthiness, to one's beliefs, or even to an orthodox set of dogmas or doctrine.

It is commonplace among Christians to read Paul as saying that one is saved by or through "faith *in* (Jesus) Christ." In particular, the classic Protestant doctrine of *sola fide, sola gratia, sola scriptura* (which may be freely rendered as "by grace alone, through faith alone, on the basis of Scripture alone") is beholden to Martin Luther's formulation, based upon his reading of Rom 3:28, that one is saved not by one's works but by one's faith—and God's unmerited grace, of course. Some have maintained that there is present an inherent contradiction is this formulation, however. If it is one's personal "faith" that is required for "righteousness" before God, "faith" itself could be considered a "work." Righteousness would thus come not purely from grace but would require a prior act on the part of each believer in order to receive that grace in the first place. Resolution of this theological conundrum is beyond the limits of this book. Nevertheless, the issue does bear on the Paul's thesis of Christ as the second Adam and so cannot be ignored entirely.

The "problem" stems from an inherent ambiguity in Paul's use of the phrase "the faith of (Jesus) Christ" (*pistis [Iēsou] Christou*).[5] This geniti-

---

5. In the undisputed letters of Paul the phrase occurs in Rom 3:22, 26; Gal 2:16

val construction is ambiguous in Greek since one may understand the genitive "of Jesus Christ" as either a *subjective* genitive or an *objective* genitive. The difference between the two may be illustrated by contrasting the differences in meaning in the English phrases "the truck of John" (a subjective genitive) and "the fear of God" (an objective genitive). In the former example John is the subject, that is, the owner of the truck. In the latter example God is the object of one's fear—for example, John might speak of feeling paralyzed by his excessive "fear of God." If *pistis (Iēsou) Christou* is an objective genitive, then Jesus Christ is the object of the believer's faith, and the phrase would have reference to the believer having "faith *in* (Jesus) Christ." But if one understands *pistis (Iēsou) Christou* as a subjective genitive, then it is a matter of Jesus's own faith or fidelity, and the reference is to Jesus having absolute trust in God.[6] The believer gains access to God's salvation not by anything she or he does, but by being united with Christ and receiving the benefits of Christ's death and resurrection literally "through the faith *of* Christ."

The debate over which view is correct, the objective genitive interpretation or the subjective genitive interpretation, can get very technical and involved. Both views have been well argued by very competent Pauline scholars. Nevertheless, there are multiple indications in Paul's letters, taken as a whole, that incline me at least to believe that the subjective genitive interpretation ("the faith *of* Christ" [Jesus's own trust in God]) was indeed what Paul intended, as that better corresponds to Paul's Christology, especially regarding his view of Jesus Christ as the second Adam.

In the first three centuries a subjective genitive interpretation was commonplace among Christians, but in the fourth century it was abandoned by orthodox Christians—a casualty of the ongoing christological debates, particularly in the struggle against Arianism.[7] Thereafter, an objective genitive interpretation became standard, to the extent that since the Protestant Reformation it has become almost exclusively the sole interpretation that Christians learned. Only with the advent of modern

---

(2x), 20; 3:22; Phil 3:9.

6. For a comprehensive review of this issue in modern Pauline scholarship, see Hays, *Faith of Jesus Christ*; Hays argues convincingly for a subjective genitive construction. For an opposing view, see Dunn, "Appendix 1: Once More, ΠΙΣΤΙΣ ΧΡΙΣΤΟΥ," in the same volume, 249–71.

7. So Wallis, Faith of Jesus Christ in Early Christian Traditions, cited by Hays, *Faith of Jesus Christ*, p. xlviii.

critical Pauline scholarship, with its goal to recover the "authentic Paul," has the subjective genitive interpretation reemerged—and is steadily gaining adherents. An important recent study of the subjective genitive interpretation in Pauline literature is that of Richard B. Hays, who steadfastly maintains that "the faith *of* (Jesus) Christ" is the correct rendering of Paul's meaning.[8] The fact that the earliest Christians mostly understood a subjective genitive construction here is in and of itself a powerful argument for thinking that such was indeed Paul's meaning, since those ancient readers, being closer in time and cultural context to the author, are more likely than later Christians to have understood correctly the mind of Paul.

Furthermore, if one leaves aside those passages containing the controverted phrase *pistis Christou* or the equivalent, there are no examples of Paul using *pistis* ("faith") with an objective genitive. By contrast, Paul used *pistis* with a subjective genitive some twenty-four times.

The most convincing example is Romans 4:16, where Paul employs a subjective genitive construction to highlight "the faith of Abraham."[9] In Paul's view, there is a kind of symmetry between "the faith of Abraham" and "the faith of Christ." God declared Abraham righteous—right (with God)—because Abraham trusted God. At the same time, God's "righting" of Abraham served a larger purpose in God's salvific plan to save all people. "Now the words, 'it was reckoned to him,' were written not just for his sake alone, but for ours also" (4:23–24). Like Abraham, Paul argues, we also will be declared "right" before God if we trust the God who raised Jesus from death. Abraham is thus a prototype of Jesus.

Jesus is greater than Abraham, of course, not just because Jesus's trust in God was absolute while Abraham had to be further tested (Gen 22:1), but also because through Jesus's fidelity God accomplished the salvation of all humankind. Jesus's place in the divine plan is therefore much more radical than that of Abraham. The effects of Jesus's absolute trusting of God reach both forward and backward. Forward, to all who follow Jesus; and backward, all the way to Adam himself. No one is excluded

8. Hays, *Faith of Jesus Christ*, 115–62. See also Hooker, "Pistis Christou," 321–42; Howard, "Notes and observations on the 'Faith of Christ,'" 459–84; Matera, *New Testament Christology*, 115–16, 122.

9. The phrase "from the faith of Abraham" (*ek pisteōs Abraam*) in Rom 4:16 is an exact grammatical parallel to the phrase "from the faith of Jesus" (*ek pisteōs Iēsou* [*Christou*]) in Rom 3:26 and Gal 3:22.

from God's saving grace effected through the second Adam. Everyone is saved through "the faith of Christ" so long as one is "in Christ."

Jesus as the New Adam in Philippians 2:6-11

Reading Genesis in the original Hebrew, one would have little difficulty in comprehending the universal significance that Paul attaches to the figure Adam, since "Adam" is usually preceded by the definite article, that is, *ha-'adam*. Grammatically speaking, this phrase is better translated as "the Human" or "humankind." Only rarely does it occur without the definite article, as if it were a proper name "Adam" (so Gen 1:26-27; 5:1-2, 3, 4). Even in those instances, however, the name (or term) "Adam" retains its primary meaning as "Human" or "humankind." This is obvious in the interchange between the singular and plural pronouns referring to *'adam* in Gen 1:26-27: "Then God said, 'Let us make *'adam* in our image, according to our likeness.' . . . So God created *ha-'adam* in his image, in the image of God he created *him;* male and female he created *them.*" Nearly identical language is found at Genesis 5:1-2. There is virtually no distinction in Genesis between the figure "Adam" and *'adam* the representative of "humankind." Paul understood this well, and it allowed him to draw the logical conclusion that all of humankind was present virtually in "Adam." Accordingly, Paul can assert that even though "sin came into the world through one man," nevertheless "all have sinned" (Rom 5:12) because all humankind was literally embodied in Adam. By the same reasoning, Death, the companion of Sin, is also said to come upon every "human." Humans are enslaved by Sin and thus powerless to do anything to better their own condition. It is pure grace, therefore, that God steps in to rescue humankind from this sinful condition by sending the second Adam.

Paul's understanding of the process by which Jesus became the second Adam is elaborated in the letter to the Philippians, particularly in the so-called Song of Christ (2:6-11). This hymn has been the subject of much scholarly discussion, due to its cryptic language. Most present-day scholars assume that this hymn speaks of Christ as divine and preexisting from all eternity with God in heaven, but then temporarily renounced his place in heaven in order to become human and die in obedience to the divine will. He subsequently rose to resume once more his place in heaven with God (the Father).

By contrast, a minority of scholars maintain that the Song of Christ in Philippians 2 says nothing about Jesus being preexistent. Rather, its language is better characterized as "Adamic Christology."[10] That is, Jesus is presented as a new Adam through whom God has effected the salvation of humankind.

There is a great difference in interpretation, depending upon whether one assumes Paul was invoking a Christology of preexistence *or* an Adamic Christology.[11] The difference can best be understood by comparing two translations of this hymn side by side. The NRSV translation, which assumes a Christology of preexistence is presented in the first column. An Adamic Christology is presented in the second column.

The Pauline context for either translation is the same. Just prior to reciting this Song of Christ, Paul admonishes the Philippians to rise above their petty jealousies and to look instead to the interests of each other. They should adopt an attitude of humility, regarding others as better than themselves. To reinforce his point, Paul appeals to the example of Christ as set forth in this hymn, introduced with the words, "Your attitude must be that of Christ, who . . ."

10. Dunn, *Christology in the Making,* 114–21; Murphy-O'Connor, "Christological Anthropology in Phil. 2:6–11," 25–50.

11. For a concise overview of the principal issues involved, see Brown, *Introduction to the New Testament,* 491–93.

TABLE 4

Preexistence Christology	Adamic Christology
though he was in the *form* of God,	though he was in the *image* (*morphē*) of God,
did not regard equality with God	did not consider equality with God
as something to be *exploited*,	something to be *grasped at* (*harpagmon*).
but *emptied* himself,	Instead, he *humbled* (*kenōsis*) himself
taking the form of a slave,	and took the *form/image* (*morphē*) of a slave,
being born in human likeness.	being born in the likeness of humans.
And being found in human form,	And being found in status as *human* (*anthrōpos*),
he humbled himself	he abased himself
and became obedient to the point of death—	and became obedient onto death—
even death on a cross.	even death on a cross.
Therefore God also highly exalted him	Therefore God also highly exalted him
and gave him the name	and gave him the name
that is above every name,	above every other name,
so that at the name of Jesus	so that at the name of Jesus
every knee should bend	every knee must bend
in heaven and on earth and under the earth,	in heaven and on earth and under the earth,
and every tongue should confess	and every tongue proclaim
that Jesus Christ is Lord,	that Jesus Christ is Lord,
to the glory of God the Father.	to the glory of God the Father.

The debate whether Paul intended to attribute to Christ divine pre-existence or merely an Adamic status is due to the ambiguity of certain key phrases in this hymn. First and foremost are the words used to describe the initial condition of Jesus Christ as *en morphē theou,* for which one may concede that the most literal translation is "in the form of God." Many scholars interpret this phrase in light of John 1:1–3 and Colossians 1:15, and conclude that Paul was speaking about a stage of preexistence in the career of Christ. The Johannine formulation patently reflects a Christology of the early church several decades after Paul wrote. Without clear and certain indications of a similar christological viewpoint in the undisputed letters of Paul, however, John should not be used to decode ambiguous Pauline passages, precisely because John postdates Paul—and that in a period of rapidly evolving "Christologies."

Similarly, Colossians should also be discounted, as there is solid evidence that the Letter to the Colossians is a pseudonymous letter written after Paul's death. The very similar Letter to the Ephesians was almost certainly written by someone other than Paul. Because Ephesians is heavily dependent upon Colossians, both literarily and doctrinally, it is very likely that Colossians, too, postdates Paul and should be considered an unreliable guide to the mind of Paul.

Almost certainly Paul understood the Greek phrase *en morphē theou* in Philippians 2:6 as a reference to God's words in Genesis 1:26, "Let us create Adam/humankind in our image."[12] If true, then one must conclude that Adamic Christology does indeed pervade the Song of Christ in Philippians 2.

Two additional vocables in the hymn with ambiguous meanings are *harpagmon* (2:6) and *kenōsis* (2:7). *Harpagmon* may mean either to "grasp at" or to "cling to." *Kenōsis* in context may mean either to "humble/lower (oneself)" or to "empty/pour out (oneself)." Proponents of preexistence understand Christ here voluntarily foregoing his status as the eternal Son/Word of God in order to take on the condition of humanity; accordingly they translate the relevant phrases as the preexistent divine Son "did not cling to (*or* exploit) (his) equality with God but emptied himself (of his divine status)" in order to assume instead the condition of a servant. That makes for an appealing Christology from the perspective of later Christians; but it does not comport with Paul's thinking elsewhere.

Given Paul's emphasis in Romans 5–6 and 1 Corinthians 15 that Christ is a second Adam, it is much more probable that Paul intended to present Christ as a second Adam here as well. If so, preexistence was not Paul's focus. Rather, Paul seems to have considered Jesus to be a human specially raised up by God, like the great men of the Hebrew Scriptures:

---

12. The fact that the Septuagint translated Hebrew *tselem* "image" in Gen 1:26 by the Greek vocable *eikōn* rather than by *morphē* does not invalidate this conclusion. As Dunn (*Theology of Paul*, 284–85) notes, "The terms were used as near synonyms, and it would appear that the writer preferred 'form of God' because it made the appropriate parallel and contrast with 'form of a slave.' Such a double function of a term is precisely what one might expect in poetic mode." According to Dunn, it is entirely appropriate to think that the phrase *en morphē theou* in Phil 2:6 is a reflex of Gen 1:26–28 and should be translated "in the *image* of God," and not "in the form of God."

Moses, Samuel, David or other kings, and the prophets. These men were at times given the title "son of God" or some other special designation in order to mark them as God's special servants.[13] Although the New Testament applies to Christ the words of Ps 2:7, "You are my son, today I have begotten you," originally these words referred to the kings of Israel and Judah as God's special agents. At enthronement, the king was thought to be elevated to a status well above that of other humans and was empowered to act in God's name as his "son." Similar expressions concerning the Davidic king as God's son are found in Ps 89:26–27 and 2 Sam 7:14.[14]

The Second Adam versus the First Adam

Paul had no conception of Jesus having had a preexistent career prior to his birth.[15] Indeed, Paul's preaching concerning Jesus depends upon Jesus's acceptance of his "human" status, which in turn requires obedience to God's will. In other words, Paul presents Christ as the exact opposite of disobedient Adam.

Adam had been created in the image of God (Gen 1:26–28). Paul would have read Genesis 2–3 as an elaboration of the account in Genesis 1. Remember that in Genesis 2 it is said that after God formed "the Human" from clay, God "breathed into his nostrils the breath of life" (2:7). As discussed in chapter 2, this may be regarded as a statement that *the Human* enjoyed partial divinity. At the urging of the serpent, Adam and Eve believed that they could "become like God," that is, achieve full divinity, by disobeying God and eating from the tree of knowledge (wisdom). Or to borrow language from Paul, Adam—remember, Eve is ignored here—overreached and "grasped at" "equality with God."

Adam never accepted his assigned status as servant/slave: "There was no one to work the ground." So "the Lord God formed "the Human (ha-'adam) from the dust of the ground (ha-'adamah)." Then "the Lord

13. For a discussion of the evolving notion of "son of God" in the Bible and related literature, see Collins and Collins, *King and Messiah as Son of God.*

14. Collectively, the Israelites themselves were on occasion called the son of God: "Israel is my firstborn son" (Exod 4:22); "Out of Egypt have I called my son" (Hos 11:1, cp. Matt 2:15); and "I have become a father to Israel, and Ephraim is my firstborn" (Jer 31:9; see also Isa 43:6).

15. Intimations of preexistence in 1 Cor 8:6, 10:4, 9; 2 Cor 8:9 and elsewhere should not be considered as Paul predicating actual preexistence for Christ; so Matera, *New Testament Christology*, 94–95; Dunn, *Theology of Paul*, 266–93.

God planted a garden in Eden, in the east, and there he put the Human whom he had formed." The intimate connection the Lord God intended between the Human and the soil that the Human was created to work is better captured in English by rendering the relevant vocables as a pun: "the Human" was created to work "the humus." The Human's assignment to be a servant of the soil is made even more explicitly by its repetition in verse 15: "the Lord God took the human and put him in the garden of Eden to work it and keep it"—the Hebrew word for "work" in the phrase "to work it" derives from the same Hebrew root word ('*bd*) as "servant/ slave," thereby making explicit the linkage between the Human/Adam and his servanthood. Paul likely had no inkling of the origins of this motif in the more remote ancient Mesopotamian myth of Atrahasis or of the associated underlying Mesopotamian conviction that humans had been created precisely to be the servants/slaves for the gods. But Paul did understand the Genesis creation account to imply that servanthood was integral to the condition of humankind from the very beginning. Adam, however, rejected his slave/servant status by overreaching and attempting to "become like God."

Jesus, Paul implies, adopted exactly the opposite attitude before God. Jesus was "sent" by God specifically to be a second Adam. But this time "the Human" (Greek *anthrōpos* = Hebrew '*adam*) did not reject his humanness by attempting to "grasp at . . . equality with God." Instead, Jesus accepted the status of slave/servant—both conditions are refer- enced by the relevant Hebrew and Greek vocables ('*ebed* and *doulos*, respectively)—and submitted in absolute obedience to God's will, as is evident in that Jesus willingly gave even his life out of obedience. Such transparent obedience to the will of God is unparalleled in the history of humankind. Such absolute fidelity God could not and did not overlook, any more than in the case of the "suffering Servant" of Isaiah (Isa 42:1–4; 49:1–6; 50:4–11; 52:12—53:12).

Although Paul seldom quotes directly from the suffering Servant passages in Isaiah, it is obvious that Paul had this figure firmly in mind as he penned the Song of Christ. Like other early Christians, Paul may even have viewed the Servant passages in Isaiah as a direct prophecy of Christ. God had said of the Servant, "Here is my servant [*or* slave], whom I uphold, my chosen, in whom my soul delights. I have put my spirit upon him; he will bring forth justice to the nations" (Isa 42:1). The Servant announces that he was specially raised up by God for a mission: "The Lord called me before I was born; while I was in my mother's womb, he named me" (Isa 49:1). Furthermore, his mission was not just to Israel but to all peoples: "It is too light a thing that you should be my servant/ slave to raise up (just) the tribes of Jacob and to restore the survivors of Israel. I will give you as a light to the nations, that my salvation may reach to the ends of the earth" (Isa 49:6). God laid upon the Servant great suffering in order that God's people might be made whole: "Surely he has borne our infirmities and carried our diseases; yet we accounted him stricken, struck down by God, and afflicted. But he was wounded for our transgressions, crushed for our iniquities; upon him was the punishment that made us whole; by his bruises we are healed" (Isa 53:4–5). "It was the will of the Lord to crush him with pain . . . Through him the will of the Lord shall prosper" (Isa 53:10). Without understanding why he was be- ing asked to bear the sins of his people, the Servant obediently accepted his mission as the will of God: "The Lord God has opened my ear, and I was not rebellious, I did not turn backward. I gave my back to those who struck me, and my cheeks to those who pulled out the beard; I did not hide my face from insult and spitting" (50:5–6). Through all his trials and suffering, the Servant never lost faith in God: "The Lord God helps me . . . and I know that I shall not be put to shame; he who vindicates me is near" (50:7). In the end God himself rewards the Servant by exalting him:

> See, my servant shall prosper,
>> he shall be exalted and lifted up,
>> and shall be very high.
> Just as there were many who were astonished at him
>> —so marred was his appearance, beyond human semblance,
>> and his form beyond that of mortals—
> so he shall startle many nations;
>> kings shall shut their mouths because of him;
> for that which had not been told them they shall see,
>> and that which they had not heard they shall contemplate.
> (Isa 52:13–15 NRSV)

Likewise for Jesus Christ as servant/slave. Because he humbled him- self and became totally obedient to God's will, Paul writes, "Therefore God also highly exalted him" (Phil 2:9), such that all who comprehend are without doubt astounded. As astounding as God raising Jesus from the dead and lifting him up to heaven (see 1 Thess 1:10) might be, it is far from the full extent to which God exalted Jesus. No, the height to which Paul refers is that God bestowed divinity upon Jesus, while at the same time conferring upon him God's own ineffable name, *kyrios* "Lord."

In Isaiah, God had said, "I am Yahweh; that is my name. My glory I give to no other" (Isa 42:8; see also 48:11). By New Testament times, it was standard Jewish practice never to pronounce the name of God, as it was considered too sacred. Instead, Jews substituted the term *adonay*, "my Lord," which was translated into Greek in the Septuagint as *kyrios* "Lord." Paul generally quoted the Hebrew Scriptures from the Greek Septuagint when writing for his Greek audience. So when Paul writes that God conferred on Jesus Christ the name *kyrios*, "Lord," Paul implies that God did something that God had said he would never do, namely, share his divine name with another.

Now every being—whether in heaven, on earth, and in the underworld—is henceforth obligated to give Jesus as Messiah the exact same honor that they give God himself, by kneeing and confessing that Jesus Christ too is "Lord." As it is written in Isaiah (45:23), "to me every knee shall bow, every tongue shall swear." Paul does not explicitly say he is quoting from Isaiah, but he clearly has the prophet's words in mind, because the previous verse in Isaiah (45:22) reads: "Turn to me and be saved, all the ends of the earth! For I am God, and there is no other." God, Paul implies, has associated Jesus Christ with himself in his saving outreach to all humankind.

This apparent reversal on God's part in sharing his name and his glory with another is indeed theologically revolutionary. Revolutionary, because God has elevated the human Jesus to his right hand, thereby making the second Adam, the Messiah, co-divine with God, as the "Son" of God. But all of this, rather than diminishing the deity, only adds "to the glory of God the Father" (Phil 2:11). We have already noted that Paul did not think Jesus to have been the Son of God from birth, but only became such by divine fiat through his resurrection and exaltation. Recall that in Rom 1:3–4 Paul says concerning "the gospel of God" that he announces, that it is "the gospel concerning [God's] Son, who was *descended from David according to the flesh* (human nature) and *was declared to be the Son of God with power according to the spirit of holiness by resurrection from the dead, Jesus Christ our Lord.*"

Despite seeming to contradict Isaiah that God would not give his glory to another, Paul maintains that salvation through Jesus Christ was God's plan all along. In Rom 1:2 Paul writes that such is what God "promised beforehand through his prophets in the holy scriptures." Among other prophets, Paul surely had Isaiah primarily in mind. In Galatians Paul writes, all has now come to pass "in the fullness of time," when "God sent his Son, born of a woman" under the law (Gal 4.4).[16] And in another place Paul says all had been prepared beforehand by the will of God, so that "Christ died for our sins in accordance with the scriptures, and . . . he was raised on the third day in accordance with the scriptures" (1 Cor 15:3–4).

Many scholars think that Paul did not himself compose the words of the Song of Christ, however, but was merely quoting from a familiar hymn already in use in the early Christian community. If so, Paul would be recalling for the Philippians something they already knew and presumably believed concerning Jesus. That would only have increased its rhetorical power for the Philippians. But whether the hymn predated Paul or originated with him, Paul certainly used it to good effect to advance his message that Jesus was a new Adam—and the beginning of a whole new era for humankind.

One final note regarding the Song of Christ. To my knowledge there is no evidence that the author, whether Paul or an anonymous Christian poet, was aware of the Jewish pseudepigraph Life of Adam and Eve, or vice versa. But it is interesting that the two texts are near contemporaries, both having been composed in the first century CE/AD. The Latin version of Life of Adam and Eve (Vita 12–16) contains the earliest attestation of the trope that Satan fell out of heaven precisely because he refused to worship Adam, or at least the image of God in Adam, but instead attempted to exalt himself. According to the interpretation proffered here, the Song of Christ says that Christ as the second Adam, though being in the image of God, did not covet divinity; nevertheless, because of his obedience, God exalted him to the status of divinity and commands all to bow down in worship before him. While such similarities may be merely coincidental, one cannot but wonder if one of these texts may have influenced the other, or even if both acquired the motif of worshiping the divine image in Adam/second Adam from yet a third, common source.

16. This is not a statement of preexistence. Rather with Dunn (*Christology in the Making,* 37–46), Paul's statement here that God "sent" his son, as in Rom 8:3, should be understood as eschatological, not protological. Adela Yarbro Collins compares this to God's "sending" of the prophets ("Jesus as Messiah and Son of God in the Letters of Paul," in Collins and Collins, *King and Messiah as Son of God,* 101–22, esp. 107.

Jesus Christ as the Second Adam in 1 Corinthians 15

Paul writes about Christ as the second Adam also in 1 Corinthians 15. This letter was written prior to Romans and is less systematic than Romans both in organization and message. Nevertheless, what Paul wrote the Corinthians concerning "the gospel that I proclaimed to you" (15:1) is consistent with the gospel he set forth in Romans. In 1 Corinthians 15 Paul is concerned primarily to affirm that our mortal bodies will rise at the end time and will become immortal, since resurrection of the dead is intimately connected to the resurrection of Christ, the second Adam.

> If Christ has not been raised, your faith is futile, and you are still in your condition of sin . . . But in truth Christ has been raised from the dead, the first fruits of those who have died. As death came through a human (*anthrōpos*), so also the resurrection of the dead has come through a human (*anthrōpos*). As all die in Adam, so all will be made alive in Christ—each in his own order: Christ the first fruits, then at his coming those who belong to Christ. Finally comes the end, when he hands over the kingdom to God the Father, after he has destroyed every ruler and every authority and power. For he is destined to reign until he has put all his enemies under his feet. The last enemy to be deposed is death. (1 Cor 15:17–26)

The specific issue that Paul is addressing here is that some at Corinth are skeptical of the Christian claim that the dead will rise, and especially that their bodies will live again. One need not be surprised that some Corinthian converts, like other Greeks, might have had difficulty believing in the resurrection of the body. According to Acts 17:32, Paul encountered similar skepticism among the Athenians concerning resurrection. But for Paul, steeped in the Hebrew scriptural tradition that the human person is an integral unity of spirit and body, it is unthinkable that one could rise and live again without one's body also being raised. This is the case with Jesus's resurrection—which Christian tradition affirms included Jesus's body as well as his spirit. It will be the experience as well of everyone "who falls asleep in Christ" (verse 18). To deny that the dead will live again is tantamount to denying that God truly raised Jesus from the dead, which in turn would make not only Paul a liar but also God who had revealed this "good news" to Paul. Not just Paul's own preaching but the whole Christian gospel would be false, making everything Christians believe to be false and everything they hope for to be in vain.

Not only would death emerge victorious but also Sin would still reign supreme over us. But not to worry, Paul writes, because Christ truly has been raised, and his resurrection is the guarantee of our own resurrection and the foundation of our hope of eternal life.

As in Romans, Paul explains the union between Christ and his followers in terms of his thesis about Christ being the second Adam. Christ is the antidote to Adam. "All die in Adam." So too "all will be made alive in Christ" (15:22). Paul explicitly contrasts the functions of Adam and of Christ, since both represent humankind in its entirety, but in radically different ways. "As death came through [one] Human (*anthrōpos*), the resurrection of the dead has also come through [one] Human (*anthrōpos*)" (15:21).

Unlike in Romans, however, Paul does not explain precisely how this happens or the process by which this transpires. There is no mention here of the faith of Christ nor that one is saved through the faith of Christ. There is no discussion of being baptized into Christ nor of dying with Christ and rising with Christ. Nevertheless, these elements should be assumed here, since elsewhere in this letter the vocabulary and imagery of baptism figure prominently (1:13–16; 10:2; 12:12:13; 15:29). Paul does speak of being "in Christ" when he speaks of the deceased as those "who have fallen asleep *in Christ*." "In Christ" likely has reference to these persons having been baptized since earlier in the letter Paul had written, "For in the one Spirit we were all baptized into one body—Jews or Greeks, slaves or free—and we were all made to drink of one Spirit" (12:13). In context, the "one body" refers primarily to all Christians who are joined together to form the one body of Christ. The one body is in a very real sense the resurrected body of Jesus, in which all believers are joined and made one with Jesus Christ and therefore also with one another.

To express further the unity of Christ with his "members" (1 Cor 12:12), Paul employs the harvest concept of "first fruits." According to the Hebrew Scriptures (Exod 23:19; 34:26; Lev 23:10; Deut 18:4), the first produce harvested each season was considered representative of the entire harvest. By offering the "first fruits" to God, one acknowledged that the whole harvest was a gift from God and technically belonged to God. In a similar way, Christ, as the representative of all who are saved, may be called "the first fruits" precisely because after baptism there is no distinction between Christ and those who are "in Christ." In baptism they all have "put on Christ," thereby becoming one with Christ and with each other (Gal 3:27–28). What happens to Christ happens to all.

"All" is the correct term for Paul. Listen again to Paul's words, "for as all die in Adam, so all will be made alive in Christ" (15:22). No one is excluded from this "Christian" event of reversing Adam's damning act of disobedience. Every descendant of Adam is included, at least potentially, in Christ's salvific act. God's grace has absolutely no limits.

But if Adam and Christ have parallel functions as embodying all humankind, the outcomes could not be more different.

> The first man was out of the earth—dust; the second man is from heaven. As was the [one] of dust, so are those who are of the dust; and as is the [one] of heaven, so are those who are of heaven. Just as we have borne the image of the [one] of dust, we will also bear the image of the [one] of heaven. (1 Cor 15:47–49)

Paul here contrasts the "earthly" first Adam with the "heavenly" second Adam. One must be careful not to misinterpret Paul. "When Paul speaks of Christ as the man from heaven, the heavenly one (vv. 47–48), he is referring to the risen Lord, who has been raised from the dead. Before his resurrection, Jesus already bore the image of Adam. But now, raised and transformed, he is the heavenly one, the image of God, and he will confer upon believers the image of his resurrection body at the general resurrection of the dead."[17] Paul is not saying that Christ descended from heaven, as if he were a preexisting being who at some point came down to earth. That is John's Christology, not Paul's. Rather, Paul is building upon a point he has just made about the mystery of the resurrected body. We do not know exactly what kind of body we will have at the resurrection, he acknowledges, but we can be sure that it will not be the same as the physical body that is placed in the grave. He uses various analogies to illustrate our resurrected bodies will be transformed into spiritual bodies of some sort, even as they have continuity with our former physical bodies. The most poignant analogy is that of a small acorn that is placed into the ground but then springs forth as an immense, beautiful, strong oak tree. Who could have imagined such a grand outcome from such an insignificant beginning!

It must be emphasized that Paul's point is not to posit preexistence for Christ. Indeed, Paul's argumentation here makes immanently more sense if Christ is understood as *not* having preexistence but instead shares a common human condition with the rest of humankind. If Christ had preexistence, then one might find it hard to believe that Jesus Christ did

17. Matera, *New Testament Christology*, 97.

not rise under his own power—as commonly assumed by later generations of Christians steeped in the Nicene formula: "on the third day he
rose again from the dead"—rather than having been raised up by God,
as Paul always puts it. If Christ had risen by his own power, Christ would
be radically different from the rest of humans and Paul's logic would fail
to convince, namely, that what happened to Jesus happens also to the rest
of humankind.

Despite Adam and Christ sharing a common humanity, Paul argues
that the life forces at work in Adam and in Christ are radically different.
Paul's point of departure is the creation of Adam ("the Human") as narrated in Gen 2:7, "then the Lord God formed the Human from the dust
of the ground and breathed into his nostrils the breath of life; and the
Human became a living being." The first Adam was formed from earth
and can rightly be characterized as earthly. Adam never transcended
that condition because he lost access to the source of immortality. The
situation is quite different with the second Adam. Christ transcended his
original human condition when God exalted him up to heaven, whereby
he became the Son of God and co-divine with God the Father. This is the
source of Christ's "power" (Rom 1:4), which subsequently is made available to the rest of humankind being held in the prison of their earthiness.
Thus can Paul characterize the second Adam as being "from heaven"
because of his newly acquired "heavenly" condition. As the new Adam,
Christ passes on his "power" to others who now may also be characterized as "heavenly."

All Creation as Well

The second Adam succeeded in the quest of immortality and divinity
to which the first Adam aspired but failed. All humankind becomes the
beneficiary of the new Adam, being co-heirs with him and in him—and
not just humankind, but all creation as well.

One of the consequences of the sin of Adam according to Genesis
3:17–19 was that "the ground is cursed because of you," bringing forth
"thorns and thistle" readily, but yielding up its good fruit only "by the
sweat of your brow." Adam's son Cain added to the burden laid earth by
murdering his brother Abel. As God tells Cain, "Your brother's blood is
crying out to me from the ground! And now you are cursed from the
ground, which has opened its mouth to receive your brother's blood from

your hand. When you till the ground, it will no longer yield to you its strength" (Gen 4:10–12).

Jewish tradition greatly embellished upon the negative consequences of Adam's sin upon creation itself. The apocryphal book of Jubilees (3:26–31) tells how in Eden the animals, like the Human and his wife, enjoyed paradisiacal conditions. Peace and harmony prevailed among the animals. They did not attack one another. They did not prey upon one another, for in the beginning all were vegetarians! There was no such thing as a "wild beast" in paradise. Animals were friendly not only with each other but also with the Human and his wife. Humans and animals alike were accustomed to conversing pleasantly with each other, as the animals were also gifted with the ability to speak Hebrew, the language of creation (Jub 3:28; 12:26).

That all changed, however, when Adam (and Eve) sinned. The animals were driven out of Eden along with Adam and Eve, and all paradisiacal conditions vanished immediately. The animals turned on one another and began to kill and eat one another. They lost their ability to speak. Moreover, harmony between humankind and animalkind was completely disrupted. This ever-present scourge of devouring wild beasts in the land is frequently alluded to in the Hebrew Scriptures (e.g., Exod 23:29; Lev 26:22; Deut 28:26; Isa 56:9; Jer 12:9; 15:3; Ezek 5:17; 32:4). By the same token, one sign that the longed-for eschatological kingdom of God has finally arrived will be that "wild beasts" will be removed from the land, because animals will revert to their former peaceful ways (Lev 26:6; Ezek 34:25; Isa 11:6–11; Hos 2:18).

Such traditions must have resonated with Paul from his youth onward since their echo can be heard in Romans 8. Paul begins that chapter with the statement that "there is no condemnation for those who are in Christ Jesus." A bit later he adds, "If the Spirit of him who raised Jesus from the dead dwells in you, he who raised Christ from the dead will give life to your mortal bodies also through the Spirit that dwells in you" (8:11). The Spirit who animates us makes us "children of God" by adoption, and therefore we are "heirs of God and joint heirs with Christ" (8:14–17). Paul then unexpectedly broadens his focus to note that not just humankind, but all creation is beneficiary to this transforming power of the Spirit of God.

> For *the creation* waits with eager longing for the revealing of the
> children of God; for *the creation* was subjected to futility, not of
> its own will but by the will of the one who subjected it, in hope

> that *the creation* itself will be set free from its bondage to decay
> and will obtain the freedom of the glory of the children of God.
> We know that *the whole of creation* has been groaning in labor
> pains until now. (Rom 8:19–23 NRSV, italics added)

The language is somewhat convoluted, but the message is clear. "*The creation*" was subjected to the penalty of Adam because of its solidarity with humankind, even though creation itself had done nothing to warrant punishment. But if it was condemned because of its solidarity with humankind, so too, for the same reason, creation will enjoy the fruits of the humankind's redemption through the second Adam. Indeed, creation has long been eagerly anticipating the rebirth of humankind as God's children, as creation itself has been in labor pains for its own regeneration, a regeneration that can only be achieved through a reversal of the sin of Adam.

In short, the second Adam undoes the evil wrought by the first Adam not only upon Adam's heirs but also upon the whole of creation. The extent of God's grace revealed through Jesus Christ is limitlessness. God's grace has no bounds.

For Paul, then, Christ truly is the turning point in history. Adam inaugurated a shameful era for humankind and humankind's environment. But in and through the faith and obedience of the second Adam, God has revealed an even better end for all in this new era. To be sure, one could never have come to understand the depth of God's love and mercy apart from the second Adam. In him all creation is brought to completion and the glorious work of the Creator perfected and fully revealed.

Assessing the Pauline Contribution

Paul's views about Christ as a second Adam had little importance beyond Christian circles. Judaism, and still later, Islam, were little impacted by Paul and his novel ideas. But it would be difficult to overstate the impact Paul's christological views had within the Christian community. Almost single-handedly, Paul transformed the garden of Eden narrative, from merely an initial episode in the long history of humankind, into one of the two most important events in the whole of human history, the second being the advent of the second Adam. The sin of the first Adam had dire consequences for humanity and creation alike.

In the following chapter we shall see that Paul's teachings about the first Adam and the second Adam are capable of more than one interpretation, however. Most famously, Augustine, Bishop of Hippo, understood Paul to say that every human inherits the "original sin" of Adam at conception. Augustine's thesis that all humans are born in original sin is grounded in Paul's doctrine that all humankind was virtually present in the first Adam but redeemed only subsequently in the second Adam. Irenaeus, Bishop of Lyons, understood Paul's thesis about the two Adams in a radically different manner. Irenaeus preached that the second Adam "recapitulated" all humankind within himself from the very beginning, and thereby immediately reversed the effects of the first Adam's sin. Both Irenaeus and Augustine agreed, however, that most importantly Paul had proclaimed a merciful God, who raised up a second Adam to reverse the heritage of the first Adam.

One might summarize Paul's teaching as follows: The ever-merciful God repaired the harm done by the first Adam by raising up a second Adam who humbly accepted his human status as servant, becoming totally obedient to God, even to death on a cross. Because of his utter humility and obedience, the second Adam was exalted to the status of God and empowered to incorporate all humanity within himself. Accordingly, all who accept this saving gift from God have died with Christ and are raised with him to eternal life. Though formerly slaves, humans have now become adopted children of God. All this is possible because of the absolute trust or faith of the second Adam, Christ, in the saving power of the all-merciful Father.

According to Paul, the Adam (and Eve) saga has henceforth been radically and forever altered, with an eternally different outcome for all.

Postscript: Eve in Pauline Literature

As mentioned previously, Eve has virtually no place in Paul's doctrine. However, she does figure in two passages, 2 Corinthians 11:3 and 1 Timothy 2:13–14. Let us look briefly at these two passages, beginning with the latter.

The overwhelming majority of critical biblical scholars hold that the so-called pastoral letters (1 & 2 Timothy and Titus) were not written by Paul at all, but rather were penned by one of Paul's disciples after Paul's death. Seemingly, this disciple, presumably a close associate of Paul during the latter's lifetime, felt compelled to carry on Paul's mission and to elaborate the import of Paul's teachings for the next generation. From various statements in these letters we may assume that this action was deemed necessary because new and alarming issues had arisen following Paul's death which needed to be addressed promptly and decisively. Among the issues dealt with are a proliferation of teachings contrary to "sound doctrine" and the necessity to choose good leaders (bishops, deacons, and other ministers) to carry on the functions of original apostles and leaders, most of whom are now dead or soon will be. It is in this context that "Paul" admonishes Timothy that women are not to be appointed as leaders over the community.

> Let a woman learn in silence with full submission. I permit no woman to teach or to have authority over a man; she is to keep silent. For Adam was formed first, then Eve; and Adam was not deceived, but the woman was deceived and became a transgressor. Yet she will be saved through childbearing, provided they continue in faith and love and holiness, with modesty. (1 Tim 2:11–15 NRSV)

Important for our topic is how Adam and Eve figure in the author's argument that women are to be submissive and silent. Ignoring completely the (first, Priestly) version found in Genesis 1, the author focuses on the (second, Yahwistic) version of creation from Genesis 2–3 to make the claim that "Adam was formed first, then Eve." According to Genesis 2, God initially formed from clay a solitary "Human" (ha-'adam) but then concluded that it was not good for "the Human" to be alone. So, God divided this "Adam" into two. As I argued in chapter 2, however, the correct understanding of the Genesis 2 passage is that the deity divided "the Human" by re-shaping its two "sides"—not just a "rib"—into two entirely new beings: a gendered human pair, male and female, or husband and wife. The author of 1 Timothy follows the conventions of his time, however, in reading Genesis 2 as a story of the Lord God taking a bone ("rib"?) from "Adam" and building it in a woman. Reading Genesis in this way, one readily understands how the author could posit that "Adam was formed first, then Eve."

First Timothy asserts, further, that "Adam was not deceived, but the woman was deceived and became a transgressor." Here one can hear loud and clear the influence of apocryphal texts like Life of Adam and Eve which blame Eve alone for the transgression in the garden of Eden.

Increasingly, from the first century onward, this became the conventional understanding of Genesis 3. Lost was recognition that, when read attentively, Genesis 3 does not say that the woman was alone when she ate, but that her husband was beside her the whole time and that blame is laid on the man and the woman equally.

This is the same cultural milieu in which one should situate 2 Corinthians 11:3, which contains the only reference to Eve in the authentic letters of Paul. In Paul's mind, Eve patently was of little consequence. In this 2 Corinthians passage she appears almost as an afterthought. The context is that Paul is defending himself and his teaching against the false teachings of opponents whom he sarcastically labels "super-apostles" (11:5). Just who these people were and what exactly they were teaching is not spelled out; but Paul decries them for "proclaiming another Jesus than the one we proclaimed" (11:4). Paul worries that the Corinthians, as neophyte Christians, are being led astray by "a different gospel" being promulgated by these false teachers. To reinforce his point, Paul introduces a marriage analogy. Like the father of the bride, Paul says he presented the Corinthians "as a chaste virgin to Christ." But now worries that they are being misled, away from their true husband who is Jesus Christ. "I am afraid that as the serpent deceived Eve by its cunning, your thoughts will be led astray from a sincere and pure devotion to Christ" (11:3).

Although Paul knows the trope about Eve being led astray by the serpent, he seems to attach little importance to Eve and her action. The serpent here does not seem to be Satan, but only a "cunning" serpent who by overestimating his own wisdom misled a naïve Eve down a wrong path. The Corinthian Christians are in similar danger from the "wisdom" of certain "super-apostles" preaching at Corinth. Presumably, these super-apostles believed their own teaching to be valid and not malicious, even if it did not agree completely with what Paul was preaching about Jesus as the Christ. If the analogy is valid, then it is not clear that Paul thought the serpent intended anything malicious by its speech, even if the result ended in error. It is not impossible, of course, that Paul may have been alluding to the recently introduced trope, according to which the serpent was actually Satan in disguise, who maliciously seduced a naive and vulnerable Eve—a trope found in Life of Adam and Eve and in deutero-Pauline letter 1 Timothy 2:14. But that is far from obvious. What is clear is that, in contrast to Adam, Eve was of little importance in Paul's scheme of things.

8

Church Fathers

FOLLOWING THE CLOSE OF the New Testament period, during the second to the fifth centuries several "church fathers" (apologists for early orthodox Christianity) took up their pens to elaborate upon Paul's teaching about Christ as a second Adam. For example, Tertullian, Cyprian, Ambrose, and Ambrosiaster opined that all humanity shares in Adam's sin, transmitted by human generation. But by far the two most important church fathers responsible for the development of the Adam and Eve tradition in relation to Christ were St. Irenaeus, Bishop of Lyon, and St. Augustine, Bishop of Hippo. Although these two writers were miles apart in their assessments of the consequences of Adam's and Eve's sin for all subsequent generations of humans, the influence that both Irenaeus and Augustine wielded in the development of subsequent Christian doctrine can hardly be overstated.

Irenaeus of Lyons

Saint Irenaeus was born in Asia Minor in the provincial capital city of Smyrna (modern day Izmir, Turkey) circa 130 and died in approximately 202. He grew up in a strong Christian family. By his own report he was acquainted in his youth with Polycarp, who reportedly had been a disciple of the apostle John. As a young man Irenaeus was ordained a priest and found his way to France, where he was chosen as bishop of Lugdunum (now Lyons). Irenaeus spent much of his later life writing treatises in which he defended the church against various heretical sects, especially various forms of Gnosticism. He wrote in Greek but only two of his works have survived intact, both in Latin translation. By far his most important work, or at least best known, is *On the Detection and Overthrow of the So-Called Gnosis*, usually cited by its Latin title *Adversus Haereses* or by its English title *Against the Heresies* (abbreviated herein as *AH*), in 12 books. In this tract Irenaeus was concerned to expose gnostic "heretics" identified as Barbelognostics or Barbeloites, whose teachings would appear to be similar to that of gnostic treatise known as *The Secret Book of John* (to be discussed in the next chapter).

Christ as Second Adam: Recapitulating Humankind

For our purposes, I will zero in on only one issue in Irenaeus's writings, how Christ reverses the work of Adam, or to use Irenaeus's terminology, Christ as the *recapitulation*[1] of all things. Recapitulation refers to the final summation in a speech, when the speaker repeats or brings together his principal points in order to drive home for his audience the full force of his oration. It is thus a summation of all that the speaker has said previously, but in a capsulized form. Irenaeus was not the first to apply the term *recapitulation* to Christ. That was done already by the author of Ephesians, who said that God set forth in Christ "a plan for the fullness of time, to *gather up* (*anakephalaióō*) all things in [Christ], things in heaven and things on earth" (Eph 1:10). Irenaeus expands upon this statement in Ephesians, insisting that Jesus both "repeats" in his own person the whole history of humankind from Adam on, and also that God "summarizes" the economy of salvation in and through Jesus. Irenaeus uses the phrase "economy of salvation" to encapsulate the entire process by which God saves humankind. Through and in the person of Jesus, God has not only undone the sin of Adam but also accomplished the salvation of all humankind. If Adam as the first human contained within himself in seminal form the whole of humankind to follow, similarly Christ is the summation of that same humankind, the fulfillment of its very mission and purpose.

> For Irenaeus, the whole history of mankind has one particular aim: the appearance of the God-man. The reverse is also true: the God-man relates to the whole history of mankind. This

1. The English word "recapitulation" derives from Latin *recapitulans*, which in turn is a translation of Greek *anakephalatiosis* ("gathering up/summing up")—a term borrowed from the rhetorical language of the day.

twofold movement leads Irenaeus to speak of Christ as the one
who recapitulates in himself all things ... For Irenaeus, Christ is
the center of history."[2]

Irenaeus builds upon Paul's idea of Christ as the second or last Adam.
Indeed, Irenaeus derives much of his Christology from Paul. But whereas
Paul posits that the salvation of humankind was achieved principally
through the *death and resurrection* of Jesus, Irenaeus posits that salvation
is centered in the *incarnation* of Christ. It is not that Irenaeus dismisses
the importance of Jesus's death and resurrection, but rather that he places
far greater emphasis on the fact that the divine *Logos* (Word) took on our
humanity, thereby becoming one with humankind.

In Irenaeus's view, the unity of God is paralleled by a unity in salvation. Because God is one, the Father and the Son are unequivocally united
in the economy of salvation. The Son became incarnate out of obedience
to the Father. But equally, the Father operates in unison with the Son
in the incarnation. When God became incarnate, the inseparable Father
and Son were both at work accomplishing the salvation of humankind.

In an analogous way, the incarnate God (Father and Son) is united
with the whole of humanity from the very beginning until the end of
time. By taking on flesh the incarnated Word recapitulates the entire history of humankind. Everyone, from Adam on, is "summed up" in Christ
and thereby saved and restored to eternal life. Only those who like Cain
consciously reject God's offer of mercy are excluded from restoration in
Christ, because they consciously and willfully harden their hearts to the
Almighty's counsel and choose to remain in death and darkness instead
(*AH* 3.23.4; similarly 2.28.7).

From Adam to Christ and Back Again

Irenaeus does not provide his readers with a narrative account about
Adam and Eve. Most of what he has to say about Adam can be found in
Against the Heresies, book 3, chapters 18–23. But he does refer to various
aspects of the Genesis narrative, from which the reader can glean how
Irenaeus understood the role and function of "the first-formed" (i.e.,
Adam). As was the case with the apostle Paul, Eve barely figures in Ire-
naeus's thinking. This is hardly surprising, as Irenaeus is heavily depen-
dent upon Paul concerning parallel functions between the first Adam

2. Nielsen, *Adam and Christ in the Theology of Irenaeus*, 57–58.

and the second Adam, within which Eve has virtually no role. But even Adam is not the primary focus of Irenaeus's attention. Adam is merely the means by which to arrive at Christ, who sums up within himself the whole of human history:

> For we have shown that the Son of God did not begin to exist then [i.e., when he was born], having been always with the Father; but when he became incarnate and was made man, he recapitulated in himself the long unfolding of humankind, granting salvation by way of compendium, that in Christ Jesus we might receive what we had lost in Adam, namely, to be according to the image and likeness of God. (*AH* 3.18.1)[3]

All humankind is in some true sense a unity. We all were contained in Adam in seminal form. As Adam was, so are we. Adam was made in the image and likeness of God, and so are we. What Adam lost, we also lost.

It would be a mistake, however, to think of our "loss" in Augustinian terms, that is, that every component of us humans—mind, will, emotions, and desires—had been so completely corrupted by sin that humankind is totally depraved and spiritually dead. To be sure, Irenaeus does speak of humans as having suffered corruption; but unlike Augustine, he does not thereby assume that humankind is thoroughly depraved and incapable of doing anything pleasing to God. Adam's sin did wound humans to the extent that all must undergo physical death. Nevertheless, every person is still capable of doing good, even if with difficulty. That is so because from the very beginning the second Adam (Christ), in union with God the Father, has been actively at work recapitulating—that is, "summing up"— the whole of humankind in the person of the incarnate Son, precisely for the purpose of rescuing humankind.

Throughout history Christ has all along been paralleling the actions of Adam and humankind, and in some salvific manner incorporating them into himself. The parallels are patent. Christ, like Adam, was born of a virgin. Adam was formed by the hand of God from the "virgin Earth (for God had not yet rained [upon] the earth nor had the Human as yet tilled it)." So, too, Christ, "since he is the Word recapitulating Adam in himself, rightly took from Mary, who was yet a virgin, his birth that would be a recapitulation of Adam" (*AH* 3.21.10; similarly 3.18.7). Furthermore, as the earth-derived body of Adam was animated by divine

---

3. Translations of Book 3 are from Unger, *St. Irenaeus of Lyons: Against the Heresies.*

breath, so the virgin Mary's womb was made fruitful by the infusion of the Holy Spirit.

This continuity between Adam and the incarnated Word, Irenaeus says, is verified by the evangelist Luke, who points out that the genealogy of Jesus extends backward through seventy-two generations, to Adam. In this way Luke "joins the end to the beginning and points out that he [Christ] it is who recapitulates in himself all the nations that had been dispersed from Adam onward, and all the tongues, and the human race, including Adam himself" (AH 3.22.3). Irenaeus notes also that Paul had called Adam "a type of the one who was to come" (Rom 5:14). This means that God has established the Son of God, who existed before anything was made, as the center, so that from the very beginning "the natural man" might be saved through "the spiritual man."

Adam and Eve as Prepubescent Children

We shall return shortly to the issue of how humankind was/is saved. But first let us examine how Irenaeus understands the original condition of Adam and Eve in the garden. As already noted, Irenaeus posits a kind of virgin birth for Adam, "the first-formed," since God molded him from virgin earth and then animated the lifeless form with living spirit/breath directly from the deity's own mouth (Gen 2:7).

Moreover, Irenaeus says that at their creation both Adam and Eve were young and inexperienced—innocent and naïve are better descriptors. Irenaeus even refers to them as "infants" (AH 4.38.1; Epid. 14).[4] Physically, intellectually, and morally they were but at the beginning stages of human development. Their infantility was obvious in their dress, or rather the lack thereof. Like little children, they were oblivious to their nakedness and moved about without shame. They had no need of clothes. Immaturity also lessened their moral culpability in their sin of disobedience. The whole time Adam and Eve were in the garden, Irenaeus argues, they were prepubescent or at most barely pubescent "because they had recently been made and had no knowledge about generating children; for they had first to grow up, and then multiply" (AH 3.22.4). Moreover, in the garden they never engaged in sexual activity, evidently due to sexual immaturity. Genesis 4 relates that Adam "knew" his wife

---

4. See Klager, "Divine Identification and the Recapitulation of Peace in St. Irenaeus," 1–22.

for the first time only after they were expelled from the garden, and this 'knowing" resulted in the births of Cain and Abel. How long Adam and Eve resided in the garden is unknown. But it was certainly long enough for them to become familiar with God's habits, like strolling through the garden while enjoying the evening breezes.

Since Adam and Eve were not yet mature in paradise, Irenaeus does not regard them as perfect, nor even capable of being perfect. Only the eternal God is perfect. Created "in the image God," only means that Adam and Eve were created in the eternal Word of God, who in time would become incarnate in Jesus Christ. In other words, Adam and Eve were imperfect images of the true image of God.

> Created things must be inferior to Him who created them, from the very fact of their later origin; for it was not possible for things recently created to have been uncreated. . . Inasmuch as they are not uncreated, they fall short of perfection. (*AH* 4.38.1)

God could have arranged matters differently, but in God's scheme of salvation "it was reserved for Christ to bring all together under one head and to perfect it . . . The fall is to Irenaeus hardly more than an intermesso, needful to set off the work of salvation that God has carried out in Christ. . . Adam is [merely] 'typus futuri' [a type of the future one]. The divine plan of salvation did not only begin when man was disobedient and went his own way, but at once when he was created."[5]

Adam's and Eve's lack of maturity, especially intellectually, is what made them such easy targets for the devil. Irenaeus has little to say about the actual temptation of Adam and Eve by Satan. But he does elaborate on its consequences. And those consequences are not what we might expect, given our long-standing conditioning to think of the couple's expulsion from the garden as a severe punishment. Rather than punishment, Irenaeus sees a merciful God at work.

From their creation Adam and Eve were "in the image of God." Sin may have tarnished the divine image, but it did not destroy it completely—not in Adam and Eve, and not in their descendants. That is evident from the fact that after Adam and Eve sinned, God did not abandon them but continually showered them with mercy.

The first evidence of that mercy was manifested when Adam and Eve made for themselves loincloths or girdles from fig leaves. In Genesis 3 the primal couple's motive for clothing themselves is attributed to their

---

5. Nielsen, *Adam and Christ*, 62.

recognition of their nakedness and their need to cover themselves out of shame. Irenaeus has a different take. When Adam tells God that he hid because he was "afraid," his fear did not arise from any desire to escape punishment. Rather Adam was ashamed "because having transgressed God's commandment, he felt unworthy of coming into the presence of and conversing with God. . . knowledge of the transgression led to repentance—and God bestows His kindness on those who repent" (*AH* 3.23.5).

With the gravity of their offense beginning to dawn on them, Adam and Eve deliberately set out to make amends by imposing harsh punishment upon themselves. To that end, they donned the most horrific clothing they could imagine. They made for themselves girdles from fig leaves.

> Adam showed his repentance by his action in regard to the girdle, namely, when he covered himself with fig leaves, though there were many other leaves that would have been less irritating to the body. But being awed by the fear of God, he made a garment conformable to his disobedience. He resisted the petulant impulse of the flesh, since he had lost his guileless and childlike mind and had come to the knowledge of evil things. And so he surrounded himself and his wife with a girdle of continence, for he feared God and expected His coming. It was as if he wished to say, Since through disobedience I have lost the robe of holiness that I had from the Spirit, I now acknowledge that I deserve such a garment as offers me no pleasure, but gnaws at the body and pricks it. (*AH* 3.23.5)

As anyone who has worked with figs knows, fig leaves are terribly irritating to the skin. Not only do they induce itching, they also can cause severe skin rash. So to increase their punishment, Adam and Eve applied these self-made instruments of torture to the most delicate, the most sensitive parts of their bodies. This was, if you will, a primitive form of what later came to be known as the practice of wearing "penitential hair shirts."

God looked favorably upon this act of repentance. But here is where God showed just how merciful he is, according to Irenaeus. Rather than letting Adam and Eve continue to suffer from their self-imposed torture, God replaced their fig leaf girdles with clothes made of animal skins (*AH* 3.23.5). Not only would these new clothes be less irritating to the skin, they would also be more durable and practical as body covering. Likely Irenaeus recognized this as God's additional concern for his newly created humans, precisely because they were still naïve and inexperienced in providing for their own needs. Like young children, they needed to be shown how to cope in a hostile environment—for shortly they would experience just how hostile their environment had become, as God was about to expel them from their paradisaical home.

God revealed his mercy also by driving Adam and Eve from the garden. In paradise they had access to the Tree of Life. If they should eat of its fruit, they would not die but live forever. That would be a curse in disguise. Having been deceived by Satan about the consequences of disobeying God's command not to eat of the Tree of Knowledge of Good and Evil, Adam and Eve now learned the true consequences of their disobedience. Though they had not been cursed like Satan, their world was cursed. Their previously idyllic lives suddenly had been turned upside down. Whereas previously Adam's agricultural tasks had been a pleasure, now they became burdensome. The cursed ground henceforth would give up its fruits only reluctantly. Thorns and thistles would overwhelm Adam's plantings; and much "sweat of the brow" would be required for even a meager return on his vast labors. And Eve, for her part, would be forced to bear children in excruciating pain. Moreover, while her "desire" for her husband was, if anything, now even greater, he would "dominate" her and treat her more as a slave than as a "partner." As Irenaeus says of Eve, "In like manner, the woman [received] weariness, labors, sighs, painful childbirths, and servitude—that is, to serve her husband" (*AH* 3.23.3).

Banishment from paradise under such circumstances was thus an act of divine mercy, not an act of punishment. If Adam and Eve had remained in the garden, they surely would have had eaten from the Tree of Life. Remember (from chapter 2, above) the Hebrew text of Genesis 2:16 contains the grammatical imperative, a command: "You shall (must) eat of every tree in the garden; only of the tree of knowledge of good and evil you shall not eat." So, if they were to stay and eat of the tree of life, they would never die but would live forever. Given the cursed conditions under which Adam and Eve must now exist, to live forever would have meant that they would be condemned to a life of unending misery. God wished to spare them such an awful fate; so in his mercy he expelled them from paradise and barred the way back. Without access to fruit from the tree of life, Adam and Eve and their progeny die, thus sparing them an unending life of misery. So banishment from paradise truly was God having pity upon his poor repentant creatures, Irenaeus argues (*AH* 3.21.6; 3.23.6). But they will be restored to life eventually, when the second Adam comes.

Satan, the Purveyor of Death

God showed no mercy to Satan, according to Irenaeus. Unlike Adam and Eve, Satan truly is cursed by being condemned to the eternal punishment "prepared for the devil and his angels" (*AH* 3.23.3, quoting Matt 25:41). Adam and Eve were naïve and inexperienced; they can be forgiven because they acted partially out of ignorance. By contrast, Satan was cunning and deceitful. With his superior intellect and moral faculties fully developed, he deliberately set out to foul up God's good creation—and especially the young and trusting first human couple. This struggle between God and Satan was not new. Satan was a creation of God, like Adam and Eve. But he was created with mature knowledge and knew full well what he was about when he rebelled against God. Irenaeus does not tell the reader any of the details about how or when Satan, that "apostate angel of God" (*AH* 5.21.3), revolted against God. Presumably, Irenaeus had in mind traditions circulating at the time from one or more of the Jewish pseudepigraphs about a primordial battle between God and the fallen angels, with Satan as their leader. In any case, this was a struggle between God and Satan for ultimate supremacy—except that Satan in his arrogance apparently did not realize the full power of the Almighty. The result was that Satan and his allies, the fallen angels, were cast down into hell, that place of "everlasting fire prepared for him . . . [and] all who abide without penitence in their apostacy" (*AH* 5.26.2).[6]

The battle for supremacy between God and Satan spilled over onto Adam (and Eve). Even though defeated, Satan attempted to continue the battle by stealing into paradise with the intention of subverting humankind, the jewel of God's good creation. Irenaeus says that Satan acted out of envy. Citing Ephesians 2:2 concerning "the ruler of the power of the air," Irenaeus posits that Satan, "envying man, became a rebel against the Divine Law" (*AH* 5.24.4). It was envy that led him to seduce humankind into disobeying God's command concerning the tree. Satan failed, however, to the extent that the image of God in Adam was not destroyed but only (partially) corrupted. Were the image of God to have been completely lost and Adam condemned to hell like Satan, Satan would have won.

> For if humankind, which was made by God that it might live,
> but which lost that life when it was injured by the serpent who

---

6. Quotations from Books 4 and 5 are from Irenaeus, *Five Books of S. Irenaeus*, trans. John Keble, slightly updated for readability.

corrupted it, would no longer return to life but would be altogether abandoned to death, God would be overcome and the
serpent's wickedness would thus prevail over God's will. (*AH*
3.23.1)

Indeed, God had foreseen what Satan would attempt, and planned from
the very beginning to thwart Satan's machinations. For that reason God's
plan involved the incarnation of the divine Word.

The Image of God Tarnished but Restored

When it is recorded in Gen 1:27 that "God created humankind in his
image, in the image of God he created him," God already was preparing
for the advent of the second Adam. The "image of God," Irenaeus affirms
(*AH* 5.16), refers first and foremost to the preexistent Word of God who
would become incarnate in Jesus the Christ, and only secondarily to the
creation of Adam. Christ is the authentic, true image of God. Adam was
but *an image of the Image,* so to speak. From the very beginning, all of humankind was already being "recapitulated" in Christ, the "second Adam,"
by divine design. God in his mercy determined that humankind should
not perish altogether but instead be saved in the coming second Adam,
a reality already adumbrated in the creation of the first Adam. Through
the incarnation, by the divine Word becoming "flesh," the second Adam
joined himself with humankind—that is, with Adam and all his descendants—with the purpose of reversing the effects of the first Adam's
disobedience. Because all humankind was "summed up" (contained) in
Christ, all humankind was thereby freed from sin and death even before
the first sin was committed. It was fitting that Adam be the first human
to be saved.

> Now since humanity is saved, it is proper that the man be saved
> who was created first. For it would be quite irrational to say that
> he who suffered severe injuries from the enemy, and first en-
> dured captivity, is not freed by him who overcame the enemy,
> though his children whom he begot in captivity were freed. The
> enemy would still not seem to be conquered, if the ancient spoils
> were still to remain in his power. (*AH* 3.23.2)

Even though death at first held sway over Adam and his descendants,
life has been restored through Christ. The enemy has been conquered,
Irenaeus insists, and therefore one may exult with Paul,

the last enemy to be destroyed is death,[7] which had first taken possession of humankind. Wherefore, when humanity has been freed, shall come to pass the saying that is written, "Death is swallowed up in victory. O death, where is your victory? O death, where is your sting?"[8] (AH 3.23.7)

But it is not just humankind that rejoices in God's victory over Satan. All creation was affected negatively by Adam's sin, so all creation is restored—recreated—in and through the second Adam. Such is the necessary extent of the "economy of salvation." God's victory over Satan is total, right from the very beginning, even if the full effect of this victory over evil will be fully manifested only at "the close of the age," the eschaton.

The corruption of the image of God in the first Adam took place at a tree (the tree of knowledge of good and evil). It was appropriate, therefore, that the image of God should be fully restored also at a tree (the cross):

For doing away with that disobedience of man which at first was wrought at the tree, He 'became obedient unto death, even the death of the cross,'[9] healing the disobedience which had been wrought at the tree, by obedience which was also at the tree." (AH 5.16.3)

From Eve to Mary

Mention of the junction of the tree with the cross allows Irenaeus conveniently to reintegrate Eve into the picture. Eve had been responsible for the disobedience that occurred at the tree in the garden. Eve's perversion was reversed, fortunately, by the obedience of a second virgin, Mary. Just as Irenaeus posits a (contrasting) correspondence between Adam and Christ, so he similarly points to a parallel contrast between Eve and Mary.

For as the former [i.e., Eve] was led astray by an [apostate] angel's discourse to flee from God after transgressing his word, so the latter [i.e., Mary] by an angel's [Gabriel's] discourse had the Gospel preached unto her, that she might bear God, obeying his word. And if the former disobeyed God, yet the other was

7. 1 Cor 15:26.
8. 1 Cor 15:54–55.
9. Phil 2:8.

persuaded to obey God, that the virgin Mary might become an
advocate for the virgin Eve. And as mankind was bound unto
death through a virgin, it is saved through a virgin; by the obedience of a virgin the disobedience of a virgin is compensated.
(AH 5.19.1)

But even here, Irenaeus is less interested in the first Eve than in her
New Testament counterpart, Mary. Just as Adam was of secondary importance to Christ, Eve similarly is of little importance, apart from her
serving as a foil for Mary, of whom the savior was born. For Irenaeus,
everything centers around the incarnation of the divine Word, who took
on flesh through the Virgin Mary whereby he united himself with humankind, thereby recapitulating all humanity and all things in himself in
order to accomplish the salvation of all things that had been corrupted by
Satan's machinations.

> She [Eve] was disobedient and became the cause of death for
> herself and for the entire human race. For this reason, the law
> calls her who is espoused to a man, though she is still a virgin,
> the wife of him who espoused her, pointing out thereby the
> return-circuit from Mary to Eve. For in no other way is that
> which is tied together loosed, except that the cords of the tying
> are untied in the reverse order, so that the first cords are loosed
> by [loosing] the second; in other words, the second cords release
> the first. And so it happens that the first cord is untied by the
> second cord, and the second cord serves as the first's untying ...
> the knot of Eve's disobedience was untied by Mary's obedience.
> For what the virgin Eve tied by her unbelief, this Mary untied by
> her belief. (AH 3.22.4)

Summing up Irenaeus

A fundamental tenant in Irenaeus's writings against the gnostic heretics
of the second century is the importance of the incarnation of the Word of
God for the salvation of humankind. Irenaeus's view of "the economy of
salvation" may be summed up thus:

1. The authentic image of God first and foremost is the preexisting
    Word (Logos).

2. God in his infinite wisdom knew beforehand that one of his crea-
    tures, the apostate angel Satan, would attempt to undo God's good

creation, and planned accordingly. Indeed, Irenaeus implies, God would not have allowed the creation of the world and humankind to go forward, had he not already put in motion a plan by which to rescue a tainted creation from the clutches of Satan. (This is a theme that will be reiterated in various forms by later traditioners of the Adam and Eve story, especially John Milton in his epic poem *Paradise Lost*.)

3. When God created humankind ("Adam"), God created him in the image of God, that is, in conformity with the Word of God who at some future time would take on the "flesh" of "Adam, thereby joining all humankind to himself.

4. Through this union, the incarnate Word becomes a second Adam—what the apostle Paul termed "the last Adam"—thereby "recapitulating" (or "summing up") the whole of human experience within his own person.

5. The last Adam by his obedience reverses the disobedience of Adam and his wife Eve, and at the same time undoes the curse on the earth, resulting in the recreation or restoration of all creation. Death lost its "sting" and eternal life was restored, beginning already with the first Adam.

6. The story of Adam and Eve is a story of a merciful God. Because Adam and Eve were young and naïve, their sin was not so grave that they lost God's friendship. Moreover, they immediately repented of their sin and did penance by donning fig-leaf girdles. God was pleased with their penitential acts and mitigated their pain by substituting skin clothes in place of irritating fig-leaf girdles. As a further act of mercy, God drove them out of paradise so that they would die and not live forever, thereby further mitigating their suffering.

7. As the virgin Eve was instrumental in bringing death to all humankind by her sin of disobedience, so the virgin Mary was instrumental in restoring everlasting life for that same humankind by her obedience that resulted in the birth of the second Adam who restores all.

Irenaeus's view of the "economy of salvation" may be viewed as a partial corrective to the doctrine of the apostle Paul. Paul seemed to see nothing good in Adam (or Eve); his (their) act of disobedience resulted in all of humankind (and their world) being trapped in sin and condemned to death, both physically and spiritually. Sin is so pervasive and dominant that humans, left on their own, are incapable of doing good. That is a view that Augustine of Hippo will take up and elaborate with his doctrine of "original sin." By contrast, Irenaeus posits that, despite the debilitating effects of sin, humans have always been capable of doing good and pleasing God—as did Adam and Eve even after their sin of disobedience. God was pleased with their acts of repentance and showed them great mercy. Irenaeus even credits the majority of humans as pleasing God through authentic contriteness. Yes, a minority like Cain—and Satan—do persist in willful rebellion against God; these are condemned to the "everlasting fires of hell." Most humans do experience the mercy of God, however, whether they live before or after Christ, because all are recapitulated or summed up in the saving incarnated Word.

Irenaeus's message is truly a positive one for all humankind, and one that deserves to be heard more frequently alongside the views of Augustine, to whom we now turn.

Augustine of Hippo

Saint Augustine, Bishop of Hippo, was born in the little town of Thagaste in North Africa (modern-day Algeria) in 354. His father, a pagan, was a minor Roman official. His mother Monica was a devout Christian. Monica's prayers for her husband's conversion were finally answered when, on his deathbed, he was baptized. Augustine himself, though enrolled in his youth as a catechumen in the Catholic religion of his mother, was not baptized until midway through his adult career—and then only after a nine-year flirtation with Manicheism.

Early on Augustine's parents recognized his exceptional abilities and at the age of eleven sent him some 20 miles away to the small town of Madaurus to receive a classical education in Latin literature—the surest path to success in the Roman world. At the age of seventeen, Augustine's father died. Nevertheless, with financial assistance from a family friend, Augustine transferred to the provincial capital city of Carthage to continue his education as a rhetorician. Later in life, Augustine wrote in his *Confessions* that during this period at Carthage he not only pursued his classical (pagan) education, but he also indulged in a decadent lifestyle that included numerous sexual liaisons. At an early age he had received encouragement for his sexual explorations from his father, who had never been completely faithful to Monica, though she bore through it all patiently. In Carthage Augustine met a young woman by whom he had a son, Adeodatus. Although he never married the mother of his son, this was far from a casual affair. Augustine stayed with her fifteen years, only ending the relationship with reluctance when his mother arranged for him to marry a ten-year old wealthy heiress. Because the legal age for marriage was twelve, Augustine had a two-year wait period. During this waiting period Augustine met Ambrose, bishop of Milan, himself an intellectual giant and powerful churchman. Listening to Ambrose preach, Augustine found answers to intellectual problems that had troubled him since youth, a result of the shallowness of his poorly trained Christian teachers back in north Africa. Ambrose baptized Augustine in Milan in the year 387. Following his conversion, Augustine decided to remain celibate. He broke off his engagement and never married. The following year Augustine decided to return to his home in Africa, together with his mother Monica and son Adeodatus. Monica became ill, however, and died on the way. By now Augustine had adopted a semi-monastic way of life. He sold most of his family inheritance at Thagaste and gave much of the money to the poor. Adeodatus died soon after, whereupon Augustine took up monastic life in earnest. Ordained a priest in 391, the classically trained rhetorician quickly became renowned for his compelling preaching. The local bishop of Hippo recognized Augustine's superior abilities and installed him as coadjutor bishop in 395 or 396. When that bishop died a year later, Augustine was installed as bishop of Hippo in his stead.

One may speak of not just one but two conversions in Augustine's life. For nine years earlier in his life and particularly during his years at Carthage, Augustine had turned away from the religion of his parents and became a Manichee, despite lingering doubts about certain tenets of that religion. His attraction to Manicheism was in part driven by a certain revulsion in his youth to the generally anti-intellectual cast of the clergy in the African church, rigidly adhering to an overly simplistic theology. God was presented in crudely anthropomorphic terms, e.g., understanding Genesis literally, that God sees and speaks like humans, and that God has a body that occupies space and time. Augustine's exposure to the classical philosophical tradition had transformed him into a sophisticated thinker. The fact that the African church seemed wedded to the ineptly translated Old Latin Bible was yet another turn-off for the budding literary scholar. By contrast, Manicheism offered the young Augustine a more intellectual alternative. They correctly taught that God does not have a human-like body, emphasizing instead the non-materiality of

God. Mani's dualistic explanation for the presence of evil in the world—namely, that this world originated from two equal principles, one good and the other evil, eternally at war with one another—was not entirely convincing to the young Augustine, however. When he went to Milan and heard Ambrose preach, Augustine discovered to his relief that the Catholic church was not wedded to those simplistic anthropomorphic views of God that he had learned as a youth. Following his (re)conversion to Catholicism at the hands of Ambrose in Milan—and especially later as bishop of Hippo—Augustine dedicated the remainder of his life to vigorously refuting the errors of the Manichees, as well as those of the Pelagians and other sects he regarded as heretical.

Augustine was a prolific writer and penned a number of works that are considered classics still to this day. Among his best-known works are *Confessions* and *The City of God*. Our interest is not with Augustinian thought as a whole, however, but only with Augustine's views concerning Adam and Eve and the consequences of their actions for the whole of humankind that came after them.

Augustine on Adam and Eve

Augustine was preoccupied for much of his Christian career with the meaning and the implications of the creation story in Genesis 1–3. It was a topic that he attempted to expound at least five times.[10] His two earliest attempts were written shortly after his conversion, for the purpose of refuting the Manichean heresy of which Augustine himself had previously been associated as an "auditor" (as opposed to one of the "elect," as full Manichee adherents were known).[11] When a literal interpretation of a scriptural passage yielded unsatisfactory meaning, Augustine would resort to figurative interpretations. Nevertheless, he abandoned both of these early attempts at explaining Genesis 1–3, due to the difficulty of the task. Initially, he had intended to destroy both manuscripts. But upon reviewing them shortly before his death he decided, with considerable

10. See the introduction by Roland J. Teske in Augustine, *On Genesis Against the Manichees; and, On the Literal Interpretation of Genesis: An Unfinished Book*, 3.

11. The first work was written in 388 or 389 and published with the title *De Genesi contra Manichaes (On Genesis against the Manichees)*. The second was written approximately three years later, and eventually published under the title *De Genesi ad litteram inperfectus liber (The Literal Interpretation of Genesis: An Unfinished Book)*. Both works are available in the English translation of Roland J. Teske; see preceding n. 10.

hesitation, to publish them as "unfinished," thinking they might have some value for others. As if driven by compulsion, Augustine returned to the story of the disobedient Adam and Eve in Eden again and again. A third attempt at exposing the tragic consequences of the "original sin" for all of humankind is found in *The Confessions,* where in Books 12 and 13 Augustine attempted both allegorical and literal interpretations of the first chapter of Genesis. Fourthly, his longest and most systematic attempt to unlock the elusive first three chapters of Genesis is a monumental volume begun in 401, entitled *The Literal Meaning of Genesis: A Commentary in Twelve Books.*[12] Lastly, Augustine returned once more to expound the meaning and significance of the opening chapters of Genesis in books XI–XIV of *The City of God,* written in 417/8.[13]

A complete accounting of Augustine's views about creation in general or even about Adam and Eve would take us far afield of our goals for this volume and would likely also be beyond the interests of many readers. We will therefore be selective in our treatment.

Is Genesis 1–3 a Single, Unified Narrative?

Like nearly every reader before the modern period and the advent of critical scientific exegesis (interpretation), Augustine understood Genesis 1–3 to be the work of a single author, traditionally Moses, who was guided and enlightened by God as he wrote out the whole Pentateuch, the "five books of Moses." Being the word of God and not mere words composed by human ingenuity, there could be no question that the account of creation recorded in Genesis 1–3 had to be accepted as accurate and completely true. According to Augustine, even when the text contains things that appear to be inconsistent, there can be no contradiction. To the human mind, finite in knowledge and fallible in understanding, biblical narratives may appear incompatible. But when understood as God intends them, they are entirely consistent. Our task is to probe for the meaning God intends.

12. *De Genesi ad litteram libri duodecim* (abbrev. *DGnL*). For a translation, see Augustine, *The Literal Meaning of Genesis,* translated and annotated by John Hammond Taylor.

13. For a very accessible translation by Gerald G. Walsh, see Augustine, *The City of God.*

> In matters that are obscure and far beyond our vision, even in such as we may find treated in Holy Scripture, different interpretations are possible without prejudice to the faith we have received. In such a case, we should not rush in headlong and so firmly take our stand on one side, that, if further progress in the search of truth justly undermines this position, we too fall with it. That would be to battle not for the teaching of Holy Scripture but for our own, wishing its teaching to conform to ours, whereas we ought to wish ours to conform to that of Sacred Scripture. (*DGnL* 1.18.17)

Much like modern biblical scholars, Augustine struggled to explain discrepancies between Genesis 1:1—2:3 and Genesis 2:4—3:24. But unlike modern biblical scholars, Augustine does not attribute such discrepancies as due to different authors but to a different purpose at work in each text. It is the same author describing the same event but from two different perspectives. To undergird his explanation, Augustine reaches back to his pagan classical education in philosophy, to Aristotelian categories of "potency" and "act," or cause and effect. Genesis 1 describes God creating the heavens and earth and all things in their potencies, that is, in their invisible, spiritual forms. Genesis 2–3, by contrast, describes how God created these same things in their visible, material forms—the actual forms we encounter in our world of experience. The two are very different and not to be confused. The first creation account concerns how God conceived them all at once in the wisdom of his mind. Regarding the creation of humankind, for example,

> one will ask how they were created originally on the sixth day. I shall reply: Invisibly, potentially, in their causes, as things that will be in the future are made, yet not made in actuality now. (*DGnL* 6.6.10)

The second creation account describes the how God formed the first humans in time and space in their actual historical forms, such as humans may perceive:

> ... what [God] has originally established ... in causes, He later fulfilled in effects. Thus *God formed the dust of the earth* (or *the slime of the earth) into man*; that is, He formed man from the dust or slime of the earth. And *He breathed (or blew) into his face the breath of life; and man was made a living being*. . . At that time he was [not] made in causes . . . for that happened with the commencement of the ages in the primordial reasons when all

things were created simultaneously. But he was created in time, visibly in the body, invisibly in the soul, being made up of soul and body. (*DGnL* 6.11.19)

These two creation accounts should not be confused, as if one were true but not the other, or one more accurate than the other. Both are simultaneously true and accurate, each according to its own purpose.

The key for understanding how Augustine arrived at his solution to reconciling the two accounts of creation may be found in Augustine's Old Latin Bible. The Latin translation at Genesis 2:3 is misleading in stating that on the seventh day God rested from "all the works *that he had begun to make*" (*quae inchoavit Deus facere*). Augustine did not know Hebrew at all, and his Greek was minimal, having begun to study that language only late in life. Although the Hebrew text is a bit difficult to translate, the meaning in English is approximately: "God rested (or *ceased*) *from all the work that he had done in creating.*" The Hebrew of Genesis 2:1–3 clearly states that at the conclusion of Day 6, the whole of creation had been completed; everything was finished. By contrast, the Old Latin translation could be understood to imply that creation at the conclusion of Day 6 was *inchoate*, that it was still ongoing. This suggested to Augustine that the differences between the two creation accounts should be explained as the difference between potency and act, or cause and effect.

Were Adam and Eve Ceated at the Same Time?

Genesis 2:15–23 narrates that after Yahweh God formed "the Human" from the clay and had placed him in the garden to till it and care for it, the deity determined that the Human needed a partner. Resorting to the same technique he used to create the Human, Yahweh God molded additional figures out of clay—the various animals. When none proved satisfactory, the deity decided upon a new stratagem. He placed the Human in a stupor and extracted one of his ribs—so the Old Latin text—and closed up the cavity with flesh. Augustine understands this as historical fact and, moreover, that thereafter "Adam" had one less rib than previously. Augustine has no answer to his own question, "Why was not another rib made to replace it?" (*DGnL* 9.13.23). except to note that God "built" the rib into a woman, much like one builds a house. The formerly solitary "Adam" was thus refashioned into male and female. This passage patently claims that the woman Eve was created only secondarily, sometime later than "Adam." [14]

Augustine recognized that there was an *apparent* discrepancy between this account that Eve was created subsequent to Adam and the prior account in Genesis 1:26–29 that the male and the female humans were created at the same time. But his conviction that both accounts had been authored by Moses at the command of God prevented Augustine from positing any true conflict between the two narratives. Any discrepancies were apparent only—and due to our limited human capacity to comprehend the full meaning intended by their divine author. One by one Augustine dismisses explanations proposed by other commentators, before proposing his own aforementioned explanation, namely that the first account describes God's creation of all things in "potency" (in their invisible, spiritual forms), while the second account describes how God created these same things in "act" (in their visible, material forms). Within the historical framework of time and space, God did form Adam first and then Eve only later, but in the mind of God both were conceived simultaneously and as equals. Recognizing that his own explanation may not be entirely adequate, Augustine invites others to proffer a better explanation, if possible.

An interesting side note here is Augustine's subsequent "discovery" that Genesis 1 records both that the Triune God was at work in creation and that humankind was created in the image of the Triune God.

> By the name of "God," who made these things, I now understood the Father, and by the name of "Beginning" the Son, in whom he made them. And believing my God to be the Trinity, as I did believe, I searched into his holy words, and behold, your "Spirit was borne above the water." Behold, the Trinity, my God, Father, and Son, and Holy Spirit, creator of all creation! (*Confessions* 13.5.6)

Augustine's discovery that "Beginning" is another name for the Son seems inspired by the words in the prologue of the fourth gospel

---

14. Although some of Augustine's contemporaries speculated whether Adam originally might have been androgynous, Augustine explicitly rejected this idea (*DGnL* 3.22.34). Note, however, that in *Confessions* 13.20.28 Augustine says that the whole of the human species was contained in Adam's *uterus* ("womb"), sparking speculation as to whether Augustine at one point might have thought of Adam as originally bi-sexual, an androgyne. In his introduction to Augustine, *Confessions*, 421 n. 8, John K. Ryan calls attention to an analogous idea in Plato's *Symposium*.

concerning the divine Word: "He was *in the beginning* with God. All things came into being through him, and without him not one thing came into being" (John 1:2–3). The creative presence of the Holy Spirit at creation was not a novel idea with Augustine, however, as it had been taught by previous church fathers. But it was a doctrinal concept easily "verified" by Augustine from the Old Latin translation he used, "And the *Spirit of God* was stirring above the waters." Augustine says he prefers another translation which renders this text as "he was brooding over." "Brooding over" not only better captures the attentive, loving care exercised at creation, it also corresponds to the New Testament image of "Divine Wisdom himself, taking our weak nature . . . come to gather the children of Jerusalem under his wings, as a hen gathers her young," that we may not remain children but become mature adults.[15]

A corollary of this concerns the very nature of humankind. According to Augustine, when *God* says, "Let *us* make humankind in *our* image, in the likeness of *God*," we are hearing the Triune God (Father, Son, and Spirit) speaking. It follows, therefore, that humans are created in the image and likeness of the Triune God.

Were Adam and Eve Created as Equals?

Early Christian writers were heavily influenced by 1 Timothy 2:11–15, which letter was universally believed to have been written by Paul (rather than by a disciple writing sometime after Paul's death, as many biblical scholars today think). This passage commands that women should have no authority within the church and should remain entirely silent, all because of Eve's sin: "I permit no woman to teach or to have authority over a man; she is to keep silent. For Adam was formed first, then Eve; and Adam was not deceived, but the woman was deceived and became a transgressor." While recognizing the authority of this Scripture and others like it in the New Testament that call for women to be submissive to their husbands and to males in general, Augustine mitigated the universal scope of such Scriptures by appeal to the words of Paul in Galatians 3:27–28: "As many of you as were baptized into Christ have clothed yourselves with Christ. There is no longer Jew or Greek, there is no longer male and female; for all of you are one in Christ Jesus." Christian baptism restores the original

15. *DGnL* 1.18.36. See the discussion of Augustine's choice of *fovebat* over *superferebatur* by John H. Taylor, in Augustine, *Literal Meaning*, 1:229 n61).

equality of male and female lost by sin (*DGnL* 11.41.58). Even so, Augustine continues, equal in dignity does not mean that men and women should act equally in their social interactions. Despite the statement in Genesis 1:26–27 that male and female were both created in the image of God, Augustine maintains that from the very beginning God intended that women should defer to their husbands and be instructed by them. This is clear from the fact that in the temporal order God created the man first, and only afterwards, the woman. This natural order is evident also in the fact that God gave the command not to eat to Adam before the creation of Eve, who was expected to learn it from her husband. This principle that a woman should defer to her husband also underlies God's reprimand of Adam for having "listened to the voice of your wife" (Gen 3:17). It should have been the other way around!

This natural, hierarchical subordination of a wife to her husband was not to be onerous or burdensome in any way, however. Rather, it was to be act of loving service, Augustine insists. He had in mind Ephesians 5:22–33, where the relationship of a subservient church to a loving Christ as its head is presented as the model for husbands and wives: "Husbands, love your wives, just as Christ loved the church and gave himself up for her." But the reciprocal is equally true: "Wives, be subject to your husbands as you are to the Lord." The disaster of Eve's sin was that the loving hierarchical relationship that should have existed between Eve and Adam immediately degenerated into a kind of slavery. For as it says in Gen 3:16, despite an increased desire—which Augustine understood as "concupiscence," or sinful lust—in Eve for her husband, "he shall rule over you" (Gen 3:16). Even though for Christians that original egalitarian relationship between male and female has been restored in Christ, a definite hierarchical order nevertheless persists, at least as regards husbands and wives.

In the temporal and spatial order of creation, according to Augustine's understanding of the second creation account, God created Eve to be a "helper" ('*ezer*). In the Bible a "helper" need not be an inferior. It could refer to a superior "helping" an inferior, as was the case when God *helped* Samuel and the Israelites defeat the Philistines near Mizpah, whereupon "Samuel took a stone and set it up between Mizpah and Jeshanah; he called its name Eben-'ezer ["Stone-of-*help*"], explaining, "Thus far has the Lord *helped* us" (1 Samuel 7:12). But in Eve's case, she was definitely not Adam's superior, nor even his equal. According to Augustine, God created Eve to assist Adam in fulfilling the divine command to multiple and fill the earth (Gen 1:28).

> If one should ask why it was necessary that a helper be made for man, the answer that seems most probable is that it was for the procreation of children, just as the earth is a helper for the seed in the production of a plant from the union of the two. (*DGnL* 9.3.5)

Was Eve More Guilty Than Adam?

Both in Jewish and Christian antiquity one finds writings in which Eve is depicted as more guilty than Adam for the sin that resulted in their being expelled from paradise. The biblical narrative of Genesis 3 depicts Eve as the one whom the serpent engages with his seductive words and as the first to eat of the forbidden fruit. The presumption of Eve' dominant role in this crime is further stoked by the fact that, when Yahweh God questions Adam about why he had disobeyed, Adam points the finger at Eve as the real culprit. That passage has sparked a firestorm of recriminations against Eve over the centuries.

As noted previously in chapter 6, according to the Greek version of the Jewish pseudepigraph Life and Adam and Eve, Adam was not even present when the serpent beguiled Eve. According to that text, Yahweh God had divided the garden in two, entrusting a half to each of the primal couple for their care. Adam and Eve were separated and on opposite sides of the garden when the serpent approached Eve and seduced her. Moreover, the serpent feigned disinterest in letting her sample the fruit, unless she promised to give some also to her husband. In that telling of the story, Adam appears more an innocent victim, while Eve is singled out as the principal culprit.

The trope about Eve being the one primarily responsible for the sin of humankind eventually found its way into late biblical tradition as well. The deuterocanonical book of Sirach (25:24) seems to reference Eve when it says, "From a woman sin had its beginning, and because of her we all die." While Sirach may be ambiguous, there can be no doubt whatsoever about Eve's guilt according to the author of 1 Timothy who, writing sometime after Paul, exonerates Adam entirely, while laying responsibility for the sin squarely upon Eve: "Adam was not deceived, but the woman was deceived and transgressed" (1 Tim 2:14).

As damning as these texts may appear, perhaps no person is more responsible than St. Jerome for damaging Eve's reputation within Western Christian imagination. When (ca. 400) Jerome translated Genesis from the Hebrew into Latin for his new Vulgate Bible, he left out one word. Jerome's Vulgate translation of Genesis 3:6 reads, "The woman saw that the tree was good to eat, and beautiful to the eyes and delightful to behold; and she took of its fruit and ate, and *she gave to her husband who ate.*" Jerome left out of that last clause "she gave to her husband" the all-important Hebrew word *'itto,* "(who was) *with her.*" Since the word (*secum* "with her") was present in the prior Old Latin version that Jerome was here revising, it appears that he made a conscious decision to leave this word out in his new Vulgate translation. Perhaps Jerome thought it was unimportant. Or, more likely, he was influenced by texts like Life of Adam and Eve and assumed that Adam was not actually "with her" at the immediate time the serpent was speaking to Eve, so including the word would give a false impression. Whatever the case, the omission of "with her" in the Vulgate translation has had profound repercussions. The Vulgate was quickly adopted by the Roman Catholic Church as its official Bible. Moreover, as the vernacular movement gained momentum, the effect of Jerome's omission was compounded with the publication of the Douay-Rheims Bible in 1582. Because the Douay-Rheims Bible was translated into English directly from the Latin Vulgate, it too omitted the phrase "with her," thereby perpetuating Jerome's mistake. Although contemporary Protestant vernacular translations were being made directly for the original Hebrew and Greek texts—and in the process were quietly restoring the missing phrase—the damage had been done.[16] Many generations of Christians have come and gone without the slightest notion that according to the plain meaning of the original Hebrew text, Adam was right there beside Eve in the garden observing and listening to the exchange between Eve and the serpent. Adam could have intervened, had he wished, but did nothing to stop his wife. The implication of the Hebrew text is that both the man and the woman were equally complicit, as indeed the following verse makes clear: "Then the eyes of both were opened, and they realized that they were naked."

16. In Martin Luther's German translation of Gen 3:6 (*sie nahm von der Frucht und aß und gab ihrem Mann auch davon, und er aß*), the key phrase "with her" was omitted. It is also lacking in some modern translations: *Revised English Bible* (1970) and *Good New Bible* (1976).

One should be thankful that Augustine relied on the Old Latin version, which does include the phrase "with her," rather than on Jerome's newly translated Vulgate. Augustine's treatment of Eve—and women in general—is bad enough, without additional ammunition from Jerome.

Original Sin

Without a doubt, Augustine's most important "contribution" to the evolving Adam and Eve tradition was his formulation of a doctrine of "original sin." We have seen how the apostle Paul set forth the idea of Christ Jesus as a new or second Adam, as a way of explaining both the importance and the necessity of Christ as universal savior. Arguing backward from the necessity of Christ as universal savior, Paul concluded that all humankind is enslaved to Sin because of the sin of the first Adam; and likewise because of Adam's sin, all die. Adam's sin had universal consequences; no one escapes its effects. Following Adam, all humans are born slaves to Sin; they cannot escape its grasp, save through the liberating power of Christ, the second Adam.

Despite Paul's "universal" assessment of the condition of humanity before the advent of Christ, few Christians in the first four centuries understood Paul to say that humans on their own can do *absolutely nothing* pleasing to God. We have seen, for example, how Irenaeus believed that the sin of Adam and Eve was not so serious, and moreover, that God readily had mercy on them. God forgave their descendants also when these sinned. According to Irenaeus most persons prior to Christ were indeed saved, having been "recapitulated" in the incarnate Christ right from the beginning; the sin of Adam and Eve was not such a big deal for humankind, given that God's mercy has always been present. With Augustine, however, matters took on a much more pessimistic cast.

Augustine in no way diminishes the sin of our first parents. In contrast to Irenaeus, Augustine says that Adam had been endowed with *superior* knowledge and a will completely under the control of reason, with the result that he was totally free of the concupiscence (lustful passions) that afflicts us, his descendants. Adam did not sin because he did not fully comprehend the enormity of his offense against God. Rather, Adam's sin was like that of Solomon; he preferred to offend God rather than displease the woman he loved.

It is not to be thought that Solomon was deceived into believing in the worship of idols, but was merely won over to this sacrifice by feminine flattery. So, too, we must believe that Adam transgressed the law of God, not because he was deceived into believing that [Lucifer's] lie was true, but because in obedience to a social compulsion he yielded to Eve, as husband to wife, as the only man in the world to the only woman. It was not without reason that the Apostle wrote: "Adam was not deceived but the woman was deceived." He means, no doubt, that Eve accepted the serpent's word as true, whereas Adam refused to be separated from his partner even in a union of sin—not, of course, that he was, on that account, any less guilty, since he sinned knowingly and deliberately. (*City* 14.11)

The situation was quite different with Eve. Lucifer deliberately targeted the woman as

the weaker part of that human society, hoping gradually to gain the whole. He assumed that a man is less gullible and can be more easily tricked into following a bad example than into making a mistake himself . . . To summarize briefly: though not equally deceived by believing the serpent, [Adam and Eve] equally sinned and were caught and ensnared by the Devil. (*City* 14.11)

Augustine continues, one cannot fully comprehend how our first parents could have slipped so easily in such a venial matter as eating a bit of food, unless one factors in *pride*, "for 'pride is the beginning of all sin.'"[17] Rather, they "must already have fallen before . . . eating the forbidden fruit." Pride is what made them so susceptible to the devil's seductive words, "You shall be as gods," had they not already begun to seek pleasure in themselves (*City* 14.13). Moreover, they did not repent. They did not deny their sin (as did Cain), but neither did their pride let them repent. Instead each blamed someone else. Adam blamed Eve, and Eve blamed the serpent. Blame was in no way lessened simply because "the woman believed the suggestion of the serpent, and the man obeyed the woman who gave him the fruit" (*City* 14.14).

In the matter of repentance and God's pardon, Augustine stands in sharp contrast to the majority of both his predecessors and his contemporaries. We have already noted how Irenaeus, for example, had said that God readily forgave Adam and Eve because they immediately repented

17. Sir 10:15, quoting from the Old Latin translation (English 10:13).

of their youthful indiscretion in sinning. Likewise, Ambrose, Augustine's own mentor, understood Eve to have quickly repented of her sin. When confronted by God,

> the woman said, "The serpent deceived me and I ate." That fault is pardonable which is followed by an admission of guilt. The woman, therefore, is not to be despaired of, who did not keep silent before God, but who preferred to admit her sin—the woman on whom was passed a sentence that was salutary . . . she admitted her sin and was considered worthy of pardon.
>
> Because Eve has admitted her crime, she is given a milder and more salutary sentence, which condemned her wrong-doing and did not refuse pardon. She was to serve under her husband's power, first, that she might not be inclined to do wrong, and secondly, that she might not dishonor her husband, but on the contrary, might be governed by his counsel. I see clearly here the mystery of Christ and his Church.[18]

Ambrose said that Adam, too, was pardoned by God for an even lesser sin, having been enticed by Eve who in turn had been duped by the serpent. For God

> knew that the serpent found numerous ways to deceive people. "Satan disguises himself as an angel of light" and "his ministers as ministers of justice,"[19] imposing false names on individual things, so as to call "rashness" a virtue and avarice "industry." The serpent, in fact, deceived the woman and the woman led the man away from truth to a violation of duty.[20]

Ultimately, only the serpent was cursed. The humans, Ambrose says, being less culpable, were pardoned.

In contrast to Ambrose, Augustine opined that the consequences of that first sin cannot be overstated. It had repercussions that extend to every single descendant of Adam. And I say *Adam* quite advisedly. For had Adam not sinned, all following humankind would not have been affected. If only Eve had sinned, she alone would have suffered punishment, but her descendants would have been exempt from any punishments imposed upon her.

18. Ambrose, "Paradise," 14.71–72, in Ambrose, *Hexameron, Paradise, and Cain and Abel,* 349–50.

19. Deut 6:13; Luke 4:8.

20. Ambrose, "Paradise," 15.73 (p. 351).

This reasoning is rooted in ancient conceptions of anthropology. Up until the advent of the modern scientific period it was widely believed that in the generation of new human life, the male semen by itself contains the entire essence of what will develop into the new human person, not only with regard to the physical body but also for the spiritual soul. The woman (mother) served merely as a kind of nursery for male semen. A male would implant his "seed" into the woman, who then, much like soil for plant seeds, would provide nourishment and protective environment in which the sprouting seed can develop into a new individual. The seedbed may affect whether the new plant grows up healthy or not, but in no way is the seedbed determinative of the type of plant generated. Augustine assumed that the same is true in human generation. All characteristics of each new human are predetermined solely by the male's semen.

Perhaps relevant here is the fact that—whether by design or merely by an ill choice of words is not entirely clear—on one occasion Augustine even spoke of Adam as having contained within his *uterus* (womb) the whole of the human species (*Confessions* 13.20.28). In any case, when Adam sinned, all humankind, his descendants, sinned *in* him.

On this point, Augustine believed himself to be following the teaching of the apostle Paul. Augustine's comprehension of Greek was rudimentary, so his knowledge of Paul's doctrine was only as good as the Latin translations he utilized—the Vetus Latina and the Vulgate being in agreement here. Augustine read Romans 5:12–13 to imply that Adam's sin is hereditary: "Through one man sin came into this world, and through sin death, and so death spread to all men, in whom all sinned (*in quo omnes peccaverunt*)." Like most Latin readers, Augustine understood *in quo* ("in whom") to refer back to the "one man" (Adam).[21] Unfortunately, this was not Paul's meaning. Modern scholars point out that *in quo* ("in whom") is almost certainly not a correct rendering of the original Greek phrase *eph' hō*, not least of all because the phrase is separated from "one man" by a great distance in the Greek text. A more accurate English translation would be: "with the result that" or "because."[22] The NAB rendering "*inasmuch as* all sinned" captures approximately Paul's meaning, eliminating any reference to all having sinned *in Adam* or to hereditary sin of any kind.

21. Augustine, *Literal Meaning of Genesis*, 1:263 n. 33.
22. See Fitzmyer, *Romans*, 408–17.

Augustine's faulty interpretation of Paul's meaning was based not just in his reliance on a faulty Latin translation, however. It stems also from ancient misconceptions of how the semen of males and the ova of females interact within human conception. As already noted, Augustine was certain that all humankind was contained in essence within Adam's semen. Each new generation replicates and passes on the entirety of Adam's essence to the next generation. It was thus relatively easy for Augustine to conclude that all humankind was present virtually within Adam when he sinned and therefore that all humankind is "contaminated by" (afflicted with) his sin and suffers its consequences.

Augustine believed his theory of the hereditary transmission of original sin was supported by the Scriptures as a whole. "Not in vain . . . does Scripture say that even an infant is not free from sin if he has spent one day of life on earth. The Psalmist[23] says, 'In iniquity I was conceived, and in sin my mother nourished me in her womb'" (DGnL 6.9.15). This cannot mean that the unborn are guilty of personal sin, since they cannot have sinned while still in their mother's womb. Rather, it must mean that they have inherited sin from their parent(s), and even more specifically, from their first parent (Adam). In short, it is a matter of the *original sin*, which continues to have universal consequences for both the physical body (pain, sickness, death) and for the soul (spiritual death) of every human.

If only the body were affected and not the soul, why does the church baptize infants? "There can be only one explanation, namely each child is Adam in body and soul, and therefore the grace of Christ is necessary for him. At that age the infant in his own person has done no good or evil, and thus his soul is perfectly innocent if it has not descended from Adam" (DGnL 10.11.19). Baptism is necessary precisely because every person is born with sin inherited from Adam.

Note again that Augustine speaks only of Adam passing on sin. Eve is ignored because the woman contributes nothing essential to the genetic and spiritual makeup of a child. Her sin does not contribute one way or the other to "original sin" as defined by Augustine and his followers. This distinction also provided an explanation for why Jesus is the sole *sinless* exception among those "born of woman." Jesus was not conceived from human sperm but by the Holy Spirit's overshadowing the virgin Mary.[24]

23. Ps 50:7.

24. Someone may ask, What about the Virgin Mary? Didn't Augustine talk about Mary being conceived without original sin? The Roman Catholic doctrine of the

Jesus's only *human* parent was a woman who did "not know man" (Luke 1:34). By divine foresight and design, therefore, Jesus was kept free from any taint of "original sin" inherited from Adam.

But what would have been the lot of Adam and Eve, had they not sinned? Augustine concisely laid out his vision in *The City of God* (14.15). For one thing, they would have continued to enjoy life in paradise surrounded by every blessing and every treat imaginable. They would not have died, as they would have had continual access to the tree of life from which they would have eaten regularly while in the garden. The tree of life was never intended to be the source of eternal life, however. Adam and Eve, along with their descendants, were destined to become spiritual beings. At some point, after a period of testing in which humans demonstrated fidelity to God through observance of his command not to eat the fruit of that single tree, God would have transformed their bodies, together with their souls, into immortal beings, much like the angels. In that ultimate condition they would have enjoyed perfect happiness, "a happiness which would have excluded even the possibility of sin or of death" (*City* 14.10).

Our first parents' lack of obedience is even more lamentable, Augustine says, because the prohibition imposed upon them was so easy to respect. God had created them in his own image, set them above all the animals, placed them in paradise with an abundance of goods and well-being. God had not burdened them with many heavy and hard precepts, but with a single, momentary, and utterly easy precept meant merely as a medicine to make their obedience strong and to serve as a reminder that it is good for them as creatures to serve God, their master, freely.

Unfortunately, all humankind must now suffer the consequences of our first parents' lack of obedience. Instead of acquiring spiritual bodies, humans are burdened with fleshy bodies that both die and are rebellious against their higher rational faculties (reason and will). No one is able to do what he or she desires to do. Neither the body nor the spirit obeys the

---

immaculate conception of Mary was unknown to Augustine, having developed only after his time. That Mary, in view of her future role as the mother of the divine savior, was herself, by divine privilege, preserved free from original sin, was infallibly defined as Roman Catholic doctrine by Pius IX only in 1854. Since Late Antiquity, however, the question of whether Mary was born without sin had been much debated. During the Middle Ages, for example, two of the most prominent Catholic theologians took opposite sides, with the Dominican Thomas Aquinas arguing against an immaculate conception and the Franciscan John Duns Scotus arguing for. The Council of Trent (1545–1563), out of deference to Aquinas, declined to take a position.

will. Old age, aches and pains, death, and other ills would not be, if only our nature, in whole and in its parts, would obey our will.

Nowhere is this more evident than in the way humankind is afflicted by *concupiscence,* as Augustine explains in *The City of God.* Concupiscence is a name for desire, especially lustful desire or passion that cannot be controlled by reason and will. "Lust is a word applicable in any kind of appetite, as in the classical definition of anger as a lust for revenge." But there are other forms of lust. "Lust for money is avarice, lust to win at any price is obstinacy, lust for bragging is vanity," and so on (14.15). Sexual lust, commonly called *libido,* is the most terrible kind of lust. It "does not merely invade the whole body and outward members, it takes such complete and passionate possession of the whole man, both physically and emotionally, that what results is the keenest of all pleasures on the level of sensation; and, at the crisis of excitement, it practically paralyzes all power of deliberate thought." Lust is problematic even for a married person desirous of adhering to the apostolic ideal to "learn how to possess his vessel in holiness and honor, not in the passion of lust like the Gentiles who do not know God" (1 Thes 4:5). Such a person "would prefer, if this were possible, to beget his children without suffering this passion. He could wish that, just as all his other members obey his reason in the performance of their appointed tasks, so the organs of parenthood, too, might function in obedience to the order of will and not be excited by the ardors of lust" (14.16).

According to Augustine, concupiscence, like disease, is always evil. One must fight to restrain spontaneous sexual arousal in any form. For that reason, celibacy is the higher good. Augustine laid all this out very clearly in a spirited and vicious denunciation of his fellow bishop, Julian of Eclanum, about whom we will have more to say momentarily. Julian, an advocate of natural goodness, had argued that God intentionally blessed marriage with passion between spouses as something good. Augustine responded that, yes, marriage is good—or should one say, "permissible"—because "it unites the two sexes for the purpose of begetting offspring," on the condition that the partners remain completely faithful to each other and do not separate (divorce). Especially "in the early days of the human race . . . the saints had an obligation to use the good of marriage" (marital sex) to carry out the divine command to populate the earth. The Old Testament period was a time of *multiplying,* and thus virginity was not recommended. But that period is past, Augustine says. The New Testament proclaims the arrival of a new period: a time to practice abstention as much as possible—even counselling virginity for those called to such a state.[25] In the current age even marital sex is "venial" (slightly sinful), which is why it should be accomplished without passion (concupiscence)—or, better, abstain completely.

Not possible? Augustine said that passionless marital sex could and would have existed in paradise,

> if no one had sinned. After sin, however, and not happily but from necessity, a combat came to marriage, so that marriage . . . must now war against the evil of concupiscence, . . . [which] never ceases to urge marriage to the unlawful, even when marriage makes good use of the evil of concupiscence in the propagation of offspring. (*Against Julian* 3.16)[26]

Undoubtedly Augustine's negative evaluation of human sexuality as being inextricably linked with concupiscence—and the root cause of humankind's moral degeneracy—was in part grounded in Augustine's own personal experiences. First, there was the example of his father who had never been faithful to his mother Monica. Second, there was the youthful Augustine's own trysts with various lovers, and especially his fifteen-year co-habitation with his final lover, the mother of his son Adeodatus. As previously noted, Augustine ended that relationship reluctantly, when his mother Monica arranged for him to marry the ten-year-old wealthy heiress—a marriage that was never finalized. The choice between indulging his libido and embracing celibacy was overwhelming for Augustine, almost to the point of a mental breakdown. Years later he described the intense interior struggle he had experienced, in tears and dread, trying to break free "from the fetters of desire for concubinage, by which I was held most tightly, and from the slavery of worldly concerns," while at the same time strongly attracted to a life of liberating celibacy (*Confessions* 8.6.13). He was thus of two minds and two wills.

> As . . . I deliberated upon serving the Lord my God, as I had long planned to do, it was I myself who willed it and I myself who did not will it. It was I myself. I neither willed it completely, nor did I refrain completely from willing it . . . I was at war within myself, and I was laid waste by myself. This devastation was made against my will, indeed, and yet it revealed not the nature of a

25. *De bono coniugali* 9.9; see comment by Taylor in Augustine, *Literal Meaning,* 2:268 n33.

26. Augustine, *Against Julian,* 133–34.

> different mind within me, but rather the punishment of my own
> nature. Therefore, it is no more I that did it, but sin that dwells
> in me, sin that issues from punishment of a more voluntary sin,
> for I was Adam's son. (*Confessions* 8.10.22)

Augustine acknowledges his own sin but traces it back ultimately to the original sin of Adam, who was guilty of "a more voluntary sin" because Adam's will power had not been diminished by concupiscence, as was Augustine's. From Augustine's own personal struggles to overcome his *attraction* to the things of this world—what he calls "the city of man"—he concluded that concupiscence is the root cause of human sin and misery. It should occasion no surprise, therefore, that human sexuality received such negative evaluations within Augustine's writings.

According to Augustine, Adam and Eve did not experience concupiscence (lustful passions) prior to their sin. So what is the good of sex? Augustine says that our first parents did not engage in sex while in the garden, not because sex per se was forbidden or even unlawful. Rather, when the proper time for them to fulfill the divine command to "be fruitful and multiply" should come, they would have had intercourse, but without any taint of concupiscence—and for the sole purpose of conceiving. Their bodies would have been fully under the control of their wills and reason. Eve's conception would have been accomplished without lustful passions on the part of either, as also would have been the case with their descendants (*City* 14.10). A little further on Augustine acknowledges that these are merely his own hypotheses but insists that a better explanation has yet to be proffered (*City* 14.26).[27]

God was not unprepared for the way things turned out with our first parents. Augustine reminds his readers, "God foresaw all things, and hence that man would sin." By the same token, "God could foresee two future realities; how bad man whom God had created good was to become, and how much good God was to make come out of this very evil" (*City* 14.11). Augustine seems to be saying here much the same thing that Milton expressed in his epic poem *Paradise Lost* more than a millennium later, namely, that God would not have created humankind had there not beeen in place a plan to redeem humankind (through the Son becoming human). Likely, Milton got this idea from Augustine, either directly or indirectly.

27. For additional discussion of Augustine's views regarding concupiscence within marriage following the sin of Adam and Eve, see Anderson, *The Genesis of Perfection*, chapter 3.

Augustine versus Pelagius and Julian of Eclanum

Pelagius, an ascetic British monk, arrived in Rome around 380. Hoping to improve the appallingly lax moral standards of his day, Pelagius stressed the natural goodness of each person and the power of every individual to choose whether to do good or evil. Pelagius's intention was to discourage a life of indulgence by choosing the path of asceticism. Almost immediately, however, Pelagius's opponents accused him of denying any need of divine grace in order to do moral good. It is difficult to determine precisely what Pelagius taught, as his positions must be gleaned primarily from critical documents produced by his opponents. For example, it is uncertain whether Pelagius denied the reality of "original sin," as his accusers alleged. But his disciple Celestius certainly denied it, and with it, the necessity of infant baptism. Augustine and some others quickly denounced this new Pelagian doctrine as "heterodox," that is, not in accord with the authentic teachings of the Catholic Church.

Nevertheless, Pelagius attracted many followers, creating a rift within Christendom. The bishops of Africa, largely at the instigation of Augustine, condemned Pelagius. The bishops of Palestine, by contrast, declared Pelagius's teaching to be orthodox. Rome was so divided that in 417 riots broke out in the streets between Pelagius's supporters and his detractors. Pope Innocent had been persuaded by Augustine and his African bishop colleagues to condemn Pelagius. But the very next year Innocent's successor, Pope Zosimus, at first declared Pelagius to be orthodox; but under pressure from Augustine and allied African bishops, Zosimus subsequently reversed positions and excommunicated Pelagius. Pelagius died soon after, but the controversy he had aroused continued.

One of Palagius's principal defenders was Julian, recently installed as bishop of Eclanum in southern Italy. Julian was one of sixteen bishops who refused to sign Pope Zosimus's condemnation of Pelagius in 417. Moreover, because Julian expressed sympathy for at least some of Pelagius's views, Augustine, Jerome, and others accused him of teaching outright Pelagianism. The result was that Julian was expelled from his episcopal see. He spent the rest of his lifetime defending himself against fierce attacks by his opponents, notably Augustine and Jerome, and attempting to regain his ecclesiastical standing, but without success. He was repudiated by more than one assembly of Catholic bishops and exiled three different times, including once from Constantinople by the emperor himself. Recent scholars have expressed a certain amount of skepticism about whether Julian had been given a fair hearing.[28]

In these debates with Julian, Augustine had claimed the support of prior and contemporary Catholic heavy weights such as Irenaeus, Bishop of Lyons; the blessed martyr and Carthaginian bishop, Cyprian ; the Gallic bishop Hilary, a revered defender of the faith; the illustrious Ambrose, bishop of Milan; Gregory, a bishop of great reputation and highest renown from the East; the brilliant and venerable Basil; John Chrysostom of Constantinople; and many others. But that seems to have been a bit of overreach on the part of Augustine. For example, while all these early pillars of the church did address in some fashion how the sin of our first parent(s) adversely affects us, none of them used the term "original sin." Moreover, on closer examination it may be seen that these Fathers often preached a doctrine about sin and salvation that was at variance with that of Augustine—as we have already noted in the case of Irenaeus. In many regards the more "optimistic" views of Julian about natural goodness and the ability of individuals to choose between good and evil actually seem closer to Irenaeus's teachings than do the "pessimistic" positions espoused by Augustine.

Against Augustine, Julian argued that both death and sexual desire were "natural," having been ordained by God "from the beginning." Moreover, the "death" with which God threatened the primal pair in paradise, and which resulted from their disobedience, was not physical death but *spiritual* death. Physical death is a condition enjoined upon all creatures on earth, including humankind, Julian said. It is a necessary step by which these "corruptible bodies" should transition to eternal life, "for that which is corruptible must clothe itself with incorruptibility, and that which is mortal must clothe itself with immortality" (1 Cor 15:53). By contrast to such natural death, what happened to Adam and Eve was that on the day that they disobeyed God, they began to die morally and spiritually.

Similarly for the other "punishments" that came upon the primal pair. Pain in childbirth is natural to all animals, including humans. In Eve's case, God did increase her pangs in giving birth, but only to Eve, and as punishment for her personal sin. Human maladies such as illness, birth defects, still-born babies, even "sweat," all these occur naturally and should not automatically be attributed to sin. Jesus himself said (John

28. For an informed discussion of the debate between Julian and Augustine, see Pagels, *Adam, Eve, and the Serpent*, 127–50.

9:3) that the man's blindness was not because either the man himself or his parents had sinned, but rather that the wonderous ways of God may be made manifest.[29] The implication is that, yes, sin does increase pain and sorrow in this world, but Augustine certainly overreaches when he attributes every human malady as due to the sin of Adam and Eve. Some human maladies are simply part of nature itself and cannot be called evil.

Augustine is similarly mistaken, Julian argued, in claiming that sexual passion is a consequence of the sin of Adam and Eve. Marriage is one of the "praises of God." God instilled sexual desires in all earthly creatures, including humans, as a means of ensuring the propagation of the species. Sexual passion is natural. It becomes sinful only when misused in ways not intended by God, such as in licentiousness and adultery.

Augustine's position was almost the exact opposite: sexual passion is *inherently* evil. Accordingly, every human exercise of sex is necessarily contaminated, even when legitimately performed in the marriage bed. For that reason, celibacy is the preferred path to holiness. Most persons will not be able to resist the undeniable pull of concupiscence, however. In addition, there is the divine command to "multiple and fill the earth." So Christian couples may engage in sexual intercourse within lawful marriage. But in so far as possible, the sex act must be accomplished without passion, that is, without consenting to the evil of concupiscence.

The Legacy of Augustine for the Adam & Eve Tradition

It is difficult to overstate the importance of Augustine for the development of the Adam and Eve tradition. No writer since the apostle Paul has had a greater impact in shaping the evolving tradition about Adam and Eve and especially beliefs about their role in determining the fate of humankind itself. Especially within Western Christianity, one may rightly speak of a pre-Augustine period and a post-Augustine period. This is most evident in three central doctrinal issues: original sin, diminished free will, and perverted human sexuality.

As has been seen, Augustine coined the term "original sin" to encapsulate his belief that every human automatically inherits the sin of Adam. Prior to Augustine, no orthodox believer—Jew or Christian, not even the apostle Paul—had taught that every human was born spiritually dead and completely incapable of doing the least good because their will

29. See *Against Julian*, 3.6.

had been totally impaired by inherited sin. Rather as Irenaeus, Julian, and others taught, each person enjoys free will, by which one is required to make personal choices daily between good and evil, thereby determining one's own fate—granted, with the aid of divine grace. This earlier, less extreme view continues even today in Eastern Orthodox Christianity, which prefers the term "ancestral sin" over "original sin." Ancestral sin "emphasizes the physical and moral consequences of Adam and Eve's actions for humanity (such as corruption and death). However ancestral sin does not impute Adam's and Eve's sin and guilt to all humanity. Ancestral sin is not a matter of biological transmission."[30]

It was a different matter in the West, however. After Augustine, Western Christian theological discourse quickly became saturated with discussions of "the fall" and "original sin." According to Augustine, Adam's sin had disastrous consequences for every human being. After Adam, every human is born with diminished reason and diminished free will, such that one not only has less ability to grasp the full implications of one's actions but even minimal will power to perform what little good one might wish. In addition to moral evil, also all the maladies that afflict humankind and disrupt our physical environment—from still births to birth defects, from diseases to accidental deaths, from natural catastrophes to lack of adequate shelters, to name but a few—all may be laid at Adam's feet, since the perfect life of paradise would still prevail had Adam not sinned. The result is that today Western Christians can scarcely think of Adam (or Eve) without at the same time also conjuring up thoughts of how profoundly that "original sin" *negatively* impacts every facet of human life and culture.

In the sixteenth century the Protestant Reformers Martin Luther and John Calvin both adopted Augustinian ideas and pushed them far beyond even what Augustine had imagined: the *total depravity* of humankind. In a nutshell, the doctrine of total depravity of humankind posits that as a result of the fall of Adam and Eve, all humans are inherently evil to their very core. Every part—soul and body (mind, will, emotions, flesh)—has been so thoroughly corrupted by sin that there is nothing good in human persons, nor can they do anything good. Being sinners to the core and unable to do absolutely anything to please God, Christians must cast themselves upon God's mercy and rely entirely upon unmerited divine grace for salvation—or, as encapsulated in the classic

30. Smith, *Genesis of Good and Evil*, 4.

Protestant formula of salvation, everything is *sola gratia, sola fide, sola scriptura.*

Similarly regarding concupiscence, Augustine's teaching had far reaching tentacles. Negative assessments of human sexuality, whether exercised within lawful marriage or not, did not originate with Augustine. But he certainly perpetuated *and* amplified them. As we have seen, Augustine regarded sexual passion as inherently evil, rendering every human exercise of sex as bordering on immorality, even when legitimately performed in the marriage bed. Celibacy is the preferred path to holiness. Most persons will not be able to resist the undeniable pull of concupiscence, however. What is more, even the divine command to "multiple and fill the earth" must be accomplished without passion, that is, without succumbing to the evil of concupiscence.

Augustine's was a viewpoint that many Western Christians would find difficult to overcome. One need think no further than the example of the Puritans in America. Our Puritan forebearers adopted the practice of "bundling." That is, during the act of intercourse spouses would remain completely clothed, exposing only as much of their body parts as was necessary for the husband to penetrate the wife for the purpose of depositing his semen. Sex was not supposed to be for pleasure, but for procreation only. One can easily think of other historical examples.

Within the Roman Catholic Church also, only after Vatican Council II in 1965 declared that conjugal love "is uniquely expressed and perfected through the marital act"[31] has it become commonplace to speak of sex within marriage as having *two* "ends"—the procreative *and* the unitive, or furtherance of love between spouses. In other branches of Christianity, negative evaluations of human sexuality are also manifest. Apart from Protestantism, emphasis upon celibacy as a higher calling than marriage is neigh universal.

Finally, one may reflect upon the evolving "storyline" of the Adam and Eve tradition. After Augustine, for Christians at least, it is scarcely necessary any longer to speak of an "Adam *and Eve*" story. Eve has virtually disappeared, having been reduced to a minor character. Rather, it has been transformed into a story about Adam alone, since he is the only one who matters for the subsequent history of humankind.

Such is the overpowering legacy of Augustine, extending all the way down to the present day. One can only speculate how Christian history

31. Vatican Council II, "Dogmatic Constitution on the Church" (*Gaudium et Spes*), #49.

and intellectual thought might have been different, had the more moderate views of church fathers like Bishop Irenaeus of Lyons prevailed or at least acquired traction equal with those of Bishop Augustine of Hippo.

9

Gnostic Inversions of Adam and Eve

THE GNOSTICS WERE A strange group by any standard. A unique community of believers, they had roots in both the Jewish and the Christian religions. This is not to say that Gnostics all believed alike. Far from it. There were many forms of Gnosticism, some arising more directly from Judaism, some directly from Christianity, others deriving more from Manicheism, and still others being a combination of all three. Most gnostic rewritings of the Adam and Eve story draw more heavily from the Genesis story and Jewish pseudepigraphs, however, than upon Christian interpretations of Adam and Eve.

During the last century, our understanding of the Gnostics and their beliefs has been greatly advanced by the discovery in 1945 at Nag Hammadi in Egypt of a large clay jar with thirteen leather bound codices. These codices contained some fifty-two different texts, mostly gnostic treatises. Previously, our knowledge of matters gnostic had been dependent primarily the writings of early Christian apologists who were intent upon portraying Gnostics in as bad a light as possible. But thanks to the Nag Hammadi discovery, we can now see what the Gnostics actually wrote and taught in their own words.

Despite the many varieties of Gnosticism, one element that all held in common is the conviction that *gnosis,* "knowledge," is the only way of salvation—hence their name Gnostics. This is not ordinary knowledge, however, but an esoteric knowledge of divine secrets reserved exclusively to the Gnostics themselves. This esoteric knowledge consists of understanding both one's true self and ultimate reality—including the transcendent, spiritual deity—as the key to achieving liberation from the material existence in which humans find themselves presently trapped. Most humans, however, are unaware of their actual condition. How one gains this liberating knowledge varied according to the specific gnostic sect to which one adhered. In any case, achieving such knowledge was considered absolutely crucial. At the risk of oversimplification, one may attempt a synthetic overview of gnostic beliefs along the following lines.

A Synthesis of the Gnostic View of Reality

According to the Gnostics, the world of experience, that is, what we humans experience as "reality," is all a huge illusion. Humans, apart from a few exceptional persons, are trapped in material bodies and kept in ignorance of their true identity as spiritual beings. This condition can only be remedied by coming to know one's true identity. This is usually done with help from a savior figure who comes from above and reveals to privileged individuals the authentic knowledge (*gnosis*) concerning reality.

How this state of human ignorance came about in the first place is a long and complicated story. Essential to understand, however, is that, according to the Gnostics, the creator of the world—the "god" depicted in Genesis—must be totally disassociated from the authentic transcendent deity who is above and beyond all. The god of Genesis is nothing more than an arrogant and ignorant "blind" demiurge (a lesser god, the controller of this material world) who created humankind in a fit of jealous rage; he must be ignored and condemned by all who possess true enlightenment (*gnosis*). According to the Gnostics, the biblical story of the origin of the world, especially the story of humankind recounted in the opening chapters of Genesis, is deliberately erroneous. It is a false narrative concocted by the demiurge and his minions, designed to prevent humankind from discovering both their true spiritual identities and the authentic, all-transcendent deity. For this reason, the enlightened reader must "unlearn" the Genesis account in order to the discover *the actual reality* of the world and humankind. Naturally, only the gnostic version of the origin of the world is to be believed.

But getting beyond the false Genesis narrative to this authentic knowledge of the origin of the world and of humankind is difficult. Even more difficult, however, is coming to an authentic knowledge of the all-transcendent deity. Some Gnostics referred to this all-transcendent deity as the One (or Monad). Other Gnostics spoke of the transcendent deity as a kind of hierarchical trinity consisting of Father, Mother, and Child. First is the Father who contains within himself the completeness of being. From the Father emanates the Mother, and from these two emanates the Self-Generated Child. Together these three comprise the All, sometimes referred to as the Pleroma ("Fullness"). From these three primal entities there emanated a series of other spiritual beings called aeons, ranked in descending order. Each of these additional spiritual beings is composed of a male principle and a female principle. Moreover, the male and female principles must be always in agreement, each with the other, in order to be whole and complete. To operate independently of one another would result in a rending of the perfect harmony existing within the Pleroma and would bring on imperfection. Yet according to the Gnostics that is exactly what happened.

One of the highest-ranking aeons, a female by the name of Pistis Sophia ("Faith Wisdom")—often shortened to just Sophia—had a desire to act independently. (Sophia in some texts goes under the name Barbelo.) Without obtaining permission from or consulting with her male counterpart, Sophia had a desire to create something in her own image. But as her thought took shape, Sophia immediately realized she had made a mistake. Her creation was nothing more than a monstrous lion-headed male snake-like figure, completely devoid of understanding. Lacking his mother's spiritual (female) element, he was radically defective, since he was composed of psychic (that is, soul) matter only. Being the first of his kind, he looked about and saw no other beings. Ignorant of his true origin, he arrogantly boasted, "I am God, there are no other gods besides me!"

His mother, knowing better, declared him mistaken and named him "Samael"—meaning "god of the blind." Hoping to salvage her disastrous creation, Sophia called out to him, "Yalda-baoth!" ("Child, come over here!").

Yaldabaoth is the creator god in the book of Genesis known by the name Yahweh (God). He is the one responsible for creating both the material world and humankind. But before creating the world and humankind, Yaldaboath generated the archons, beings similar to himself but lower in rank. These are what Ephesian 6:12 refers to as the evil "rulers of this world."

While the (unfortunate) creation of humankind is a major theme in all gnostic writings, there was no uniform tradition concerning Adam and Eve, since each community followed a version formulated by its local leader. Gnostic writings about Adam and Eve and creation may be divided into two categories: those that depend primarily upon Jewish tradition, and those that incorporate large elements of Christian tradition. To the former (Jewish influenced) group belong two works: *The Nature of the Rulers* (or *The Reality of the Rulers,* aka *Hypostasis of the Archons*) and *On the Origin of the World.* To the latter (Christian influenced) group belong the *Secret Book of John* (aka *The Apocryphon of John*) and *The Tripartite Tractate.*[1]

Two Jewish-inspired Gnostic Texts

Somewhat arbitrarily, we will begin our study of gnostic traditions about human beginnings with the treatise *On the Origin of the World.* This may also serve as our entry point into the multi-faceted world of Gnosticism.

On the Origin of the World

In many ways, this text defies classification. It does not fit neatly with other gnostic treatises. It seems to draw not only on biblical themes but also upon Greco-Roman, Egyptian, and Christian motifs. With its many literary allusions, it appears to present itself as a sophisticated and learned introduction to Gnosticism, but in a way that at the same time would appeal to the masses.

On the Origin of the World does not begin with a description the eternal Pleroma or Primal Spirit, as might be expected. Rather, the existence of the Pleroma (the Fullness) and the eternal spirits, including Pistis Sophia, is simply assumed. As its title implies, this text picks up "the story" right smack in the middle of the problem, explaining how "chaos"—the material world—came into being. That unfortunate development was the doing of Pistis Sophia but narrated in images reminiscent of the opening verses of Genesis.

---

1. Recent translations of all four texts may be found in the authoritative volume edited by Meyer, *Nag Hammadi Scriptures: International Edition.* Unless otherwise noted, the translations quoted herein are from this volume. Other convenient collections of translations are Robinson, ed., *Nag Hammadi Library*; and Barnstone and Meyer, eds., *Gnostic Bible.*

FIGURE 2

A Gnostic View of Reality
(On the Origins of the World)

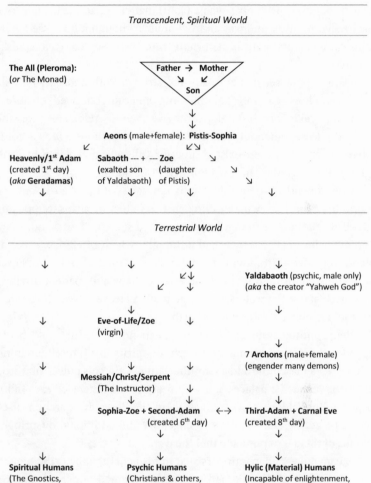

Transcendent, Spiritual World

The All (Pleroma):
(*or* The Monad)

Father → Mother
↘ ↙
Son

↓
↓

Aeons (male+female): **Pistis-Sophia**

Heavenly/1ˢᵗ Adam
(created 1ˢᵗ day)
(*aka* **Geradamas**)
↓

Sabaoth --- + --- **Zoe**
(exalted son
of Yaldabaoth)
↓

(daughter
of Pistis)
↓

↓

Terrestrial World

↓   ↓   ↓   ↓ **Yaldabaoth** (psychic, male only)
(*aka* the creator "Yahweh God")

↓   **Eve-of-Life/Zoe**   ↓
(virgin)

↓

7 Archons (male+female)
(engender many demons)
↓

↓   **Messiah/Christ/Serpent**   ↓
(The Instructor)
↓   ↓
Sophia-Zoe + Second-Adam ←→ **Third-Adam + Carnal Eve**
(created 6ᵗʰ day)   (created 8ᵗʰ day)
↓   ↓

↓   ↓   ↓
Spiritual Humans   **Psychic Humans**   **Hylic (Material) Humans**
(The Gnostics,   (Christians & others,   (Incapable of enlightenment,
already enlightened)   can be enlightened)   forever damned, no hope)

When Pistis Sophia acted upon a selfish impulse, her intention was to do something great, something along the lines of those first primal emanations within the All, the Pleroma. She wanted to bring about something "to resemble the first light." Because of her great powers, immediately her wish appeared as "a heavenly likeness with incomprehensible greatness." But her product was not an augmentation of the infinite at all. It was more like a shadow, or better yet, a deep darkness suspended over a limitless chaos or vast abyss. (The reader is intended to recall the opening verses of Genesis, where "darkness was on the face of the deep.") An alternate image is that this new entity was like an aborted fetus that has within it no spirit, only psychic (soul) matter. It had the likeness of a lion-headed monster and was androgynous. Although it possessed great authority, it was ignorant of its origin from Pistis Sophia, well as of its own defective being.

Pistis Sophia, seeing her "offspring" struggle within that watery bile of chaos and hoping to salvage something of her ill-conceived "creation," called out, "Yalda, baoth (Child, come over here!)." Yaldabaoth was the first of the lesser rulers of this world known as archons. He was completely ignorant that there existed superior, fully spiritual beings in a still higher realm, including his own mother, Pistis Sophia.

Consequently, when Yaldabaoth emerged and looked about, he saw nothing but his own reflection in the waters of chaos. Supposing himself to be the sole being, he arrogantly declared, "I am God; there is no other but me!" He then had a thought, which briefly appeared as an androgynous spirit moving to and fro across the face of the waters of chaos. Yaldabaoth then divided the watery chaos and made a dwelling for himself above the waters, which he named Heaven. Next, he made a footstool for himself and called it Earth.

Being androgenous and desirous of expanding his rule, Yaldabaoth engendered seven additional androgynous spirits like himself, archons, each having a masculine and a feminine name. Using his powerful word,[2] Yaldabaoth created a palace—a heaven—above the waters for each of his offspring. But Yaldabaoth ruled over them all. These lesser archons used their male and female faculties to engender still additional offspring— myriads of them—to populate their heavens.

Meanwhile, Yaldabaoth persisted in his belief that he is the highest and only god. Pistis Sophia had long since repented of her mistake. So when Yaldabaoth declared himself to be the supreme deity, Pistis Sophia pronounced him not only ignorant but also "Samael"—a "blind god." Furthermore, she announced the existence of "an enlightened, immortal human" prior to Yaldabaoth, who ultimately will trample Yaldabaoth underfoot. [The astute reader will catch the allusion to a long-standing Christian interpretation of Genesis 3:15, according to which the serpent is told that the woman's (messianic) offspring "will crush your head while

2. Compare the recurring formula in Genesis 1, "And Yahweh God said, Let there be . . . , and so it happened."

you bruise his heel." Although the identity of this "enlightened, immortal human" is not revealed here, another gnostic text uses similar language to speak about Geradamas (or Pigeradamas, the "heavenly Adam").] By now Pistis Sophia has had enough of her wayward child and withdrew to her own heaven above, but not before providing Yaldabaoth and his rulers a brief glimpse of her superior being.

Sabaoth, the noblest and most perceptive of Yaldaboth's sons, heard Pistis Sophia's words and understood. Thereupon he condemned his father and loathed everything his father (darkness) and his mother (abyss) together had wrought, including the work of his sister, that spirit who moved to and fro, stirring up the waters of the abyss.[3] Sabaoth's siblings, the other archons begotten by Yaldaboth, turned against Sabaoth and a great war ensued in the heavens. (This may be a late reflex of the ancient trope concerning a rebellion in heaven, previously encountered in the Mesopotamian Enuma Elish and in the Jewish pseudepigraph 1 Enoch.) Once the disturbance had been quelled and the "troublemaker" (Yalda-baoth, apparently) had been removed to Tartaros (Hell), we learn that Pistis Sophia has been firmly ensconced in the highest (seventh) heaven, while Yaldabaoth and the archons are confined in the six lower heavens. We learn, further, that in the course of the battle Pistis Sophia had sent down seven great archangels to assist Sabaoth, snatching him up into the highest heaven. Pistis Sophia then rewarded Sabaoth for his repentance and gave him her daughter Zoe ("Life," the exalted Eve) as his feminine counterpart, thereby restoring the authentic male-female unity of the original Pleroma. That is how Sabaoth came to be known as "Lord of powers" [or "Lord of hosts," the biblical Yahweh Sabaoth]. To Sabaoth was then granted a huge, magnificent dwelling place, seven times greater than all those in the lower heavens, together with cherubim and sera-phim and archangels to minister before him and to glorify him. In short, Sabaoth had totally eclipsed his father Yaldabaoth as the principal ar-chon. But bear in mind that, exalted as Sabaoth might be, he ranks still far below the Pleroma and the invisible, transcendent deity, whom only those with real *gnosis* ultimately come to know. But we are getting ahead of ourselves in this story.

When Yaldabaoth perceived that his son Sabaoth had become the greatest of the archons, he became jealous and wrathful. From that jealousy Death emerged and spread across the six lower realms. Being

3. Cp. Gen 1:2.

androgynous, Death was able quickly to engender still other demonic psychic powers: Jealousy, Wrath, Suffering, Lust, Curse, and many more. Sabaoth and Zoe, however, countered by engendering opposing, good and guileless spirits: Peace, Gladness, Blessedness, Truth, Love, Faith, and others.

Although Yaldabaoth had never seen Pistis Sophia, he had heard her voice, as when she informed Yaldabaoth that a superior, enlightened, immortal human exists prior to him. Foolishly, Yaldabaoth issued a challenge: "If something exists before me, let it appear!" Immediately a blinding light appeared, and within it a heavenly messenger, the holy or Heavenly Adam [Geradamas]. But he was seen only by Yaldabaoth and Pronoia (Forethought) who was with Yaldabaoth. Pronoia became enamored of the messenger, even though the messenger spurned her because she belonged to the darkness. Nevertheless, from Pronoia's ardor was born Eros (Passionate Love). It was from Eros that eventually (unfortunate) marriage would come both to the wicked archons and their demonic angels and to humankind, followed by reproduction and death. But first the grape had to sprout, because it was from drinking its fruit, wine, that the desire for intercourse arose. [The reader will recognize that in linking love to wine, the gnostic author has imported a motif from Greek literature, namely the association of Eros with Dionysos. Allusions to Greek myth are a frequent phenomenon in this text.]

But back to the biblically inspired tradition concerning the origin of the world. It was at this point that paradise appeared.

> Then justice created paradise. Paradise is beautiful, and is outside the circuit of the moon and the circuit of the sun in the land of pleasure, which is in the east in the rocky region. Desire dwells in the middle of the beautiful, stately trees. The tree of life eternal, as it appeared by the will of God, is in the north of paradise to give immortality to the souls of the holy people, who will leave their poor modeled bodies at the end of the age. The tree of life looks like the sun, and its branches are lovely. Its leaves are the leaves of the cypress, its fruit is like a cluster of white grapes, and its height reaches the sky.
>
> Next to it is the tree of knowledge, which is endowed with the power of God. It is glorious as the moon shining brightly, and its branches are lovely. Its leaves are like fig leaves and its fruit is like a bunch of good, delicious dates. The tree of knowledge is in the north of paradise to arouse the souls from demonic

stupor, so that they might come to the tree of life, eat its fruit,
and condemn the authorities and their angels.

Quite obviously, the gnostic tradition about paradise differs radically from that of Genesis, as does also the nature and function of the two special trees in the garden. In particular, "the tree of knowledge" (*gnosis*), carries special significance for the Gnostics. Rather than castigating eating from this tree as something harmful, Gnostics saw therein the authentic source of their superior, enlightened status as the true believers. True believers *should* partake of its fruit and thereby attain the enlightenment necessary to understand their present condition as spiritual beings wrongly imprisoned in material bodies and weighed down with psychic souls. The command not to eat the beneficial fruit of this tree came from the "creator" Yaldabaoth and his minions, who were intent on keeping humankind ignorant and in bondage to them.

The Creation of Humankind

The creation of humankind came about in this way. Sophia, daughter of Pistis, had desired to illumine the darkness. She requested and received permission from her mother Pistis to create various lights. That is how the sun, the moon, and all the stars came to be fashioned. That was also when the aforementioned luminous heavenly figure called "Adam of light" (aka Geradamas) appeared briefly before withdrawing from chaos. During that brief moment, however, he had been glimpsed by the archons who, recalling Yaldabaoth's boast that he was god because nothing else existed, now laughed at Yaldabaoth and his arrogant stupidity. Attempting to salvage the situation, Yaldabaoth proposed that he and the archons destroy the mysterious Adam of light and his power by creating a rival figure, a human made from earth but formed in their image. Their idea was that Adam of light would see this new human, become enamored of it, and beget descendants who would serve the archons and forever do their malicious bidding.

Meanwhile, Pistis, having anticipated the scheme of Yaldabaoth and the archons, directed her daughter Sophia Zoe (Wisdom-Life) to execute a counterplan to subvert the evil plan of Yaldabaoth and the archons. Sophia Zoe let a ray of light fall upon the waters, where it initially appeared as an androgynous human being, which Sophia Zoe then transformed into a female body. Thus came into existence the "mother Eve of life," that is, the instructor of life. Without any male, this spiritual Eve gave birth to a male child who would become the lord—though the archons would label it "the beast" in order to deceive future humans and lead them astray. Her child was the Messiah who would enlighten humankind. In this telling, Eve was the first virgin to give birth without a male.

Yaldabaoth and his subservient archons set about executing their plan. Each of them casts his semen into the navel of the earth to generate a human in imitation of the likeness (reflection) of the heavenly human they had glimpsed in the water. Since they themselves lacked a spiritual component, the best they could do was to fashion a material (earthly) body with a psychic soul. Because the "Adam" they created lacked a spiritual element, it lay lifeless like an aborted fetus for forty days. Then Sophia Zoe infused her breath into this Adam, causing it to move but without ability to stand. Upon seeing it move, the archons became alarmed and queried it, "Who are you? Where have you come from?" Adam replied, "I came through the power of the (heavenly) human to destroy your work." Observing that Adam could not even stand, the archons were greatly relieved and celebrated by resting from their worries. They declared it to be the day of rest (the Sabbath) and withdrew up to their heavens.[4]

The following day (i.e., the eighth day), Sophia sent her daughter Zoe ("Life"), also known as Eve, as an instructor to raise up Adam that he might produce vessels of life. Seeing her helpless male partner lying there, Eve had compassion on him and commanded, "Adam, live! Get up!" Through the power of her word, Adam rose up and opened his eyes. Seeing Eve, he declared, "You will be called the Mother of the living, because you have given me life."[5]

The archons were alarmed when they learned that Adam had come to life and they went to investigate. They found Adam speaking with Eve. They recognized that the "enlightened woman" they were looking at bore resemblance to the likeness they had glimpsed previously in the light but were at a loss as what to do about her. They attempted to rape her so that by their pollution she would be rendered incapable of ascending back into her light. Moreover, her offspring by them would become their obedient slaves.

Eve merely laughed at their stupidity and futility. Using her superior spiritual power, she blinded the archons and slipped away, leaving but a

4. Cp. Gen 2:2–3.
5. Cp. Gen 3:20.

mere likeness of herself with Adam. When the archons recovered from their stupor, they spied Eve's likeness dallying with Adam and proceeded to rape it. Their intention was to trap the light of the spiritual Eve within material bodies of their own making. In their ignorance, however, they did not recognize that they were merely replicating their own likenesses in material bodies animated by psychic, not spiritual, souls. First came Abel, followed eventually by the rest of the sons of the archons.[6]

When the real Eve slipped away, she transformed herself into a tree—the tree of knowledge. Suspecting what had happened and fearing that their plan had gone awry, the seven highest archons approached Adam and (earthly) Eve with great trepidation. They attempted to frighten Adam away from the tree by warning him, "You may eat the fruit of every tree created for you in paradise but be careful not to eat from the tree of knowledge. If you eat, you will die."[7]

Fortunately, at this point the serpent—here called "the beast"— showed up to save the day. In gnostic belief, the serpent is a hero, not a villain, because he instructed the primal human couple about the true significance of the tree of knowledge.

> The beast, the wisest of all creatures, came by. When it saw the likeness of their mother, Eve, it said to her, "What did God say to you? 'Do not eat from the tree of knowledge'?"
>
> She said, "He not only said, 'Do not eat from it,' but 'Do not touch it, or you will die.'"
>
> The beast said to her, "Don't be afraid. You certainly will not die. He knows that when you eat from it your minds will become sober and you will be like gods, knowing the difference between evil and good people. He said this to you because he is jealous, so that you would not eat from it."[8]
>
> Eve believed the words of the instructor. She looked at the tree and saw it was beautiful and appealing, and she liked it. She took some of its fruit and ate, and she gave it to her husband too, and he also ate. Their minds opened.
>
> When they had eaten,
> the light of knowledge (*gnosis*) shone on them.
> When they clothed themselves with shame,
> they knew they were stripped of knowledge.

6. Cp. Genesis 4 and perhaps also Gen 6:1–4.

7. Cp. Gen 2:16–17.

8. Cp. Gen 3:1–5.

> When they became sober,
> they saw they were naked
> and they fell in love.
> When they saw their makers looked like beasts,
> they loathed them.
> They understood a great deal. (118.25—119.18)

In this gnostic retelling of the garden scene, when the archons real-ized that Adam and Eve had disobeyed their command, they immedi-ately set out to mitigate this latest threat to their plan, descending upon the garden in a terrific earthquake. Frightened by all the commotion, Adam and Eve hid. Unable to find the couple, the archons called out, "Adam, where are you?" "Over here," Adam replied, "I was ashamed and hid because I was afraid of you." Lacking in comprehension, the archons persisted, "Who told you about the shame with which you clothed your-self? Unless you ate from the tree!" In accord with the Genesis narrative, Adam pointed the finger at Eve, and Eve pointed to the serpent. Compre-hending that their ruse had been discovered but powerless to undo the damage to their own machinations, the archons cursed all: Adam, Eve, the serpent, and the ground. In a departure from the Genesis narrative, however, this gnostic text asserts that the archons attempted to determine just how much knowledge Adam had acquired from his act of disobedi-ence. "They gathered all the domestic animals, wild beasts of the earth, and the birds of the sky, and brought them to Adam to see what he would call them." Dismayed at Adam's skill in aptly naming all, the archons as-sembled in council to deliberate:

> "Look, Adam has become like one of us, and he knows the dif-ference between light and darkness. Now perhaps he will go astray as he did with the tree of knowledge and will come to the tree of life, eat from it, and become immortal and rule and despise us and consider us and all our glory to be foolish. And he will denounce us and the world. Come, let's throw him out of paradise down to the earth, where he came from, so that he can no longer know anything better than we can." So they threw Adam and his wife out of paradise.

Still not satisfied, in their fear the archons

> went to the tree of life and set great dreadful things around it, fiery living creatures called cherubim, and among them they put

a flaming sword, constantly turning in a terrifying way, so that
no one from the earth might ever enter that place.[9]

They were unable to change the lifespan for humankind, however, which
had been established in the beginning as 1000 years. The seven chief archons did have a partial recourse, however. Each of the seven had the
power to take back ten years of life as punishment for having received
enlightenment. This they did, so that "the remaining time allotted to every human was nine hundred and thirty years," years to be "spent in grief
and weakness and evil distractions" until the end of the age. In addition,
they created many "demonic angels," who

> taught much about error, magic, potions, idolatry, bloodshed,
> altars, temples, sacrifices, and libations to all the demons of
> the earth. The angels work with fate, which came into being by
> agreement of the gods of injustice and justice.
> So when the world came into being, it went about in error
> and confusion all the time. All the people on earth served the
> demons from the creation until the end of the age—both the
> angels of justice and the people of injustice. Thus the world was
> in confusion, ignorance, and stupor. All erred, until the appear-
> ance of the true human.

If the reader has found all the preceding somewhat confusing and
difficult to follow, the important take-away can be boiled down to a few
key points. There are three principal types of humans, each deriving from
a different "Adam."

1. The highest type of humans are "spiritual" humans. These are descendants of the (first) Adam of light, who appeared on the first
   day, when light appeared over the darkness of waters of chaos. Spiritual humans are inherently enlightened; they inherited *gnosis* (true
   knowledge) directly from their progenitor, the Adam of light. In
   turn, spiritual humans can help the less enlightened to gain *gnosis*.

2. At the opposite end of the spectrum are hylic or "earthly" humans.
   These are descended from the "third Adam," who was created (came
   alive) on the eighth day—that is, Monday of the second week—by
   Yaldabaoth and his seven chief rulers (archons) who fashioned
   this Adam in their own image from the earth. Accordingly, earthly

9. Cf. Gen 3:6–19.

humans lack both spirit and soul. They are doomed to perpetual ignorance and are incapable of coming to *gnosis*.

3. In between spiritual humans and earthly humans are "psychic" humans, that is, humans endowed with a "soul" (Greek *psyche*); these are descended from the "second Adam," the Adam created on the sixth day, into whom Pistis Sophia surreptitiously managed to slip a modicum of her own self. The majority of humankind belongs to this category, being the descendants of the Eve of Life. Although their minds have been darkened by Yaldabaoth and the archons, their "souls" can be enlightened with proper instruction. That is the role of the "instructor," identified variously as the serpent (the beast), or the Christ (Messiah), or the woman Eve, or even (Pistis) Sophia herself. In any case, this group is the main outreach for Gnostics, as their souls (*psyches*) are capable of acquiring true knowledge (*gnosis*).

For the Gnostics, therefore, salvation is not a matter of a Messiah or a Christ dying and rising in order to redeem humankind from sin. Rather, salvation consists in individuals acquiring "knowledge" derived from the heavenly instructor concerning the true origins of the world and of humankind. Knowledge is salvation, literally.

There is much more in this text, especially about the apocalyptic end of the world. But we will pass over the remainder in silence as it does not pertain directly to Adam and Eve or to the furtherance of that tradition.

The Nature of the Rulers

There is a second gnostic text very close in ideology to the text just considered, though considerably more abbreviated: *The Nature of the Rulers*. The fact that these two texts share much in common likely is the reason why they appear together on the same scroll from Nag Hammadi. While much is repetitious, there are significant differences.

The Nature of the Rulers opens immediately with its unmistakable gnostic message. An unidentified revealer speaks, proclaiming that he has been sent by "the spirit of the Father of truth" to warn the reader that "our struggle is not against flesh and blood but against the authorities of the world and the spirits of wickedness."[10] In short, humans are engaged

10. Quoting Eph 6:12.

in a conflict with powerful evil authorities who rule this world. These authorities, of course, are none other than blind Samael and his minions, the "rulers of the world" (archons) already known to the reader from *On the Origin of the World*. Our new text bypasses the story of the origins of the rulers themselves, to begin instead with the rulers' decision to create a human from the earth. What they molded was indeed humanoid, but it had no life. So Samael breathed into its face, giving it soul. But it remained lifeless until the spirit (the superior female spiritual presence at work in the world) took notice and came to dwell in it, causing it to become a living soul. The spirit called its name Adam because he was from the ground (Hebrew *'adamah*). Following loosely the narrative of Genesis 2–3, the rulers then gather animals and the birds to see what Adam would call them. Then they put Adam in the garden to cultivate it and to watch over it. At the same time, they commanded Adam not to eat from the tree of knowledge, not realizing that the inspiration for this command was coming from the Father's will, precisely so that Adam might learn not to trust or obey the rulers of this world.

Next the rulers caused a deep sleep to fall upon Adam and then opened his side. The text is somewhat unclear here. But the point seems to be that from an androgynous Adam, the archons removed one side— the feminine half—and crafted it into a woman's body. They replaced the side they had removed with flesh, not realizing that they had removed the spiritual element from Adam, leaving him only a defective soul body. But the "woman"—in actuality, the female spiritual presence—came to Adam and awakened him, saying. "Arise, Adam." Opening his eyes, Adam exclaims, "You have given me life. You will be called the Mother of the living. For she is my mother. She is the physician, woman, one who has given birth."

When the rulers arrived and saw Adam's newly come-to-life female partner, they became sexually excited and wanted to inseminate her with their seed. But she eluded them by merging into a tree, leaving behind a mere shadowy resemblance of herself. This the rulers foully defiled.

Afterward the female spiritual presence approached Adam and the earthly Eve "in the shape of the serpent, the instructor. The serpent taught Adam and Eve." Here again the serpent is a gnostic hero who instructs the primal couple to disregard the evil rulers' commands designed to keep humankind in ignorance of their true spiritual destiny. The narrative continues with "the ruler" learning of Adam's and Eve's disobedience; and after cursing them, he expels them from the garden. According to the narrator, the ruler's actions were designed to throw "humankind into great confusion and a life of toil, so their people would be too preoccupied with things of the world to attend to matters of the holy Spirit."

Norea: A Female Model Gnostic

Underscoring the importance of the feminine in gnostic thought, *The Nature of the Rulers* introduces the reader to a new model Gnostic: the woman Norea. In a major departure from *On the Origins of the World*, this gnostic text relates that after Eve bore Cain and Abel and Seth, she became pregnant again and bore a daughter, Norea. From the beginnings it is obvious that Norea would become a model Gnostic. Eve announces at Norea's birth: "[The Invisible Father] has produced for me a virgin to help many human generations." The narrator is no less effusive concerning Norea, commenting that she "is the virgin whom the forces did not defile," and continues, at that point "humanity began to multiply and develop." That is to say, with the coming of Norea, humankind began to improve! Admittedly, Genesis 6:1–5 says the opposite, that as humankind multiplied on earth, they became so evil in the eyes of Yahweh that he determined to send the great flood to wipe them off the face of the earth. In the gnostic view, however, what Moses wrote in the Bible was false because, like most other humans of that time, Moses was under the spell of the blind demiurge (i.e., Yahweh) and his archons. What is called "wickedness" in Genesis is actually true spirituality, i.e., living in accord with the divine spirit.

Improvement among humankind was indeed a serious challenge to the authority of the rulers, so much so that they determined to wipe out all humankind apart from Noah and a few "righteous" persons with him in the ark. Our document implies that Norea alone understood the magnitude of what was about to transpire. When she was rebuffed by Noah and refused entry onto the ark, she destroyed the ark with fire from her breath. Noah was forced to rebuild the ark a second time.

Naturally, the rulers could not brook such a challenge to their authority. Attempting to lead Norea astray, their supreme chief spoke seductively to her, "Your mother Eve came to us." But enlightened Norea did not fall into their trap, defiantly retorting, "You are the rulers of the darkness. Damn you! You did not have sex with my mother but with one of your own ilk. I am not from you. I am from the world above."

Now thoroughly enraged, and with flames shooting forth from his face, the supreme chief commanded, "You must serve us sexually, as your mother Eve did." But Norea cried out for help to the holy one, who answered her prayer by sending down the great angel Eleleth to rescue her from the clutches of the evil ruler.

The Nature of the Rulers ends with Norea recounting the conversation she had with Eleleth following her rescue. Eleleth explained that he was one of the four luminaries who stand in the presence of the great Invisible Spirit. Norea need not fear the rulers, as they have no power over her. The savior will appear in the final age and restrain those authorities.

Being a good Gnostic, Norea asks Eleleth to explain about the rulers, their origin, and their power. Eleleth explains in a concise and summary fashion how this material world came to be through the machinations of Yaldabaoth and his minions, and why most humans live in ignorance of their origin as creatures of Yaldabaoth. Now more anxious than ever about her own origins, Norea inquires, "My lord, am I also from their matter?" Eleleth assures her that she had a different origin.

> "You and your offspring are from the Father, who was from the beginning. Their souls come from above, from incorruptible light. So the authorities cannot approach them because of the spirit of truth within them, and all who know this way are deathless among dying humanity."

On this reassuring note that true Gnostics like Norea are guaranteed eternal life, *The Nature of the Rulers* quickly comes to an end.

Two Christian-inspired Gnostic texts

There is considerable overlap in the Christian-inspired gnostic texts with the Jewish-inspired texts. In the interests of avoiding much repetition, we will concern ourselves here primarily with those motifs and religious concepts that are distinctive in two texts: (1) *The Secret Book of John*, and (2) *The Tripartite Tractate*.

The Secret Book of John

The Christian roots of *The Secret Book of John* is evident right from the start, as this gnostic document purports to have been written by the apostle John, the brother of James and son of Zebedee, and based directly on a secret revelation given to John by the resurrected Jesus. This patterning upon the New Testament book of Revelation is patent. John has a vision in the temple in which he sees the heavens open, accompanied by awesome quakings on earth. Within a bright light Jesus appears as the tri-morphic figure of Father, Mother, and Son—all one and the same. Puzzled by Jesus's strange and changing appearance, John asks the meaning of this vision. Using the "I am" formula of the Gospel of John, Jesus explains the purpose of his three-fold appearance: "I am the Father, I am the Mother, I am the Child" who has "come to teach you what is, what was, and what is going to come, that you may understand what is invisible and what is visible, and to teach you about the unshakable race of perfect humankind . . . that you may relate them to your spiritual friends, who are from the unshakable generation of the perfect human."

In the vision the Invisible One is further explained. The Father—the one revealing—saw a reflection of himself in the spring of living water and loved it so much that it becomes Barbelo, the Mother. The father then gazed upon Barbelo with such pure light that Barbelo conceived an only child—more precisely, this is the "divine Self-Generated Child." The Father and Mother Barbelo rejoiced over the Self-Generated Child and anointed it with goodness until it was perfect, lacking nothing. The Child then asked to be given mind (*nous*) as a companion, and the Spirit (Father) consented. From these three came other emanations, the four luminaries—Harmozel, Oroiael, Deveithai, and Eleleth—to guard the four eternal realms (heavens).

Next the Virgin Spirit (the Mother-Father), using foreknowledge of the perfect mind (the will of the Self-Generated Child), generated the perfect human, named Geradamas, and placed him in the first eternal realm with the first luminary Harmozel. Geradamas was given "an invincible power of mind" with which he "glorified and praised the Invisible Spirit" as the perfect power in three-fold oneness: Father-Mother-Child.

Geradamas appointed his son Seth (another gnostic hero) to the second eternal realm, where was the second luminary Oroiael. In the third eternal realm with the third luminary Deveithai were stationed Seth's offspring and the souls of the saints. In the fourth eternal realm with the fourth luminary Eleleth were stationed the souls of those who were ignorant of the fullness but who will eventually repent. They are creatures that glorify the Invisible Spirit.

The main difference here is the rise of Seth as a gnostic hero, a feature common to a subcategory of gnostic texts often called Sethian literature. In Genesis, the line of Adam and Eve had to be renewed with Seth because Abel is killed by Cain and then Cain becomes an outcast. Among Sethian Gnostics, Seth takes on even greater significance. Here Seth is not the descendant of the biblical Adam and Eve. Rather this Seth is prior to that Adam, being descended from the heavenly human, Geradamas. He therefore belongs to the spiritual race of spiritual beings, rather than to the race of psychic or material humans who populate earth. This prior Seth not only possesses spiritual essence himself, in various texts he functions as "instructor" to those lacking "knowledge" about their true identity. In short, he is a savior figure.

The creation of humankind in *The Secret Book of John* is narrated in much the same fashion as in other gnostic texts. Sophia attempts to create without permission of the divine Father, only to beget the monstrous demiurge Yaldabaoth, who in turn begets the authorities, or rulers of this world. But this text does diverge significantly when it comes to the creation of Adam and Eve. At this point the rulers' deliberations echo the wording of Genesis 1: 26 more faithfully than other gnostic texts: "Come, let us create a human being after the image of God and with a likeness to ourselves." But the similarity to Genesis ends here, as the authorities literally create Adam in their own likeness. Each authority contributed a physical feature. The first authority created bone. The second authority created the soul for the bone. The third created sinew; the fourth, soul for the sinew. And so it went for skin, marrow, blood, hair, skull, right eye, left eye, and so forth, until the whole physical body of Adam was completed. Nevertheless, as in other texts, this physical body of Adam did not, could not move until Sophia intervened, after praying to the "most merciful Father-Mother of all," who sent five luminaries down to trick Yaldabaoth into breathing on Adam, not realizing that by so doing he was imparting the spirit of his mother into Adam. Sophia's spirit went into Adam, making him "like the one who is from the beginning," that is, the heavenly human. Fearing that the authorities might overwhelm Adam, the merciful Father-Mother also sent a helper to Adam. This was enlightened Insight, "who was called Life" (Zoe); she was hidden within Adam, lest the rulers see her and frustrate her future purpose of restoring fullness by teaching Adam's seed the path of spiritual ascent.

Though hidden within Adam, his newly acquired spiritual quality was evident to the rulers when they perceived that Adam's ability to think was now greater than that of themselves, his creators. So they devised a plan whereby Adam would die. They placed Adam in paradise with its marvelous trees and told him to eat from the trees, especially the "tree of life," which refers to *their* life—which is not life at all, but death. At the same time the rulers tried to hide the tree of knowledge from Adam, lest he eat from it and become even more enlightened.

Next Yaldabaoth determined he must remove "enlightened Insight" (Zoe) from inside Adam. Reminiscent of Yahweh taking a rib from Adam and replacing it with flesh, Yaldabaoth attempted to remove enlightened Insight from Adam's side and replace it with another figure in the form of a female. The plan did not succeed, as enlightened Insight eluded Yaldabaoth, leaving only a shell of herself visible. This was the "Eve" whom the rulers immediately defiled, thereby producing Cain and Abel. The text traces the origin of sexual intercourse to this event, because the first ruler "planted sexual desire within the woman who belongs to Adam." *The Secret Book of John* emphasizes that evil comes through sexual intercourse.

But sexual intercourse need not be evil. Enlightened Insight remained hidden within Adam and was gradually rejuvenating his mind. When Adam "came to know [had intercourse with] the counterpart of his own foreknowledge," he regained some of his enlightened powers and produced "a son like the child of humanity." That is, the child from this union was endowed with characteristics derived from the heavenly Adam. For that reason Adam called him Seth, after the manner of the heavenly race in the eternal realms. (Remember that these Gnostics believed themselves to be descendants of Seth, the spiritual son of the enlightened Adam by this spiritual "Eve," not the material Eve.)

In the course of discussing the events surrounding the trees in paradise, Jesus mentions that he, Jesus, had instructed Adam to eat from the tree of knowledge. John expressed surprise at this revelation:

> I said to the Savior, Lord, was it not the serpent that instructed Adam to eat? The Savior laughed and said, The serpent instructed them to eat of the wickedness of sexual desire and destruction so that Adam might be of use to the serpent.
>
> The first ruler [Yaldabaoth] knew Adam was disobedient to him because of the enlightened Insight within Adam, which made Adam stronger of mind than he. He wanted to recover the power that he himself had passed on to Adam. So he brought deep sleep upon Adam.
>
> I said to the Savior, "What is this deep sleep?"
>
> The Savior said, It is not as Moses wrote and you heard. He said in his first book, "He put Adam to sleep." Rather this deep sleep was a loss of sense. Thus the first ruler said through

the prophet, "I shall make their minds sluggish, that they may neither understand nor discern."[11]

Here again we encounter the gnostic teaching that Genesis presents a false account of reality. Human sex is a device created by the rulers to populate the world with unenlightened persons who would serve their ends. In this text the snake is not the enlightener but rather another component of the rulers' grand plan for deceiving humankind. Jesus says that he instructed Adam and Eve to disobey the ruler's command so that by eating they would gain the enlightenment necessary for their own salvation and the salvation of their descendants.

Obviously, the rulers would try to undo the damage done to their plan by the savior. Borrowing a trope from Greek mythology, our text says that the rulers countered by making human beings "drink water of forgetfulness . . . so that they might not know where they had come from." (According to Greek myth, if a thirsty soul drinks from the River Lethe, it forgets its previous lives and will be reincarnated in another body.) This revised plan apparently was successful to the extent that most humans are born without knowledge of their true origin. But it was not entirely successful because there remains in every human a seed capable of being "raised up" (awakened) to a knowledge of "the entire realm of Fullness," whereby it can become "holy, lacking nothing."

John asks Jesus, "Master, will all the souls then be led safely into pure light?" Jesus explains at length that salvation for each person is conditional upon one's response to the spirit of life who descends upon every person at birth. But a false spirit is also at work, leading many astray. Those who belong to "the unshakable generation" of perfect humankind readily respond to the spirit of life and are assured of ascending to eternal rest, never to be reborn again in the flesh. By contrast, those who heed the false spirit and reject knowledge will be taken to the place where the angels of misery go. Because they "have blasphemed against the spirit," they "will be tortured and punished eternally."

Finally, there are the souls of people who do not know to which spirit they belong. At death such a soul "is handed over to the authorities" who will imprison her in a cycle of reincarnations until finally "she awakens from forgetfulness and acquires knowledge." The text is vague on this point, but it appears that such a soul at rebirth is placed alongside "another soul in whom the spirit of life dwells, and she is saved through

11. See Isa 6:10.

that one. Then she will not be thrust into flesh again." However the process may be accomplished, because "the Mother-Father is great in mercy," salvation is extended even to those now suffering in forgetfulness and lack of knowledge.

Jesus also revealed one final secret to John—though the reader will recognize this as a conceit borrowed from 1 Enoch. After the rulers failed in their quest to bring every offspring of Adam and Eve into subjection under their power, the first ruler devised another plan. He sent his angels to take human daughters for their pleasure and to raise up offspring.

> The angels changed their appearance to look like the partners of these women, and filled the women with the spirit of darkness that they had concocted, and with evil.
>
> They brought gold, silver, gifts, copper, iron, metal, and all sorts of things. They brought great anxieties to the people who followed them, leading them astray with many deceptions. These people ... died without finding truth or knowing the God of truth. In this way all creation was forever enslaved, from the beginning of the world until the present day.
>
> The angels took women, and from the darkness they produced children similar to their [own] spirit. They closed their minds and became stubborn through the stubbornness of the contemptible spirit until the present day.

With this message of warning—and hope—the savior brought his revelation to John to a close. Jesus's parting words before ascending back to the perfect realm were for John to record everything he had just been told and to share them secretly with his spiritual friends. John then went to the other students and reported what the savior had told him concerning the mystery of the unshakable race.

The Tripartite Tractate

The Tripartite Tractate is unique among gnostic texts in that it attributes the "fall"—the rupture within the pleroma that resulted in the creation of the material world and humankind—not to the sin of a female principle (Barbelo or Sophia) but to the masculine Word (the Logos), which will in turn result in the Word eventually becoming the savior (the revealer of true knowledge). The Christian roots of this conceit are so patent that one could fairly describe this branch of Gnosticism as a Christian heresy known as Valentinianism. Indeed, that seems to have been the primary target of church fathers such as Irenaeus and Augustine who wrote vigorously and extensively refuting various gnostic sects.

In common with all gnostic texts, *The Tripartite Tractate* posits the existence of an utterly transcendent entity that is the source of all. Most other gnostic documents posit this primal source as a masculine-feminine dyad functioning in unity. *The Tripartite Tractate*, by contrast, posits a monadic (single) first principle, "the Father." Without beginning and without end, this unbegotten Father is the complete perfect one—inscrutable, immutable, incomprehensible, utterly unknowable, and unfathomable.

From the inscrutable Father proceeds an initial trinity of Father-Son-Church (replacing the trinity of Father-Mother-Son of other texts). The Son is begotten from the thought of the Father having a perfect perception of himself, such that it becomes a spiritual entity who glorifies the Father. This is the firstborn and only Son, "firstborn" because no one exists before him, and "only Son" because no one is after him.

The Church likewise exists from the beginning, proceeding from both the Father and the Son. Just as the Father reveals himself as a thought that becomes the Son, so also the Son was found to be a brother to himself in the thought of the Father. This is the Church that issues from the Son and the Father like so many kisses. Kisses are many, but at core the many kisses have a unity in love. "This is the Church that consists of many people and exists before the aeons," which is to say that the "holy imperishable spirits" that constitute the Church originate within the initial trinity itself. In this schema, the Church is prior even to those additional emanations from the thought of the Father known as the aeons. Patently, the Church is a major preoccupation for this Valentinian gnostic sect, as they see themselves as the mainstay of the Church, both in this world and the next.

The aeons who came forth from the thought of the Father, through the Son and the Church, were in no way inimical to the Father. Rather, they are an extension of his loving and creative nature. They have the power to beget additional, limitless emanations to glorify the Father. All of this was done with the approval of the Father.

The Fall of the Word

One of the highest of these aeons was the masculine Word (the Logos). This aeon had an idea for giving greater honor to the Father. The Word wished to grasp the incomprehensibility of the Father and so give glory to the incomprehensible Father. Without consulting even his feminine counterpart, he proceeded. While his intention was good, he was attempting the impossible. Inevitably, his use of his creative power resulted in a defective product. What he intended was to replicate a perfect copy of himself to praise the Father. What resulted, however, was a defective copy of himself. It was nothing more than a shadow or a likeness of his weaker female self, devoid of its virile component. Consequently, everything that proceeded from this defective copy was likewise lacking in completeness. It is analogous to a reflection in a mirror: while beautiful to behold, it lacks substance, being nothing more than a copy and not the real thing. This was the origin of the defective aeons, known elsewhere as Yaldabaoth and the archons, who go on to create the material world and humankind.

According to *The Tripartite Tractate*, however, when the Word saw the consequences of his action, he immediately repented of his sin and prayed to the Father for assistance. He first turned for help to his brother aeons and then all of them together prayed to the Father that he might save the Word's defective creation. The Father was pleased. In fact, this had all come about through the Father's prior knowledge, as the Father had planned all along to use this "event" as an instrument of salvation for those destined to be saved. The Father, together with the Son, willingly brought forth the one who is called "Savior" and "the Redeemer"—"the Christ." In the end, therefore, the "fall" of the Word was beneficial in that it produced the Savior. In other words, the fall was a kind of *felix culpa*, a "happy fault."

When the Word repented, he stripped off his arrogant thought and reunited with the Rest, the Pleroma, thereby regaining the male-female unity of his former full self. The Word then conceived a new thought, a harmonious new entity, namely, "the Church." As in other gnostic writings, within the Church humankind is divisible into three types. The first group are those who are already spiritual and need little or no further enlightenment; these are the Gnostics themselves. A second group have totally rejected the truth; these are the hylic or material humans destined for eternal damnation. A third group is not willfully blind but do require the savior to enlighten them; these are the psychic humans, mostly ordinary Christians, for whom the hope of salvation is held out.

The Creation of Humanity

The second part of *The Tripartite Tractate* is a short discourse on the creation of material (hylic) humanity. Little attention is paid to details about how "the demiurge and his angelic servants" (that is, the chief ruler Yaldabaoth and his archons, as they are called in other gnostic texts) happened to create Adam and Eve. Instead, this text goes behind the scenes, so to speak, to tell about how the invisible Father was at work guiding the process, unbeknownst to those ignorant rulers who imagined themselves as the real creators.

Much like in Plato's analogy of the cave, the material world and material human bodies are but a shadow of the true reality. Most humans are ignorant of this truth, however, and mistakenly consider the projected shadows they see moving about to be the real thing. Only gradually do humans come to understand that what is truly real lies beyond this material world of human experience. All this is by the Father's design.

When the demiurge (Yaldabaoth) set out to create the material world and humankind, he was in fact carrying out the predetermined plan of Father, utilizing the invisible spiritual Word's defective desire to create. The Father allowed the Word's illegitimate desire to happen so that humankind might be created—but to a good end.

When the demiurge breathed into the face of Adam, he unwittingly expelled into Adam that spiritual element the demiurge had received from the Word. So Adam was a "mixed creation," possessing both spiritual and psychic elements within a material body. And although the spiritual element in psychic humans is dormant, even in its dormant condition it serves as a goad to remind psychic humanity of its deficiency, that is, of its need to seek out its spiritual dimension.

In paradise it is said that there were three types of trees, corresponding to the three types of humans. Adam's "creator" intended to allow Adam access to ordinary trees only. He tried to prohibit Adam from eating both from "that tree which had the double character" (that is, the tree of knowledge of good and evil) and from the tree of life. As is well known, Adam transgressed his creator's command and was expelled from paradise, resulting in his death. This was providential—that is, this happened by the will of the Father and enabled by the Son—so that humans through the experience of death might realize that their ultimate goal is "life eternal, which is the complete knowledge of the All and the partaking of all good things."

Conclusions

The Gnostics certainly provided a different take—actually, several different takes—on the Adam and Eve story. Most significant was an emphasis that "Adam and Eve" is about more than a historical event that happened at the beginning of human history. It is a meta-historical event with continuing implications for every human; it involves the spiritual world above as much as humanity in the material world. The Gnostics were not the first to posit that supernatural actors were involved in the Adam and Eve cycle, nor the first to lay principal blame for the origination of evil on earth on a figure or figures other than Adam and Eve.

But the Gnostics were the first to turn the Adam and Eve story on its head by claiming that the Genesis narrative is completely false and that the creator God of Genesis is a false god. The truth is something that only Gnostics know. Everyone else is in error, some to a greater degree than others. Moreover, one's salvation depends upon coming to know this truth.

What made the gnostic version of the truth so pernicious in the minds of contemporary Christian apologists such as Justin Martyr, Tertullian, Clement, and church fathers like Irenaeus, Ambrose, and Augustine, was that these "heretics" spouted a gospel that at times bore remarkable resemblance to "orthodox" (correct) Christian doctrine as presented in the Bible. To cite but two examples: the "apostle Paul," for example in the first chapter of the letter to the Colossians prays that the Colossians may be "filled with the knowledge of God" and even that they might "grow in the knowledge of God." The author continues, likely quoting from an early Christian hymn (Col 1:15–20) with gnostic-like language, in his description of the Christ:

> "He is the image of the invisible God, the firstborn of all creation; for in him all things in heaven and on earth were created, things visible and invisible, whether thrones or dominations or rulers (*archons*) or authorities (*exousias*) . . . For in him all the fullness (*pleroma*) of God was pleased to dwell, and through

him God was pleased to reconcile to himself all things, whether
on earth or in heaven."

Likewise, the Gospel of John is often cited as containing language and
concepts with affinity to Gnosticism. Consider the following statements:
"In the beginning was the Word, and the Word was with God, and what
God was, the Word was" (1:1); "And the Word became flesh" (1:14); "I
am the way, and the truth, and the life . . . If you know me, you will
know the Father also" (14:6–7). Proto-gnostic ideas were certainly current in the first century. Whether proto-gnostic ideas influenced the New
Testament, *or* the New Testament influenced the Gnostics, is a matter of
debate. Perhaps the influence was mutual.

While Gnosticism was a major problem during the first five centuries of Christianity and numerous church fathers expended considerable
ink refuting its errors, Gnosticism did not have an enduring impact in
shaping of the *storyline* per se concerning Adam and Eve. But the Gnostics did have a lasting effect on *theological* understandings of the "event"
itself. After the Gnostics, Adam and Eve took on *universal* significance,
both in fostering a negative evaluation of the material world as being
evil, and in solidifying the view that humans need to be "saved" from this
material world and from the influence of the evil (demonic) powers that
rule it.

One should also credit to the Gnostics a subsequent fascination
among Christian theologians with speculation about the internal work-
ings of the Trinity. To this day Christians continue to debate how the Son
is begotten of the Father, and whether the Holy Spirit proceeds from the
Father and the Son or from the Father only.

Moreover, one may wonder whether the tendency among some
Christians to ascribe to Mary, the mother of the divine Jesus, a status
bordering on divinity, especially under the title "mother of God" (*theoto-
kos* "God-bearer" in Greek), may derive in part from the gnostic doctrine
of the Trinity as Father, Mother, and Son. Certainly, there is some overlap
between the Christians' "virgin Mary" and the Gnostics' "spiritual Eve"
as the first virgin mother—and perhaps also with the divine virgin who
generated the perfect human Geradamas, as well as the virgin Norea.

Despite an insistence upon cohesion between the masculine and
the feminine principles as a fundamental requirement for all reality, the
Gnostics, much like Augustine, did not value human sexuality as positive. At best, engaging in sexual activity was something to be regarded

with indifference by enlightened spiritual humans; at worst, sexual inter-course was an activity indulged in by psychic and material humans under the domination of the rulers of this world. The Gnostics were not alone in the ancient world in devaluing human sexuality, but they did nothing to elevate it as a positive human act.

Gnosticism itself may have faded into the annals of history, but its legacy continues in varied and subtle ways right down to the present.

10

Classical Judaism

CLASSICAL JUDAISM WAS BORN out of the brutal Roman suppression of the First Jewish Revolt (67–73 CE), an event which totally disrupted the structures of Second Temple Judaism, including the demolishing of the Temple in Jerusalem in 70 CE. Vast numbers of Jews were killed or taken captive and deported as slaves. As a result, the ruling class was virtually annihilated and with it much of the priestly class, leaving the task of resurrecting the Jewish community primarily to the few remaining Pharisees and scholars of the Torah. Under their leadership Judaism was revitalized and transformed into a community devoted to the study, interpretation, and praying of the Scriptures, especially the Torah (the five books of Moses). New schools for this purpose were established and led by non-priestly scholars of the Torah known as rabbis ("masters" or "teachers" of the Law). One important outcome from this period was the formation of the Talmud as the chief authoritative document for how to be Jewish with the Temple gone. The Talmud is a compendium of religious laws, wise sayings, and stories as formulated by the more famous rabbis of that period (approximately 70–500 CE). It is comprised of two overlapping parts. The first and earliest, the Mishnah, completed by 200 CE, is a collection of the opinions of famous rabbis about how to interpret and live the Torah. The second part, the Gemara, is a later supplement to the Mishnah, incorporating the opinions and interpretations of rabbis who lived circa 300–500 CE.

This talmudic period is to Judaism what the Patristic Period is to Christianity. The basic tenets that would guide Judaism right down to the present day were established during this period, in much the same way that the core beliefs of Christianity were largely formulated during this same 500-year period by the church fathers. As Augustine, bishop of Hippo, and his contemporaries were largely responsible for developing Christian doctrine about the universal significance of Adam (and Eve) for all humankind, so also Jewish understandings of the importance of Adam and Eve was established by the talmudic rabbis.

Talmudic Judaism formalized its evolving belief system under the rubric of Oral Torah. Oral Torah refers to the belief that the Torah, in its fullest sense, cannot be fully contained within the written words of Scripture. The rabbis taught that when God gave the Torah to Moses at Sinai, God revealed it in two parts. The first part was written down; that is the Written Torah now contained in the Tanakh.[1] The second part was not written but given by God orally to Moses, who memorized it and passed it on orally to his successor Joshua who also memorized it and passed it on. Each succeeding generation passed this Oral Torah on in like manner down through the centuries.[2] Finally, beginning about 200 CE certain rabbis began writing down this Oral Torah for fear that memory might fail, and the oral portion of the divine Torah would be lost.

The concept of Oral Torah was conveyed using various metaphors. One claimed that when God gave Moses the two stone tablets of the Law "written by God's own finger" (Exod 31:18), God wrote them using "black fire" and "white fire." The black fire represents the written text of the Torah. The white fire represents the spaces between the letters and between the lines of the written text. In this view, the portion of the divine Torah that is invisible to the eye is as great as or greater than what is actually scribed on scrolls of the Torah.

Such mythic imagery was not intended to trivialize but rather to emphasize the importance of the Torah as divine and coeternal with God. To that end, another metaphor portrayed God himself reading and studying the Torah much like a rabbi. Prior to beginning the work of creation, the Lord God in heaven opened the divine Torah and read, "In the beginning the Lord God created the heavens and the earth . . ." The Lord God faithfully followed those very words of the Torah as his pattern for making the heavens and the earth and all that they contain. In other

1. Tanakh is an acronym for the traditional three divisions of the Hebrew (Masoretic) Bible: Torah (the Law), Nevi'im (the Prophets), and Ketuvim (the Writings); or T+N+K, with vowels added to aid in pronouncing this acronym.

2. "Moses received Torah from Sinai and handed it on to Joshua, and Joshua to the elders, and the elders to the prophets, and the prophets handed it on to the men of the Great Assembly," *Pirke Aboth* 1.1; translated by Judah Goldin, *Living Talmud*, 43.

words, the divine Torah represents the very thoughts of God himself. Divine Torah is not only coeternal but also coterminous with the Lord God, being the very expression of his divine will.

Precisely because the fullness of divine Torah cannot be confined to the written text, the rabbis expended great energy searching out meanings that might be hidden or only opaquely stated within these sacred scriptures. What is more, seemingly contradictory passages, for example, differing accounts of the creation of the man and his wife, might need to be reconciled. Finally, it must be remembered that originally Hebrew was written consonantally only. Because vowels were not written, confusion over intended meanings was not infrequent. To illustrate, without any indication of the associated vowels, the consonants "cr" might represent any number of English words: car, cur, care, cere, core, acre. One would normally be able to determine from context which word the writer intended, but not always. For all of these reasons, and others besides, the rabbis might disagree about the precise meaning of a text. Indeed, they competed to find additional possible meanings in a text, meanings that may have been overlooked by others. The very word *midrash* refers to a "searching" of the Scriptures with the goal of adducing a fuller sense or meaning present in the text. In the view of the rabbis, it is through study, interpretation, and debate that the "whole Torah" is uncovered and understood.

Midrash Rabba: Genesis

Eventually the diverse interpretations and opinions of the more honored rabbis were collected and written down. The most famous of these collections is the Mishna Rabba, a series of volumes devoted to various books of the Bible, particularly the Torah. We will explore the Adam and Eve tradition of classical Judaism as it is represented principally in the Midrash Rabba on Genesis, alternatively known as Genesis Rabba (the Great Midrash on Genesis, herein abbreviated Gen. Rab.).[3]

Exact dating of midrashic materials is difficult because they were composed and continuously supplemented over the course of several centuries. Most scholars think Genesis Rabba was mostly complete by

---

3. Unless otherwise indicated, all references are to Genesis Rabba are from the first volume of *Midrash Rabbah: Genesis,* trans. H. Freedman, being volumes 1–2 of the larger ten volume work *Midrash Rabbah,* translated by Freedman and Simon.

500 CE. And although Jewish traditions about Adam and Eve continued to be embellished during the Middle Ages and beyond, we will limit our study to the classical period, as the basic outlines of Jewish tradition were set by then. One notable exception is a late tradition about Lilith, the "first wife" of Adam, which we will treat at the end of this chapter.

As already noted, midrashic rabbis were of many opinions regarding how any given biblical text should be interpreted and how apparent contradictions should be explained. The multitude of opinions about the proper interpretation of passages in Genesis that deal with Adam and Eve illustrate this phenomenon very well. In addition to expounding upon the biblical story of Adam and Eve, there was much moralizing about how their descendants ought to conduct themselves, as well as explanations of the origins—the etiologies, if you will—of later Jewish practice.

As with other talmudic texts, it is assumed that the reader or "student" has the biblical text open and is following it closely. Genesis Rabba is a verse-by-verse commentary on selected verses, not a retelling of the story itself.

The Creation(s) of Adam and Eve

According to Gen 1:26, when God set out to create humankind, God said, "Let *us* make humankind in *our* image, according to *our* likeness." For midrashic interpreters, two questions immediately arose: (1) With whom is God speaking, and (2) To whom does "our" refer? Genesis Rabba (8.4–9) records several different responses to these questions.

Rabbi Simon proffered what might seem an obvious conclusion: God is speaking to his ministering angels (who were believed to be the very first beings God created, as it says in Gen 1:1, "In the beginning God created the heavens and the earth"). Patently God had summoned his ministering angels in council to announce his decision to create humankind. The angels misunderstood, however, and thought that God was seeking their advice. One group of angels advised for creation; another group advised against, arguing that humankind ('*adam*) would only compound falsehood on earth. While the angels debated, God, like a king, went ahead and did as he had planned all along. God knew that some humans would turn out bad while others would be good, but ultimately it was God's mercy that would prevail.

Attributed to Rabbi Hanina is an amusing wordplay on the name "Adam" that preoccupied the angels in their deliberations. As already noted, Hebrew scribes wrote down only consonants without the associated vowels, making it possible to misread the intended word. Confusion might be compounded still further by scrambling the order of the consonants. Thus "Adam" in Hebrew, omitting the vowels, is *'dm*, and can represent either the proper name "Adam" or a common noun "human/ humankind." Moreover, the word "very" (*me'od*) contains the same three consonants (though in a different order) and is thus the equivalent of "Adam." It is written, "And God saw everything that he had made, and behold it was good—*very*" (Gen 1:31), which suggested to Rabbi Hanina the reading "and behold *Adam* was good!" This in turn meant that the "pro-creation" angels won the argument, since what God created was at one and the same time both "Adam (or Man)" and also "*very* good." Rabbi Huna the Elder extended this punning exercise even further, saying that while the angels were arguing amongst themselves, God ignored their debate but instead went ahead with the creation of Adam. Then he turned to the angels and put an end to their arguments with these words, "Man/ Adam has (already) been made!" What Rabbi Huna did here was simply to read the Hebrew consonants of the verb *n'sh* in Genesis 1.26 with different vowels, namely, *ne'asah* ("is made") rather than *na'aseh* ("let us make"). He thereby altered the deity's statement from "Let us make Man/ Adam" to "Man/Adam has been made!" The matter is settled!

But precisely what manner of man did God create? Genesis Rabba 8.1 reports Rabbi Jeremiah b. Leazar had argued God originally created Adam as a hermaphrodite (or androgyne), since in Genesis 5:2 it is said, "Male and female he created them and called their name Adam." Normally, "androgynous" refers to someone having both male and female genitals; but Rabbi Jeremiah b. Leazar opined that Adam had two bodies, a male body and a female body joined together back-to-back. In this opinion he is joined by Rabbi Samuel b. Nahman, who specified that Adam originally was "double-faced"; then God split Adam and made him to have "two backs—one back for this side and one back for the other side." When someone objected that according to Genesis 2:21, God "took one of his ribs" and built that into the woman, the rabbi correctly pointed out that elsewhere the word in question (*tsela'*) more properly refers to a "side" (as in one "side" of the tabernacle, Exodus 26:2). The implication, therefore, is that God split Adam in half, building one *side* into a "man/ male" and the other *side* he built into a "woman/female."

"Side" itself provoked debates. Some argued for the left side, where the heart is located, thereby giving the woman an edge over men with regard to emotions. Others opined that it was the bottom half, as women are inherently inferior to men. Yet others posited, applying a similar logic, that it was the back side (that is, the rear end), making women inferior. Patently, there was little incentive at this time to accord women equal status.

In making the decision about which body part to use for making the woman, God had deliberated very carefully:

> I will not create her from the eye, lest she be a coquette; nor from the ear, lest she be an eavesdropper, nor from the mouth, lest she be a gossip; nor from the heart, lest she be prone to jealousy; nor from the hand, lest she be light-fingered[4]; nor from the foot, lest she be a gadabout; but from the modest part of man, for even when he stands naked, that part is covered. (Gen. Rab. 17.2)

Rabbi Hisda felt compelled to add: "[God] built more chambers in her (i.e., a womb) than in man, fashioning her broad below and narrow at the top, so that she could receive child" (17.3).

In Rabbi Joshua b. Karhah's opinion, God should have provided Adam and Eve with "garments of skin" right from the beginning, since observing them naked and especially engaging in sexual intercourse is what aroused in the serpent a passion for the woman and led him eventually to seduce her. Rabbi Jacob of Kefar Hanan countered that it would have been inappropriate to conclude this passage by focusing on the serpent, which is why God refrained (17.6).

It is said that the first human was of humongous stature. Indeed, the rabbis seemed to compete in finding words to describe his massive size (Gen. Rab. 8.1; 21.3). One said he filled the whole world, from one end to the other. Another, that his body stretched from the east to the west. Still others, that he filled the entire space between the ground and the sky. His gigantic stature was tremendously reduced following upon his sin, however.[5] When that first human was created, he was so magnificent that the angels mistook him for a divine being and wanted to bow down in worship. God quickly corrected the angels' error by causing Adam to fall into a deep sleep, showing that he was but a mortal man (8.10).

---

4. I.e., thievish.

5. Adam's original gigantic size and later reduction is reported more briefly in the Babylonian Talmud, *Sanhedrin* 38b.

Indeed, humankind falls midway between angels and beasts, having four attributes of the higher beings and four attributes of the lower beings. Like the angels, humans stand erect, can speak, have the capacity to understand, and can see to both sides by moving only the eyes. Like the beasts, humans eat and drink, procreate, excrete, and die. The celestial beings were created in the image and likeness of God, but do not procreate, while terrestrial beasts procreate; also angels were not created in God's image and likeness. Rabbi Tifdai, following Rabbi Aha, maintained that this mid status was intentional on God's part, for God reasoned: "If I create him of celestial elements (only), he will live (forever) and not die; and if I create him of terrestrial elements (only), he will die and not live (in a future life). Therefore I will create him of (both) celestial and terrestrial elements:[6] if he sins, he will die; while if he does not sin, he will live" (Gen. Rab. 8.11; similarly 14.3).

And then there is the opinion of Judah b. Rabbi that the Human originally had a tail, citing as evidence the scripture "and *'adam* became a *nefesh hayyah* (literally, "a living soul"). But as *hayyah* can also mean "beast" or "animal," Judah b. Rabbi argued—without benefit of modern biology—that *nefesh hayyah* means that man at first also had animal characteristics, and hence a tail, but that God "subsequently removed it from him for the sake of his dignity" (14.10).

When God brought the animals to Adam to be named, they came in pairs, two by two. In naming them appropriately, Adam demonstrated his superior knowledge. But at the same time, Adam recognized also that he alone lacked an appropriate companion. So, he asked God for a suitable partner. God caused Adam to fall into a deep sleep and removed "one of his ribs"—others say it was "one side of him"—which he built into the woman Eve. Why did God not create a companion for Adam at the beginning? Because God foresaw that Adam would bring charges against the woman. Therefore, God did not create her until Adam expressly requested her (17.4–6).

Despite the statement of Genesis 2:25 that the man and the woman were both naked and felt no shame, some say that when God presented Eve to Adam, he brought her fully clothed and decked out as a bride in twenty-four pieces of finest cloth and jewelry.[7] Moreover God brought them together under multiple bridal canopies having walls of gold and

6. I.e., the soul is from heaven while the body if from earth.
7. These opinions were based upon passages such as Ezek 28:13 and Isa 3:18–24.

coverings of precious stones and pearls (Gen. Rab. 18.1). These wedding allusions are implied in the statement: "For this reason a man shall leave his father and his mother and cleave unto his wife" (Gen. Rab. 18.5, quoting Gen 2:24). Genesis Rabba 14.7 had specified that Adam and Eve had been created as full adults—specifically, at an age of twenty years; they were therefore sexually mature and ready for marriage.

Their happiness was short lived, thanks to the serpent. Rabbi Hoshaya the Elder said of the serpent that he stood erect, "like a reed, and he had feet." Rabbi Jeremiah b. Eleazar added that the serpent was "an unbeliever," while Rabbi Simeon b. Eleazar described him as being "like a camel" of tremendous strength (Gen. Rab. 19.1). Such was the awesome opponent that naïve Eve had to confront—alone! Where was Adam during the whole episode when Eve was being seduced by the serpent? Abba Halfon b. Koriah says that Adam was fast asleep, having dozed off after a session of vigorous sex with his new bride. (Male physiology has remained pretty much unchanged since the very beginning, apparently.)

Adam and Eve and the Serpent

Sometime prior, it would appear, Adam had foolishly put a "fence" around God's command (Gen. Rab. 19.3). Although God had only commanded Adam not to *eat* from the tree of knowledge of good and evil, when conveying the divine command to Eve, Adam had added a further restriction: "neither shall you *touch* it." The serpent used this unnecessary further restriction to trick Eve. Undoubtedly Eve was surprised by the serpent's ability to address her in her own Hebrew language.[8] Caught off guard by the serpent's question about whether any tree was off limits for her, Eve blithely blurted out that not only were she and Adam forbidden to eat from one particular tree, but they will also die if they even touch it. Not so, the serpent replied, God has lied to you; he is merely concerned to prevent you two from becoming gods yourselves and rivaling him by

8. Although Josephus (*Ant.* 1.4), writing toward the end of the first century CE, attributed to all creatures in paradise the ability to speak Hebrew, Louis Ginsberg (*Legends of the Jews*, 5:94 n. 58) claims that older rabbinic literature, including Genesis Rabba, knew only of the serpent—the wisest of all beasts—as having the ability to communicate in human language. The original human language was Hebrew; the confusion of human speech came about only with the attempt to construct the tower of Babel (Gen 11:1–9). The Babylonian Talmud, *Sanhedrin* 38b, says that the original language was Aramaic, not Hebrew, probably because Babylonian Jews had long since switched to speaking Aramaic.

creating other worlds. To demonstrate the "veracity" of this lie, the serpent shoved Eve against the tree. "So, have you died?" the serpent taunted her; "just as you have not been stricken from touching it, so you will not die from eating it."

From that very moment, as the serpent had predicted, Eve did indeed begin down a different path with "opened eyes" (Gen. Rab. 19.5). Not only was the serpent correct that she had not died, she saw also that the tree was good in a threefold way: (1) it was good for food; (2) it was a delight to the eyes; and (3) it was to be desired for making one wise. Foolishly she ate, only to recognize the real truth: that she was now destined to die. She also realized that if Adam did not eat and die as well, God would surely create another Eve for him—a thought she found totally unbearable. Accordingly, she squeezed some grapes for wine and approached Adam with great lamentation. With much weeping and many tears, she prevailed upon him to partake of the forbidden tree. Not content to ruin Adam, she also gave the cattle, the beasts, and the birds to eat of it also, so that that they would have to suffer death as well. (According to a parallel passage in Gen. Rab. 20.8, Adam was the one responsible for giving animals the forbidden fruit to eat.)

Implied here is that the "tree of knowledge of good and evil" was a grape vine. Others opined that it was wheat, which grew as lofty as the cedars of Lebanon; or corn, whose ears were a handbreadth in width; or a citrus. Some said it was a fig, because only the fig would allow its leaves to be used to cover the nakedness of the man and the woman, it being complicit in their sin. Still others cautioned that it is useless to speculate about the species of the tree, since "The Holy One, blessed be He, did not reveal to man what that tree was" (15.7).

Standing beside the Tree of Knowledge was the Tree of Life. This second tree was even more special; it spread far and wide, providing shelter for every living thing. To travel beneath the shadow of its crown from one edge to the other would require a journey of five hundred years. Others say it was not the width of its boughs but the diameter of its trunk that required a five-hundred-years journey (15.6).

When Adam sinned, six things were taken away from him: his luster, his immortality, his height, the fruit of the earth, the fruit of the trees, and the luminaries (Gen. Rab. 12.6). A scripture is cited to prove each of these six loses. Perhaps the most interesting "loss" in light of what has already been said, is that Adam's height was reduced to a *mere* one hundred cubits (approximately 150 feet).⁹ (Others posited that Adam's stature had been reduced only to 200 cubits, or 500 cubits, or even 900 cubits.) Whatever Adam's final stature, how do we know that his height had been drastically reduced? Because it says that when God called out to the man and his wife, "Where are you?" (Gen 3:8), they were able to hide among the trees, so small had they become!

Regarding the statement in Genesis 3:8 that "they heard (the sound of the Lord God walking in the garden)," instead of "and they heard" (*wayyishme'u*), Rabbi Berekiah read "and they caused to hear" (*wayyashmi'u*), referring to the trees speaking: "See the deceiver who deceived his Creator!" Rabbi Hanina b. Papa said, no, it was ministering angels they heard, with some angels saying that "The Lord God is certainly going to the garden (to punish them)," while other angels were saying, "The one in the garden is a goner, dead!" or even, "Is [that man] still walking about (and not already dead)?" But the Holy One, blessed be He, said to the angels, "Behold I am giving [Adam] a one-day respite—one of my days, which is a thousand years. He will live nine hundred and thirty years, leaving seventy for his children." Thus did God prove true to his word, that should the man (and his wife) disobey the divine command by eating from the forbidden tree, they would die in that very day. At one and the same time, God was showing mercy.

For the serpent, however, God had no mercy, but instead made it the most cursed of the whole animal kingdom (Gen. Rab. 20.5). God instructed his ministering angels to descend from heaven and cut off the serpent's hands and feet. When they did so, the serpent's "cries (of pain) resounded from one end of the world to the other," for as is said about the fall of Babylon, "The cry thereof shall go (sound forth) like that of the serpent." God condemned the serpent, saying that he had made him to be king over all cattle and beasts. Because the serpent had spurned God's offer, henceforth it shall crawl on its belly, eating dust as his food. But even in this curse Rabbi Eleazar finds a measure of God's mercy: God did not impose a death sentence upon the serpent but rather allowed it to escape by crawling under walls and hiding in holes.

Also in the curse that befalls Adam, certain rabbis found elements of blessing (Gen. Rab. 20.10). Rabbi Isaac said that when Adam heard that the ground, no matter the amount of toil, would produce (only) thorns and thistles, and that Adam would be forced to eat grass or such

9. Similarly, Gen. Rab. 19.8.

from the field, "his face broke out into a perspiration [of anguish] and he exclaimed, 'What! Shall I be tied to the feeding-trough like a beast?" God took Adam's sweating as a favorable sign and partially relented, substituting bread in place of grass: "You shall eat bread until you return to dust from which you were taken" (Gen 3:18–19). Rabbi Simeon b. Yohai said even the threat of impending death was somewhat mitigated. In the words "You are dust, and to dust you shall return" there are hints of resurrection. This scripture does not say, "For you are dust, and unto dust you shall go," but rather "you shall return"—which he seemingly interpreted as "you shall go to the dust, yet you shall return," that is, at the resurrection.[10]

Similar cords of God's mercy have been posited for how God clothed Adam and Eve at their expulsion from Eden. In place of the standard reading of Genesis 3:21, "And the Lord God made garments of *skin* for Adam and his wife," Rabbi Meir's copy of the Torah had "garments of *light*." Although both words in Hebrew may have been pronounced alike, the word ʿ*or* ("skin") is written with the letter ʾ*ayin,* while the word ʾ*or* ("light") is written with the letter ʾ*aleph.* Relying upon his copy of the Torah, Rabbi Meir insisted that God had cloaked Adam and Eve with radiant brilliance before sending them forth from the garden. Other rabbis kept "skin," but instead of a basic rustic leather loin cloth; they understood God to dress the man and his wife in fine clothes, with "skin girdles" referring to the smooth linen undergarments worn next to their skin. Still others interpreted "garments of skin" as referring to clothes make of soft fur, such as rabbit pelts, or lambs' wool, or the wool of camels (Gen. Rab. 20.12). In any case, the Lord God had dispensed with the original uncomfortable, itchy fig-leaf garb crudely crafted by the man and his wife.

Even the manner by which God expelled the couple from Eden became a matter of debate. Did the Lord God "*send [Adam] forth*" as it says in Genesis 3:23 "to till the ground"? Or did he "*drive him out*" as it says in the next verse, and then posted cherubim guards to prevent any possibility of return? Was it an act of justice, or mercy, or both? Rabbi Joshua b. Levi says it was both. Rabbi Johanan espoused the harsher view, because there can be no return to Eden, neither in this world nor the next. By contrast, Rabbi Simeon b. Lakish argued the case for God's leniency, namely,

---

10. So Freedman, *Midrash Rabbah: Genesis I,* 169 n. 8.

that there may be the possibility of a return in the world to come (Gen. Rab. 21.7–8).

Life Outside the Garden

Adam and Eve produced no offspring while in the Eden, likely because they resided there only for a very short while. It was a quite different story, however, once they were outside the garden. It is said that Adam called his wife Eve because she was the mother of "all living." Rabbi Simeon b. Eleazar took this quite literally. Eve was mother not only of all humans but also of the demons. How Rabbi Simeon arrived at this conclusion is much easier to grasp in Aramaic and Mishnaic Hebrew, where the word for "serpent" is ḥiwya, a word that both in form and sound closely resembles the name Ḥawwah (Eve). It was a short step, therefore, to posit that Eve was mother of the demons as well. Rabbi Simeon says that "Adam held aloof from Eve"—that is, did not have sex with her—for 130 years following their departure from Eden. The reason for this abstinence is not stated here, but later talmudic rabbis attribute Adam's action to repentance. Adam blamed himself for the death of Abel because death had entered the world because of Adam's sin. For 130 years Adam separated himself from Eve as he sat fasting and doing penance by wearing fig leaves (Eruvin 18b). Unfortunately, the result was not as salubrious as Adam had desired. During those 130 years, the serpent satisfied his lust for the beautiful Eve by copulating frequently with her, as did other male demons, so that Eve bore many demon offspring. One must not ignore Adam, however. During this same period female demons were "made ardent" by Adam, so that they also bore (Gen. Rab. 20.11; 24.6). Later talmudic rabbis attempted to excuse Adam of culpability for his demonic offspring, however, by asserting that his semen had been released accidentally during dreams as he slept (Eruvin 18b). The implication is that female demons scooped up Adam's spilled semen, with which they impregnated themselves. However it happened, there certainly was no shortage of demons to trouble Adam's and Eve's descendants. When Adam finally reunited with Eve after that hundred-thirty-year hiatus, he sired another "son in his likeness, according to his image, and named him Seth" (Gen 5:3).

But let us return for a moment to the births of Cain and Abel. In Genesis 4:1–2 it is written: "And the man knew his wife Eve, and she conceived and bore Cain, and she said, 'I have gotten a man with the help of the Lord.' And she continued to bear his brother Abel." We moderns have been conditioned to assume this text speaks of Cain and Abel having been born at different times. But the text is ambiguous and can be understood otherwise. Consider, for example, Rabbi Joshua b. Karhah's commentary on this passage: "Only two entered the bed, but seven left it: Cain and his twin sister, Abel and his two twin sisters" (Gen. Rab. 22.2). Rabbi Joshua patently understands the text to imply there was only a single pregnancy, but it resulted in the birth of quintuplets.

This point is reinforced in Gen. Rab. 22.3, that this passage "implies an additional birth, but not an additional pregnancy." Not only were Cain and Abel conceived and born at the same time, but Cain's twin sister and Abel's two twin sisters as well. What is the evidence for this interpretation? Genesis 4:17 mentions a wife for Cain but does not mention any additional conceptions or births by Eve. Popular culture gave rise to numerous explanations not only for the origin of Cain's wife but also for the rapid propagation of humankind. One explanation was that Eve had borne twins—a girl as well a boy—when birthing Cain and/or Abel; this daughter was destined to become Cain's wife. A variant legend posits that Cain and Abel, while born at different times, each had a twin sister, and each brother married his twin. Abel's sister/wife was more beautiful, causing Cain to become jealous of his brother, so much so that desire for his brother's wife became a factor in Cain's killing Abel. Yet another variant (Gen. Rab. 22.7) is that Abel had two twin sisters, one more beautiful than the other. Cain maintained that he, as the older brother, had the right to marry Abel's second, more beautiful twin. Abel insisted that she should be his wife because she was his twin. In this version, too, jealousy was a factor in Cain's murder of his brother. Rabbi Joshua seems to have merged these traditions in concluding that "only two (Adam and Eve) entered the bed, but seven left it: Cain and his twin sister, Abel and his two twin sisters."

Traditions surrounding Eve's conception and the birth of Cain are more complex still. Commenting on the verse, "and she conceived and bore Cain" (Gen 4:1), Rabbi Eleazar b. 'Azariah is reported to have said, "Three miracles were performed on that day: on that very day [Adam and Eve] were created, on that very day they had sex, and on that very day they produced offspring" (Gen. Rab. 22.2). All that in one day! Now Rabbi Eleazar was not thinking of one of the Lord's days—a thousand years by human reckoning. No, Rabbi Eleazar was counting in human years, but tapping into a Jewish tradition according to which Adam and Eve were in Eden only a very short time, a few hours at most. They sinned almost immediately following their creation. Unlike some Christian moralists, Judaism has no aversion to linking sex with life in Eden. Cain was conceived in Eden, when Adam and Eve performed their initial "marital duty" immediately following Eve's creation, before they sinned and were expelled from Eden. What is more surprising is that Eve's pregnancy was so short, less than a day, as Cain was born in that same day but outside Eden. No wonder that in Gen. Rab. 24.7 these events were labelled as "miracles." Rabbi Eleazar's was far from the only voice on this matter, however.

While agreeing with the view that Abel had been born on the very day that the world was created, Rabbi Eliezer and Rabbi Joshua disagreed about the month. The former argued for the month of Tishri and said that Abel had lived from the Festival of Tabernacles (which begins on the fifteenth of Tishri) until Hanukkah (the festival of lights which begins on the twenty-fifth of Kislev). In opposition, the latter asserted that the world had been created at the commencement of Passover, in the month of Nisan, and that Abel died on Pentecost. "In either case, all agree that Abel was not in the world more than fifty days" (Gen. Rab. 22.4).

When Adam finally ended his prolonged period of penance and abstinence after 130 years, it was only because Lamech—the wicked descendant of Cain who according to Genesis 4:23-24 boasted to his two wives that he was ten times more violent than his murdering ancestor—had shamed his ancestor Adam for neglecting his duty of begetting additional children by Eve (Gen. Rab. 23.4). Jolted back to reality, Adam's desire for Eve revived. "And Adam knew his wife again, and she bore a son and named him Seth, for she said, 'God has appointed for me another seed in place of Abel, because Cain killed him.' To Seth also a son was born, and he named him Enosh" (Gen 4:25-26).

With the birth of Enosh the primeval period comes to an end, for Enosh was the last of Adam's descendants to possess fully those qualities which had defined Adam. At least some rabbis read the biblical text as signaling a major transition in human history at this point, namely, that the era of creation had ended and the post primeval era—our era—had begun. Not only is Enosh the last of Adam's descendants to be named in this passage, but the next verse seems to imply that a new era has begun, the era introduced as "the Book of the Generations of Adam" (Gen 5:1).

Like most everything written in the Torah, however, midrashic rabbis found much in these verses to debate (Gen. Rab. 24.5–7). Rabbi Judah opined that "the Book" refers to the Written Torah with its 613 precepts—248 positive and 365 negative. This book, the Torah, was not given to Adam but to his descendants. Abba Cohen Bardela taught that "four things changed in the days of Enosh: the mountains became [barren] rocks, the dead began to feel [the worms], men's faces became ape-like,[11] and they became vulnerable to demons" (24.6). Another interpretation: While those of this (our) era are true descendants of Adam, those of the former era were not, referring to the numerous demons generated by Adam during the 130 years he remained aloof from Eve. A related opinion: The former were not labelled as "descendants of Adam" because everyone descended through Cain has been destroyed off the face of the earth by the flood.

Uncharacteristically, Genesis Rabba passes over in silence the final two verses in the Torah about Adam living another 800 years after the birth of Seth and that during that time Adam sired other sons and daughters (Gen 5:4–5). Apparently, there was little controversial about the final years of the life of Adam (or Eve), at least in the biblical text.

Lilith: Adam's First Wife

The tale of Lilith,[12] Adam's first wife, first appears in a little-known Medieval text known as the Alphabet of Ben Sira,[13] but soon became firmly entrenched in Jewish folklore. This anonymous text is attributed to Jesus ben Sirach, the author of the Wisdom of Sirach (written ca. 180 BCE); but that is patently not possible as our text dates only to sometime between 700 CE and 1000 CE. In the centuries since, the figure Lilith has acquired

11. Likely meaning they lost their luster.

12. Much has been written about Lilith, some more fanciful than tradition warrants. For a convenient, up-to-date presentation, see the article on "Lilith" in Wikipedia (https://en.wikipedia.org/wiki/Lilith). See also Jo Milgrom, "Adam's First Wife," 225–53; and Ben-Amos, "Lilith in the Garden," 54–58.

13. The story of Lilith is found in the "second alphabet" of Ben Sira, an apocryphal collection of twenty-two "proverbs" (tales) in Hebrew; the tale Lilith is the fifth response of Ben Sira to King Nebuchadnezzar. For a critical translation, see Yassif, *Tales of Ben Sira*, 64–67. Translations of the relevant passage may also be found in Kvam et al., *Eve and Adam,* 204. Online, see Wikipedia, "Alphabet of Sirach": https://en.wikipedia.org/wiki/Alphabet_of_Sirach.

ever-increasing importance as both her legend and her role have greatly proliferated.

The genesis for the idea that Adam had two wives is rooted in the biblical story of creation. Eve is first mentioned in Genesis 2:18–25, wherein, according to the conventional understanding of this text, God took a "rib" from the side "Adam" and built it into the woman Eve. Plainly, here "Adam" is said to have been created prior to "Eve." But this text seems to contradict the prior statement in Genesis 1:27–28, to wit, "And God created the human (*ha-ʾadam*) in his own image, in the image of God he created **him**, male and female he created **them**. God blessed **them**, saying, 'Be fertile and increase; fill the earth and control it. Rule over the fish of the sea, the birds of the sky, and all the living things that creep on earth.'"

On its surface, this text would seem to say that when God created humankind, he made the male and the female of the human species simultaneously. At least, it can be read that way, and that is how some Jewish interpreters understood it. Moreover, this reading was reinforced from Genesis 5:1–2: "This is the book of the generations of Adam/ humankind (ʾadam). In the day that God created Adam/humankind (ʾadam), in the likeness of God he made him; male and female he created **them** and blessed **them** and called **their** name Adam (ʾadam)." These texts would allow that the creation of Eve narrated in Genesis 2 happened only subsequently to the creation of a prior woman recounted in Genesis 1. Such is the basis for the legend of Lilith as Adam's first wife.

That certainly was the understanding of the Alphabet of Ben Sira, that when God first created humankind, God made the first male (Adam) and the first female (Lilith) at the same time, with the intention that they would be husband and wife—as well as the progenitors of the human race. Harmony between Adam and Lilith quickly dissipated, however, as they immediately began quarreling over which of them had priority. Adam attempted to assert his authority over Lilith, but she resisted, saying that God had created them both at the same time and from the same substance; therefore, they should be equal. The quarrel is amusingly told in sexual terms. When it came time for them to procreate, Adam asserted that he should be on top, "for you are fit only to be in the bottom position while I am the superior one." Lilith countered, "We are equal to each other inasmuch as we were both created from the earth." As they were unable to compromise, Lilith asserted her independence by leaving Adam and fleeing into the desert.

Adam complained to God, "Sovereign of the earth, the woman you gave me has run away." God sent three angels to try and persuade Lilith to return. The angels found her in the Red Sea but were unsuccessful in their mission—despite threats that if she refused to return, one hundred of her children would "die every day." Defiantly, Lilith retorted that she would cause others' babies to die. "If an infant is male, I have dominion over him for eight days after his birth, and if female, for twenty days." Nevertheless, Lilith swears by the living and eternal God that she will forego stealing any child that is protected by an amulet bearing the image or the name of one or all three angels. Thereafter, Lilith acquired a reputation as a child snatching demon. According to some myths, Lilith mated with the fallen archangel Samael—a Satan-equivalent fallen angel—and bore great numbers of demon offspring, demons which to this day still roam the earth wreaking havoc. According to others, Lilith is a seductress who plagues men by night and is the cause of their wet dreams, and worse.

Although the legend of Lilith as the first wife of Adam dates only to approximately the tenth century, the figure of Lilith as a female demon that harms humans, adults as well as infants, is alleged to have a much longer and more diverse history. Some eighty bowls from Babylon and elsewhere in Mesopotamia dating to the Sasanian Empire period (fourth to sixth centuries CE) have been excavated from beneath the floors of numerous houses. In the center of each bowl is the figure of a female demon named Lilith or her male counterpart Lilit. Surrounding the demonic figure is a spiraling inscription—an incantation written in Jewish Babylonian Aramaic, Syriac, or other language of the region—warning the demon to stay away. The incantation is fortified with quotations from Scripture or the Talmud. These bowls were then turned upside down and buried underneath the floor of the house, sometimes one at each of the four corners. Ostensibly their purpose was to trap the demon and keep it from entering the house and harming the occupants, particularly any newborn. Although there is nothing in these incantation bowls linking Lilith to Adam in any way whatever, they do provide evidence of an earlier "career" for Lilith as a malevolent demon against whom one must guard.

From approximately this same period, in the Gemara of the Babylonian Talmud there are five rather opaque references to Lilith.[14] All refer to her as some kind of demonic figure to be avoided. Only one specifies

14. Niddah 24b, Eruvin 100b, Gittin 69b, Bava Batra 73a-b, and Shabbat 151b.

the danger she poses, and it is directed to men who are particularly susceptible to Lilith's wanton ways: "R. Hanina said: One should not sleep
in a house alone, for whoever sleeps in a house alone is seized by Lilith"
(Shabbath 151b). This might refer to nothing more than lonely men being especially prone to masturbation or wet dreams; but it likely points
to something more sinister, namely, a belief that nocturnal emissions
somehow engender the birth of demons.

> "R. Jeremiah b. Eleazar further stated: In all those years [follow-
> ing his expulsion from the Garden of Eden] during which Adam
> was under the ban he begot ghosts and male demons and female
> demons [or night demons], for it is said in Scripture: And Adam
> lived a hundred and thirty years and begot a son in own like-
> ness, after his own image, from which it follows that until that
> time he did not beget after his own image . . . When he saw
> that through him death was ordained as punishment, he spent a
> hundred and thirty years in fasting, severed connection with his
> wife for a hundred and thirty years, and wore clothes of fig on
> his body for a hundred and thirty years. That statement [of R.
> Jeremiah] was made in reference to the semen which he emitted
> accidentally." (Eruvin 18b)

The Midrash Rabba contains three possible references to Lilith. The
first two are quite questionable since they do not explicitly name Lilith.
As a (partial) motive for Cain murdering his brother Abel, Genesis Rabba
22:7 vaguely references a quarrel between the two about "the first Eve"
(Ḥawwah ha-rishona), which is said to have occurred "after the first Eve
had returned to dust." Granted that in the medieval Hebrew literature and
folklore, Ḥawwah ha-rishona was identified with Lilith, it is unlikely that
such an identification was made already this early in Jewish antiquity.
Equally implausible as a reference to Lilith is the curious statement in
Genesis Rabba 18.4 that God "recreated her (Eve) a second time" because
"he (God or Adam?) saw her full of discharge and blood." This would
appear to say that an original version of Eve was found unacceptable because she menstruated continuously.

A third, more explicit, reference to Lilith is found in Numbers Rabba
16:25. The context is God's threat to destroy the Israelite people for their
reluctance to carry out the divine command to attack the Canaanites following the report of the returning spies about the gigantic size of the
enemy warriors. Moses intercedes for the Israelites, appealing to God not
to act like Lilith who kills her own children:

[God,] do not do it [i.e., destroy the Israelite people], that the nations of the world may not regard you as a cruel being and say: "The generation of the flood came and he destroyed them, the generation of the separation came and he destroyed them, the Sodomites and the Egyptians came and he destroyed them, and these also, whom he called my son, my firstborn (Exod 4:22), he is now destroying! As that Lilith who, when she finds nothing else, turns upon her own children, so because the Lord was not able to bring this people into the land . . . he hath slain them" (Num 14:16).

While Lilith here is depicted as a demonic figure who kills—this time her own children—there is no indication that she is in any way connected to Adam, however. While Numbers Rabba seems to have been written down sometime in the Middle Ages, it incorporates materials from earlier periods. It is probable that this midrash has its origins in older tradition still.

The word *lilith* occurs only once in the Hebrew Bible (Isaiah 34:14), and its precise reference there is not entirely certain. The context is an oracle against Edom for having aided Babylon in the destruction of Judah in 587 BCE. Various punishments upon Edom are threatened, including being ravaged by ferocious unclean beasts known to inhabit wilderness regions: jackals, ostriches, wildcats, and hyenas. But the list also includes mythical and semi-mythical creatures believed to haunt deserted places: satyrs (goat-headed demons) and Lilith, along with owls and buzzards. A related text (Isa 13:21) speaks of ruins being populated with "howling beasts." Given the strange combination of wild beasts and mythic figures, for centuries commentators have struggled to find an appropriate translation for the word *lilith* here. The Latin Vulgate rendered it as "lamia"—a reference to the Greek myth of Lamia, the beautiful queen of Lybia who became a monster, half woman and half serpent, roaming the earth devouring children as revenge for Hera having killed Lamia's own children conceived in adulterous trysts with Zeus. In this same vein are "night monster" (ASV), "night hag" (RSV), "night creature" (NIV), and "vampire" (Moffatt). Given the threatening context of Isaiah 37:12–17, naturalistic renderings of *lilith* as a "screech owl" (KJV), "nightjar" (New World Translation), or "night bird" (ESV) are probably wide of the mark. Some element of the demonic does seem intended. This conclusion is not negated by the fact that the great Dead Sea Scroll for Isaiah 34:14 has the plural *liliyyot* "liliths" rather than the singular as in the Masoretic Text. This merely suggests that the Dead Sea Scrolls community understood *lilith* in Isaiah 34:14 to refer to a whole category of female demons rather than to a single archetype.[15]

These biblical and Jewish traditions about a *lillit*-demon likely have some connection with the *lilû* (fem. *lilītu*) demon mentioned in still earlier Mesopotamian texts. Various cuneiform omens and ritual texts prescribe methods for warding off both a male *lilu*-demon and a female *lilītu*-demon. Both demons lurk in hidden corners. They have no bed of their own but rather roam about incessantly. When they come across an unsuspecting person, young or old, they can inflict various illnesses and evils such as headaches, epilepsy, or even death. Hence the need for protective rituals. It is noteworthy that a special ritual is prescribed for infants, "in order that the *lilu*-demon should not come near the baby."[16]

In this context one may also mention two inscribed limestone plaques from seventh or eighth century BCE Arslan Tash in upper Syria. These plaques appear to have been amulets worn to ward off child-devouring demons, one of whom is named Lilith. The authenticity of these Arslan Tash amulets is much debated, however. Moreover, the purported name "Lilith" occurs in a broken context and must be partially restored, rendering the value of these Arslan Tash plaques as evidence for a pre-Jewish Lilith highly uncertain at best.[17]

This lengthy review of alleged "sightings" of Lilith has produced no evidence that the legend of Lilith as the first wife of Adam goes back any further than the Middle Ages and the Alphabet of Ben Sira. But in the centuries since that first appearance, the legend of Lilith the first wife of

15. The demonic nature of lilith—whether singular or plural—appears to be confirmed by a yet another fragmentary Dead Sea Scrolls text known as Songs of the Sage (4Q510–511), written perhaps a century later than the great Isaiah scroll; if correctly restored, it reads: "And I, the Instructor, proclaim his glorious splendor so as to frighten and to te[rrify] all the spirits of the destroying angels, spirits of the bastards, demons, Lilith, howlers, and [desert dwellers] . . . and those which fall upon men without warning to lead them astray from a spirit of understanding and to make their heart and their . . . desolate during the present dominion of wickedness and predetermined time of humiliations for the sons of lig[ht], by the guilt of the ages of [those] smitten by iniquity—not for eternal destruction, [bu]t for an era of humiliation for transgression"; translation from Chilton et al., *Comparative Handbook to the Gospel of Mark*, 84.

16. CAD 9/L, 190, sub voce *lilû*.

17. A number of scholars of the last century had opined that the so-called Burney Relief depicts Lilith, but that identification is now universally rejected. The unnamed winged, nude, goddess-like figure with bird's talons, flanked by owls, and perched upon two lions depicted on this Old Babylonian terracotta plaque is almost certainly the goddess Inanna/Ishtar, and not Lilith.

Adam turned demon has never been absent from popular lore, and never more so than in contemporary popular culture.

Assessing Adam and Eve in Classical Jewish Midrash

Classical Judaism adheres closely to the biblical narrative concerning Adam and Eve and the serpent as found in the book of Genesis. The rabbis responsible for creating the Talmud and its midrashic commentaries were less interested in expanding the story than in elucidating its meaning for a new age. As a result, the principal rabbinic witness to Jewish interpretation of the Adam and Eve tradition from this period, Genesis Rabba, is less a new narrative than an exploration of the Genesis text for overlooked meaning(s) that might be contained therein—in other words, a searching out of the Oral Torah revealed to Moses along with the Written Torah. The resulting discoveries were not considered to be new revelation so much as a deeper understanding of the revelation given to Moses.

While talmudic rabbis changed very little of the basic biblical narrative concerning Adam and Eve and the serpent, their "searches" (*midrashim*) did add a surprising amount of (hidden) new detail to the story. One need only think of the original humongous stature of the first human reaching into the sky. Or of the briefness of the first couple's stay in Eden: one day or less. Or of the possibility that the forbidden tree was a grape and its fruit as intoxicating wine. More intriguing still is the view that the first human was created as an androgyne (or hermaphrodite) and subsequently divided into two to form the male and the female of the human species.

As intriguing as such suggestions may be, of far greater significance is the way classical Judaism handled the introduction of evil into the world. The serpent is not Satan. The serpent remains a serpent throughout, even though he was a much more imposing creature prior to his being cursed and forced to grovel in the dirt and eat dust. The serpent's ruin was a result of his envy of the human couple and especially his lust for Eve. The serpent did cause the man and the woman to be cast out of Eden, but the serpent is never transformed into Satan, nor posited as the source of every human evil. Unlike Christianity, Judaism does not espouse a theory of original or hereditary sin, such that every descendant of Adam is born in sin and from which one must be redeemed.

According to the rabbis, humankind itself is largely responsible for the evil that plagues our world. Once outside Eden, Adam withdrew from Eve for 130 years, leaving her exposed to demonic machinations. The powerful demon Samael impregnated (raped?) Eve repeatedly during this time, causing her to give birth to many demon children. One tradition claims that Cain was sired by one such demon. One must not be overly critical of Eve, however, as it was Adam's actions that left her so vulnerable. Furthermore, another tradition claims that during the time of Adam's self-imposed 130-year separation from Eve, he also sired demon children, though not consciously but in his sleep. In any case, the multitude of demonic forces in the world are in large part the consequence of human actions. True, demons lurk everywhere, but they can be warded off.

Unfortunately, the rabbis continued to perpetuate the ages-old stereotype that women are more akin to evil than men and should be controlled by men. Nowhere is this more evident than in the medieval story of Lilith, the alleged first wife of Adam. Even though created at the same time as Adam and from the same substance as Adam, Lilith nonetheless desired the position of dominance. When Adam (rightly) refused to accede to such unnatural behavior, Lilith abandoned her divinely ordained role and fled, with the result that she was transformed into a demon and a killer of babies. Fortunately, the story of Lilith never succeeded in becoming a central tenet of classical Judaism—or of any religious tradition.

On the whole, classical Judaism posited a view of humankind that balances notions of good and evil. Without denying the presence of evil in the world, Judaism resisted any view that humans are incapable of resisting evil—especially overwhelming evil—but always remain free to choose the good.

11

Islam: Enter Iblis

ISLAM IS ONE OF the three Abrahamic religions, along with Judaism and Christianity. Muslims honor Moses and Jesus, along with Muhammad, as great prophets sent by God (Allah in Arabic) to instruct his righteous people. Muhammad is revered as the last and greatest of God's prophets because God's last and most authentic revelation was revealed to Muhammad who wrote it down in the Qur'an. Earlier revelations given to Moses, Jesus, and other prophets are also authentic, but have suffered corruption in transmission and must be corrected by what is recorded in the Qur'an.

It will come as no surprise, then, that the Qur'an also contains in broad outline the biblical tradition about the creation of Adam and Eve, their sojourn in the garden and eating of the forbidden tree, and their expulsion from paradise. At the same time, Islam recasts the story of the first man and woman in its own unique way in order to make it conform more closely to Islamic theology. "Paradise" in Islamic tradition is the name for the eternal abode of the blessed, what Christians commonly refer to as "heaven," the place of everlasting bliss. This is where God first placed Adam and Eve at their creation. After Adam and Eve sinned, they were cast out of paradise and sent down to earth. There they repented and were forgiven by God. Moreover, Adam became God's instrument to correct other sinners—so much so that in Islamic tradition Adam is regarded as the first in a long line of God's holy prophets.

There is no narrative about Adam and Eve in the Qur'an like that in Genesis. Indeed, the Qur'an contains few continuous narratives like those in the Bible. Instead it is composed of various moral teachings given as revelations to Muhammad at various times and places over the course of many years. According to tradition, these revelations were recorded at the time of their revelation. But when it came time to assemble these revelations into a book—the Qur'an—they were collected into "surahs" (chapters), each numbered and uniquely named, and further subdivided into verses. The arrangement of surahs in the Qur'an is neither chronological nor thematic. Generally, they were arranged approximately according to length, with the longer surahs placed at the beginning of the book, and the shorter ones last. Accordingly, the qur'anic "story" of Adam and Eve must be gleaned from various places in the Qur'an and thematically reassembled in order to obtain a coherent portrait of the first humans and their experiences in and out of paradise.[1]

The task of reconstructing qur'anic traditions about Adam and Eve is no easy matter, therefore, and this is confirmed by the fact that almost immediately various Islamic commentators took up their pens to clarify—and supplement—what is written in the Qur'an. Sayings attributed to Muhammad himself but not recorded in the Qur'an are known as "hadith"; these hold a privileged position in Islamic theology, second only to the Qur'an itself. Opinions ascribed to Muhammad's earliest followers are also accorded special respect. Finally, various commentators, especially those of the early Islamic centuries, are held in high esteem for their relentless efforts both to track down the opinions of prior "traditioners" and for the astuteness of their own insights concerning the most authentic interpretation of these traditions. All these levels of transmission must be considered in any attempt to set forth how "Adam and Eve" fare within Islam.

Synthesis with Later Commentary

According to Islamic tradition, humans were not the first intelligent beings created by God. The Qur'an states that before Adam, there already existed multitudes of angels, including a subcategory of angels known as the jinn "created before [the humans], from the fire of scorching wind" (Q 15:27). From the time of Muhammad on, Islamic commentators have expended great energy attempting to amplify and clarify such

---

1. The most relevant passages in the Qur'an are 2:29–39; 7:10–27, 189–91; 15:26–48; 20:115–23; 23:12–14; 30:20–22; and 38:71–85. References to the Qur'an are cited as Q, followed by the number of the surah and verse. Quotations are from Abdel Haleem, trans., *The Qur'an*; punctuation and spelling have been modified to conform to American standards.

often-cryptic statements contained in the Qur'an, and these commentators did not always agree one with another. Hence the need to attempt a synthetic treatment of the diverse Islamic traditions about creation.[2] The synthesis offered here is a compilation of the meager statements in the Qur'an itself, plus matter drawn from later texts written by various commentators. One of the most important of these is a medieval composition known as *Tales of the Prophets*, composed around 1200 by a certain al-Kisa'i, who was as much a *raconteur* or storyteller as a transmitter of tradition. Much of the extra-qur'anic materials quoted here in are from this source, though otherwise not acknowledged.[3] Along with passing on the comments of earlier commentators, al-Kisa'i frequently embellished these stories with folkloristic elements from surrounding culture(s) as a means of adding excitement and interest to the bare qur'anic substratum.

The Angels, the Jinn, and Iblis

The Qur'an says little about the creation of angels, apart from the statement that the jinn were created from fire. Rabi'a b. Anas adds that God created the angels on Wednesday and the jinn on Thursday, before creating Adam on Friday. This led to other commentators to posit that the angels and the jinn lived on earth prior to humankind for 2000 and 1000 years respectively, since with God a thousand years are but a single day. There is universal agreement that the jinn were a problematic population. Created from fire, they considered themselves superior beings. At first, they were fine. But over time their arrogance led them to fighting among themselves and with the other angels, causing much bloodshed— so much so that it is said that blood ran ankle deep on earth. The jinn were not universally prone to evil, however. The Qur'an reports that some of their number listened to God and exhorted their fellows to adhere to the teachings of Moses and especially to Mohammad (Q 46:29–31; 72:11–14). Al-Tabari notes that Iblis was one of the jinn on earth and especially powerful. It appears that Iblis was successful in subduing the jinn

2. For a concise overview of the Adam and Eve tradition in Islam, see Schöck, "Adam and Eve," 22–26; for a more extensive treatment, see Wheeler, *Prophets in the Quran*, 15–48. For an excellent treatment of feminist issues in the writings of al-Tabari and al-Kisa'i specifically, see Kvam et al, eds., *Eve and Adam*, 178–203.

3. Matter herein derived from al-Kisa'i has been abbreviated and paraphrased from Wheeler Thackson's translation of Muhammad ibn 'Abd Allah al-Kisa'i, *Tales of the Prophets*, 23–84.

troublemakers, and because of this, according to Ibn Abbas, God made him keeper of paradise, with authority to rule over the lower heavens and the earth. Unfortunately, this elevation caused Iblis to become swollen with pride. The other angels may not have noticed, but God knew what was in Iblis's heart.

According to various commentators, this is the background for the statement in the Qur'an that after God had created the heavens and the earth (Q 2:29), God announced in council to the angels that he planned to put a successor or viceroy (khalīfa)[4] on earth, to which the angels objected.

> When your Lord told the angels, "I am putting a successor on earth," they said, "How can You put someone there who will cause damage and bloodshed, when we celebrate Your praise and proclaim Your holiness?" But He said, "I know things you do not."

The ambiguity in God's response, "I know things you do not," baffled not just the angels but also later commentators about whom God intended to appoint as khalīfa. The interpretation espoused by Ibn 'Abbas and Ibn Mas'ud was that the angels thought God was thinking of appointing one of his existing creatures—angel or jinn—as his deputy to rule over creation. And given their prior disastrous experience with the rebellious jinn who had caused such corruption and bloodshed on earth, they could only foresee a bad result, especially if God were to appoint Iblis to rule over earth, seeing how God had already bestowed great authority on Iblis. The angels did not know what would happen, but their prior experiences pushed them to assume the worst, were a powerful jinn such as Iblis to turn to the dark side. Yet another interpretation was that the angels feared corruption and bloodshed would come from proposed Adam's descendants, who would soon disobey God's law.

According to most commentators, however, God had in mind to create an entirely new creature, Adam, to be his viceroy on earth to exercise judgment with justice. That is why God answered the objections of the angels with something of a double entendre: "I know what you do not know." On the one hand, God is telling the angels that they are mistaken

---

4. The term khalīfa is normally translated as "vicegerent" or "deputy." While this is one meaning of the term, its basic meaning is "successor"—the Qur'an often talks about generations and individuals who are successors to each other, see Q 6:165; 7:129, etc.—or a "trustee" to whom a responsibility is temporarily given, e.g., Moses and Aaron, Q 7:142.

about who and what this deputy ruler will be. On the other hand, God is informing the angels that he knows full well the consequences of his actions, including what both Iblis and humankind will do in the future. Indeed, a great drama will unfold as humankind and Iblis interact on earth.

The Creation of Adam

The Qur'an in several places tells how God fashioned Adam's body from clay. Q 15:26+28 describes it as "sounding clay," alluding to the sound dried clay pottery gives off when struck. The prophet Muhammad says that God used dirt gathered from across the entire earth, with the result that the children of Adam come in various colors: red, black, white, and other colors, in addition to plain, rugged, pleasant, and ugly. This same trope is also used to explain the origin of the many languages of humankind (Q 30:22).

Ibn Mas'ud elaborated this trope, saying that God originally sent Gabriel to earth to gather clay for this purpose, but the earth refused to give up its clay because it did not wish to be an accomplice in spreading corruption and violence on earth. So, God sent Michael, but again the earth refused. Finally, God sent the Angel of Death. When again the earth refused, the Angel of Death scraped from its surface bits of red, white, and black soil. From these bits of earth mixed with moisture God concocted a plastic substance which he fashioned into a body, but left it lying until it became putrid. This seemingly is what led Ali b. Abi Talib to opine that "the skin of the earth" contained both good and bad elements, accounting for why some people are good and some are bad.

Like a potter, God molded clay to shape a body. Because of Iblis's retort that he was made of fire, unlike Adam who was made of dried clay without the use of fire (Q 15:26-7; Q 55:14-5), commentators insist that Adam's clay body was not fired but allowed to dry naturally. According to Al Tabari, Adam's unanimated body lay on the ground for 40 nights—others say, for 40 years. During this time, whenever angels passed by the lifeless form, they became frightened, none more so than Iblis. He would prod and kick it, all the while listening to the dull sounds the dried-out clay gave off—finally concluding that the figure posed no threat whatsoever: "You are not fit even for a (musical) instrument, so why were you created? If I had the power, I would utterly destroy you."

Furthermore, Iblis thoroughly investigated this strange figure by entering through its mouth and exiting through the anus, and then reversed his course through its body cavity. Finding nothing therein, Iblis confidently assured other worried angels that they had absolutely nothing to fear from this hollow shell.

The Fall of Iblis/Satan[5]

When God finally did breathe his spirit into Adam and Adam stood up, God commanded the angels to prostrate themselves before Adam.

> [28]Your Lord said to the angels, "I will create a mortal out of dried clay, formed from dark mud. [29]When I have fashioned him and breathed My spirit into him, bow down before him," [30]and the angels all did so. [31]But not Iblis; he refused to bow down like the others.
>
> [32]God said, 'Iblis, why did you not bow down like the others?" [33]and he answered, "I will not bow to a mortal You created from dried clay, formed from dark mud." [34]"Get out of here!" said God. "You are an outcast, [35]rejected until the Day of Judgement." [36]Iblis said, "My Lord, give me respite until the Day when they are raised from the dead." [37]"You have respite," said God, [38]"until the Day of the Appointed Time." [39]Iblis then said to God, "because You have put me in the wrong, I will lure mankind on earth and put them in the wrong, [40]all except Your devoted servants." [41]God said, "[Devotion] is a straight path to Me; [42]you will have no power over My servants, only over the ones who go astray and follow you. [43]Hell is the promised place for all these, [44]with seven gates, each gate having its allotted share of them. [45]But the righteous will be in Gardens with springs. [46]"Enter them in peace and safety!"—[47]and We shall remove any bitterness from their hearts; [they will be like] brothers, sitting on couches, face to face. [48]No weariness will ever touch them there, nor will they ever be expelled. (Q 15:28-48)

Some commentators say God commanded the angels to bow down to Adam because God was testing the angels for their unwavering obedience, especially the jinn whose loyalty might be regarded as questionable. Others maintain that God merely wished to expose Iblis's perfidiousness.

5. In Islam the preferred name for the devil is Iblis, though Satan is also used; in the Qur'an both names are used interchangeably.

When questioned by God about why he refused to prostrate himself before Adam, Iblis revealed the depth of his overweening pride and arrogance, saying "I am better than [Adam]; I shall not prostrate before a mortal You have made of clay." Others elaborate Iblis's prideful response as an implied rebuke of God: "I am made from fire; [Adam] is made of stinky clay"—to paraphrase Q 38:76.

God's response was immediate. He stripped Iblis of all his goodness and honor and expelled him from the heavenly paradise, down to earth. One tradition says that in that very instant Iblis's countenance was transformed into that of the devil; his evil appearance and abominable stench were so foul that the other angels rushed at him with fiery spears and drove him away, beyond the Euphrates, until he disappeared from their sight. Others say that God condemned Iblis with the words, "Leave us immediately. You are stoned"—a reference to the practice of Muslim pilgrims at Mecca casting stones at a certain place which represents Satan while circumambulating the Qaaba, as a symbol of their rejection of Satan.

Not one to repent of his arrogance, Iblis defiantly challenged God: Give me a reprieve until the Day of Judgment. God granted Satan his request, with the intention of using Iblis's reprieve as an opportunity to test the fidelity of the righteous and prove the infidelity of the wicked among Adam's descendants. Paraphrasing Q 38:77–84, Satan immediately gloated: Excellent! With the reprieve you have just granted me, I will bring about the destruction of all humankind—save a few of your most devoted servants who may, with your (puny) help, be able to elude my clutches. God knew better, however. He answered Satan: I, not you, decree what is just and proper. Yes, hell will indeed be filled—with you and your (unrighteous) followers!

Adam Is Taught by God

By right, Iblis should indeed have bowed down before Adam, not just because God commanded it, but also because Adam actually was superior to Iblis, despite appearances to the contrary at the time. In Islamic belief, God created humans with free will and endowed them with the ability to reason, thereby making them superior to the angels who lack all emotion and have no knowledge save what God chooses to reveal to them—and that includes Iblis the rebellious jinn. Moreover, Adam was lovingly crafted by God's own hand and then given part of God's own breath, setting humankind far above the angels.

Humankind's superiority to the angels is charmingly expounded in Q 2:30–34. When God announced to the angels that he was about to place his viceroy on earth and the angels objected, God reassured them that he knew best with the statement, "I know things you do not." To drive home the point, God asked the angels the names of various things. They had to admit that they did not know: "We have knowledge only of what you have taught us. You are the All-knowing and All-wise." Then God turned to Adam standing there: "Adam, tell me their names." Without a moment's hesitation, Adam proceeded to name all things.

The commentators disagree among themselves just how Adam was able to accomplish this marvelous feat. Q 2:31 states that God "taught Adam all the names," but without revealing exactly how Adam was taught by God. One opinion was that God had previously taken Adam by the hand and showed him the various creatures while instructing him: This is a lion. This is a donkey, a crow, a mountain, a sea, and so forth, for everything. Others opined that God taught more generically, that is, about the essences, functions, and attributes of things, for example, This is an animal for riding, and so on, until Adam had learned the names (the essences) of everything that God had created. Others say God taught Adam the names of the descendants who would come after him, as well as the names of all the angels. Al-Tabari's opinion was that God was reprimanding the angels for objecting to God appointing someone other than an angel or a jinn as his vicegerent on earth, since they never disobey God but always faithfully praise God and extoll God's holiness, while humans will surely wreak corruption and shed much blood. By God saying to the angels, "Tell me the names of these if you speak the truth," God was making clear to the angels how mistaken they were in challenging God, and that one of their own (Iblis) would be the cause of the corruption and bloodshed. The angels immediately recognized their error and turned to God in repentance—all except Iblis.

Another tradition relates that after Adam recited the names of everything, God caused a bunch of grapes to approach Adam, so that Adam reached out and ate. This was the first food Adam had eaten. God commended Adam, saying that he had specially created food for Adam and his children to enjoy. Adam then fell asleep. When Iblis learned that Adam had eaten food, he was ecstatic: "Now I know how to lead him astray!"

The Creation of Eve

Eve is not named in the Qur'an, though she seems to be referred to obliquely in Q 4:1, where humans are said to be descended "from one soul, and from it made its mate." Q 7:189 repeats this statement, adding that this was done "that he might dwell with her." Subsequent tradition, however, greatly expanded upon Eve and her role. Ibn Abbas says that after Iblis was expelled from paradise, Adam led a happy but solitary life in paradise. He would wander about the garden gazing at all the wonderful sights. But without a proper companion, Adam was lonely (Q 7:189 and 30:21). One day Adam awoke to find a woman sitting by his head, he asked, "Who are you?" "Woman," she replied. "And why were you created?" "To be your companion." The angels, who had been watching, were curious to learn how much knowledge Adam possessed. So, they asked Adam, "What is her name?" "Hawa" (Eve), he replied. "And why is she called Hawa?" "Because she was created from something living (*hayya*)." Then God said to Adam, "Adam, dwell, you and your wife, in the garden, and eat freely whatever you desire. Do not approach this tree, however, or you will become evildoers."

This episode was embellished by others, often in minute detail. One says that Adam lived alone for 500 years before Eve was created. Another says that Eve was created from a rib taken from Adam's side while he slept. This rib was taken from Adam's left side and was the shortest of his ribs, suggestive of woman's inferior status. Still another notes that the rib was "crooked," that is curved. From this, men are admonished to watch over women carefully but gently. Women must be guarded, since they are from crooked stock. At the same time, women must not be overly chastised, since they may easily be broken if one attempts to straighten them too rigidly.

Yet another authority relates that before Adam awakened from his deep sleep, Adam and Eve spoke to each other in his dream. That is how Adam learned that Eve was created to be his wife in a marriage blessed by God himself. Marriage thus is a sacred institution that originated with the first human couple, and by divine design.

The Qur'an (33:72) records that at creation God offered Adam—and by extension, all humankind—a "trust" (or covenant), which Adam accepted. In effect, God demonstrated just how highly he regarded humankind. A trust implies that something is freely given and may be used at the trustee's discretion, subject to the terms of the trust. In this case, humankind was given access to the whole of paradise, with the single proviso that God's command not to go near that one tree be obeyed. God had bestowed humans with reason and free will, which God would never take away. By so doing, God intended that his viceroy/deputy on earth should have a dignity next to God himself. To that end God breathed into Adam something of his own spirit, making humans higher than the angels. Humankind was also given a choice between good and evil, and made capable of forbearance, love, and mercy. In short, humankind was created to be a microcosm of Allah himself, ruling over the Almighty's good creation. Sadly, Adam betrayed this trust, with terrible consequences.

Existence in paradise was—is—to state matters simply, paradisaical. In paradise, every good thing is present in superabundance. There is no hunger, no thirst, no discomfort of any kind. Everything one could wish for is close at hand. Further, as befitting God's viceroy on earth, Adam and his wife were decked out in the finest silk robes. Adam wore a royal crown on his head, while Eve's tresses were adorned with precious jewels. Both lounged on daises studded with pearls and pillars made of precious gems. Nothing marred their happiness during the first five hundred years—a mere half day as God reckons time—of their idyllic existence in the garden of Eden.

Iblis, the Serpent, and the Fall of Adam and Eve

The Quran blames Satan for causing Adam and Eve to "slip" (Q 2:36). After Iblis revealed his contempt for God by refusing his command to bow down to Adam, God warned him,

> "Adam, this is your enemy, yours and your wife's; do not let him drive you out of the garden and make you miserable. In the garden you will never go hungry, feel naked, be thirsty, or suffer the heat of the sun." But Satan whispered to Adam, saying, "Adam, shall I show you the tree of immortality and power that never decays?" and they both ate from it. They became conscious of their nakedness and began to cover themselves with leaves from the garden. Adam disobeyed his Lord and was led astray—later his Lord brought him close, accepted his repentance, and guided him—God said: "Get out of the garden as each other's enemy." (Q 20:115-23)

Elsewhere all people are warned to not fall into the same trap as their first parents:

> Children of Adam, do not let Satan seduce you, as he did your parents, causing them to leave the garden, stripping them of their garments to expose their nakedness for them. He and his forces can see you from where you cannot see them. (Q 7:27)

Later tradition records yet other versions of how the fall of Adam and Eve happened. One in particular stands out for its narrative quality. According to a tale recorded by al-Kisa'i in the twelfth century, though likely much older, after Iblis had been driven from paradise by angels with their fiery spears, he feared to show himself openly. He was forced to slink around, hiding as best he could. One day he heard a loud voice proclaim: "O people of heaven, I establish Adam and Eve in paradise under the trust and covenant. I permit them everything that is in paradise, except the tree of eternity.[6] If they approach it and eat from it, they will be among the unjust." When Iblis heard this, he rejoiced and said, "I shall certainly have them expelled from that kingdom, seeing that they have been forbidden something!"

Iblis was fixated on slipping back into paradise to ruin Adam and Eve. Eventually he settled upon a plan that involved the serpent. In Islamic tradition the serpent is female. It is said that originally the serpent was a thing of beauty, more beautiful than a Bactrian camel.[7] Tall and sleek, she walked about erect on four strong, nimble legs. She was well acquainted with the whole of paradise. In fact, she used to stroll with Adam and Eve and explain to them all the marvelous trees of paradise. Because of this long association, Eve had no reason to doubt the word of the serpent.

Iblis saw an opportunity in the serpent. He sought out the serpent and persuaded her to let him enter her mouth and speak through her mouth. Ever the liar, Iblis promised the serpent that she was destined to grow old and die. Iblis swore to her by Allah that he, Iblis, possessed magic that could prevent all that, conditional upon her helping Iblis slip back into paradise. Iblis would enter the serpent's mouth and hide between her fangs. The serpent trusted Iblis, never suspecting that anyone would

6. In Islamic tradition the forbidden fruit was that of "the tree of eternity" (the tree of life).

7. Jewish midrash (Gen. Rab. 19.1) similarly compares the serpent to a camel, see above, p. 238.

swear to a lie while invoking Allah's name. The ruse worked. The serpent opened her mouth and Iblis settled between her fangs. (That is how the fangs of snakes became poisonous.) In this way Iblis was able to reenter paradise undetected by the angels guarding its gates—though God knew.

When the serpent reached the middle of the garden, she expected Iblis to jump out. Instead, Iblis spoke directly to Eve from the mouth of the serpent,[8] "O beautiful Eve, haven't I been with you in paradise all this time and haven't I informed you of all the marvels herein? And haven't I always spoken the truth to you?" "Certainly, Serpent," replied Eve. With innocent sounding guile, Iblis urged Eve to tell what God allows and whether nothing at all was off limits to her and Adam. When Eve told him about the one thing forbidden to them, Iblis prodded her, "Why did your Lord forbid you the tree of eternity?" Eve had to admit she did not know why.

This was the moment Iblis had been waiting for. "I can tell you why," he announced. "God forbade it because he wanted to prevent you from becoming like that slave sitting over there under the tree of eternity. He has been sitting under that tree for 1000 years, caring for it."

As Eve turned to look at the tree, faster than lightning Iblis leaped from the serpent's mouth and seated himself under the tree, pretending to be the slave. Presuming him to be an actual slave, Eve inquired, "Who are you?"

"I am a simple creature of my Lord, created from fire," it replied. "I have been in paradise 2000 years. God created me with his own hand, just as he created you two, and he also breathed his breath into me, and caused the angels to bow down before me. He placed me in this paradise and forbade me to eat from this tree—a command that I obeyed until an angel whispered to me that anyone who eats from this tree will have everlasting life in paradise. I trusted the angel and ate. As you can see, I am still in paradise, safe from old age, illness, death, and expulsion." Iblis continued, "God forbade you this tree for no other reason than to prevent you from becoming angels and acquiring immortality." Even more insistently, it urged, "Eve, hurry and eat before your husband returns, for whoever eats first will have precedence over his companion."

Eve's naivete is evident in her rebuke to the serpent, to whom she turned, "You have been with me all this time since I entered paradise, and you never told me about this marvelous tree?" The serpent, fearful of

8. The motif of Satan using the mouth of the serpent to speak to Eve appears also in the Greek version of Life of Adam and Eve (Apocalypse of Moses 16:5).

losing her own reward promised by Iblis, remained silent. Not needing additional encouragement, Eve ate, and then rushed to Adam with her good news—along with fruit from the tree. Forgetting the covenant binding them to the Lord, Adam took the fruit from Eve's hand and tasted. The result was not as expected.

According to Ibn Abbas, no sooner had Adam taken a single bite than the crown flew off his head and the rings slipped from his fingers. At the same moment Eve's pearls dropped from her tresses, while her belt broke. All the beautiful, sumptuous clothes that had previously covered Adam and Eve fell to the ground, crying out in protest, "O Adam! O Eve! Long may you sorrow, and may your affliction be great! We made a covenant with God that we should clothe only obedient, humble servants."

Seeing their newly revealed nakedness, Adam and Eve attempted to cover themselves with tree leaves. But the leaves also fell away, so that the couple was not able to cover themselves. When Adam would come near a tree, it would shout, "Go away from me, O disobedient one!" Every creature, Adam's horse, the dove that previously loved to perch on Adam's crown, even the angels, all heaped blame and reproach upon the pair. In desperation, Eve tried to cover herself with her own tresses, but even these refused. All creation recoiled in horror before the disobedient pair, until Adam cried out to God, "Have mercy, O Most Merciful!"

At this, the Awesome One called out to Adam, "O Adam, did I not forbid you this tree; and did I not warn you that Satan is your sworn enemy?" (Q 7:22). "Lord," Adam sobbed, "you did not teach us that anyone would swear by You to a lie!" One detects in Adam's retort an accusation that God is partially to blame for Adam's sin—a topic to which we will return shortly.

Expulsion from Paradise

After Satan had caused Adam and Eve to "slip," God removed "them from the state they were in," that is from paradise (Q 2:36). God commanded the three of them:

> "All of you get out! You are each other's enemies. On earth you will have place to stay and livelihood—for a time." He said: "There you will live; there you will die; from there you will be brought out." (Q 7:24–25; similarly 2:36)

Commentators say God sent the angel Gabriel to expel Adam and Eve from the garden. As they approached the gate Adam begged Gabriel to allow him one last glance at paradise and then added, "Let me flee paradise, for I am ashamed before my Lord." Gabriel reminded Adam that no one can escape the purview of the All Knowing. Adam appealed directly to God, "Lord, by your Splendor I beg you to return me to the dust from which You created me, that I become dust as at first." God silenced Adam with the words, "How can I return you to dust, when from all eternity I have known that I would fill the earth, including hell, from your loins!"

God also reprimanded Eve, who was lamenting that all her finery was gone and that she was left naked as she departed paradise. "And who is responsible for that?" God asked. Eve acknowledged that it was her own fault, having been led astray by Iblis's lies that he was advising her rightly: "I never dreamed that anyone would swear, invoking the name of Allah, while lying."

God answered the woman, "Leave paradise, forever deceived. Henceforth I make you morally deficient and deprived of all the best things: no Friday congregational prayer, no mingling in public nor greeting. I subject you to menstruation and pain in pregnancy and labor, not excluding death even. Women will have much sorrow and tears; they will have little patience; and God will never make a prophet or a wise person from among them."

Because of this, Ibn Abbas counseled husbands: God ordained affection and familiarity between men and women, so keep women at home and be kind toward them in so far as you are able; for every woman who is pious, worships her Lord, performs her religious obligations, and obeys her husband will enter paradise.

As Eve departed paradise, God did give her hope, however, saying that through her he would fill paradise with prophets, pious individuals, martyrs, those to be pardoned, and those of her descendants who pray for and ask forgiveness for the two of them (Adam and Eve).

As Gabriel ushered Eve out of paradise, she made one last desperate attempt to grab a leaf to cover her nakedness. Although Gabriel would have prevented her, God mercifully commanded the leaf to accede to Eve's request. With that leaf, Eve covered herself as best she could while hurriedly descending from paradise down to earth.

Gabriel was less gentle with Adam, grabbing him by his forelock to cast him out of the garden. The angels lined each side of the path, heaping censure upon Adam the whole way. "O angels of my Lord," Adam pleaded, "do not revile me but rather have mercy on me. What I did was destined by the foreknowledge of the Preserved Tablet." (This is a reference to Q 2:30 wherein God replied to the angels' objection to God's decision to place a viceroy on earth, "I know things you do not.") God had indeed foreseen Adam's breach of the trust, but God also foreknew that Adam's disobedience would provide the opportunity for God's mercy to abound even more. So, Adam here reminds the angels—and God—that somehow his breach of the trust was foreordained by the wisdom of his Maker.

God answered Adam that indeed he shows mercy to those who repent, but that does not excuse disobedience, for God condemns to hell the unrepentant. God continued, "Adam, have you forgotten all that I have done for you. Have you forgotten your trust with me by obeying my enemy Iblis, instead?" Adam acknowledged his complicity with Iblis, but again pleas that his disobedience was foreknown by God, foreordained even. God concedes that he created Adam for this very purpose, and that Adam's "disobedience has come about through my decree, my omnipotence and my will, which have existed in my pre-eternal knowledge." Encouraged, Adam pleads further, "Lord, by the right of him to whom you have given greatest honor, cannot my fall be lessened?" To which God asks, "To whom are you referring in making this petition?" "Your chosen one, Your beloved Muhammad," Adam replied, "I have seen his name written on the canopy over the Throne, on the Preserved Tablet, on the Book of Heaven, and on the portals of paradise. So how may I ward off Iblis?" God responded, "You can indeed ward off Iblis by declaring my unity, when you say, 'There is no god but God, and Muhammad is the Messenger of God.'"

Adam's success in pleading with God encouraged Iblis to try his own hand at bargaining with God. Iblis attempted to lay blame on God for Iblis having become a devil because God knew beforehand that Iblis would go astray yet did not prevent it. Therefore, God owes Iblis at least a partial reprieve from his punishment. God does concede to the extent of postponing Iblis's consignment to hell until the Day of Judgment. Iblis gloats that he will use this reprieve as an opportunity to lead humankind astray; he will come at them from all sides, attacking them from the front and the back, from the right and the left; and moreover, most of them will succumb to Iblis's wiles (Q 7:13–18; similarly 15:37–48; 38:79–84).

Later tradition has Iblis pressing God even further, in an effort to sort out what kind of existence he will have in the meanwhile—plus to develop a stratagem by which to lead humankind astray:

"Where will I stay?"

God answers: "On earth, in filthy holes!"

"What shall I read?"

"Poetry and song!"

"What shall I eat?"

"Anything over which My name is not invoked!"

"What will my drink be?"

"Wine!"

"Where will I reside?"

"Public baths!"

"My gathering place?"

"Markets!" . . .

"What is my prey?"

"Women!"

"Splendid," cried Iblis, "then I shall put love of women into the hearts of men!"

"You truly are accursed!" replied God. "Nevertheless, I will not take away the opportunity for repentance from any human until the moment of death. As for you, begone! For you are accursed, and your curse shall remain until the Day of Judgement!"

Also the serpent was summoned for judgment. As the angels dragged her along on her belly while others threw stones at her, her body became elongated and deformed, with her legs being abraded completely off. She lost her ability to speak, becoming mute and forked-tongued. The angels cursed her, "May God show you no mercy, nor mercy to anyone who has mercy on you!" It is said that the Prophet [Muhammad] said: "He who kills a serpent will have seven blessings, and he who leaves it alone, fearing its evil, will have no reward. He who kills a viper will have one blessing." Indeed, according to Ibn Abbas, "to kill a serpent is better than to kill an infidel."

As Adam passed by the serpent, he said, "Lord, what about this serpent? She aided my enemy Iblis against me. How will I be able to withstand her?" God answered, I will cause her to live in dark places and eat dirt. Whenever you see a serpent, crush its head!"

Eve's and Adam's Repentance

For Islam, the story is far from over when Adam and Eve were expelled from paradise. In many ways it was just the beginning. Even outside paradise Adam did not cease to call upon God with sorrow for his disobedience. God was pleased with Adam's prayer and sent Gabriel to console Adam with the comforting words, "Peace be with you who have wept and grieved so much. Your repentance has been accepted and your transgression forgiven." In addition, Gabriel taught Adam a special prayer of repentance intended for all; whoever recites its words will be forgiven. There is disagreement among the commentators over exactly what these special words were, but they agree that God truly hears contrite prayer and readily forgives, just as he forgave Adam. Because Adam taught his descendants to seek forgiveness as God taught, Adam is regarded as God's first prophet, and one of the most important.

The angels were heaping censure upon Adam for his transgression and the consequences that sin had wrought upon all creation. Gabriel chided the angels, "Leave Adam alone! Stop censuring him for his transgression, for God has erased his sin." At that, the angels changed their words of censure into prayers of thanksgiving over Adam's forgiveness.

God then commanded Michael to bring the glad tidings of repentance and forgiveness to Eve, and to clothe her. She praised God, bathed, and immediately began to weep out of longing for Adam, from whom she had been separated since their departure from paradise. Meanwhile, Gabriel was assuring Adam, who had been inquiring about Eve, that God would bring the two of them together in the most noble of all places, Mecca. Gabriel then instructed Adam how to build God's House, the Qaaba, in Mecca. Gabriel also instructed Adam how he and his progeny after him should circumambulate the Qaaba while offering prayers after the manner Adam had seen the angels doing in heaven, as well as the procedure for stoning Iblis who had refused to prostrate himself to Adam at his creation. When Adam reached Mecca, he built the Qaaba in accordance with God's command. Upon its completion, Adam circumambulated it while continuously praising God. God blessed Adam, saying, "Today I have sanctified Mecca and its environs; it shall be sacred until the Day of Resurrection."

"O Lord," Adam lamented," you promised me that you would join Eve and me in this place. But where is she?" "There, on Mount Marwa," came the reply. "You are standing on Mount Safa. You may see her, but do not touch here until the two of you have performed the rites of pilgrimage." So, Adam went across the valley to meet Eve. and the two of them together completed the seven days of ritual circumambulation, exactly as Gabriel had taught Adam.

Then Adam and Eve came together on a Friday evening and Eve conceived that very night. Because of this, God grants coition on Friday evening, to the exclusion of all other nights.

Eve conceived twins, a male and a female. But in the eighth month she aborted. She similarly conceived twins a second time, and again she aborted. Eve was devastated. When she conceived a third time, Iblis came to her, saying, "If you want this one to live, then name him Abdul Harith" ("Servant of Harith," Harith being a name associated with Iblis). After she had given birth to a healthy boy, God sent an angel to inquire of Eve why she had so named her child. "So he would live," Eve answered. "Then you should have named him either Abdullah or Abdul-Rahman" ("servant of the Most Gracious"). Adam and Eve regretted their decision, and God allowed the child to die.

When Eve again conceived twins, she named her son Abdul-Rahman and his twin sister Amatul-Rahman ("Handmaid of the Most Gracious"). Eve continued to bear twins, a hundred and twenty pairs in all. Among them were the prophet Abel and his twin sister, and Cain and his twin sister. Thus did their progeny quickly multiply.

After Cain and Abel were grown, Adam summoned them, his two most beloved children, to go offer a sacrifice to God because of all that God had done in forgiving Adam. Abel was a shepherd, so he selected the finest, fattest ram from his flock and sacrificed it. Cain was a farmer, so he chose some of his best grain and offered it. White lightning fell from heaven and consumed Abel's sacrifice, but left Cain's offering untouched. Cain was envious of his brother—and angry. As they were returning to their father's house, Abel walked ahead. Cain grabbed a large rock and struck his brother from behind, killing him.

As the two were late in returning, Adam went searching and found Abel dead. Adam and Eve mourned the death of their son for forty days, until God consoled them, saying that he would give them another son, "one as pure as Abel, who would produce prophets and apostles." Eve conceived and gave birth to Seth, whose "face shone [like] the light of our Lord Muhammad." The angels carried the good tidings of the new prophet's birth to Adam, who immediately glorified God.

The Deaths of Adam and Eve

According to tradition, as Adam's days were drawing to a close God said to him, "Adam, your allotted time is at an end. Make your bequest to your son Seth (who was then four hundred years old)." So, Adam summoned Seth and said, "Son, I am about to die and rejoin my Lord. Be steadfast in your witness that there is no god but God, and in affirming faith in his coming prophet Muhammad, whose name I have seen written on the Canopy of (Adam's) Throne (in paradise) and on the gates of paradise. This is my bequest to you, and which you are to bequeath to your children after you. Gabriel, Michael, Israfel, the Angel of Death and hosts of cherubim will pray over me. When they have finished, you also pray over me and then seal my tomb with the pronouncement of peace." Then he removed the ring from his finger and gave it to Seth.

Adam continued, "My son, I once lusted after a certain fruit in paradise, and my Lord promised me that he would feed me from it. Go, search out an angel on my behalf." Seth found an angel, one of the guardians of paradise, who had brought some fruit from the tree of life in paradise. Seth brought the fruit to Adam, who rejoiced, "God will not fail in his promise" (to give Adam eternal life on the Day of Judgment). That was on Thursday.

The next day, Friday, at the same hour that God had created Adam— it also being the hour of the midday prayer—God commanded the Angel of Death to descend with the Nectar of Separation and give it to Adam to drink, while taking up the spirit God had breathed into Adam. The Angel of Death descended along with Gabriel, Michael, and many other angels. They were carrying the great throne of paradise for Adam, which they placed between heaven and earth. Adam obediently drank the draft as God had commanded.

At that, Gabriel said, "Look up, Adam." When Adam looked heavenward, he saw ranks of angels standing with their wings spread wide and in their hands were banners of honor and glad tidings. There, too, stood Abel, waiting for his father to come join him. Such was Adam's glorious departure from this life.

Gabriel consoled Seth, saying, "God has exalted your purpose and has blessed your father by bestowing these honors upon him."

Eve was unaware of Adam's death until she heard the commotion in nature, as the birds and beasts wept, and the sun eclipsed. Alarmed that something awful had befallen Seth, Eve ran to Adam's tabernacle to find him—only to find it empty. Seth soon arrived to console her that all was right, for Adam had gone to his Lord. Eve remained by Adam's tomb mourning for forty days, without sleeping.

Eve grew increasingly ill. Out of compassion, the angels wept for her. Finally, the Angel of Death descended and gave her also the same draft he had administered to Adam, so that she too died. Her daughters washed her body and wrapped it in a shroud from paradise, burying her alongside Adam.

With the death of Adam and his wife, the guardianship passed to Seth.

Adam as Prophet

Although the Qur'an does not name Adam as a prophet, a very early hadith claims that Muhammad himself had pronounced Adam to have been the very first prophet.[9] This has been accepted by Muslims ever since, although it poses something of a problem for Muslim orthodoxy. In Muslim belief, because prophets are chosen by God and divinely guided, they are immune to sin. They are impeccable. According to most, prophetic impeccability applies both during *and* before their prophetic career—though some would allow that a prophet might commit a *minor* sin. The problem, therefore, is how to reconcile Adam's well-known sin of disobedience with the doctrine of prophetic impeccability.

The earliest commentaries do not question that Adam sinned, but they posit that Adam's sin was predetermined and hence not fully culpable. In his foreknowledge God had allowed—perhaps even ordained—Adam's fall in order to show forth his great mercy. This approach minimized Adam's sin, while also emphasizing that Adam's "slip" had been provoked through Iblis's machinations and augmented by Eve's urging. Still others suggested that Adam was guilty only of an error in judgment, thinking that God had forbidden him to approach but a single tree, whereas God had placed off limits an entire species of "trees of eternity."

Another approach was to say that Adam became a prophet only after he had been expelled from paradise, after he had fully repented of his sin. As a prophet Adam never sinned. Hence, prophetic impeccability is maintained.

9. From a hadith narrated by Abu Dharr al-Ghifari (d. 32/653); cited by Schöck, "Adam and Eve," 26.

Adam's office as prophet is evident in that he urged his descendants, and especially the line of Seth, to maintain steadfast fidelity to God, praying to God alone, and refusing to follow Iblis and his ways. Because of his example and his instructions for all humankind coming after him, Adam is revered as one of the greatest of the prophets.

Assessing the Adam and Eve Tradition in Islam

The Islamic story of Adam and Eve clearly is rooted in the biblical story. But as the story was passed down through the centuries, the story was greatly amplified to incorporate specifically Muslim practices, as well as many folkloristic elements (mostly omitted here) which enhanced its popular appeal. Although many of these folkloristic elements arose from within the various Islamic communities, oftentimes they were borrowed from Jewish or Christian sources and adapted for Muslim audiences. An example concerns how Adam's original gigantic proportions at creation later came to be much reduced in size; al-Kisa'i in *Tales of the Prophets* relates how Adam, when told that he would be able to stone Iblis for having led him astray, leaped with joy. He was so tall, however, that his head poked through the sky. God commanded Gabriel to put his hand upon Adam's head and push him down, thereby reducing his height to that of a normal human of today. Adam was much grieved that he could no longer hear the angels glorifying God in the heavens. One may compare the Jewish trope in the Mishnah Rabbah for Genesis about Adam being originally of such gargantuan size that his head reached into the clouds and his body filled the whole earth.[10]

Similarly for the motif of the skeptical angels at the creation of Adam as the vicegerent of God on earth. This seems to derive in part from a Jewish tradition in the Babylonian Talmud, *Sanhedrin* 38b, that when God declared that he was going to create the human, he asked one company of ministering angels: "Is it your desire that we make a man in our image?" When they questioned the Almighty's wisdom about creating creatures who would disobey and corrupt the earth, God consumed

10. *Midrash Rabbah: Genesis*, tr. Freedman, 1:173–74 (= chap. 21.3; see also chap. 8.1 for R. Leazar's statement that "[God] created [Adam] filling the whole world . . . from east to west . . . (and) from north to south"; similarly 24.2). For additional statements about the original gigantic dimensions of Adam's body in both rabbinic Judaism and early Christian sources, see Ginsberg, *Legends of the Jews*, 1:59, with n. 22 (in vol. 5:79). See also my preceding chap. 10, "Classical Judaism," p. 236 with n. 5.

them with fire. The same thing happened with a second company. A third company of angels got the message, apparently, and reluctantly approved of God's plan. In the age of the flood, however, when the corrupt deeds of humankind were most apparent, these angels seemingly chided God: "Lord of the Universe, did not the first [company of angels] speak correctly?" To which God retorted, "Even when I am old and gray, I will bear with them"—thereby expressing his enduring mercy.

Eve—and women in general—fare poorly in Islamic tradition. Eve is never mentioned by name in the Qur'an; she also is clearly subjugated to Adam and said to be inferior to him, both in morals and in intellect. In the hadith and later traditions, Eve is named and figures more prominently in the narrative, but she is restricted nonetheless to a secondary status relative to males. Women's roles for the most part are limited to being dutiful wives and caring mothers. Women may not exercise authority over men, and especially not over their husbands. Moreover, no woman has ever been named a prophet, that being strictly reserved for males. Even Adam, despite his sin, once he repented, could become a prophet. Eve, never.

Humankind as a whole, however, is accorded a very high status, higher than angels even. Of all God's creatures, humans rank the highest, next to God himself. There can be no greater dignity than that bestowed upon humankind.

In Islam, the Adam and Eve tradition diverges from the larger tradition in other ways as well. Paradise was a not some fantastical place on earth that no longer exists. Rather, it is a heavenly sanctuary where angels glorify God and where every imaginable delight is present. Because of their sin, Adam and Eve were removed from paradise and descended to earth where life is at best a struggle. But the repentant Adam and Eve will be readmitted to paradise on the Day of Judgment, as will everyone who turns toward the all-merciful God. Admittance into paradise is the goal of every Muslim.

In paradise Adam and Eve were not nude like innocent children. On the contrary, they were sumptuously decked out in the finest brocade and silken robes, adorned with exquisite jewelry, and lounged on luxurious daises decorated with precious gems.[11] As befitting God's viceroy, Adam

---

11. This motif that in paradise Adam and Eve were exquisitely dressed may derive from a prior Jewish tradition (Gen. Rab. 18.1, 5) according to which, when God presented Eve to Adam, he brought her fully clothed and decked out as a bride in twenty-four pieces of finest cloth and jewelry; see chapter 10 above, p. 237.

and his wife lived in a manner more splendid than even the wealthiest sultan of the entire Near East could imagine. In contrast to the biblical version, nudity only happened for Adam and Eve upon their disobeying God and eating the forbidden fruit. At that point, all their clothes and finery fell off and they discovered themselves nude. Their nudity was a sign of guilt, not of innocence as in the biblical account.

Also, the forbidden tree with its fruit was not about "knowledge"— as in the biblical "tree of knowledge of good and evil." According to the Qur'an, Adam already had knowledge since God "taught" Adam everything at his creation. The Qur'an does not provide a name for the forbidden tree, only that they—Q 2:25 uses the grammatic dual, so both Adam and Eve are included here—should not go near the tree. If anything, the forbidden tree would seem to have been conflated with the biblical "tree of life," since later commentators speak of Adam and Eve having desired the "tree of eternity." Also, the prohibition was not just against eating the fruit, but even against going anywhere near the tree.

Iblis (Satan) figures prominently in Islamic religious belief, as God's principal opponent. Iblis was not always God's enemy, however. Originally, he was among the most faithful angels in paradise, a jinn who had put down a rebellion of other unfaithful jinn. For his faithful service, God elevated him as leader over all the angels. Thinking himself better than all of God's creatures, Iblis refused to bow before Adam as God commanded, and for his disobedience Iblis was cast out of paradise. Determined to get revenge, Iblis schemed to pervert God's most treasured creation, Adam, along with all his descendants. This set off an unending battle between God and Iblis, and between Iblis and God's faithful servants. This, of course, is essentially the same story we have encountered previously in various Jewish pseudepigraphs and in the Christian New Testament, albeit with different names attached to the principal characters at times; but never had the story been told more vividly than in Islamic tradition. It is likely that the Islamic version at least indirectly contributed to Milton's epic poem *Paradise Lost*, to which we will turn in the following chapter.

Finally, unlike Christianity which holds that Adam's sin was hereditary and passed on to every descendant of Adam and Eve, Islam has no concept of "original sin" and therefore no need for a doctrine of redemption. Much like Judaism, Islam holds that each person is responsible for his or her own sins. In the words of the Qur'an, "Each soul is responsible for its own actions; no soul will bear the burden of another" (Q 6:164; see also 17:15; 29:12). Most assuredly Adam's sin unleashed a multitude of evil upon humankind and even upon creation as a whole, but each person has the ability to choose God and reject the enticements of Iblis/ evil. At core, this is the principal burden of Islamic tales about Adam (and Eve): to encourage fidelity to the all-merciful God. Humans are indeed fallible and all too prone to "slip." But God is ever merciful and always ready to forgive us humans our frailties at the slightest sign of repentance, even to our last breath.

12

Paradise Lost: Milton's Epic Poem on Adam & Eve

AN EXAMINATION OF HOW Adam and Eve fare in John Milton's epic poem *Paradise Lost* seems an appropriate way to conclude this book, as it will demonstrate just how much the Adam and Eve tradition has evolved over the course of some three millennia. In *Paradise Lost* not only has the storyline changed greatly from the original story in the book of Genesis, but also the principal characters and their roles have been drastically altered. Moreover, in today's larger culture, if people allude to the Adam and Eve story at all, more likely than not they have in the backs of their minds the bold and highly dramatic version penned by Milton, rather than the brief, straight-forward narrative found in the first book of the Bible. It is scarcely to be wondered that Milton's version has attracted so much attention, as his version was beneficiary of an exceedingly rich narrative tradition that passed through successive cultures and faith traditions over more than 3000 years, with each transmitter adding new elements and meanings to the tradition.

Its author, John Milton (1608–1674), is regarded as one of the greatest English poets, surpassed only by William Shakespeare. In addition to his two most famous works, *Paradise Lost* and *Paradise Regained,* he also authored numerous other poems and treatises. But he was much more than just a writer. He was an intellectual and a historian of no mean accomplishments. As a student, Milton had been steeped in the Greek and Roman classics and he also learned Italian, Hebrew, French and Spanish. As a Puritan, he firmly believed in the supreme authority of the Bible and opposed the Church of England and the monarchy with which it was intertwined. He advocated religious freedom and supported Oliver

Cromwell in the English Civil War by writing pamphlets. With the demise of Cromwell and the restoration of the monarchy in 1660 under Charles II, however, Milton was imprisoned and narrowly escaped death for his role in the beheading of Charles I. Through the influence of powerful friends, Milton was released from prison, but he spent much of the later part of his life in hiding. By 1652 Milton had become totally blind, and subsequently was reduced to poverty. It was in this period of blindness that he wrote, with the help of several amanuenses, some of his most important works: *Paradise Lost* (the original ten-book version in 1667), *Samson Agonistes* (1671), *Paradise Regained* (also in 1671), and in 1674, the year of his death, the revised 12-book classic edition of *Paradise Lost*.

A Novel (Christian) Classic

Being well versed in Hebrew, Greek, and Latin, Milton did not hesitate to draw freely from not just the Jewish and Christian scriptures but also the classical literature of ancient Greece and Rome, especially the great epic poems of Homer, the *Iliad* and the *Odyssey*, and of Vergil, the *Aeneid*. Milton modeled his own epic poem on those classics, both in terms of style (blank verse, allusions to classical motifs and events, and the like), and in adopting the epic format to emphasize the enduring value of his composition for all ages to come—or at least so he hoped.

Milton did not approach his task lightly. To the contrary, he intended that his new composition would surpass the works of the pagan poets Homer and Vergil. Indeed, he fancied his masterpiece would rival the work of Moses, that divinely inspired amanuensis of the Lord God, who copied out the divine Torah on the top of the Sinai mountain. Three times in the course of *Paradise Lost*, each time more forcefully, Milton invoked the same Heavenly Muse that inspired Moses atop of Sinai to inspire him. Milton aspired to write eloquently and faithfully about those awesome events of that primeval epoch which had such powerful consequences for all of humankind to come. Like the classical poets Homer and Vergil before him, Milton believed himself to be entrusted with the task of transmitting to the people of his own time as well as for future generations of English readers the most important traditions of the past, so that coming generations of humankind may derive benefit through his instruction. It was Milton's ardent desire that the divine Spirit might descend once again with that same pregnant power, manifested so long ago at the creation of the world, this time upon Milton himself that he might champion God's providential mercy in this tale of the beginnings, and thereby "justify the ways of God to men."

> Sing Heav'nly Muse, that on the secret top
> Of Oreb,[1] or of Sinai, didst inspire
> That shepherd,[2] who first taught the chosen seed,
> In the beginning how the heav'ns and earth
> Rose out of chaos: or if Sion hill
> Delight thee more, and Siloa's brook[3] that flowed
> Fast by the oracle of God; I thence
> Invoke thy aid to my advent'rous song,
> That with no middle flight intends to soar
> Above th' Aonian mount, while it pursues
> Things unattempted yet in prose or rhyme,
> And chiefly thou O Spirit, that dost prefer
> Before all temples th' upright heart and pure,
> Instruct me, for thou know'st; thou from the first
> Wast present, and with mighty wings outspread
> Dove-like sat'st brooding on the vast abyss
> And mad'st it pregnant: what in me is dark
> Illumine, what is low raise and support,
> That to the highth of this great argument
> I may assert Eternal Providence
> And justify the ways of God to men. (I.1–26)[4]

This trope of inspiration by the divine muse not only undergirds Milton's claim to writing with greater authority, it is also a device to support Milton's imaginary version of events that happened prior to the creation of the world, whether in heaven or in hell. This allows Milton to write authoritatively about the fall of Satan and his allied rebel angels from heaven into hell—an event not recorded in Sacred Scripture, unless one counts an obscure passage in the book of Isaiah.

Isaiah 14:3–23 is a taunt against the king of Babylon (which may have originally been directed against Assyria, the primary threat in

1. Oreb, i.e., the Latin Vulgate spelling of Horeb (Exod 3:1; Deut 4:10), an alternate name for Sinai where Moses received his revelation.

2. I.e., Moses, who shepherded his father-in-law's sheep at Horeb (Exod 3:1).

3. The pool of Siloam, fed by the Gihon spring, located at the foot of Mount Zion near the Temple Mount, and built by King Hezekiah. Milton alludes to a Greek tradition that muses prefer mountains located near springs.

4. Quotations of *Paradise Lost* are from the Norton critical edition of John Milton, *Paradise Lost,* edited by Scott Elledge.

Isaiah's day). The foreign ruler, despite great displays of might, is caricatured as an empty shell doomed to failure. Using imagery drawn from Canaanite myth, the prophet mocks the invading king as a hollow threat by comparing him a now disgraced Canaanite deity who formerly had fancied himself capable of becoming the highest god in that pagan pantheon, but now has been banished to the deepest pit in the underworld. In verse 12 the prophet says of the king:

> How you are fallen from heaven, O day Star, son of Dawn!
> How you are cut down to the ground, you who laid the nations low!"

Although the prophet's taunt originally had nothing do with Satan, centuries later Christian interpreters began to see herein an allusion to the fall of Satan in primordial time. This accommodation was facilitated by the Latin Vulgate translation of this verse,[5] which rendered "day Star" as *lucifer* (meaning "light-bringer" but which left untranslated eventually became the name "Lucifer")—an epithet widely associated with Satan since the early days of Christianity, particularly with reference to the fall of the principal archangel as recounted in 1 Enoch. The trope of a primordial archangel falling or expelled from heaven was reinforced by the terse statement of Jesus in the Gospel of Luke (10:18), "I watched Satan fall from heaven like a flash of lightning." The fall of Satan from heaven into hell before the world began will be a major theme in *Paradise Lost*.

Satan: Anti-Hero or Protagonist?

Milton wastes no time in introducing Satan to his readers. Immediately after invoking the Holy Spirit as his Muse, Milton pivots to what caused "our grand parents" to fall from their original "happy state" in paradise (I.27–30). Without hesitation Milton points the finger directly at Satan:

> Th' infernal Serpent; he it was, whose guile
> Stirred up with envy and revenge, deceived
> The mother of mankind, what time his pride
> Had cast him out from heav'n, with all his host
> Of rebel angels, by whose aid aspiring
> To set himself in glory above his peers,
> He trusted to have equaled the Most High,
> If he opposed; and with ambitious aim

5. *Quomodo cecidisti de caelo lucifer qui mane oriebaris* ("How you have fallen from heaven, O Lucifer, who were appearing by morning"; Vulgate Isa 14:12).

Against the throne and monarchy of God
Raised impious war in heav'n and battle proud
With vain attempt. Him the Almighty Power
Hurled headlong flaming from th' ethereal sky
To bottomless perdition, there to dwell
In adamantine chains and penal fire . . . (I.29–48)

In these few short lines Milton lays out the case against Satan. Satan deceived Eve, "the mother of mankind," out of a desire to get revenge for God having cast him out of heaven and into hell. Before there was a "world" and before there was any human, Satan was already paving a road to perdition. Blinded by his own pride, Satan fancied himself the equal of the Most High—nay, even greater than the Most High. Mislead by vanity, Satan attempted to assert his superiority by recruiting an army of rebellious angels as allies with which to wage war against the Most High and enthrone himself as the supreme ruler. Satan grossly underestimated the power of the Almighty, however, and Satan and his rebel angels quickly found themselves deep in hell, chained fast in everlasting fire.[6]

As the curtains lift for the opening scene in Book I, the reader finds Satan and his rebel companions lying dazed in hell, uncomprehending of what has happened to them and how they have come to be chained in these infernal fires—so sudden and so overwhelming had been their defeat and expulsion from heaven.

Rebellion in Heaven

The story of how and why Satan and his allies fell into hell will not be revealed to the reader until much later, in Books V and VI, when, at Adam's request, the archangel Raphael will give Adam a full account of how Satan recruited an army of rebel angels for the purpose of mounting a full-scale revolution with the goal of dethroning the Most High and making Satan the supreme ruler instead. Because these events happened prior to the creation of the world and humankind, humans would have no knowledge of them except by a direct revelation from God or one of his angels who took part in those primordial events. Raphael was reluctant to relate those sordid events, but finally acceded to Adam's request, reasoning that

6. The motif of the fallen angels chained in eternal hell fire is found in Jude 6–7 and 2 Pet 2:4, which in turn is derived from 1 Enoch 6–12 and, more remotely, Gen 6:1–4; see above, chapter 4.

perhaps it will be "for thy good" (V.570) to know what had transpired before the creation of the world.

In Raphael's telling, all was well in heaven until the Most High Father called all the angels into assembly and solemnly announced his intention to install a vicegerent who will rule in his stead:

> "Hear all ye angels, progeny of Light,
> Thrones, Dominations, Princedoms, Virtues, Powers,
> Hear my decree, which unrevoked shall stand.
> This day I have begot whom I declare
> My only Son, and on this holy hill
> Him have anointed, whom ye now behold
> At my right hand; your head I him appoint;
> And by my Self have sworn to him shall bow
> All knees in heav'n, and shall confess him Lord:
> Under his great vicegerent reign abide
> United as one individual soul
> Forever happy; him who disobeys
> Me disobeys, breaks union, and that day
> Cast out from God and blessed vision, falls
> Into utter darkness, deep engulfed, his place
> Ordained without redemption, without end." (V.600–615)

Although drawing ultimately upon biblical language (Psalms 2 and 110; Hebrews 1:5–11; 5:5–6; Philippians 2:6–11) to speak of Jesus as the Son whom God exalts to his right hand, Milton is also harkening back to a tradition previously encountered in Islam about God appointing or creating a vicegerent to rule in his stead. In the Qur'an, however, "vicegerent" refers to the creation of Adam/humankind, while here the referent is transferred to the begetting of the Son of God, aka "the second Adam." For Milton, the idea that the Father specially "generated" the Son for this purpose was entirely consistent with his theological views. Milton did not subscribe to the standard Christian trinitarian doctrine of God, that is, that God is one in being but consists of three co-equal and co-eternal persons: Father, Son, and Holy Spirit. Rather, Milton held that the Son was lesser than the Father, having been generated by the Father, not out of any physical necessity but by the Father's decree and of his own free will.[7] But to return to our main point, as in Islamic tradition, so in *Paradise Lost*, the deity's begetting and appointment of a "vicegerent" is the

7. For Milton's views regarding the Son of God, see his *De Doctrina Christiana*, V [I.v].

trigger that sets off a rebellion by the highest ranking angel (Iblis/Satan/Lucifer) and a host of allied angels, which rebellion ultimately ends in the defeat and punishment of the rebellious angels.

When God announces his decision to appoint a vicegerent whom all are to obey, all the angels at first submit and praise God—all save Satan. Satan's pride had been sorely wounded by the Almighty preferring someone else over him. Afterall, Satan until now had been esteemed as "the first Archangel, great in power, in favor and pre-eminence" (V.660–1). How could the Almighty have passed him over, to choose this novel "Son of God" instead?

Smarting from such a grievous wound to his pride, Satan was unable to sleep that night, but stayed awake plotting revenge. Before the night was out Satan managed to convene a third of the angelic beings—those heretofore most beholden to him as their awesome leader—on the pretext of needing to assemble and plan how best to greet their newly appointed Messiah-King upon his arrival. Satan, however, very quickly revealed his real purpose, to persuade the assembled angels of the need to resist the Almighty's design as an insult to their dignity and freedom. Borrowing from the freemasonry political philosophy of his day, Milton cast Satan and his allies as rebels desirous of throwing off the excesses of a tyrannical king in order to establish an egalitarian rule of their own making:

> Will ye submit your necks, and choose to bend
> The supple knee? Ye will not, if I trust
> To know ye right, or if ye know yourselves
> Natives and sons of heav'n possessed before
> By none, and if not equal all, yet free,
> Equally free; for orders and degrees
> Jar not with liberty, but well consist.
> Who can in reason then or right assume
> Monarchy over such as live by right
> His equals, if in power and splendor less,
> In freedom equal? Or can introduce
> Law and edict on us, who without law
> Err not, much less for this to be our Lord,
> And look for adoration to th' abuse
> Of those imperial titles which assert
> Our being ordained to govern, not to serve? (V.787–802)

Satan's message may be stated more simply—and arguably better expressed—in his more famous clarion call to resist tyranny in any form, no matter the cost: "Better to reign in hell, than serve in heav'n" (I.263).

Of the multitude of assembled angels only one, the fearless seraph Abdiel, rose to oppose mighty Satan. Abdiel—whose name means "servant of God"—easily saw through the duplicity and the lies of Satan, calling upon him to desist from "this impious rage" but, instead, to seek the Father's forgiveness "while pardon may [still] be found" (V.846–49). Despite the zeal with which Abdiel spoke, "none seconded" him, to the delight of the apostate archangel. With that, brave Abdiel turned his back on the assembly and fled back to the Almighty, where he was heartily welcomed back into the fold of the faithful angels.

While the disaffected angels may have been easily hoodwinked by the dissembling words and outright lies of Satan, the omniscient God was not deceived about Satan's intentions. Meanwhile in heaven God the Father, monitoring the growing rebellion, turned to "his only Son" and advised that they need be on their guard, "lest unawares we lose this our high place, our sanctuary." To which the Son confidently responded that the rebels pose no real threat:

> ". . . Mighty Father, thou thy foes
> Justly hast in derision, and secure
> Laugh'st at their vain designs and tumults vain." (V.735–737; cf. Ps
> 2:4–6)

What is more, the Son then volunteered, if necessary, to assume the Father's full "regal power" and himself attempt to quell the rebellion. But the Father had other plans.

While God and his Son observed from their superior vantage place, God directed Michael and Gabriel, his two most powerful archangels, along with Abdiel to lead the army of faithful angels in outright war to defeat Satan and the apostate angels. A terrific, cosmic three-day battle ensued. In Milton's telling of this ultimate battle between the forces of good and the forces of evil, the first day—if time before time can be delineated in "days"—ended in a draw. Satan had suffered a grievous wound such as would kill mortals, but which soon healed over, as angelic beings do not suffer death. That first day ended with neither side able to achieve victory. Satan and his minions retired at night to plan a more successful battle strategy for the following day. They are credited with inventing a weapon, cannons mounted on wheels—the most destructive weapon of war known in Milton's day—and from deep down under, they mined the nitrous elements required for producing gunpowder necessary to rain down deadly cannonballs upon the foe. The rebel angels' nocturnal industry paid off, for by the end of the second day Michael and Gabriel and their allies had been thoroughly routed, desperately uprooting and defensively hurling mountains as they fled in disarray before the advancing rebel army.

On the third day, however, God weighs in by sending his Son, the Messiah, to take charge of the battle and thereby get the glory reserved for him. The angels stand aside as the Messiah, with terrifying countenance, charges forth in his chariot, arrayed in thunder and lightning. He repels the thunderstruck rebels back against heaven's wall, from where, desperate to escape, they leap down to their punishment into the yawning depths of hell, whereupon the Messiah returns triumphantly to reign by his Father's side.

Raphael concluded his account of the fall of Satan with a warning to Adam that Satan even now is plotting revenge against God. Moreover, Satan's revenge likely involves Adam himself:

> ". . . [Satan] envies now thy state,
> Who now is plotting how he may seduce
> Thee also from obedience, that with him
> Bereaved of happiness thou may'st partake
> His punishment, eternal misery;
> Which would be all his solace and revenge,
> As a despite done against the Most High,
> Thee once to gain companion of his woe.
> But listen not to his temptations, warn
> Thy weaker[8]; let it profit thee to have heard
> By terrible example the reward
> Of disobedience; firm they might have stood,
> Yet fell; remember, and fear to transgress." (VI.900–912)

The motif of a rebellion in heaven we have encountered previously in 1 Enoch and subsequent literature. What is new in Milton's version is the vivid description of a three-day cosmic battle between the forces of good and evil—which George Lucas adapted so graphically in his *Star Wars* trilogy—and also the introduction of the Messiah, the Son of God, as the decisive factor in the ultimate defeat of Satan and the fallen angels.

---

8. The allusion to Eve as "thy weaker" derives from 1 Pet 3:7, where husbands are exhorted to honor their wives as "the weaker vessel."

In Milton's reformulation, the rebellion in heaven motif has been thoroughly transformed into a Christian drama—literally, in that the Messiah (Christ) unilaterally defeats Satan and the forces of evil, but with a novel twist. In traditional Christian belief, this ultimate defeat of Satan by the Son of God is projected to be an apocalyptic event that will take place at the end of time, as in the book of Revelation, when the Christ finally overcomes the great red dragon and chains it in the eternal fires of hell. Milton transfers this battle to the "beginning," before the world was created. But these are epic times, and epic battles are seldom decisively concluded once and for always. Just so, no sooner does Satan awaken in hell following his fall from heaven than he immediately embarks on a new scheme to avenge himself against the Almighty. If the Almighty has proved too powerful to confront head on, perhaps his honor and glory can at least be sullied by an indirect attack—which is how Adam and Eve come to be featured in this epic battle between good and evil. For that, we need to return to the moment when Satan and his rebel angels awaken in hell, still dazed from their precipitous expulsion from heaven and descent into the fiery depths of hell.

As the rebel angels gradually gain cognition of their new reality, of being imprisoned in total darkness despite horrific flames searing them on every side, they are unable to accept their punishment as justified. Signs of a new rebellion manifest themselves almost spontaneously. A temple, more accurately, a palace, appears as if by magic on a hill before them. Its name, Pandaemonium—literally, "(place) of all demons"—says it all; it is the opposite of the heavenly temple-palace of the Most High in heaven. The fallen angels quickly gather in council within Pandaemonium to figure a way out of their present predicament and to plot revenge against the Almighty who is responsible for placing them in this sordid condition. Some propose another battle against God, while others caution against a second direct attack against the force that has proved so overwhelmingly powerful already. A second defeat surely would result only in even greater punishment, with consequences more dire even than their present torments.

Given the impasse in their deliberations, Beelzebub advocated a third option, first proposed by Satan (for whence could such a malicious idea have originated but from the author of all evil). With uncanny malevolence Beelzebub argues the case: Why not investigate the truth of a rumored prophecy that the Almighty was about to create a new world? If true, perhaps some avenue might be found in that new world by which

to thwart the designs of the Almighty and thereby gain at least a partial
victory over their archenemy.

> ". . . There is a place
> (If ancient and prophetic fame in heav'n
> Err not) another world, the happy seat
> Of some new race called Man, about this time
> To be created like to us, though less
> In power and excellence, but favored more
> Of him who rules above; so was his will
> Pronounced among the gods, and by an oath,
> That shook heav'n's whole circumference, confirmed.
> Thither let us bend all our thoughts, to learn
> What creatures there inhabit, of what mold,
> Or substance, how endued, and what their power,
> And where their weakness, how attempted best,
> By force or subtlety: though heav'n be shut,
> And heav'n's high arbitrator sit secure
> In his own strength, this place may lie exposed
> The utmost border of his kingdom, left
> To their defense who hold it: here perhaps
> Some advantageous act may be achieved
> By sudden onset, either with hell fire
> To waste his whole creation, or possess
> All as our own, and drive as we were driven,
> The puny habitants, or if not drive,
> Seduce them to our party, that their God
> May prove their foe, and with repenting hand
> Abolish his own works. This would surpass
> Common revenge, and interrupt his joy
> In our confusion, and our joy upraise
> In his disturbance, when his darling sons
> Hurled headlong to partake with us, shall curse
> Their frail original, and faded bliss,
> Faded so soon . . ." (II.346–376)

Though the council was easily persuaded by Beelzebub's brave
words about attacking the Almighty indirectly though ruination of his
darling new creatures, none was found willing to undertake so perilous
a journey to an unknown world, with such an uncertain outcome, until
Satan himself, puffed up with self-importance and monarchial pride,
volunteered himself to go scout out this rumored new world. The rebels

quickly accepted Satan's offer, and the "Stygian council" was dissolved, having entrusted all into Satan's hands.

Satan managed to slip out of his chains and carefully pick his way out of that infernal prison. The gates of hell were guarded by two monstrous figures, Sin and Death; but these Satan easily won over to his side, since they are in reality his very own offspring. They not only unlocked and flung open the gates of hell, allowing the father of lies to pass through into the chaos beyond, but even more, Sin and Death followed in Satan's tracks like steadfast companions.

From his vantage point on high, God the Father watched as the determined Satan made his way across the vast expanse of the void—"The monster moving onward came as fast // With horrid strides, hell trembled as he strode" (II.675–76)—blazing a path by which to connect hell and the newly created world above. The Father apprised his Son about Satan's evil intent and Satan's certain success. The Father explained that even though the sin of the newly created human will be lesser than that of Satan who with full knowledge sinned most deliberately, and while the man will be tricked or seduced to sin by another, more powerful being, nevertheless, divine justice demands that the man and his descendants must die, suffering the same eternal punishment as the rebellious angels, unless someone may be found who will provide satisfaction for the human's imminent offense of aspiring to become like God. The Son praises God for his all-knowing mercy and then volunteers himself to become human precisely to make the necessary satisfaction for Adam's offense.

This primordial offer of the Son to make satisfaction for the humans' sin even before that sin has occurred is not entirely new, as it bears resemblance to Irenaeus's concept of all humankind having been recapitulated in the incarnated Word of God even before creation commenced.

Moreover, the Son's offer (in Book III) to make satisfaction accords well with a strain of Christian theology long since made popular by Anselm of Canterbury (ca. 1100) in his treatise *Cur Deus Homo* ("Why God [Became] Human"). According to Anselm, the incarnation was necessary to resolve an inherent conflict between divine justice and divine mercy. Relying on a medieval theory of justice which postulates that the gravity of an offense is predicated less upon the severity of the malfeasance (the act itself) than upon the dignity of the person offended, Anselm postulated that because Adam offended the infinite God, therefore an infinite restitution (or satisfaction) by the offending party was required to repair the damage done. This presents an impossible dilemma. As the offending party was human, reparation had to come from humankind itself. But because humans are finite, no human is capable of making infinite reparation. Only a divine being can make infinite reparation. The only solution would be for a divine person to become human in order to satisfy the debt owed to the offended deity. This is precisely what the Son proposed to do. As human, he would fulfill the requirement that humankind pay the debt owed God, as justice demanded. As divine, the Son would also fulfill the requirement that the satisfaction paid be of infinite value. Thus would divine justice be safeguarded while at the same time also revealing the magnitude of divine mercy. (Whether Anselm's theory is an adequate statement of Christian doctrine regarding the incarnation is much debated; but clearly it was the view adopted by Milton; it also accorded well with his Protestant orientation that salvation is *sola gratia*, "by grace alone.") From another perspective, this is nothing less than a restatement of the Christian concept of the "Fortunate Fall," a theme long since celebrated in Christian worship and hymns, that it took something as awful as Adam's sin to reveal that the love of God for humankind is limitless and has no bounds, in that he willingly sacrificed his own Son in order to redeem humankind.

Satan's Quest of Revenge

With humankind's eventual salvation assured through the Son's voluntary self-sacrifice, Milton turns in Book IV more directly to the story of the first human couple, or to be more exact, how Satan first gained sight of the primal human couple frolicking happily in their primeval innocence, and immediately began plotting their downfall. The story of how Adam and Eve fell into disobedience and thereby lost paradise had previously never so elaborately and so imaginatively been envisioned as in Milton's novel rendition.

The nearer Satan drew to Eden, the heavier the enormity of his wicked intentions weighed upon him, even to the point of questioning whether it might be better to turn back and seek divine forgiveness. Nevertheless, Satan quickly cast off such doubts and steeled himself in his resolve to get revenge upon the Most High.

Eden, Satan discovered, was surrounded by a high wall with but a single entrance via a locked and guarded gate. Determined to get in, Satan managed to scale the wall and perch himself high in a tree like a cormorant. From that birds-eye vantage he could not help but be over-whelmed by the incredible beauty of all that stretched before him: tall verdant trees and abundant beautiful flowers, amongst which new and strange animals of every kind frolicked happily and peacefully with each other. But of all the living creatures there stood

> Two of far nobler shape erect and tall,
> God-like erect, with native honor clad
> In naked majesty seemed lords of all,
> And worthy seemed, for in their looks divine
> The image of their glorious Maker shone,
> Truth, wisdom, sanctitude severe and pure,
> Severe but in true filial freedom placed;
> Whence true authority in men; though both
> Not equal, as their sex not equal seemed;
> For contemplation he and valor formed,
> For softness she and sweet attractive grace,
> He for God only, she for God in him:
> His fair large front and eye sublime declared
> Absolute rule; and hyacinthine locks
> Round from his parted forelock manly hung
> Clust'ring, but not beneath his shoulders broad:
> She as a veil down to the slender waist
> Her unadorned golden tresses wore
> Disheveled, but in wanton ringlets waved
> As the vine curls her tendrils, which implied
> Subjection, but required with gentle sway,
> And by her yielded, by him best received,
> Yielded with coy submission, modest pride,
> And sweet reluctant amorous delay. (IV.288–311)

Witnessing from his lofty perch this vista of serenity and harmony, Satan again experiences twinges of remorse for the havoc he is about to wreak upon this innocent, unsuspecting human couple below and upon the idyllic world in which they live. Nevertheless, proceed he must.

> Then from his lofty stand on that high tree
> Down he alights among the sportful herd
> Of those four-footed kinds . . . (IV.395–398)

Once on the ground, Satan moved silently among the innocent and trust-ing, beautiful four-footed creatures in the garden. He assumed the form first of one creature and then another, as he attempted to discern which shape might best serve his devilish purpose. It was while mingling among the animal kingdom that Satan chanced to overhear Adam and Eve conversing, as Adam tells Eve of the sole charge laid upon them by God,

> . . . "who requires
> From us no other service than to keep
> This one, this easy charge, of all the trees
> In Paradise that bear delicious fruit
> So various, not to taste that only Tree
> Of Knowledge, planted by the Tree of Life,
> So near grows death to life, whate'ver death is,
> Some dreadful thing no doubt; for well thou know'st
> God hath pronounced it death to taste that Tree,
> . . .
> One easy prohibition, who enjoy
> Free leave so large to all things else, and choice
> Unlimited of manifold delights:
> But let us ever praise him, and extol
> His bounty, following our delightful task
> To prune these growing plants, and tend these flow'rs,
> Which were it toilsome, yet with these were sweet." (IV.419–439)

Satan could scarcely believe his good fortune at having so easily discovered a means by which to overturn the deity's paradisaical realm. Overjoyed in a maniacal way, he retreated into the shadows to await a better opportunity.

With evening fast approaching, the primal couple happily retired to their bridal bower. After appropriately praising the Creator for all his marvelous works, they entered their nuptial bed and engaged in their divinely ordained marital union without hesitation or the slightest of shame, just as their Creator intended. (Here Milton, with his effusive praise of the marital act, seems to delight in poking fun at the puritanical sensibilities of his contemporary Puritan co-religionists.)

Meanwhile, the angel Uriel, who had been tasked with guarding the entrance to paradise, flew to Gabriel to report the bad news that he feared some evil spirit had managed to slip past by disguising himself as a lowly angel from heaven wishing merely to glimpse the wonders of paradise. Gabriel assured Uriel that such developments cannot happen unless the Almighty had a purpose in allowing them; but in any case, Gabriel would organize a search throughout the whole of Eden and find that evil spirit ere the sun rises again.

It was Gabriel himself with two of his lieutenants who found the wandering spirit at the bedside of the sleeping human couple. Satan was "squat like a toad, close at the ear of Eve," whispering into it. Gabriel questioned Satan about his business in the garden. Satan haughtily invoked his former superior status and challenged Gabriel to another battle. At this point divine scales appeared in the heavens, weighing whether fight or flight, engagement in renewed battle or the foregoing of further conflict, would be the better option. Gabriel and Satan both saw that the scales clearly indicated that the latter option should be chosen. Eschewing further argument, the fiend wisely fled into the night.

When morning arrived, Eve awoke from her sleep pensive and distraught. She related how in her troublesome dream a voice had awakened her. The voice had led her to "the tree of interdicted knowledge, . . . much fairer to my fancy than by day" (V.52–53). There an angelic figure similar to those Eve was accustomed to seeing in the garden stood gazing longingly upon the tree heavy laden with luscious fruit. In her dream, Eve continued, the angelic figure boldly announced,

> "Forbid who will, none shall from me withhold
> Longer thy offered good, why else set here?"
> This said he paused not, but with vent'rous arm
> He plucked, he tasted: me damp horror chilled
> At such bold words vouched with a deed so bold:
> But he thus overjoyed, , "O fruit divine,
> Sweet of thyself, but much more sweet thus cropped,
> Forbidden here, it seems, as only fit
> For gods, yet able to make gods of men:
> And why not gods of men, since good, the more
> Communicated, more abundant grows,
> The author not impaired but honored more?
> Here, happy creature, fair angelic Eve,
> Partake thou also; happy though thou art,
> Happier thou may'st be, worthier canst not be:
> Taste this, and be henceforth among the gods
> Thyself a goddess, not to earth confined,
> But sometimes in the air, as we, sometimes
> Ascend to heav'n, by merit thine, and see
> What life the gods live there, and such live thou." (V. 63–81)

Eve recounted her own reaction as angelic shape held the fruit below her nose:

> . . . The pleasant savory smell
> So quickened appetite, that I, me thought,
> Could not but taste. Forthwith up to the clouds

> With him I flew, and underneath beheld
> The earth outstretched immense, a prospect wide
> And various: wond'ring at my flight and change
> To this high exaltation; suddenly
> My guide was gone, and I, methought, sunk down
> And fell asleep; but O how glad I waked
> To find this but a dream!" (V. 84–93)

Adam likewise found Eve's dream deeply troubling, but assured her that one need not be overly anxious, as dreams lie outside of one's control:

> "Evil into the mind of god or man
> May come and go, so unapproved, and leave
> No spot or blame behind: which gives me hope
> That what in sleep thou didst abhor to dream,
> Waking thou never wilt consent to do." (V.117–121)

With their confidence reassured, Adam and his wife arose and went forth to attend their appointed duties in the garden.

Raphael Sent to Warn Adam

Above in heaven the Most High was far less confident that the human creatures he had created in his own image and likeness would exercise appropriately the free will with which he had endowed them. He summoned Raphael—the same archangel he would later send down to accompany Tobias (Tobit) and protect him during the night of his wedding to Sarah from the demon Asmodeus who had killed Sarah's previous seven husbands, each in turn on the very night of their weddings. God instructed Raphael to go down to Eden and warn Adam of the danger he and Eve faced from Satan recently escaped from hell and who even now is prowling about in the garden, determined at any cost to bring death upon them and their descendants.

When Raphael descended into paradise, he was warmly received by the happy human couple. In imagery drawn from Genesis 18 wherein the patriarch Abraham and his wife Sarah entertained the three angels sent from God, our primeval parents most graciously entertained Raphael who arrived at the hottest time of the afternoon. They invited Raphael to rest in the shade of their bower. Eve went about preparing a succulent feast for their guest, leaving Adam to engage in rapt conversation with their angelic guest. It was during the course of this conversation that

Adam learned from Raphael about the primordial rebellion of Satan and the fallen angels described previously, as well as how in the beginning he and Eve had been created in God's image and given the charge to rule over the whole of God's good creation. Eager to know still more, Adam inquired about the celestial movements of the heavens. Raphael responded that the quest of knowledge is admirable but admonished Adam to direct his mind to matters more appropriate to humankind.

Desirous of prolonging this marvelous conversation with his heavenly visitor, Adam proposes to tell Raphael the story of his own creation, at least as he knows it. Adam says his earliest memory is of lying prone on the ground and gazing at the vast sky, as he gradually gained consciousness. Instinctively, he stood up and observed many pleasant sights on every side.

> But who I was, or where, or from what cause,
> Knew not; to speak I tried, and forthwith spake,
> My tongue obeyed and readily could name
> Whate'er I saw. "Thou sun,' said I, 'fair light,
> And thou enlightened earth, so fresh and gay,
> Ye hills and dales, ye rivers, woods, and plains,
> And ye that live and move, fair creatures, tell,
> Tell, if ye saw, how came I thus, how here?
> Not of myself; by some great Maker then,
> In goodness and in power preeminent;
> Tell me, how may I know him, how adore,
> From whom I have that thus I move and live,
> And feel that I am happier than I know." (VIII.270–282)

Almost as if on cue, Adam sensed an "inward apparition" stirring within, and guiding him toward "the garden of bliss." Adam understood the apparition to be the "Presence Divine." It spoke to Adam:

> This paradise I give thee, count it thine
> To till and keep, and of the fruit to eat:
> Of every tree that in the garden grows
> Eat freely with glad heart; fear here no dearth:
> But of the tree whose operation brings
> Knowledge of good and ill, which I have set
> The pledge of thy obedience and thy faith,
> Amid the garden by the Tree of Life,
> Remember what I warn thee, shun to taste,
> And shun the bitter consequence: for know,
> The day thou eat'st thereof, my sole command
> Transgressed, inevitably thou shalt die. (VIII.319–330)

Next the heavenly Vision paraded all living creatures before Adam, two by two, that he might name them. Not only could Adam readily name them all, he understood the nature of each, thanks to the "knowledge God endued" upon him. That task completed, Adam suddenly felt lonely, however, for he realized that he alone was without a partner—a deficiency that Adam delicately pointed out to his divine Maker. Rather than being displeased, God commended Adam for recognizing his need for an appropriate companion, for God had only been testing Adam to see whether Adam understood not only the world around him, including the animal kingdom, but also his very own nature as requiring human fellowship.

Scarcely had their dialog ended before Adam felt himself succumbing to sleep, but not ordinary sleep. Although his eyes were closed, some "cell of internal sight" remained open. In his trance he perceived the glorious shape to whom he had been talking,

> Who stooping opened my left side, and took
> From thence a rib, with cordial spirits warm,
> And life-blood streaming fresh; wide was the wound,
> But suddenly with flesh filled up and healed;
> The rib he formed and fashioned with his hands;
> Under his forming hands a creature grew,
> Man-like, but different sex, so lovely fair,
> That what seemed fair in all the world, seemed now
> Mean, or in her summed up, in her contained
> And in her looks, which from that time infused
> Sweetness into my heart, unfelt before,
> And into all things from her air inspired
> The spirit of love and amorous delight. (VIII.465–477)

Awaking from his trance, Adam was overwhelmed to find a creature so similar to himself but even more beautiful than what was apparent in his trance-dream. Overjoyed, he could not contain his gratitude to the Creator:

> "This turn hath made amends; thou hast fulfilled
> Thy words, Creator bounteous and benign,
> Giver of all things, fair, but fairest this
> Of all thy gifts, not enviest. I now see
> Bone of my bone, flesh of my flesh, my self
> Before me; woman is her name, of man
> Extracted; for this cause he shall forgo

Father and mother, and to his wife adhere;
And they shall be one flesh, one heart, one soul." (VIII.491–499)

Once again Milton seems to delight in detailing the physicality of lovemaking inside paradise, how Adam gently and lovingly led this innocent and modest virgin "to the nuptial bow'r" where the primal couple consummated their marriage beneath happy constellations, surrounded with joyous melody of birds, all under the watchful eyes of guarding angels. A more pure, glorious, and happy state is impossible to imagine—though Adam does inquire of Raphael whether angels also experience comparable pleasures. This last question Raphael judiciously declines to answer, except to say that angelic spirits do enjoy a state of happiness, but of a spiritual kind.

With their conversation concluded, Raphael rose to take his leave. "So parted they, the angel up to heav'n . . . and Adam to his bow'r." Nevertheless, not all was rosy in the garden.

Temptation and Fall

When we last encountered Satan, he was strategically fleeing from Gabriel, lest he suffer another defeat, with consequences more dire than the first. Having fled Eden but still intent upon getting revenge upon the Most High, Satan spent the next seven days circumventing the earth, pondering what his next move should be. He feared to provoke another confrontation with one of the cherubim guarding paradise. On the eighth day, however, he summoned up courage to slip back into the garden under the cover of night.

Once inside, Satan carefully studied each creature, whether one of them "might serve his wiles." In the course of his investigation, he happened upon "the serpent subtlest beast of all the field" (IX.85–86), fast asleep. Satan carefully slipped into its mouth without waking it, and took possession of its faculties, to await the morn.

With the sun, Adam and Eve rose and happily set about planning their day, how best to continue their pleasant God-given duties of tending the garden. As the garden was vast and thriving under such optimal conditions, its luxuriant plants required much pruning and training. For maximum productivity, Eve proposed that the two of them separate and each work in a different portion of the garden, since together they often distracted each other with frequent pleasantries and amorous fawning.[9]

Adam commended Eve for her desire to accomplish their tasks more efficiently but reminded her that God did not make them for work only, but also for enjoying each other's company. Moreover, Adam continued, they must remember the warning that an enemy is on the prowl seeking to harm them. He worries that the enemy may overwhelm them separately. Moreover, since Eve was taken from his side, he has a special obligation to protect her, since a "wife, where danger or dishonor lurks, safest and seemliest by her husband stays" (IX.267–68).

As might be expected, Eve was offended that Adam could think that she might slip if left alone, and especially that she, as a woman, was more susceptible to temptation than Adam himself. How could he possibly harbor within his breast such demeaning thoughts!

Adam hastened to heal Eve's wounded spirit with reassuring words, saying that he had not meant to demean her. He merely meant that together the two of them would be stronger than either alone. Afterall, their common foe must not be taken lightly. Was it not already manifest just how difficult are Satan's wiles to resist, given that previously half the angels in heaven had been seduced by his smooth words! Nevertheless, Adam conceded, God had endowed them both with reason and free will, so he would not prevent her going alone if that were her decision.

And that was Eve's decision. Surely "a foe so proud," she reasoned, would consider it beneath his dignity to "first the weaker seek." Shame would certainly deter him.

> Thus saying, from her husband's hand her hand
> Soft she withdrew, and like a wood-nymph light

slipped into Eden's more distant groves, taking nothing but her simple gardening tools (IX.385–391). Of that foolhardy decision the poet laments:

> O much deceived, much failing, hapless Eve,
> Of thy presumed return! event perverse!
> Thou never from that hour in Paradise
> Found'st either sweet repast, or sound repose;
> Such ambush hid among sweet flow'rs and shades

9. The motif of Eve wishing to work separately in the garden, which ends with her being seduced by Satan, appears already in the Jewish pseudepigraph Life of Adam and Eve; see chapter 6 above, pp. 117–18.

Waited with hellish rancor imminent
To intercept thy way, or send thee back
Despoiled of innocence, of faith, of bliss.
For now, and since first break of dawn the Fiend,
More serpent in appearance, forth was come,

. . . .

He sought them both, but wished his hap might find
Eve separate, he wished, but not with hope
Of what so seldom chanced, when to his wish,
Beyond his hope, Eve separate he spies. (IX.404–424)

Satan could scarcely believe his good fortune in finding Eve alone. As he studied her, however, her beauty excited such passion in him[10] that he was sorely tempted to abandon his mission of enmity toward human-kind—but only momentarily. "The hot hell that always in him burns" and the recognition that such pleasure was "not for him ordained" quickly brought him back to his senses—and to his avowed goal:

"Then let me not let pass
Occasion which now smiles, behold alone
The woman, opportune to all attempts,
Her husband, for I view far round, not nigh,
Whose higher intellectual more I shun,
And strength, of courage haughty, and of limb
Heroic built, though of terrestrial mold,
Foe not informidable, exempt from wound,
I not, so much hath hell debased, and pain
Enfeebled me, to what I was in heav'n." (IX.479–488)

Exactly opposite of what Eve had supposed, Satan was relieved to find Eve alone, for he feared being overcome by the man's superior intellect and formidable strength, especially given Satan's diminished capacity from what he had enjoyed formerly in heaven.

Encased in his serpent shell, Satan silently approached Eve and curled up nearby. Accustomed to having creatures playing about her, she initially paid him no attention. Next, he moved his head from side to side, then "fawning, licked the ground whereon she trod," finally gaining her attention. "With serpent tongue" he flattered her with gushing com-pliments, how he adored her celestial beauty—"a goddess among gods,

10. One is reminded of the mythic fragment preserved in Gen 6:1–4, according to which the angelic beings ("sons of gods") assigned to watch the human daughters ended up lusting after them and marrying as many as they wished, resulting in the corruption of all humankind as elaborated in 1 Enoch 6–12.

adored by angels numberless." What a shame that there was but one man to admire such ravishing beauty!

Flattered, Eve took the bait and began to converse with her tempter: How is it that you, a serpent, can speak with human language? I thought God had made all beasts mute and without reason.

The "serpent" replied: You are correct. Formerly, I was dumb and mute like all beasts. We all grazed off plants growing close to the ground; we were unable to reach leaves and fruits located high above. That was my condition as well,

> Till on a day roving the field, I chanced
> A goodly tree far distant to behold
> Laden with fruit of fairest colors mixed,
> Ruddy and gold: I nearer drew to gaze;
> When from the boughs a savory odor blown,
> Grateful to appetite, more pleased my sense
> Than smell of sweetest fennel, or the teats
> Of ewe or goat dropping with milk at ev'n,
> Unsucked of lamb or kid, that tend their play
> To satisfy the sharp desire I had
> Of tasting those fair apples,[11] I resolved
> Not to defer; hunger and thirst at once,
> Powerful persuaders, quickened at the scent
> Of that alluring fruit, urged me so keen. (IX.575–588)

Although other animals, the serpent continued, were similarly drawn to the tree by the savory odor emanating from it, none could reach its high-hanging fruit. I alone was able to climb the tree by winding my body around the mossy trunk of the tree and eat of its luscious fruit until I was sated. Almost immediately I began to perceive strange alterations happening within myself. Though I retained my outward appearance, I realized that I had acquired a capacity to think, to speculate on matters high and deep. With my newly enlightened mind I now

> Considered all things visible in heav'n
> Or earth, or middle, all things fair and good;
> But all that fair and good in thy divine
> Semblance, and in thy beauty's heav'nly ray
> United I beheld; no fair to thine

11. Milton followed long-standing Western Christian tradition in identifying the forbidden fruit as an apple, based upon a pun or confusion of "apple" (*malum*) with its homonym "evil" (*malum*) in the Latin Vulgate translation of Gen 2:17: "the tree of knowledge of good and evil (*malum*)."

> Equivalent or second, which compelled
> Me thus, though importune perhaps, to come
> And gaze, and worship thee of right declared
> Sovran of creatures, universal dame. (IX.604–612)

Although Eve recognized in these "overpraising" words from the mouth of "the sly snake" an element of self-ingratiating flattery, she nevertheless was intrigued and curious to see for herself the source of the serpent's new-found wisdom. So she asked the serpent to show her this marvelous tree, which the serpent was only too eager to do. When they arrived at the tree, Eve immediately recognized that it was the forbidden tree and said,

> "Serpent, we might have spared our coming hither,
> Fruitless to me, though fruit be here to excess,
> . . . .
> But of this tree we may not taste nor touch;
> God so commanded, and left that command
> Sole daughter of his voice; the rest, we live
> Law to ourselves, our reason is our law."

To which the Tempter guilefully replied:

> "Indeed? Hath God then said that of the fruit
> Of all these garden trees ye shall not eat,
> Yet lords declared of all in earth or air?"

Had sinless Eve been wiser, she would have abruptly ended this discussion. Yet she could not refrain from mounting at least a partial defense against the implication that she was not capable of making decisions for herself:

> . . . "Of the fruit
> Of each tree in the garden we may eat,
> But of the fruit of this fair tree amidst
> The garden, God hath said, 'Ye shall not eat
> Thereof, nor shall ye touch it, lest ye die.'" (IX.647–663)

Feigning solicitude for this naïve woman, the Tempter waxed eloquent about the folly of foregoing the benefits to be gained from partaking of the fruit of this marvelous tree. Pretending that his wisdom and eloquence derives from the forbidden tree's fruit, the faux serpent addressed the naïve mother of humankind:

"Queen of this universe, do not believe
Those rigid threats of death; ye shall not die:
How should ye? By the fruit? It gives you life
To knowledge. By the Threat'ner? Look on me,
Me who have touched and tasted, yet both live,
And life more perfect have attained than fate
Meant me, by vent'ring higher than my lot.
Shall that be shut to man, which to the beast
Is open? Or will God incense his ire
For such a petty trespass, and not praise
Rather your dauntless virtue, whom the pain
Of death denounced, whatever thing death be,
Deterred not from achieving what might lead
To happier life, knowledge of good and evil. IX.684–697)

Ever duplicitous, the serpent continued, God forbade you this tree to "keep you low and ignorant," knowing that if you eat its fruit, your eyes will be "opened and cleared, and ye shall be as gods, knowing both good and evil as they know." And about the death threatened for eating, that actually would be a blessing in disguise. Yes, "ye shall die perhaps, by putting off Human"; but you will "put on gods" instead, in which case death is something "to be wished." In any case, what harm can come to the Almighty because of such a petty offense?

What can your knowledge hurt him, or this tree
Impart against his will if all be his?
Or is it envy, and can envy dwell
In heav'nly breasts? These, these and many more
Causes import your need of this fair fruit.
Goddess humane, reach then, and freely taste." (IX.727–732)

Having planted the seeds of doubt firmly within Eve, the Tempter quietly waited. His words, though softly uttered, resonated persuasively in the woman's ears, louder than any gong. Had she not with her own eyes seen that the serpent had not died. Even more, had he not joyfully shared his good news with her. And why indeed would her Creator not want to share even greater knowledge with humankind, unless he were envious that humans might become equal to gods, or perhaps even surpass them. With the noon hour approaching and her appetite whetted by the wafting odor of that savory ripe fruit, her decision was taken,

. . . her rash hand in evil hour
Forth reaching to the fruit, she plucked, she eat:

> Earth felt the wound, and nature from her seat
> Sighing through all her works gave signs of woe,
> That all was lost. Back to the thicket slunk
> The guilty serpent, and well might, for Eve
> Intent now wholly on her taste, naught else
> Regarded, such delight till then, as seemed,
> In fruit she never tasted, whether true
> Or fancied . . . (IX.780–789)

Buoyed by high expectations, Eve felt exuberant at first. She imagined herself growing in knowledge like the gods. But the doubts also grew. Should she share her newly acquired wisdom with Adam? Or should she keep it to herself and use it to make herself an equal copartner with Adam, or even his superior? But what if God has seen and imposes death upon her? Would not God create another Eve for Adam?[12] This last thought was too painful to bear, so great was her love for him. Then and there she resolved to share the fruit with her husband. Whether in bliss or woe, the two of them shall be one. Without him, life is no life. So resolved, she turned to go from the tree.

Meanwhile, Adam was growing concerned over Eve's delay in returning. Fearing something ill had overtaken her, he set out with faltering steps. He was relieved to see her approaching in the distance, clutching in her hand a newly gathered bough of fruit. She proffered a lame apology for her tardiness. Although she could scarcely bear being apart from Adam, she had a just cause. She had encountered a wise serpent who taught her strange and wonderful things:

> "This tree is not as we are told, a tree
> Of danger tasted, nor to evil unknown
> Op'ning the way, but of divine effect
> To open eyes, and make them gods who taste;
> And hath been tasted such: the serpent wise,
> Hath eaten of the fruit, and is become,
> Not dead, as we are threatened, but thenceforth
> Endued with human voice and human sense,
> Reasoning to admiration, and with me
> Persuasively hath so prevailed, that I
> Have also tasted, and have also found
> Th' effects to correspond, opener mine eyes,
> Dim erst, dilated spirits, ampler heart,

---

12. The idea that God might create a substitute wife for Adam appeared previously in the legend of Lilith. Whether Milton was aware of the Lilith story is unknown.

And growing up to godhead
. . . .
Thou therefore also taste, that equal lot
May join us, equal joy, as equal love;
Lest thou not tasting, different degree
Disjoin us, and I then too late renounce
Deity for thee, when fate will not permit." (IX.863–885)

Adam could scarcely believe what he was hearing. Aghast he stood, "while horror chill ran through his veins." His joints buckled. The garland he had woven specially for Eve slipped from his hand to the ground. He could find no words to verbalize his inmost thoughts: O fairest of all, God's final and best work of creation! How could you have allowed yourself to be beguiled by the enemy? How can I live without you? Even were God to create another Eve for me, taking a second rib from my side, my heart would never recover from the loss of my first and only love, my inseparable companion, bone of my bone, flesh of my flesh!

Eventually Adam recovered from his shock. Resigning himself to the fact that what had been done could not be undone, he set about trying to comfort Eve as best he knew how. Though God had warned them not even to touch, much less taste, perhaps not all was lost.

"Perhaps thou shalt not die, perhaps the fact
Is not so heinous now, foretasted fruit,
Profaned first by the serpent, by him first
Made common and unhallowed ere our taste;
Nor yet on him found deadly, he yet lives,
Lives, as thou saidst . . ."

Perhaps, Adam reasoned, perhaps the penalty is not so dire as threatened after all. What is more, Adam continued, would not our deaths in these circumstances be claimed by Satan as a sort of victory over God? Surely that is not something that God could allow.

"Nor can I think that God, Creator wise,
Though threat'ning, will in earnest so destroy
Us his prime creatures, dignified so high,
Set over all his works, which in our fall,
For us created, needs with us must fail,
Dependent made, so God shall uncreate,
Be frustrate, do, undo, and labor lose,
Not well conceived of God, who through his power
Creation could repeat, yet would be loath

> Us to abolish, lest the adversary
> Triumph and say, 'Fickle their state whom God
> Most favors, who can please him long? Me first
> He ruined, now mankind; whom will he next?'"

Leaving such musings aside, Adam resolutely determined that if Eve must indeed die, then, he, her husband, would willingly die with her.

> "However I with thee have fixed my lot,
> Certain to undergo like doom; if death
> Consort with thee, death is to me as life;
> So forcible within my heart I feel
> The bond of nature draw me to my own,
> My own in thee, for what thou art is mine;
> Our state cannot be severed, we are one,
> One flesh; to lose thee were to lose myself." (IX.928–959)

Eve was overcome with loving affection for her husband, hearing his vow to die with her rather than suffer separation from his beloved spouse. This decision demonstrated beyond any doubt his undying love for her. Moreover, such unequaled faithful love evoked in Eve a new hope for life itself, namely, that even death is incapable of fully extinguishing life. Sustained by such hope—and her husband's undying love—Eve embraced Adam and, weeping tenderly, the apple bough laden with deadly fruit she extended to him

> With liberal hand: he scrupled not to eat
> Against his better knowledge, not deceived,
> But fondly overcome with female charm.
> Earth trembled from her entrails, as again
> In pangs, and nature gave a second groan;
> Sky loured, and muttering thunder, some sad drops
> Wept at completing of the mortal sin
> Original; while Adam took no thought,
> Eating his fill, nor Eve to iterate
> Her former trespass feared, the more to soothe
> Him with her loved society, that now
> As with new wine intoxicated both
> They swim in mirth, and fancy that they feel
> Divinity within them breeding wings
> Wherewith to scorn the earth: but that false fruit
> Far other operation first displayed,
> Carnal desire inflaming, he on Eve
> Began to cast lascivious eyes, she him
> As wantonly repaid; in lust they burn. (IX. 997–1015)

Burning with lust indeed! For the first time their amorous play was characterized less with solicitude for the other than with gratification of oneself. Concupiscence cannot satiate for long, however. Before the night is out, the formerly caring couple will have descended deep into mutual recriminations.

But first another issue will occupy their attention. Concupiscence and associated feelings of shame—unanticipated and unwelcome consequences of their having acquired knowledge of good and evil—drove them to seek a solution. Adam proposed they look for broad leaves that could be sewn together to serve as covering. Searching the woods, the best they could find were from the fig tree, not the common fruiting kind, Milton specifies, but rather the variety that today grows in India, whose broad branches send down aerial roots and produce daughters all around, making abundant shade.[13] With what limited skill they possessed, they hurriedly fashioned loincloths for themselves.

Nevertheless, their industry failed to hide their shame—and mutual recriminations. Adam soon turned against Eve and began to reproach her.

> "Would thou hadst hearkened to my words, and stayed
> With me, as I besought thee, when that strange
> Desire of wand'ring this unhappy morn,
> I know not whence possessed thee, we had then
> Remained still happy, not as now, despoiled
> Of all our good, shamed, naked, miserable." (IX.1134–1139)

Unaccustomed to sharp rebuke, Eve responded defensively with accusations of her own. Had you been with me when the Tempter approached, who can know whether he might not have seduced us both, so persuasive are his lies. Why should he have targeted me? Besides, why blame me? Why did you not assert your authority as head and forbid me to leave your side? You are at fault for not being more assertive, more firm!

To which accusations Adam retorted: Is this the recompense, the love you show me, you ingrate! I was not the one who sinned. What more could I have done, without violating your free will? Perhaps I did err in allowing you so much freedom. Yes, indeed, a woman should not be left to herself, since women are weak!

---

13. Milton apparently has in mind the Indian fig (*ficus*) tree, commonly known as a banyan tree, but he seems unaware that its leaves are relatively small and thus not particularly appropriate for sewing into loincloths.

Thus they in mutual accusation spent
The fruitless hours, but neither self-condemning,
And of their vain contest appeared no end. (IX.1187–1189)

The Divine Judgment: Mercy Tempering Justice

From heaven the Most High was monitoring all, carefully observing the movement of Satan, from his escape from hell to every malevolent deed he wrought in Eden. When the angelic guard ascended from earth to heaven to report the sad events just transpired in Eden, the Omniscient reassured the shaken angels that they were not to blame as these developments were beyond their control. God had allowed them because he so valued human free will. Nevertheless, if justice is to prevail, humankind must be judged, and death imposed per the divine decree. Turning to the Son, he continued,

> "But whom send I to judge them? Whom but thee
> Vicegerent Son, to thee I have transferred
> All judgment, whether in heav'n, or earth, or hell.
> Easy it may be seen that I intend
> Mercy colleague with justice, sending thee
> Man's friend, his mediator, his designed
> Both ransom and redeemer voluntary,
> And destined man himself to judge man fall'n." (X.55–62)

The Son readily affirmed the Father's will, knowing that in the end it would be he that will pay the heavy ransom price. Straightway the Son arose and descended to earth to judge the two guilty humans, as well as Satan in absentia.

The voice of "Yahweh God" that Adam and Eve heard in Eden (in Genesis 3) was none other than that of the Son. That this voice came not in the heat of the day, but rather at the time of the cool evening breeze, Milton interprets as clear signal that the divine wrath was being mitigated with divine mercy. Milton stresses that the divine words, although stern, were at every junction tempered by gentleness. For example, when Adam attempted to defended himself and Eve for having hid among the bushes out of shame for their nakedness, the Son gently probed,

> "My voice thou oft hast heard, and hast not feared,
> But still rejoiced, how is it now become
> So dreadful to thee? That thou art naked, who

Hath told thee? Hast thou eaten of the tree
Whereof I gave thee charge thou shouldst not eat?" (X.119–123)

From this point forward Milton adheres closely to the storyline of Genesis 3, though greatly embellished. Adam is depicted as not having learned the lesson he was being offered, of humbly accepting responsibility for his own actions. He first attempts to shift blame onto Eve, and then, implicitly, onto the Son himself:

This woman whom thou mad'st to be my help,
And gav'st me as thy perfet gift, so good,
So fit, so acceptable, so divine,
That from her hand I could suspect no ill,
And what she did, whatever in itself,
Her doing seemed to justify the deed;
She gave me of the Tree, and I did eat." (X.137–143)

The Son chides Adam for heeding the voice of his wife rather than God. God made Eve to be Adam's lovely mate, not his superior. God intended Adam to rule over and direct Eve, not the other way around.

"Was she thy God, that her thou didst obey
Before his voice, or was she made thy guide,
Superior, or but equal, that to her
Thou didst resign thy manhood, and the place
Wherein God set thee above her made of thee,
And for thee, whose perfection far excelled
Hers in all real dignity: adorned
She was indeed, and lovely to attract
Thy love, not thy subjection, and her gifts
Were such as under government well seemed,
Unseemly to bear rule, which was thy part
And person, hadst thou known thyself aright." (X.145–156)

As was to be expected, Eve, though "with shame nigh overwhelmed," refused to accept blame for her role, deflecting blame instead to her tempter: "The serpent me beguiled and I did eat."

Milton expresses sympathy for the serpent, however, since in the end it is the one who is cursed for deceiving Eve. Being but a brute beast, the serpent is necessarily mute and unable to tell how it happened that it became the hapless victim of satanic possession. Whatever guilt it might bear rightly ought to be transferred to the one who made it "the instrument of mischief." Why God allowed the cursing of the serpent to stand, that it shall grovel upon its belly and eat dust all the days of its life, is beyond what humans are permitted to know, Milton asserts. Even so, Satan was not exempted from judgment, for the prophesied bruising of the serpent's head would be "verified when Jesus son of Mary second Eve, saw *Satan* fall like lightning down from heav'n" (X.182–184).

Also, lest Eve's curse of childbirth pain and subservience to her husband and Adam's curse of thorns and thistles as the produce of his agricultural labors overwhelm the sinful couple, the Son offered two signs of comfort and mercy. First, the Son removed their crude leafy loincloths and gifted them with garments of skin instead. Second, he postponed their deaths until a day in the distant future.

His God-given task completed, the Son then "with swift ascent up returned" to his Father's side to reassume his heavenly "glory as of old" (X.223–226).

Satan's Triumph Reduced to Ashes

Meanwhile, far below, Satan's own offspring, Sin and Death, were keeping vigil at the gates of hell, which "now stood open wide," thanks to our primal parents' sin. Catching the scent of death in the air, Sin and Death sprang up and into action. Tracing the footprints left by Satan, they had already constructed a sturdy, wide bridge to connect hell to earth, for they anticipated heavy two-way traffic in the near future, with demons surging up to earth even as human crowds flocked downward toward hell. Catching sight in the distance of their father returning to hell, Sin and Death rushed out to welcome him back. Satan's success was evident in the broad smile on his face, and his children congratulated him profusely on his grand achievement. But there was not time for celebration. Satan urged Sin and Death to follow the bridge back to earth to take up the mission where he had left off—something they were only too happy to do, spreading their bane as they went.

Satan went in the opposite direction, following the causeway back to hell. He passed through the now-wide open and unguarded gate of hell and ascended the throne in Pandaemonium, vacant since his departure. Rousing the demonic hordes from their lethargy, Satan announced that he had returned

> Successful beyond hope, to lead ye forth
> Triumphant out of this infernal pit.

Now all could escape this "dungeon of our tyrant" and "as lords" take possession of a spacious new world, "little inferior" to their native heaven from which they had been expelled. Satan recounted how this feat had been achieved at great peril to himself. He bragged about how he had so easily seduced the Creator's pride and joy, man, with—get this—with nothing more than a simple apple. Unbelievable! And what had this grand prize cost him? Nothing more than bit of minor pain. Yes, there is to be some insignificant enmity between me and the seed of the woman, Satan said dismissively. I am to bruise his heel, and he will bruise my head at some unspecified future time. But this is what I would call a great bargain: the world in exchange for a mere bruise. And to think that all this was pulled off by me, the great "light-bringer," Lucifer, as I was known formerly in heaven!

Satan finished his oration expecting universal approval with enthusiastic shouts of joy and vigorous applause. Instead, he hears

> On all sides, from innumerable tongues
> A dismal universal hiss, the sound
> Of public scorn; he wondered, but not long
> Had leisure, wond'ring at himself now more;
> His visage drawn he felt to sharp and spare,
> His arms clung to his ribs, his legs entwining
> Each other, till supplanted down he fell
> A monstrous serpent on his belly prone,
> Reluctant, but in vain, a greater power
> Now ruled him, punished in the shape he sinned,
> According to his doom: he would have spoke,
> But hiss for hiss returned with forked tongue
> To forked tongue, for now were all transformed
> Alike, to serpents all as accessories
> To his bold riot: dreadful was the din
> Of hissing through the hall, thick swarming now. (X.507–522)

Not only was Satan punished by being turned in a serpent, also his allies, the whole lot of fallen angels, watched in horror as their own formerly erect glorious bodies slowly morphed into ugly serpents, crawling on their bellies.

Moreover, they were compelled to undergo further punishment, corresponding to the means used by their glorious chief to seduce the naïve couple in Eden. A grove of apple trees laden with luscious fruit suddenly sprang up in their midst. Desperate to soothe their throats "parched with scalding thirst and hunger fierce," they scaled their way up into the trees and greedily plucked the fruit. But much to their dismay, instead of sweet tasty fruit, they found themselves chewing "bitter ashes" laced with offensive taste. No matter how "oft they assayed," so oft their "hunger and thirst" they failed to alleviate in the slightest. Although this period of "famine" and "ceaseless hiss," was only temporary and they were permitted to resume their "lost shape" after a time, some say that this humiliation is revisited on them once every year as a reminder of their role in seducing humankind.

Contrasting Joy in Heaven

The contrasting reaction in heaven could not have been greater. Seated upon his transcendent throne in heaven, the Almighty smiled at the vain efforts of Satan and his army of rebels to thoroughly corrupt the new world. To the holy angels gathered around, he announced,

> "See with what heat these dogs of hell advance
> To waste and havoc yonder world, which I
> So fair and good created, and had still
> Kept in that state, had not the folly of man
> Let in these wasteful furies, who impute
> Folly to me, so doth the Prince of Hell
> And his adherents, that with so much ease
> I suffer them to enter and possess
> A place so heav'nly . . ." (X.616–628)

These "hell-hounds," the Almighty continued, did not know that it was he who permitted them "victory" so that his glory might be even greater when he sends his Son to conquer both Sin and Death and seal them all in hell forever. First, however, God sent his mighty angels to make temporary changes both in the heavens and the earth so that humankind should experience various punishments: changing seasons to produce sweltering heat and bitter cold; fluctuating weather to induce flood and famine; warring within the animal kingdom and against humankind; and more. But these temporary scourges will cease when at the end the heavens and the earth are renewed, with no stain remaining. At this good news, the angelic choir burst forth in exuberant halleluiahs: "Just are thy ways, righteous are thy decrees on all thy works!"

From Despair to Hope

Down in Eden the effects of sin were already being felt. Animal turned against animal. Beast, fowl, fish, all now shunned the human pair, whereas formerly they had sought out their company, to play before them and with them. The enormity of his and Eve's sin weighed ever more heavily upon Adam, so that he burst forth in a loud and long lament. Whereas once the man had delighted in the divine command to "increase and multiply," now he dreaded that his descendants would curse him for inflicting universal sorrow and death upon them. Why did God ever form him from that clay clod? Why did God have to extract from his side a rib, crooked by nature, to make for him that lovely but seductive mate? Why could God not have made his companion masculine, like the angels? Why did God not remain faithful to his word and cause him to die in the very moment he ate, rather than letting him live on in lingering misery? Why? Why? Why?

Seeing Adam thus afflicted, Eve approached and attempted to comfort him with soft words. But Adam would have none of it. Turning upon the woman he once blessed the Almighty for creating to be his companion, he now denounced with passion fierce: "Out of my sight, thou serpent; that name best befits thee, with him leagued, thyself as false and hateful" (X.867–69). Bursting into tears and falling at his feet, Eve pleaded:

> "Forsake me not thus, Adam, witness Heav'n
> What love sincere, and reverence in my heart
> I bear thee, and unweeting[14] have offended,
> Unhappily deceived; thy suppliant
> I beg, and clasp thy knees; bereave me not,
> Whereon I live, thy gentle looks, thy aid,
> Thy counsel in this uttermost distress,
> My only strength and stay: forlorn of thee,
> Whither shall I betake me, where subsist?" (X.914–922)

Even more, Eve readily acknowledged that she alone ought to bear the full burden of God's ire. Were it possible, so she prayed, she would willingly take upon herself all punishment so that Adam might be spared.

Adam could not help but be moved by such profusion of contriteness and love. His heart softened, he gently raised Eve from her knees and embraced her. Retracting his harsh words, he affirmed that they

14. Obsolete form or "unwitting."

should contend no more but rather henceforth strive to share each other's burdens of woe. Whatever God sees fit to lay upon them, they will bear together, lovingly. Book X concludes with both deeply contrite and together begging their Lord's pardon with "sorrow unfeigned and humiliation meek."

Book XI opens with the Son interceding before the Father for the repentant parents of humankind. In his capacity as priest who one day will unite all mankind with himself, the Son beseeches the Father to accept the sighs and prayers of contrite Adam and Eve and to reconcile mankind to himself. The Father was pleased with the Son's request, saying that such was already his intention. Nevertheless, humankind cannot be allowed to remain in Eden to live forever in peace and perfect harmony, as if the commandment had not been transgressed.

A signal was given to the ministering angel to blow his trumpet to assemble the heavenly hosts. When all had taken their seats,

> Th' Almighty thus pronounced his sovran will.
> "O sons, like one of us man is become
> To know both good and evil, since his taste
> Of that defended fruit; but let him boast
> His knowledge of good lost, and evil got,
> Happier, had it sufficed him to have known
> Good by itself, and evil not at all.
> . . . .
> Lest therefore his now bolder hand
> Reach also of the Tree of Life, and eat,
> And live forever, dream at least to live
> Forever, to remove him I decree
> And send him from the garden forth to till
> The ground whence he was taken, fitter soil." (XI.83–98)

The Almighty charged Michael to expel the sinful pair from Eden, but gently, lest they become discouraged. Moreover, Michael must station cherubim with flaming swords at the garden's entrance, less to prevent the humans reentering Eden than to preclude future use of Eden's fruits by Satan and his allies for their own malevolent purposes. In the words of Milton's God:

> "Dismiss them not disconsolate; reveal
> To Adam what shall come in future days,
> As I shall thee enlighten, intermix
> My cov'nant in the woman's seed renewed;

So send them forth, though sorrowing, yet in peace:
And on the east side of the garden place,
Where entrance up from Eden easiest climbs,
Cherubic watch, and of a sword the flame
Wide-waving, all approach far off to fright,
And guard all passage to the Tree of life:
Lest Paradise a receptacle prove
To Spirits foul, and all my trees their prey,
With whose stol'n fruit man once more to delude." (XI.113–125)

Meanwhile down in Eden, the human pair greeted the new day with mixed emotions. Their morning orations complete, Adam tried to assure Eve that he was certain God had accepted their prayers of contrition and would show his mercy through Eve's promised seed, for she is "rightly called, mother of all mankind." Eve replied that she was "ill-worthy" to bear that title, seeing that she as transgressor has "brought death on all." Nevertheless, they must carry on as best they are able, and that means resuming their duties of tending to the garden. But as they turned to that task, it was obvious that nature was now different. Down from a hill charged one beast pursuing a weaker beast as its prey, while overhead vultures circled awaiting the kill. The air was heavy with ominous dark clouds.

They had not ventured far when Michael appeared before them, not in his celestial shape but as a man, to announce their fate. Summarily dismissing Eve that he might speak with Adam alone, Michael informed Adam that, although God had accepted their prayers, they were to be punished by expulsion from the garden. Eve was not so far away that she was unable to overhear the ill news of their imminent exile and burst forth in loud lamentation. Michael turned to Eve, and while insisting that she was responsible for her own loss, reassured her that her punishment would be bearable because her husband would always be there beside her.

Adam recovered composure more quickly. Acknowledging the justice of the Almighty, Adam worried that henceforth he and his descendants would be deprived of God's presence to which they had been accustomed in paradise. Michael assured Adam that God was not abandoning them. God's presence is not confined to this place, but rather is everywhere. His goodness and paternal love will be with them wherever they are. Michael then signaled to Adam to follow him quietly. Michael had caused Eve to fall into a deep slumber so that just the two might ascend to the top of the highest mountain in paradise where they might continue their conversation in private. "This hill" was even higher than the one

> Whereon for different cause the Tempter set
> Our second Adam in the wilderness
> To show him all earth's kingdoms and their glory.
>
> . . . .
>
> Michael from Adam's eyes the film removed
> Which that false fruit that promised clearer sight
> Had bred; then purged with euphrasy and rue[15]
> The visual nerve, for he had much to see. (XI.382–384, 412–415)

And, oh, how much he did see. With renewed clairvoyance Adam was able to see scenes of the world as it would soon become and even of the whole of human history yet to unfold—both good and bad.

The first sight Michael showed Adam was of two men standing before altars, one offering the first fruits of his tillage, the other sacrificing a lamb from his flock, whereupon the first turned and struck the other with a rock and killed him, blood spilling profusely upon the ground. Puzzled, Adam inquired of Michael the meaning of this vision. Michael informed him that these two were brothers, Cain and Abel, the first offspring from Adam's loins. Out of envy the elder would slay the younger, whose offering was more acceptable to God. Adam began to weep, for the reality of death was beginning to sink in, but even more, because he was responsible for its introduction to humankind. Michael exhorted Adam not to dwell upon the death and sorrow but rather to live well the life—long or short—that God allots each person.

Scene by scene Michael unfolded for Adam the future for humankind on earth. One particularly distressing scene was of all the floating bodies drown in the flood God sent to cleanse the face of the earth of polluting wickedness—a wickedness largely caused by warring giants born from the marriages of "the sons of God" to "daughters of men." But what is particularly distressing to modern readers, and especially to those of us sensitized to feminist issues, is how Milton has rewritten Genesis 6:1–4 to shift blame away from the guilty male characters and onto (apparently) innocent women actors. In Milton's telling, it was wanton women descendants of Cain—the "daughters of men"—who led astray the heroic male descendants of Seth—here named "sons of God"—with their lascivious dress and seductive singing and dancing. It was from the

---

15. Herbs believed to improve vision.

resulting lust-inspired marriages that sprang those giants whose warring so completely corrupted the earth that the Almighty had little choice but to send a flood to cleanse away the pollution wholesale.

Milton certainly was no feminist. Time and again he blames primarily women for the sins of humankind. Granted that both the Bible and tradition often castigate women as the perpetrators of the sins of their male counterparts, with Eve being the parade example (Genesis 3; 1 Timothy 2:13–15). Milton, however, has carried such gender bias a step further with his unwarranted recasting of the story of the corruption of the sons of God in Genesis 6 as being due to the inherent seductive nature of women.

In Michael's preview of human history, he touches on many of the major events recorded in the Bible, among them the covenant with Noah following the flood, the Tower of Babel episode that led to the confusion of languages, Moses and Aaron bringing the Israelites out of Egypt, David and Solomon building the Temple, the exile in Babylon and return. Michael climaxes this lengthy preview for Adam with an account of the coming Messiah, the promised seed of Eve who finally will bruise the head of the Serpent and repair the damage done in the garden in Eden. Moreover, after his death and resurrection, the Messiah will send the Spirit upon the faithful to preserve them throughout time in the face of much persecution and attempts to lead them astray once again. (While these last sentiments could apply to nearly every period of Christianity, they likely were inspired by Milton's own personal experience. At the time our Puritan poet penned these lines, he likely was in fear of his life, hiding both from the state and from allied corrupt clergy within the established church.)

Michael ended his oration to the father of humankind with the firm assurance that at the end of time this promised Messiah will return from heaven and restore all things.

> "The Woman's Seed, obscurely then foretold,
> Now amplier known thy Savior and thy Lord,
> Last in the clouds from heav'n to be revealed
> In glory of the Father, to dissolve
> Satan with his perverted world, then raise
> From the conflagrant mass, purged and refined,
> New heav'ns, new earth, ages of endless date
> Founded in righteousness and peace and love,
> To bring forth fruits joy and eternal bliss." (XII.543–556)

Adam, now enlightened that not all was lost but indeed that life after death awaits those who fear God and walk obediently in his presence, rejoices in the great mercy of God, and resolves to follow faithfully the example of "my Redeemer ever blest." Michael commends Adam for having learned well. Previously Adam may have known the names of all things, but now "thou hast attained the sum of wisdom." Adam is therefore equipped to leave paradise for the world outside. Indeed, Michael suggests, Adam may find, once outside Eden, "a paradise within thee, happier far."

Together Michael and Adam descend the hill to the bower where they had left Eve sleeping. Eve was already awake, however, and greeted them with the news that she had been informed in a dream of all the wonders that Michael had revealed to Adam; she was no longer sad but looking forward to a future outside of Eden, so long as Adam is at her side.

There was little time to spare. The cherubim were already taking up their stations at the gate, with "the branished sword of God before them" blazing, as Michael urged our primal parents forth from paradise.

> In either hand the hast'ning angel caught
> Our ling'ring parents, and to th' eastern gate
> Led them direct, and down the cliff as fast
> To the subjected plain; then disappeared.
> They looking back, all th' eastern side beheld
> Of Paradise, so late their happy seat,
> Waved over by that flaming brand, the gate
> With dreadful faces thronged and fiery arms:
> Some natural tears they dropped, but wiped them soon;
> The world was all before them, where to choose
> Their place of rest, and Providence their guide:
> They hand in hand with wand'ring steps and slow,
> Through Eden took their solitary way. (XII.637–649)

Thus did Milton end his epic poem. The conclusion is abrupt when compared with the Genesis narrative, which contains additional episodes about the life of Adam and Eve after their expulsion from Eden. As we have seen, however, Milton did have the archangel Michael give Adam a glimpse of how their first two sons Cain and Abel will fare. But nothing is said about the remainder of their children, Seth and the "other sons and daughters" (Gen 5:1–5). Milton seems content to leave the reader to wonder how our primal parents and their offspring actually will fare in their new world. The sense of mystery and expectation is palpable.

Milton's Enduring Legacy

The seventeenth-century English poet John Milton fundamentally changed the way all subsequent readers hear and understand the Adam and Eve story. Milton was a product of the Renaissance and in keeping with the spirit of the Renaissance, he transformed Adam and Eve into authentic humanistic characters. Before Milton, the Adam and Eve story was primarily a religious text whose function was to teach believers about the origin of sin and to admonish them to lead morally upright lives by avoiding the mistakes of our common ancestors. The genius of Milton was to turn the story into a primarily literary work wherein religious values are subordinated to universal human values; and where cleverly crafted phraseology is as important, or even more important, than moral messaging. A consistent, coherent storyline, or plot, is also of utmost importance. Everything must hang together for the story to be believable—as well as pleasing to the ear. Consequently, today *Paradise Lost* is read and studied in departments of literature rather than in departments of religion or theology; and "the story of Adam and Eve" is honored more as an artistic or literary topic than as the subject of religion or ethics.

In keeping with his Renaissance training—as well as believing himself to be a poet of no mean ability—Milton aspired to write a Christian epic to rival the best of classical Greek and Roman literature. Precisely for this reason, *Paradise Lost*, originally published in 1667 as a ten-book work, was subsequently revised and republished in 1674 as an epic in twelve books, in imitation of Virgil's masterpiece, the *Aeneid,* also written in twelve books. For Milton, form was as important as storyline. It is important to note that Milton did not entitle his composition after the two nominal main characters, for example, "The Story of Adam and Eve," but after the whole larger drama itself, that is, how paradise was lost. That encompasses a much larger story involving not only what transpired in Eden but also the prior primordial events that constitute the backstory for those fateful events in the garden.

In keeping with Milton's literary objectives, the major characters in the story are transformed from the two-dimensional, wooden figures featured in biblical narrative and in tradition into fully developed human persona, complete with complex emotions and conflicting moral values. The parade example is the serpent, aka Satan. In the Genesis 3 narrative the serpent is not identified with Satan. The serpent is special, however, in that it is said to be "more clever than any of the beasts that Yahweh God had made." It did have the ability to speak the humans' language. But then later Jewish tradition assumed that all animals in paradise could speak Hebrew. Only after the fall did animals lose their ability to speak. The identification of the serpent with Satan was a development that also came about later, in postbiblical Jewish literature and in the New Testament and in Christian literature generally, as well as in Islam. Milton, of course, continued this long-standing association of the serpent with Satan, though in *Paradise Lost* the serpent is nothing more than an external receptacle used by Satan to conceal his identity.

Moreover, before Milton the figure Satan had never been so thoroughly developed as an independent, rational, and willful being, to say nothing of his origin and history as the archenemy of God and of humankind. In Milton's world, Satan emerges as arguably the most significant figure in the history of humankind, even though Satan himself is not human. On a theological level, naturally Milton assigns a higher, more powerful status to the Father and to the Son than to Satan. But in literary dynamics, Milton places Satan at the center of his epic, thereby effectively ceding to him the most consequential role in human history, especially for shaping the actual world in which we humans live. Few would dispute that evil is rampant in our world. Milton laid responsibility for such wholesale evil directly at the feet of Satan.

Satan is more that the author of evil, however. Milton's poetic genius was to cast Satan as a full character, with personality and feelings. Satan gains the reader's empathy as we watch him struggle with conflicting emotions, trying to balance his admiration for all that God has so wonderfully created, on the one hand, and his unquenchable desire for revenge against that "unjust" God, on the other. After all, who among us has not at one time or another experienced hostile feelings against someone we judge to have wronged us in a similar grievous manner? In so far as Satan represents our own interior conflicts, he takes on the character of an admirable tragic hero.

Just as Milton imported Satan into the Adam and Eve story from later sources, so too for other angelic figures, both fallen and virtuous. The motif of fallen angels is derived from Genesis 6:1–4, as mediated through and expanded in 1 Enoch 6–12, though the narrative is much altered in *Paradise Lost*. Milton recast the battle motif by magnifying it to epic proportions worthy of his Greek and Roman predecessors. Similarly, Milton extracts from Judeo-Christian tradition the motif about helpful angelic messengers from God—Michael, Gabriel, Raphael, and others—and posits them as having acted as mediators between the Most High and Adam and Eve in paradise. If God used these angelic beings as his personal messengers for communicating with individual humans in post-Eden times, it is reasonable to assume that God similarly used these same archangels to relay messages to Adam and Eve in paradise, when divine-human communication was even more frequent and intimate.

It should surprise no one familiar with New Testament Christology that Milton has retrojected "the Son," aka "the Messiah,"—though never named Jesus—into the Adam and Eve story as both creator and redeemer. The Gospel of John (1:3) says that "through him all things came to be; without him no created thing came into being." And central to the apostle Paul is the assertion that salvation was achieved because the second Adam took upon himself the burden of the first Adam: "Adam foreshadows the man who was to come . . . For if the wrongdoing of that one man brought death upon so many, its effect is vastly exceeded by the grace of God and the gift that came to so many by the grace of the one man, Jesus Christ" (Romans 5:14–15). The author of Genesis may have had no conception of a second Adam as part and parcel of the Adam and Eve story, but for Milton, like all Christians, the story is incomplete if the second Adam is left out.

What is surprising, however, is how little a direct role the Father plays in Milton's telling of the story about the origins of the heavens and the earth. Granted that the Most High is omniscient and that nothing happens without his knowledge and consent. But Milton has, as it were, elevated the Almighty to such a transcendent status that he seldom figures directly in the storyline. The divine will is mediated mostly through others who act in God's stead. Perhaps the most striking example is Milton's rewrite of the garden scene immediately following Adam's and Eve's eating of the forbidden fruit. In Genesis 3 it is "Yahweh God" himself who walks in the garden in the cool evening breeze and calls out to the hiding, guilty couple and speaks with them. But in Milton's version, Yahweh God has been replaced by the Son, so that the judging of Adam and Eve and the serpent/Satan is done not by God himself but by his vicegerent, the Son. Theologically speaking, this may be a refinement; but it is a radical departure from the biblical narrative and it also makes God appear more distant and removed.

The nominal main characters in this epic, Adam and Eve, are also much more complex and more developed than in the biblical narrative, or even in the larger, millennia-old Judeo-Christian and Muslim traditions. Milton has given each of them a very sophisticated persona.

Adam, per the cultural bias of the day, is clearly superior, not only physically but also intellectually, and this by divine design. He possesses more of the divine image than Eve. For that reason Satan fears to take Adam on directly. By contrast, Eve is delicate and comely, as befits a woman, but also less intellectually and morally astute. Her feminine beauty is both an asset and a liability. It makes her more attractive to her husband—and to Satan—but at the same time promotes vanity and makes her susceptible to flattery—her downfall. She requires the protective presence of her husband, but at the same time she strives to assert her co-equality and her independence—a fatal flaw in a woman.

Eve's naivete makes her offense less grievous that that of her husband. Being less astute, she fails to comprehend the full implications of eating the forbidden fruit. First, she was predisposed to accept the suggestions coming from the serpent's mouth due to the dream Satan had planted in her head during the previous night. Second, as a woman she was more easily duped by the lies and flattery coming out of the serpent's mouth. (One is reminded of Irenaeus's judgment that the offense of the primal couple was not so serious, for they were but children lacking full development of their mental and moral faculties.) Adam's sin, by contrast, was far more serious. With his superior intellect, he immediately comprehended the full gravity of his impending choice. With full knowledge and consent of the will, he deliberately chose his wife in preference to God, and death over life because of her—a romantic gesture, to be sure, but nonetheless a most grievous moral lapse. (Perhaps Milton has in mind the passage in Romans 5 wherein the apostle Paul lays responsibility for the downfall of humankind entirely upon Adam, while ignoring Eve completely.)

In the end, however, it is the love uniting Adam and Eve that makes *Paradise Lost* so appealing to the modern reader. Having chosen each other for better or for worse, they emerge from Eden lovingly bound to each other, determined to face together whatever the future may hold for them and their descendants. This is indeed an epic story worthy of the ages.

Epilogue

HAVING OBSERVED HOW THE Adam and Eve tradition has undergone multiple transformations during the course of several millennia, one may legitimately ask: Is anything in the Adam and Eve story true? Certainly, the story is not historical by modern standards of history. Nor can its story of origins be easily reconciled with modern scientific views of how the universe came to be, or of the gradual evolution of the human species from primates over the course of several million years. Homo sapiens, the most recent form of humankind, is estimated to have evolved some 200,000 years ago—and not in the Middle East as Genesis says, but in Africa, no less.

The story of Adam and Eve is not history; it is myth.[1] Contrary to popular opinion, however, myth is not necessarily false. Myth, as defined by historians of religion, is a society's attempt to get at a truth that lies beyond merely what is historical or observable by scientific investigation. Myth attempts to undergird the human experience in story form, using categories familiar to the culture of a given society. Myth is a society's quest for ultimate meaning, and not merely a recording of events in human history or the physical world of human experience. Moreover, myths can change, expand, and even expire as societies change.

One way by which biblical myths—and the creation stories are a prime example—changed or were adapted to changing circumstances is through a process of what may be called *mythopoeic speculation*. As a story is passed on from one generation to the next, biblical authors at times deliberately adapted the story to apply to new situations and new

1. I have discussed myth and theories of myth in the Introduction to my *Slaying the Dragon*, 1–14, with bibliography; see also my two articles, "Myth"; and "Myth in the Hebrew Bible."

audiences by adding new motifs (often borrowed from other stories or myths) or by radically altering episodes, for example, changing the name of the creator god from the Babylonian god Marduk to the Israelite deity Yahweh/God. This process may be described as creating new myth, or "myth-making," which is the literal meaning of *mythopoeic*. Because this was often a deliberate and conscious imaginative alteration by the author of a motif or idea that cannot be verified from experience, it may aptly be characterized as *speculative*. Hence, the designation *mythopoeic speculation*. Such changes were not meant to deceive, however, but rather to strengthen the convictions—or better, the faith—of the intended audience or reader. The evolution of the Adam and Eve tradition is witness to this very enterprise.

When the Yahwistic Writer adapted the Babylonian myth Atrahasis by replacing Babylonian gods with Israel's God as the Creator, that was surely considered to be a theological advancement. When the Priestly Writer went a step further by having the Creator make both the male and the female of the new human species at the same time, and both equally in the image of God, that too was a theological statement. When the author of 1 Enoch posited that human evil originates in part from superhuman forces and not just from human malfeasance, that may be considered an attempt to explain evil as something beyond the power of any individual to control. Likewise, Paul's positing of Jesus as a second Adam was theological refinement in the sense that God is portrayed as a merciful God determined to renew sinful humankind, along with all creation. The disagreement between Bishops Irenaeus of Lyons and Augustine of Hippo regarding the gravity of the "original sin" and its consequences can serve as a reminder that in matters theological there is room for a wide variety of opinions. The view of Islam that humans may be overwhelmed by the machinations of Iblis-Satan is meant to emphasize the importance of total dedication to God. Even Milton's *Paradise Lost*, for all its inclusion of rare words, convoluted syntax, and many allusions to classical mythology, is at core an affirmation of the human quest of ultimate meaning.

Undoubtedly, the morphology of "the Adam and Eve tradition" has evolved greatly over the course of some three thousand years, sometimes in radical and unexpected ways. But one would do well not to dismiss it as inconsequential for modern audiences. Moderns are in good company, if they see therein at least a modicum of guidance for living in an age of rapidly evolving and competing theories of contemporary science, anthropology, and psychology, to say nothing of the many different and changing theological perspectives.

Indeed, one may suggest that many of the issues that the traditioners of the Adam and Eve story struggled with have considerable relevance for us moderns and continue to be issues that still confront us on a daily basis. A prime example is the belief that every person, no matter one's race or skin color, has inalienable dignity and must be treated with respect, because as the myth phrases it, every human is "created in the image and likeness of God." A corollary of this is that women have equal dignity with men and deserve to be accorded equal rights, despite the practice in many societies of privileging men over women.

Another major issue is the presence of evil in the modern world. Hardly anyone would deny that evil is real. But a debate still rages over whether such evil originates primarily from within humans themselves, or whether there are additional forces in our midst, more powerful than humans, working to promote good or ill—spiritual beings that the tradition calls angels and demons, respectively. Related to this is the question of whether humans have the power to resist or control evil, whatever its origin.

A third issue—and one with particular relevance for today—concerns the place and function of us humans in relation to the world in which we live. Are we humans a bane or a benefit to our planet? Genesis 3 suggests that all creation is "cursed" because of the actions of us humans. By contrast, Genesis 1:26–30 maintains that we humans have a positive role to play by protecting and nurturing every part of our world. God made humankind to rule over the earth and to have dominion over the fish of the sea, the birds of the air, the beasts of the field, the creepy crawly things on the ground, even trees and vegetation. Everything has been given into the care of us humans. Other texts phrase this as God having appointed humankind to be God's viceroy or vicegerent on earth. In this day of renewed concern for the environment and the rapid depletion of earth's natural resources at the hands of humans, this aspect of the creation story must become front and center in our thinking. The "care of our common home" is an urgent moral issue in the present day and age.[2]

Perhaps the most basic question of all concerns the origin of the universe itself and how life began. Did the universe as we know it originate from a cosmic explosion as postulated by the Big Bang theory or

2. So Pope Francis in his encyclical letter, *Laudato Si'* (May 24, 2015).

similar mechanical hypotheses? Or is the universe the work of a personal creator? For that matter, does God bear any resemblance to the anthropomorphized male figure commonly depicted in biblical narratives? Philosophers and theologians have long asserted that "God" is completely beyond anything the human mind is capable of imagining. How to understand the evolving figure of the creator and his function(s) in Genesis presents yet another dilemma for the modern reader.

One could suggest still other ways in which the Adam and Eve story remains relevant even today. But just the few singled out here underscore how much the Adam and Eve story continues to challenge us moderns to explore ever more deeply what it means to be truly human. Rather than laying aside the story of Adam and Eve as an ancient, naïve folktale, the biblical narrative about Adam and Eve deserves to be continually reimaged and adapted in ways that challenge contemporary audiences struggling to live in the most authentic human manner possible.

Bibliography

Abou-Assaf, Ali, et.al. *La statue de Tell Fekherye et son inscription bilingue assyro-arameenne*. Etudes assyriologiques 7. Paris: Editions Recherche sur les civilizations, 1982.

Abdel Haleem, M. A. S., trans. *The Qur'an: English Translation and Parallel Arabic Text*. New, rev. ed. Oxford: Oxford University Press, 2010.

al-Kisa'i, Muhammad ibn 'Abd Allah. *Tales of the Prophets*. Translated and with notes by Wheeler M. Thackston Jr. Great Books of the Islamic World. Chicago: Kazi, 1997.

Ambrose. *Hexameron, Paradise, and Cain and Abel*. Translated by John J. Savage. The Fathers of the Church 42. New York: Fathers of the Church, 1961.

Anderson, Gary A. *The Genesis of Perfection: Adam and Eve in Jewish and Christian Imagination*. Louisville: Westminster John Knox, 2001.

Augustine. *Against Julian*. Translated by Matthew A Schumacher. Fathers of the Church 35. New York: Fathers of the Church, 1957.

———. *The City of God*. An abridged version from the translation by Gerald G. Walsh [and others] with a condensation of the original foreword by Etienne Gilson. Edited with an introduction by Vernon J. Bourke. Garden City, NY: Image Books, 1958.

———. *The Confessions of St. Augustine*. Translated, with an introduction and notes, by John K. Ryan. Garden City, NY: Image Books, 1960.

———. *The Literal Meaning of Genesis*. Translated and annotated by John Hammond Taylor. 2 vols. ACW 41, 42. Ramsey, NJ: Newman, 1982.

———. *On Genesis Against the Manichees; and, On the Literal Interpretation of Genesis: An Unfinished Book*. Translated by Roland J. Teske. The Fathers of the Church 84. Washington, DC: Catholic University of America Press, 1991.

Barnstone, Willis, and Marvin Meyer, eds. *The Gnostic Bible*. London: Shambhala, 2003.

Batto, Bernard F. "The Divine Sovereign: The Image of God in the Priestly Creation Account." In *David and Zion: Biblical Studies in Honor of J. J. M. Roberts*, edited by Bernard F. Batto and Kathryn L. Roberts, 143–86. Winona Lake, IN: Eisenbrauns, 2004.

———. *In the Beginning: Essays on Creation Motifs in the Ancient Near East and the Bible*. Siphrut 9. Winona Lake, IN: Eisenbrauns, 2013.

———. "Myth." In *The Dictionary of Theology*, edited by Joseph A. Komonchak, 697–701. Wilmington, DE: Glazier, 1987.

———. "Myth in the Hebrew Bible." In *Oxford Bibliographies in Biblical Studies*, edited by Christopher Matthews. New York: Oxford University Press, 2013. http://www.oxfordbibliographies.com (DOI: 10.1093/OBO/9780195393361-0125).

———. "Paradise Reexamined." In *The Biblical Canon in Comparative Perspective*, edited by K. Lawson Younger Jr et al., 33–66. Scripture in Context 4. Lewiston, NY: Mellen, 1991.

———. *Slaying the Dragon: Mythmaking Speculation in the Bible.* Louisville: Westminster John Knox, 1992.

Ben-Amos, Ben. "From Eden to Ednah—Lilith in the Garden." *BAR* 42:3 (May/June 2016) 54–58.

Black, Jeremy, and Anthony Green. *Gods, Demons and Symbols of Ancient Mesopotamia: An Illustrated Dictionary.* Austin: University of Texas Press, 1992.

Black, Matthew. *The Book of Enoch or 1 Enoch: A New English Edition.* Studia in Veteris Testamenti Pseudepigrapha 7. Leiden: Brill, 1985.

Böttrich, Christfried. "The Figures of Adam and Eve in the Enoch Tradition." In *Adam and Eve Story in the Hebrew Bible and in Ancient Jewish Writings Including the New Testament*, edited by Antti Laato and Lotta Valve, 211–51. Studies in the Reception History of the Bible 7. Winona Lake, IN: Eisenbrauns, 2016.

Brown, Raymond E. *The Birth of the Messiah: A Commentary on the Infancy Narratives in Matthew and Luke.* Garden City, NY: Doubleday, 1977.

———. *An Introduction to the New Testament.* New York: Doubleday, 1997.

Charlesworth, James H., ed. *The Old Testament Pseudepigrapha.* 2 vols. Garden City, NY: Doubleday, 1983, 1985.

Chilton, Bruce, et al. *A Comparative Handbook to the Gospel of Mark: Comparisons with Pseudepigrapha, the Qumran Scrolls, and Rabbinic Literature.* New Testament Gospels in Their Judaic Context 1. Leiden: Brill, 2010.

Collins, Adela Yarbo, and John Joseph Collins. *King and Messiah as Son of God: Divine, Human, and Angelic Messianic Figures in Biblical and Related Literature.* Grand Rapids: Eerdmans, 2008.

Dalley, Stephanie. *Myths from Mesopotamia.* Oxford: Oxford University Press, 1989.

Downs, David J. "Faith[fullness] in Christ Jesus in 2 Timothy 3:15." *JBL* 131 (2012) 143–60.

Dunn, James D. G. *Christology in the Making: A New Testament Inquiry into the Origins of the Doctrine of the Incarnation.* 2nd ed. Grand Rapids: Eerdmans, 1989.

———. *The Theology of Paul the Apostle.* Grand Rapids: Eerdmans, 1998.

Fitzmyer, Joseph A. *Romans: A New Translation with Introduction and Commentary.* Anchor Bible 33. New York: Doubleday, 1993

Freedman, H., and Maurice Simon, eds. and trans. *Midrash Rabbah.* 10 vols. London: Soncino, 1939.

Foster, Benjamin R. *Before the Muses: An Anthology of Akkadian Literature.* 2 vols. Bethesda, MD: CDL, 1993.

Francis, Pope. *Laudato Si'.* May 24, 2015. http://www.vatican.va/content/francesco/en/encyclicals/documents/papa-francesco_20150524_enciclica-laudato-si.html.

George, Andrew. *The Babylonian Gilgamesh Epic: Introduction, Critical Edition and Cuneiform Texts.* 2 vols. Oxford: Oxford University Press, 2003.

———. *The Epic of Gilgamesh.* New York: Barnes & Noble, 1999.

Ginsberg, Louis, and Boaz Cohen. *The Legends of the Jews.* Translated by Henrietta Szold and Paul Radin. 7 vols. Philadelphia: Jewish Publication Society of America, 1909.

Goldin, Judah. *The Living Talmud: The Wisdom of the Fathers and Its Classical Commentaries.* Mentor Book. New York: New American Library of World Literature, 1957.

Hallo, William W., and K. Lawson Younger, eds. *The Context of Scripture.* 4 vols. Leiden: Brill, 1997–2017.

Hays, Richard B. *The Faith of Jesus Christ: The Narrative Substructure of Galatians 3:1— 4:11.* The Biblical Resource Series. 2nd ed. Grand Rapids: Eerdmans, 2002.

Heidel, Alexander. *The Babylonian Genesis.* 2nd ed. Chicago: University of Chicago Press, 1951.

Hooker, Morna D. "*Pistis Christou.*" *NTS* 35 (1989) 321–42.

Howard, George. "Notes and Observations on the 'Faith of Christ." *HTR* 60 (1967) 469–84.

Irenaeus. *Five Books of St. Irenaeus, Bishop of Lyons, against Heresies.* Translated by John Keble. A Library of Fathers of the Holy Catholic Church 42. Oxford: Parker, 1872.

Izre'el, Shlomo. *Adapa and the South Wind: Language Has the Power of Life and Death.* Winona Lake, IN: Eisenbrauns, 2001.

Joines, Karen Randolph. "Winged Serpents in Isaiah's Inaugural Vision." *JBL* 86 (1967) 410–15.

Justin, Martyr, St. *The First and Second Apologies.* Translated by Leslie William Barnard. ACW 56. New York: Paulist, 1997.

Keel, Othmar. *Jahwe-Visionen und Siegelkunst.* Stuttgarter Bibelstudien 84–85. Stuttgart: Katholisches Bibelwerk, 1997.

Klager, Andrew P. "Retaining and Reclaiming the Divine Identification and the Recapitulation of Peace in St. Irenaeus of Lyons' Atonement Narrative." In *Stricken by God?: Nonviolent Identification and the Victory of Christ,* edited by Brad Jersak and Michael Hardin, 422–89. Abbotsford, BC: Fresh Wind, 2007.

Knibb, M. *The Ethiopic Book of Enoch: A New Edition in the Light of the Aramaic Dead Sea Fragments.* 2 vols. Oxford: Clarendon, 1982.

Kvam, Kristen E., et al. *Eve and Adam: Jewish, Christian, and Muslim Readings on Genesis and Gender.* Bloomington: Indiana University Press, 1999.

Laato, Antti, and Lotta Valve, eds. *Adam and Eve Story in the Hebrew Bible and in Ancient Jewish Writings Including the New Testament.* Studies in the Reception History of the Bible 7. Winona Lake, IN: Eisenbrauns, 2016.

Lambert, W. G. *Babylonian Creation Myths.* Mesopotamian Civilizations 16. Winona Lake, IN: Eisenbrauns, 2013.

Lambert, W. G., and A. R. Millard. *Atrahasis: The Babylonian Story of the Flood.* Oxford: Oxford University Press, 1969.

Matera, Frank J. *New Testament Christology.* Louisville: Westminster John Knox, 1999.

Meyer, Marvin, ed. *The Nag Hammadi Scriptures: The International Edition.* New York: HarperOne, 2007.

Milgrom, Jo. "Some Second Thoughts about Adam's First Wife." In *Genesis 1–3 in the History of Exegesis: Intrigue in the Garden,* edited by Gregory Allen Robbins, 226– 29. Studies in Women and Religion 27. Lewiston, NY: Mellen, 1988.

Milton, John. *Paradise Lost: An Authoritative Text, Backgrounds and Sources, Criticism,* edited by Scott Elledge. Norton Critical Edition. New York: Norton, 1975.

Murphy-O'Connor, Jerome. "Christological Anthropology in Phil. 2:5–11." *RB* 83 (1976) 25–50.

Nielsen, J. T. *Adam and Christ in the Theology of Irenaeus of Lyons. An Examination of the Function of the Adam-Christ Typology in the Adversus Haereses of Irenaeus,*

Against the Background of the Gnosticism of his Time. Van Gorcum's theologische bibliotheek 40. Assen: Van Gorcum, 1968.

Nickelsburg, George W. E. *1 Enoch 1: A Commentary on the Book of Enoch, Chapters 1–36; 81–108.* Hermeneia. Minneapolis: Fortress, 2001.

Pagels, Elaine. *Adam, Eve, and the Serpent.* New York: Vintage, 1988.

Peppard, Michael. "Adopted and Begotten Sons of God: Paul and John on Divine Sonship." *Catholic Biblical Quarterly* 73 (2011) 92–110.

Pritchard, James B., ed. *The Ancient Near East in Pictures Relating to the Old Testament.* 2nd ed. Princeton: Princeton University Press, 1969.

———. *Ancient Near Eastern Texts Relating to the Old Testament.* 3rd ed. Princeton: Princeton University Press, 1969.

Roberts, J. J. M. "The Visual Elements in Isaiah's Vision in the Light of Judean and Near Eastern Sources." In *From Babel to Babylon: Essays on Biblical History and Literature in Honor of Brian Peckham,* edited by Joyce Rilett Wood et al., 206–10. Library of Hebrew Bible/Old Testament Studies 455. New York: T. & T. Clark, 2006.

Robinson, James M., ed. *The Nag Hammadi Library.* 3rd rev ed. San Francisco: HarperSanFrancisco, 1988.

Schöck, Cornelia. "Adam and Eve." In *Encyclopaedia of the Qur'ān,* 1:22–26. Leiden: Brill, 2001.

Smith, Mark S. *The Genesis of Good and Evil: The Fall(out) and Original Sin in the Bible.* Louisville: Westminster John Knox, 2019.

Steenberg, M. C. "Children in Paradise: Adam and Eve as 'Infants' in Irenaeus of Lyon." *JECS* 12 (2004) 1–22.

Taggar-Cohen, Ada. "Why Are There No Israelite Priestesses?" *TheTorah.com* (2016). http://thetorah.com/article/why-are-there-no-israelite-priestesses.

Unger, Dominic J. *St. Irenaeus of Lyons: Against the Heresies, Book 3.* ACW 64. Mahwah, NJ: Newman, 2012.

van Dijk, H. J. *Ezekiel's Prophecy on Tyre (Ez. 26, 1–28, 19).* Biblica et Orientalia 20. Rome: Biblical Institute, 1968.

VanderKam, James C. "Genesis 6:1–4 and the Angel Stories in the Book of Watchers (1 Enoch 1–36." In *The Fallen Angels Traditions: Second Temple Developments and Reception History,* edited by Angela Kim Harkins et al., 1–7. Catholic Biblical Quarterly Monograph Series 53. Washington, DC: Catholic Biblical Association of America, 2014.

———. *Jubilees: A Commentary in Two Volumes.* Hermeneia. Minneapolis: Augsburg Fortress, 2018.

VanderKam, James C., and William Adler, eds. *The Jewish Apocalyptic Heritage in Early Christianity.* Compendia rerum Judaicarum ad Noum Testamentum III/4. Assen: Van Gorcum, 1990.

Wallis, Ian G. *The Faith of Jesus Christ in Early Christian Traditions.* Society for New Testament Studies Monograph Series 84. Cambridge: Cambridge University Press, 1995.

Wheeler, Brannon M. *Prophets in the Quran: An Introduction to the Quran and Muslim Exegesis.* Comparative Islamic Studies. New York: Continuum, 2002.

Yassif, Eli. *The Tales of Ben Sira in the Middle Ages: A Critical Text and Literary Studies.* Jerusalem: Magnes, 1984.